# ROUTLEDGE LIBRARY EDITIONS:
# THE ECONOMY OF THE MIDDLE EAST

Volume 5

# ARAB MANPOWER

# ARAB MANPOWER
## The Crisis of Development

J.S. BIRKS AND C.A. SINCLAIR

Routledge
Taylor & Francis Group

LONDON AND NEW YORK

First published in 1980

This edition first published in 2015
by Routledge
2 Park Square, Milton Park, Abingdon, Oxon, OX14 4RN

and by Routledge
711 Third Avenue, New York, NY 10017

*Routledge is an imprint of the Taylor & Francis Group, an informa business*

*British Library Cataloguing in Publication Data*
A catalogue record for this book is available from the British Library

ISBN: 978-1-138-78710-0 (Set)
ISBN: 978-1-138-81048-8 (Volume 5)
Pb ISBN: 978-1-138-82002-9 (Volume 5)

**Publisher's Note**
The publisher has gone to great lengths to ensure the quality of this reprint but points out that some imperfections in the original copies may be apparent.

**Disclaimer**
The publisher has made every effort to trace copyright holders and would welcome correspondence from those they have been unable to trace.

# Arab Manpower

## THE CRISIS OF DEVELOPMENT

J.S. BIRKS and C.A. SINCLAIR

CROOM HELM LONDON

Croom Helm Ltd, 2-10 St John's Road, London SW11


British Library Cataloguing in Publication Data

Birks, J S
   Arab manpower.
   1. Labour supply – Arab countries
   2. Arab countries – Economic conditions
   I. Title    II. Sinclair, C A
   331.1'1'09174927       HD5836.A6

   ISBN 0-85664-946-5


Reproduced from copy supplied
printed and bound in Great Britain
by Billing and Sons Limited
Guildford, London, Oxford, Worcester

# CONTENTS

# TABLES

*Tables*

*Tables*

*Tables*

*Tables*

Location of Principal Arab Countries

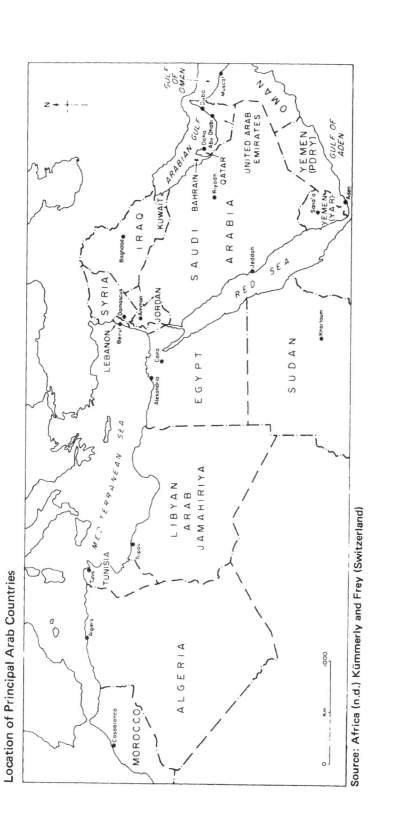

# PREFACE

## 1 Introduction

At the close of the 1970s, the Arab world — defined here as stretching from Morocco to the Sultanate of Oman, and including North Africa, Egypt and Sudan, the Levant and the Arabian peninsula — is a region of acute contrasts. States with populations enjoying some of the highest *per capita* incomes in the world abut states which rank amongst the least developed. The magnitude of these contrasts, made so acute by their geographical proximity, is engendering growing tensions in the Arab world. These stresses are both within individual wealthy and poorer states, as well as, most obviously, in international political relationships between members of these two groups. Upon the success of resolving these contrasts rests the continued stability of the region.

The dichotomy between these two groups of states, the capital-rich and capital-poor, essentially paralleled by the division of the Arab world into oil-endowed and non-oil-endowed states, is fundamental to much of the analysis in this book, being the essential determinant of varied patterns and rates of economic growth and social change within the region.

It is these contrasting types of development and change which are leading towards an inherent instability of the Arab world. Not only are international relations between Arab states threatened by the widening gap in wealth between rich and poor, but the stability of individual states is also prejudiced. In the capital-rich states, the rapid pace of development militates in favour of increasing stress as continued economic growth raises social and political issues which militate against further expansion of the economy. Yet the growth has its own momentum, and continues, even accelerates. In the capital-poor states it is the lack of economic growth which is causing increasing dissatisfaction; *per capita* incomes in these non-oil-endowed states are, at best, only being maintained, rather than rising.

This study describes and evaluates economic development in both the capital-rich and capital-poor states of the Arab world by focusing on the national labour markets. Economic development and labour markets are always mutually interactive; the nature of and processes acting within the labour market provide an interesting study in any context. In the Arab world, however, the labour market is a particularly useful means of approaching an analysis of economic development.

Normally, labour is one of several limiting parameters and constraints upon economic development. In the capital-rich states, however, shortage of human capital is the major, even pre-eminent, constraint upon development; the excess of financial capital has meant that the most common constraint to growth, lack of investment income, has been effectively removed. Monitoring and analysis of the labour market in capital-rich states are therefore an especially pertinent means of enquiry.

In the capital-poor states, evaluation of economic development by analysis of the labour market is equally apt, though for slightly different reasons. Throughout the 1960s, government efforts in stimulating economic development were geared to employment creation. However, in the 1970s, and especially since 1973, so much labour has been drawn from these states by the burgeoning demands for labour in the oil-exporting states that shortages of labour have become significant. Present-day efforts at development in the capital-poor states are therefore limited (as before) by financial constraints, but also now by shortages of labour. Evaluation of labour market developments in these capital-poor states is therefore a central and sensitive means of monitoring economic development.

The various national labour markets are evaluated by demand and supply analysis. The empirical supply of labour is comprised of the national population and demographic indices, such as age/sex composition and the rate of growth. Qualitative refinements of this labour supply are effected by examination of educational status, the skills and crafts acquired by the population and the extent of modern-sector work experience. In short, full evaluation is made of each state's stock of human capital.

Demand for labour is approached through the rate and pattern of growth of the domestic economy. Analysis therefore begins with basic assessment of gross national product, GNP *per capita*, and by economic activity. Growth by sector of the economy and major planned projects affecting labour demand are evaluated before resolving manpower demand and supply through the labour market.

Employment is analysed by economic activity, occupation, sex and nationality. Trends of employment are established and their past, present and future significance described. Thus all facets of human resources development are dealt with in terms of their impact upon the rate and nature of economic growth.

The structure of the book is therefore based upon a thematic analysis of individual national labour markets in the Arab world. These state-by-state studies are drawn together by international comparisons and examination of the international linkages between these national labour markets. The result is a regional perspective on manpower in the Arab Middle East. Within this the individual states' positions can be cast. The manpower position is projected up to 1985 for the capital-rich states, and this highlights their conflicting social and economic aims. Stresses generated by economic and social trends will become increasingly acute as these states pass into the 1980s.

In contrast, tensions in capital-poor states will be generated by increasing absolute and relative poverty. As the gap between rich and poor increases, so their geographical proximity will trigger a regional crisis. Although the book predicts acute social and political conflicts arising from present patterns of change and growth, it is difficult to enumerate effective means by which this crisis can be avoided.

## 2 The Data Base

The arguments put forward in this book are based upon a wide range of contemporary social, political, economic and demographic data. Indeed, one of the purposes of the book is to present a selection of largely new, previously untranslated and unpublished information about the Arab world.

The logistical obstacles to the collection of such a body of the most recently available data from such a wide range of countries in the Arab world are formidable. Contemporary data sources are frequently difficult of access, often not being officially released as government publications or papers, but kept in departments and agencies as typescripts of which, commonly, only few copies exist. These documents are often quickly forgotten and misplaced, so there is a significant wastage of unique data. That information which is published by governments is often only available several years after its collection, either because of deliberate suppression, or because of lengthy bureaucratic processes. Such a time lapse reduces considerably the utility of data in the Arab world because of the rapid pace of change.

The collection of extant material is itself not easy in the Arab world. The researcher has to overcome a range of logistical problems involved in visiting the country in question — contemporary data are rarely available outside the state about which they refer. Much data collection is only achieved through informal personal contacts; in official channels the researcher has to compete successfully against other clients more able to offer tangible reward for information provided.

In this case, the necessary field trips to all countries of the Arab world dealt with here were facilitated by the authors' co-direction of the International Migration Project. This project was commissioned by the International Labour Office, General Income Distribution and International Employment Policies Branch, as part of the International Migration for Employment Project. This project was a study of the modern trends of international labour migration in the Arab world, and necessitated travel to all the states of the Arab world. This travel enabled the data upon which this book is based to be collected, and facilitated the development of the authors' regional view of the Arab world that underlies the analysis.

As in most Third World countries, statistics collected in and pertaining to the Arab world can rarely be taken at face value. Official data perhaps display greater variations in quality (quite apart, of course, from uneven coverage of topic and geographical area) in the Arab region than elsewhere in the developing world. Variations in wealth mean that the capacities and inclinations of the various Arab governments to collect and process statistical data vary significantly. The exceptional wealth enjoyed by certain states, which are abutted by other governments of different ideology, militate in favour of rigorous suppression or quasi-official distortion of a wide range of national statistics.

In order that qualitative judgements and subjective assessments of empirical data sources be correct, consideration of a wide range of ancillary data sources is important. Visual evidence, hearsay, unofficial and official statements, newspaper comment and local opinion all temper the interpretation of released or unofficially obtained data. Practically all data which are released by Arab governments are initially made available in Arabic. Consequently the social scientist requires facility in the language if he or she is to keep up with the most recently available material.

In this book, because of these problems of data collection in the Arab world, efforts are made to source fully and correctly. This is in order that prospective researchers in the region are given an impression of sources and materials which might be available to them. One of the problems encountered in the early stages of inquiry in an Arab state is knowing the range of materials available, and through which agencies and offices they may be obtained.

## 3 The Regional Coverage of the Book

The book deals with the Arab Middle East. The Arab world, or region, is defined here as the Arabian peninsula, Arabian Gulf and Levantine countries, including Iraq together with the Maghreb, the Libyan Arab Jamahiriya, Egypt and the Sudan. Reference is made to Palestine under the sections on Jordan. Discussion of countries peripheral to this defined area is more limited. Thus, little note is taken of Somalia, Mauritania and Turkey, except in so far as they make, or are likely to make, contributions to the labour force and human capital of the Middle East. Iran, being separate ethnically and culturally and forming a discrete labour market, is excluded from this study. Evaluation is, however, made of the relatively limited contribution of Iranian labour to the Gulf and Peninsula states. Note is also made of the extent to which events in Iran revolving around the overthrow of the Shah might be a precursor of similar upheavals in the Arab capital-rich states.

In order to cast the impact of human resources upon Middle East economic development in a global context, the discussion of labour supplies extends to South-East Asia and West Africa. These are areas supplying labour to and comprising potential extra manpower sources for the Arab states. Important issues surround Arab utilisation of labour from these regions. The major focus throughout is the Arab world.

## 4 Acknowledgements

The authors would like to acknowledge at the outset generous grants and assistance from Shell (International) and the Ford Foundation. The University of Durham helped with printing and Xeroxing costs.

A great many people have been of assistance in compilation of the data upon which this book is based. Government officials, academics, colleagues and international agency staff in the Arab world and elsewhere have been most helpful in making available the vast range of information necessary for this study. The authors would like to thank all these persons for their time, ideas and perspectives.

The authors would like to thank those who wrote country studies, upon which the relevant chapters of this book were subsequently based. Dr R.I. Lawless wrote on Algeria and Morocco; Anne and Allan Findlay contributed on Morocco and Tunisia; Mary Sales wrote a country study on Syria and proof-read the text; Jim Socknat contributed a draft on the Yemen, and Dr Sami al Kashif a paper on international migration. Their collaboration is greatly appreciated. Professor D.P. O'Brien, Professor of Economics, Durham University, is thanked for his continuing support. The willing assistance of the Documentation Centre Staff and University Library in Durham is gratefully acknowledged. Of particular assistance in preparing the manuscript of this book was the previous research grant under International Labour Office funding described on page 4: we would like to thank Roger Böhning for his support of, interest in, and enthusiasm about our work. Mrs Pauline Morrell was involved in the administration of the research for this book from its outset, and worked assiduously preparing the manuscript. Kind assistance with typing was also given by Jean Wheatley.

All prices are given in United States dollars at prevailing rates of exchange. The views in this book do not necessarily represent those of the International Labour Office, nor of any other international agency with which the authors have been or are associated. The authors alone are responsible for what is written here.

In preparing this manuscript the authors have made every effort to cite the material they have used accurately and comprehensively. Our apologies are offered for oversights which have occurred in referencing.

# PART I: BACKGROUND

# 1 A DECADE OF DEVELOPMENT: MIXED PROGRESS AND A WIDENING GAP

## 1 Introduction

The oil-exporting states of the Arab world have enjoyed a decade of dramatic economic development.[1] The economic progress of the Arabian peninsular states and Libya could hardly have been a more complete transformation of these desert sheikhdoms and states. The rapid growth of their economies and continued industrialisation have, however, sown the seeds of acute social and political pressures which will be felt increasingly in the 1980s. Only when these tensions have been resolved can the real costs of the development of the 1970s in these oil-exporting states be evaluated.

In contrast, the capital-poor states of the Arab world have not experienced significant development, hardly managing to maintain *per capita* levels of income throughout the 1970s. Consequently, frustrations are growing in the capital-poor states. Geographical proximity and modern communications have facilitated popular comparison of the different rates of economic progress between the capital-rich and capital-poor states. This fuels growing disenchantment in the latter. Thus not only is the difference in wealth between the oil exporters and the rest increasing, but popular opinion is aware of the widening gap. As a result of the transformation of the economies of the oil exporters, therefore, the Arab world as a whole is delicately poised over a series of issues. In particular, the capital-rich states will have to come to terms with the social costs of their economic development. Not least of these is the hosting of expatriate populations almost as large as, or even greater than, the indigenous populations. The deeply entrenched pattern of rapid economic growth in these states means that their room for manoeuvre is less than might be imagined, despite an ability to 'buy themselves out of trouble' which, in reality, holds relatively little promise. The capital-poor states, continually constrained by foreign exchange shortages, will have to find − possibly in co-operation with the oil exporters − a means of increasing real *per capita* incomes. Practicable ways of encouraging a wider spread of wealth throughout the Arab world are not obvious.

In short, the future decade in the Arab world appears at best one of mixed prospects; at worst, the social and political pressures of growth in the capital-rich, combined with economic stagnation and *population* growth in the capital-poor, mean that the existing international order of the region could be threatened by crisis.

## 2 Capital-Rich and Capital-Poor States

The distinction between 'capital-rich' and 'capital-poor' states in the Arab world was first made by Mabro in 1975.[2] Since that time, because of the widening gap between extremes of income, this division, roughly paralleled by 'oil-exporting' and 'non-oil-exporting' countries, has become of increasing significance.

Here, distinction is made between capital-rich and capital-poor countries upon the basis of gross national product *per capita*. Although this indicator embodies a series of well known shortcomings when used as an index of economic development or national wealth, it demonstrates the range of wealth in the contemporary Arab world. Rather than dividing the nations into 'rich' and 'poor', three groups are chosen in this analysis. The third group is intermediate in *per capita* wealth, but aspires to and shares many characteristics of the capital-rich states; it is referred to as 'pseudo-capital-rich'.

Table 1.1: Major Arab States: Gross National Product *per capita*, 1976

| State | GNP *per capita* ($) |
|---|---|
| Kuwait | 15,840 |
| United Arab Emirates | 13,990 |
| Qatar | 11,400 |
| Libya | 6,310 |
| Saudi Arabia | 4,480 |
| Oman | 2,680 |
| Bahrain | 2,140 |
| Iraq | 1,390 |
| Algeria | 990 |
| Tunisia | 840 |
| Syria | 780 |
| Jordan | 610 |
| Morocco | 540 |
| Sudan | 290 |
| Yemen (PDRY) | 280 |
| Egypt | 280 |
| Yemen (YAR) | 250 |

Source: World Bank, *World Development Report 1978* (Washington, DC, 1978), Table 1, pp. 76-7 and p. 114.

Table 1.1 shows GNP *per capita* ranging from almost $16,000 in Kuwait down to $250 for the Yemen Arab Republic.[3] Although alternative means of calculation can give slightly different figures for GNP, the ranking of the states remains essentially the same. The true capital-rich states enjoy *per capita* incomes in excess of $4,000 and therefore include Kuwait, almost a caricature of a capital-rich state, the rapidly developing United Arab Emirates, tiny Qatar as well as the much larger Libya and Saudi Arabia. Also capital-rich is Iraq; only her substantial population deflates GNP *per capita* to the relatively low value (in capital-rich terms) shown in Table 1.1. Iraq, with its oil endowment, together with the largest population of the capital-rich states and large cultivable area, has perhaps the happiest balance of physical and human resources in the Arab world.

The capital-poor states which lie at the foot of the table each have *per capita* incomes of less than $1,000, ranging from $840 to $250. Four countries listed have a particularly low level of GNP *per capita*: Sudan, a typical African post-colonial state, but considered part of the Arab world; the People's Democratic Republic of Yemen, still searching hopefully for oil reserves; Egypt, rapidly becoming the Bangladesh of the Middle East; and the Yemen (YAR), whose role as a supplier of labour to Saudi Arabia appears increasingly to have been to the detriment of domestic Yemeni economic development.

Included in this group of capital-poor is Tunisia, which might be thought of as the Yemen (YAR) of Europe, to which she supplies large numbers of workers. Syria shows more economic potential than some other capital-poor states, and enjoys the advantage of a more manageable scale of economy than, for example, Egypt. Jordan is an economy dependent upon international aid and remittances from Jordanian workers overseas, and consequently has an artificially large service sector with few primary or secondary activities. Also capital-poor is Morocco, which, like Egypt, suffers rapid population growth whilst finding it hard to improve the performance of the economy. Her problems have been compounded by the return of many migrants from Europe.

The remaining, intermediate group comprises the pseudo-capital-rich. Despite having an income of less than $1,000 in 1976 (Table 1.1), Algeria is included in this group, as almost all facets of the economy are planned to resemble development in the true capital-rich states. Oman, despite falling firmly outside true capital-rich status, is basing development upon aspirations and planning decisions which would be more suited to the wealthiest of oil sheikhdoms. In contrast is Bahrain who, with only a small oil endowment, has invested her income with discretion, creating one of the most mature and diversified economies of the area.

Although industrialisation is proceeding apace, as yet the capital-rich and pseudo-capital-rich states are dependent upon income from oil rather than wealth generated by other domestic economic activity. Oil incomes are shown in Table 1.2.

Table 1.2: Major Middle East Oil Producers: Production and Revenues ($ billion), 1977

| State | Exports of Oil (million barrels a day) | Revenues ($ billion) |
|---|---|---|
| Saudi Arabia | 8.8 | 37.8 |
| Iran | 5.2 | 23.0 |
| Iraq | 2.1 | 9.6 |
| Libya | 2.0 | 9.4 |
| Kuwait | 1.9 | 8.5 |
| United Arab Emirates | 1.9 | 8.3 |
| Algeria | 1.1 | 5.6 |
| Qatar | 0.4 | 1.9 |

Source: Shell Briefing Service, *Oil and Gas in 1977* (London, 1978), p. 9.

In the Middle East (including Iran), Saudi Arabia dominates in terms of oil exports and revenue. Saudi Arabia enjoys oil revenues almost four times those received by the next most important Arab oil exporter — Iraq. The oil revenues of Iraq, Libya, Kuwait and the United Arab Emirates are between $8 billion and $10 billion *per annum* each. Their manoeuvrings to reduce or increase oil exports in response to political or conservation policies, or in response to variations in international market prices, are unlikely to change the general order of these rankings.

## 3 The National Populations of States in the Arab World

The range of totals of indigenous Arab populations is considerable (Table 1.3). Egypt's population, approaching 40 million, is double that of Morocco's, the next largest, at 18 million. Also large in terms of Middle East populations are Algeria, with approaching 17 million, the Sudan, whose people number over 14 million, and Iraq, with over 11 million nationals. In contrast, Qatar has a population of only 60,000 nationals. The United Arab Emirates is rather larger, having a population defined as 'national' of some 200,000. Of the same scale is Bahrain, with 225,000 nationals. Kuwait and Oman are slightly larger, with national populations of 472,000 and 550,000 respectively. Between these extremes of size are Syria, Tunisia, the Yemen (YAR) and Saudi Arabia, with populations of between 7.5 million and 4.5 million. The remaining countries of Jordan, Lebanon, Libya and the Yemen (PDRY) have between 2.7 and 1.7 million nationals.

In terms of potential for economic development it is a cruel irony that the states without oil have the larger populations. There are some exceptions to this – Egypt does produce over 400,000 barrels of oil per day, an amount equivalent to Qatar's production. All Egypt's oil, however, is used domestically. The fact that Egypt's population is 630 times as large as Qatar's means that Egypt remains firmly near the foot of the league table of *per capita* incomes. The national population of Saudi Arabia (at 4.6 million in 1975) depresses the *per capita* income to less than that of Kuwait's despite Saudi Arabia's far higher income from oil. However, the Kingdom's population does not comprise a sufficient number from which to draw a labour force to man a modern industrial sector. Nor does the population comprise a substantial domestic market. In short, relative to the scale of wealth, and in relation to the pattern of industrial and general economic development envisaged in capital-rich states, even Saudi Arabia's population is small; the populations of the Gulf states (and even Libya with over 2 million) are tiny from the perspective of the development of a modern economy. Of the capital-rich states, only Iraq's population of 11 million is of a more useful scale in development terms.

## 4 Demographic Characteristics of the Arab National Populations

The national populations of the Arab world have in common a high rate of increase. Most states are growing at 3.5 per cent per annum. At recorded rates of increase, Kuwait's indigenous population is doubling every 16 years while Egypt's doubles every 30 years. However, when (at present growth rates) Kuwait's indigenous population doubles in 1991, her national population will be about 950,000; Egypt's population will then be some 55 millions.

There is no reason for the capital-rich states to attempt to limit the growth of their national populations. Indeed, they can consider rapid population growth beneficial rather than deleterious to their efforts at

Table 1.3: Major Arab States: National Populations Ranked by Size,
Various Years

| State | Indigenous Population | Year |
|---|---|---|
| Egypt | 38,228,000 | 1976 |
| Morocco | 18,400,000 | 1977 |
| Algeria | 16,940,000 | 1977 |
| Sudan | 14,113,600 | 1973 |
| Iraq | 11,124,000 | 1975 |
| Syria | 7,335,000 | 1975 |
| Tunisia | 5,570,000 | 1975 |
| Yemen (YAR) | 5,037,000 | 1975 |
| Saudi Arabia | 4,592,500 | 1975 |
| Jordan | 2,616,700 | 1975 |
| Lebanon | 2,400,000 | 1975 |
| Libya | 2,087,900 | 1973 |
| Yemen (PDRY) | 1,660,000 | 1975 |
| Oman | 550,000 | 1974 |
| Kuwait | 472,100 | 1975 |
| Bahrain | 224,700 | 1976 |
| United Arab Emirates | 200,000 | 1975 |
| Qatar | 60,300 | 1975 |
| Total | 131,604,200 | |

Source: Authors' estimates from official sources. See J.S. Birks and C.A. Sinclair,
International Migration Project, Country Case Studies (Durham).

development. They do not suffer financial constraints in providing educational and health facilities for an expanding population. Nor does an expanding population result in reduced *per capita* wealth; the oil exporters can plan and achieve growth which assures a rising *per capita* income notwithstanding rapid population growth. Planners in capital-rich states see increasing demands and opportunities in the future for a large national work-force – all economic factors make the government disinclined to curb indigenous population growth.

Social reasons also discourage governments of capital-rich states from limiting national population growth. Planners in these states are coming increasingly to fear the consequences of hosting the large immigrant populations which their booming economies have drawn in. Most dramatically they fear the 'swamping' of their national populations by alien majorities. Rapidly increasing national populations are seen as helping to alleviate this threat. It will be some years before the governments of the capital-rich states abandon pro-natalist policies.

No such defences justify continued high population growth in the capital-poor states, especially those with larger populations. Already in these states, population growth is cited as one of the major obstacles to improvement of living standards and *per capita* income.[4] As the population increases, and numbers in the lower age groups rise, so the resources devoted to health care (which, of course, may further exacerbate population growth) and education increase. These resources have a very high opportunity cost in these poor states as they detract from development efforts in other sectors or even from improvements in quality of education.

It is the large absolute scale of growth of these populations which makes the impact upon economic development so deleterious. Presently struggling to maintain *per capita* incomes in real terms, further population growth of this scale becomes increasingly likely to bring about a fall in real living standards.

It will be some years before a fall in fertility will be significant enough to slow the rate of population growth in these capital-poor states. Birth control programmes are expensive and difficult to effect, whilst at the same time, the improvement in living standards which would bring about a 'spontaneous demographic transition', causing a fall in the rate of population growth, becomes harder to bring about. Thus increasing populations in the capital-poor states pose a threat to living standards which is self-reinforcing.

Ironically, the falling away of fertility rates, with consequent reductions in population growth, will occur first in the capital-rich states, despite their present pro-natalist policies. In these states improved living standards with high and rising aspirations will engender conscious means of family limitation. Evidence suggests that acceptance of birth control is spreading rapidly in Kuwait, for example.[5] Kuwait, the most mature of the truly capital-rich Gulf economies, often provides a pointer to the direction in which the capital-rich states as a whole are progressing.

The impact of the pattern and trends of population growth in the Arab world upon the widening gap between rich and poor states is twofold. First, in the immediate future, the high rates of population growth militate in favour of increasing wealth and economic growth in the oil exporters (or at any rate do not hamper it), whilst in the poor states population growth erodes the benefits of real economic expansion. Secondly, in the medium term, the populations of the capital-poor states will continue to grow rapidly, when rates of growth in the wealthier states have slowed. This will further reinforce the inequality of wealth in *per capita* terms.

## 5 National Work-Forces of the Arab States

The overall crude participation rate amongst the capital-poor populations is approaching 30 per cent (Table 1.4). This rate would be higher if all women who work on the land were consistently recorded in censuses and in employment surveys as 'in employment'. In fact they are rarely so recorded and therefore are generally omitted from discussions of the work-force; it should be borne in mind, though, that women feature significantly in agricultural employment in all the capital-poor Arab countries.[6]

Table 1.4: Major Arab States: National Labour Force and Crude Participation Rates, 1975

| State | Population | Labour Force | Crude Participation Rate (per cent) |
|---|---|---|---|
| Capital-Rich | | | |
| Iraq | 11,380,000 | 2,860,000 | 25.1 |
| Saudi Arabia | 4,592,500 | 1,026,500 | 22.3 |
| Libya | 2,223,700 | 449,200 | 20.2 |
| Kuwait | 472,100 | 91,800 | 19.4 |
| United Arab Emirates | 200,000 | 45,000 | 22.3 |
| Qatar | 60,300 | 12,500 | 20.7 |
| Total | 18,928,600 | 4,485,000 | 23.7 |
| Pseudo-Capital-Rich | | | |
| Algeria | 15,800,000 | 4,100,000 | 26.1 |
| Oman | 550,000 | 137,000 | 24.9 |
| Bahrain | 214,000 | 45,800 | 21.3 |
| Total | 16,564,000 | 4,282,800 | 25.9 |
| Capital-Poor | | | |
| Egypt | 37,364,900 | 12,522,200 | 33.5 |
| Sudan | 15,031,300 | 3,700,000 | 24.6 |
| Syria | 7,335,000 | 1,838,900 | 25.1 |
| Yemen (YAR) | 5,037,000 | 1,425,800 | 28.1 |
| Jordan (East Bank) | 2,616,700 | 532,800 | 20.4 |
| Yemen (PDRY) | 1,660,000 | 430,500 | 25.9 |
| Total | 69,044,900 | 20,450,200 | 29.6 |
| Grand total | 104,537,500 | 29,218,000 | 27.9 |

Source: Compiled by the authors.

Not only are the national work-forces of the capital-rich states smaller because of the scale of their populations, but the crude participation rates are also lower at less than 22 per cent (Table 1.4). The

crude participation rates of these capital-rich states range from an extremely low 19 per cent in the case of Kuwait to 25 per cent in the case
of Iraq. (Iraq, as noted previously, is something of an exception
amongst capital-rich states with her larger population and, as can be
seen in Table 1.4, work-force.) Not only are the work-forces in the
capital-rich states small, they are smaller than would be expected from
total populations of this size.

These low values stem from the very youthful nature of the populations. A larger proportion is aged less than 15 years in these states
than in more normally age-distributed populations. Of Qatar's 60,300
for example, over 44 per cent are aged less than 15 years. Almost 49 per
cent of the Iraqi population is aged less than 15 years, and the figure
for Saudi Arabia is also over 48 per cent.[7] As a result, only a relatively
small proportion of the population falls within the economically active
age groups. Secondly, oil revenues in the capital-rich states have facilitated a widespread expansion of higher education, which has held
within the educational system boys, and to a lesser extent girls, who
would otherwise have entered the work-force at, say, age 18. Thirdly,
the labour force is reduced by the exclusion of women from wage
employment, except in a limited number of professions. However,
some are involved in the traditional sector, though these activities are
decaying. Traditional employment for women which has been lost has
not been replaced by new opportunities in the modern sector.[8]
Women's low level of educational attainment — even lower than that of
their menfolk — also limits their modern-sector participation. Investment in education is rapidly changing this, however; increased participation of women in the modern sectors of the capital-rich states is to be
expected.

Amongst the three pseudo-capital-rich states of Oman, Bahrain and
Algeria, there is a wide range of size and characteristics. Algeria shares a
high crude participation rate and relatively large population with her
Maghreb neighbours. The crude participation rate is raised in Oman by
the large remaining traditional and agricultural sector, but lowered in
Bahrain by the youthful age distribution of the population, together
with widely available higher education.

The essential point is the relative scales of the work-forces of the
capital-rich and capital-poor states. The 1.8 million workers in capital-
rich states (excluding Iraq) amount to less than one-tenth of the work-
forces of the capital-poor states, yet it is in the capital-rich states where
the vast majority of industrial and general development of the 1970s
has taken place. In view of the small sizes of their work-forces, it might

seem surprising that the capital-rich states decided to embark upon relatively labour-intensive development. In view of the low educational attainment of these small labour forces, the difficulties encountered in the face of industrial growth will become yet more apparent.

## 6 Educational Attainment of the Arab National Populations

### (a) Literacy Rates

The level of educational attainment in the region overall is rather low. The regional literacy rate is only 30 per cent (Table 1.5). Most countries have national values of below 40 per cent. At the lower end of the range of literacy rates is a mixture of rich and poor states – apart from Sudan and the Yemens, the Emirates also have a literacy rate of below 15 per cent. In the capital-poor countries, lack of financial resources coupled with rapidly increasing populations mean that it is difficult to imbue a large section of the population with literacy. In the case of the Emirates, it is the short period over which infrastructure has been provided that explains the low level of literacy. Although enrolment ratios are now high, literacy in older age groups is the exception. Even in Kuwait almost half of the population remains illiterate, despite having enjoyed modern education since the 1950s.

However, the Kuwaiti literacy rate is surpassed only by Jordan and Lebanon. The Levant is a region which enjoys markedly higher literacy rates than elsewhere in the Arab world. Contact with colonial powers gave these countries the early beginnings of a modern education system. Also important in elevating educational status were the traditional and extensive links of the Levant with the wider world.

Libya, Algeria and Saudi Arabia give sure indication that recent oil wealth alone has not yet ensured literacy. In this sense, then, even the capital-rich states are 'undeveloped'. It is unusual for states with such high *per capita* incomes to have national populations of such low educational attainment. Effectively, the rapid pace of economic development has run ahead of social progress. This is a recurring theme in discussions of the capital-rich states.

The educational attainment of the Arab populations is likely to remain low in the medium term. Even in Kuwait, with ample financial resources and a geographically concentrated population, the development of human resources has proved surprisingly difficult. As will be shown in individual country chapters below, the very wealth that should facilitate rapid expansion of education serves in fact to stunt the development of human resources. Thus prospects for improvement of educa-

Table 1.5: Major Arab States: Literacy Rates of National Populations 1970 to 1975

| State | Literacy Rate (per cent) | Year | Population Age |
|---|---|---|---|
| Lebanon | 68 | 1974 | 15+ |
| Jordan | 62 | 1974 | 15+ |
| Kuwait | 55 | 1974 | 15+ |
| Tunisia | 55 | 1972 | 15+ |
| Syria | 53 | 1974 | 15+ |
| Bahrain | 47 | 1971 | 10+ |
| Egypt | 40 | 1974 | 15+ |
| Libya | 39 | 1973 | 15+ |
| Algeria | 35 | 1974 | 15+ |
| Saudi Arabia | 33 | 1974 | 10+ |
| Qatar | 33 | 1970 | 15+ |
| Morocco | 26 | 1974 | 15+ |
| Iraq | 26 | 1974 | 15+ |
| Oman | 20 | 1975 | 15+ |
| Sudan | 15 | 1974 | 15+ |
| United Arab Emirates | 14 | 1968 | 15+ |
| Yemen (YAR) | 10 | 1974 | 15+ |
| Yemen (PDRY) | 10 | 1974 | 15+ |

Sources: The World Bank, *World Development Report 1978* (Washington, DC, 1978), Table 18, p. 110, and official censuses.

tional standards in the capital-rich states are not as rosy as the scale of financial resources might suggest.

In the capital-poor states, development of educational facilities is strongly constrained by lack of financial resources. This is to the extent that in the case of Egypt, for example, expansion of school enrolments is insufficient to prevent an increase in the absolute numbers of illiterates. The widening gap in incomes will be reflected in diverging standards of educational attainment. Despite the difficulties in human resource development in the capital rich states, they will progress at a much faster rate than their poorer neighbours.

*(b) The Nature of Arab Education*

Not only is educational attainment low throughout the Arab world but, in general terms, the nature and direction of education in the region is little suited to furthering the declared aims of the governments — modern industrial economies.

Almost without exception, the educational tradition in Arab states evolved through Koranic schools. Modern schools have replaced this traditional form of education almost everywhere (although Koranic schools still exist in the Sultanate of Oman and Yemen (YAR)), but the character of contemporary education owes much to its predecessor. The Koranic schools (*kuttab*) normally enrolled only boys and taught little but the reading, writing, learning and recitation of the Koran. The curricula were invariable and repetitive. Such concepts as understanding application and initiative were not widely employed. The teachers were themselves products of these schools. The higher centres of learning were generally either explicitly religious seminaries or were controlled by Koranic injunctions, as interpreted by religious leaders.

Modern education systems adopted many of these characteristics, and also owe much to Egypt, whence curricula, teachers and educational administrators were imported. This is especially true of the capital-rich states which, when oil wealth was first received, imported Egyptian teachers, books and methods. Despite these slightly differing origins, most educational systems existing in the Arab world today can be characterised as being linear in design, heavily biased towards arts and literature, and having a general university education as the pinnacle of the educational pyramid.[9]

Courses are essentially repetitive, the same blend of subjects being studied at each educational level, only at a higher standard. Some choice is introduced at the secondary level where either 'arts' or 'sciences' can be studied. Successful secondary school graduates expect to proceed to university almost by right. Until recently, the same subjects were studied at university once again. At all levels there is a strong underlying emphasis on the literary aspect of education, reflecting the respect in the Arab world for the written word which derives from the Koran.

Unfortunately, neither the Koranic schools nor modern education are particularly well adapted to producing students attuned to the needs of modern economic development. The Koranic schools did not (and those remaining do not) impart literacy in any meaningful sense, because although the classical Arabic of the Koran, the substance of study in these schools, has not changed since its completion, spoken Arabic and everyday written Arabic have altered significantly. The two are related by script and some vocabulary but by little else. The common man who attended a Koranic school cannot read a newspaper easily. Nor, importantly, could many such men count, since mathematics was often not included in these schools. The economic value of *kuttab* graduates in the modern economy is limited.

No such fundamental inadequacies as these are prevalent in modern educational systems, but weaknesses remain. First, the structure of the modern education systems inculcates the notion in schoolchildren that

a university education is the summit of school activity. This is unfortunate, since it puts a premium on the courses which lead to university,
and a low premium on non-university options such as technical secondary school. Moreover, because of the literary tradition, it is the general
arts and social science courses which are the most popular and prestigious. These, though, are the courses which are least directed towards
fulfilling the manpower demands of a developing modern sector.

Unfortunately, the kudos of general university courses means it is
typically only those who are academically less able or who actually
'drop out' who enter technical or vocational education. The aversion to
manual work, particularly evident in the peninsula, reinforces the
stigma attached to vocational training, which is seen as leading to
manual employment. Indeed, it is probably more apt to assert that any
employment other than completely sedentary office work is looked
down upon by most nationals in the capital-rich states. This attitude
obviously has great influence upon the nature and disposition of the
work-force. It is reinforced, rather than removed, by the present set of
values in education.

These weaknesses and others are increasingly widely recognised by
educationalists. However, it is extremely difficult to change the content
or direction of even the recently established educational systems in the
Arab world. The teachers and students are proving highly resistant to
change, so the customary pattern is tending to perpetuate itself. Governments are appending to the education system a variety of vocational training institutions, such as teacher training colleges, agricultural, technical and commercial schools. However, the more able students skilfully circumnavigate these in order to obtain university education.

One point is clear: pupils who opt for general secondary courses
leading to a university education are not misguided in their educational
choice from an individual economic standpoint. Indeed, they are maximising their lifetime income, because both capital-rich and capital-poor
Arab governments offer priority employment opportunities to university graduates. Private-sector job opportunities are typically relatively limited in the capital-poor states, and in the capital-rich, governments offer nationals better conditions and higher wages than are normally available in the private sector. It is from the point of view of
social accounting and national economic development that the academic system is so ill directed.

In sum, the structure and emphasis of educational systems in the
Arab states combined with the employment policies of these govern-

ments mean that: there is an unusually large number of university enrollees, vocational training attracts only the drop-outs of the formal
system and the academically less able. Moreover, this carries the stigma
of being the last resort of those unsuccessful in educational terms and
school-leavers tend to have formal and academic qualifications, more
applicable to clerical and administrative work than to technical or scientific jobs. This undue emphasis on university education means that, in
the capital-poor states, relatively fewer resources are available to improve the quality of primary education, adult literacy schemes, or other
facets of the education system.

Therefore the nature of education in the Arab world as a whole is
ill suited to meet the manpower requirements of the modern industrial economies to which the governments aspire. Some technical
schools are highly successful, and particular countries have been successful in reordering educational priorities and attitudes, but these are
the exception. The degree to which these inadequacies have contributed
to the qualitative shortfall of indigenous manpower in the capital-rich
states will become clear as individual country labour markets are considered. So too will the disappointingly limited contribution of education to modern-sector development in the capital-poor states.

### 7 The Nature of Modern Economic Development in the Arab World

*(a) Introduction*

The distinction between capital-rich and capital-poor also serves well to
categorise the contrasting forms of modern economic development
found in the Arab world. The pseudo-capital-rich can also be discussed
as a separate group. Other works[10] give a detailed, if rather dated view
of general economic development in the Arab world. In particular, the
pre-1973 pattern is dealt with thoroughly elsewhere. This section is
concerned mainly with the developments of the 1970s.

*(b) Capital-Rich States*[11]

Oil wealth in the peninsula states and Libya was first used by emirs and
sheikhly leaders as a means of improving the welfare of their people.
Commodities whose absence set strict limits on what was possible, personally, socially and economically were provided in abundance: fresh-
water desalination plants, electricity generation plants and rather better
housing characterised the earliest moves towards modernity. Burgeoning demands and aspirations of the population encouraged an ever more
lavish provision of infrastructure and social services. Before 1973 the

provision of physical and social infrastructure absorbed much of the oil revenues. It also posed administrative problems which brought about a government bureaucracy and the beginnings of large-scale modern employment of nationals.

Indeed, a logical extension to the role of emirs and sheikhs was that of formal employer so capital-rich governments provided employment, often sinecures, in ministries. Wages were often paid more as of right than in return for particular services. This type of employment with growing oil wealth meant that transformation from traditional to modern economy occurred, on a superficial level, remarkably quickly. The desires of the major oil-exporting states to consolidate their wealth, to create an alternative source of income, to achieve the qualities of a 'modern' state, spawned industrial development, in some cases before infrastructure projects were completed. By the early 1970s petro-chemical and small-scale import-substituting industries were well established in the peninsula and Libya.

The oil price rises of 1973 transformed the potential for economic development, and in particular the industrial ambitions of the capital-rich states. All began building large-scale industrial developments.

This industrial development aims at maximisation of oil revenue in the long run. Most of the major oil exporters chose, in the mid-1970s, to extract and sell virtually as much oil as possible, resulting in surplus revenues. Although large amounts were invested overseas, the oil revenues were used primarily to invest in domestic economic development. In this transformation of financial capital into physical assets to yield an income independent of oil, planners considered that general social and economic development could best be engendered by industrialisation. Establishment of heavy industry was facilitated, apart from the financial resources, by the cheap source of power represented by natural gas.

The historical moment when modern development began in each capital-rich state varied, largely according to the scale of wealth and how liberal leaders were in distributing it. Moreover, the most wealthy states are not always the most modern: Saudi Arabia's development for example, was slow until 1973. But the path of development and aims of all these states are remarkably similar. The shared features of capital-rich states' economic development plans include a large and expanding government sector, ambitious industrial development programmes based upon heavy industry, and an ever-increasing standard of welfare and income. All these states see industrialisation as a central component of domestic development. This creation of industrial sectors has necessitated rapid further expansion in infrastructure provision. Both the industrialisation and the infrastructure provision are now, as a result of the 1973 price rises, on a spectacular scale, almost unprecedented in the Third World.

In the rush to develop the modern sector of these capital-rich economies little attention has been given to traditional activities. Traditional employment included pearling, date cultivation, farming, fishing, pottery, boat building and trading. Most of these industries have vanished, but some fishermen and boat-builders still exist on the coasts of the peninsula. Agricultural employment was always limited, so its decline has been barely noticed. In the larger capital-rich states of Saudi Arabia, Libya and Iraq, many nationals do continue to work on farms, however. Generally, though, modern economic development in the capital-rich states has largely absorbed or made redundant the traditional sector. This is hardly surprising in view of the labour demands of the expanding modern sector. Indeed, despite absorbing virtually all the labour from traditional employment, the modern sector in all the capital-rich states has suffered critical shortages of manpower and many of the planners and commentators in these states saw labour shortages as the major constraint to modern-sector expansion and development in general.

The resulting demand for labour of virtually all skills and qualifications in the oil-exporting states, remarkable in its strength because of the financial resources of the exporters combined with their urge to develop rapidly, was of great impact upon the region's labour market. Apart from the growth in employment in these capital-rich states being from a very small base, the rapid growth in the demand for labour was aggravated by these states' embarking contemporaneously on their most labour-intensive stages of development — the construction phases.

In the capital-rich states, the governments' response to this manpower shortage was to allow market forces to reign.[12] Labour was imported with little official constraint. The result was an inflow of workers of massive proportions. Most of these workers derived from capital-poor states of the Arab world, whose contrasting experience of economic development is now examined.

*(c) Capital-Poor States*

Unlike their oil-exporting neighbours, the capital-poor states are not enjoying rapid economic growth, and only expect to maintain their present level of development. Growth of gross domestic product is small in real terms and, on a *per capita* basis, often falling. Economic development in the capital-poor Arab states resembles that in other developing countries in the Third World, being characterised by high rates of population increase, low domestic savings rates, low rates of growth of fixed domestic capital formation with high rates of under- and unemployment. Recently, they have also been characterised by high rates of domestic inflation and weak currencies.

Rapid population growth is largely responsible for many weak facets of these economies. It has resulted in a large share of resources being absorbed by health services and education, which is often misdirected in view of the available employment opportunities. Governments have mopped up many of the erstwhile unemployed. This artificial employ- ment weakens the administrative capability of governments; decisions become slower and initiative is stifled. The socialist policies of the Nasserist era have resulted in small private sectors in Egypt and Syria in particular. The subsequent inability of governments to effect economic development has meant that progress has been slow.

Industrial development in the capital-poor states is limited, and often unsuccessful. Typically capital-intensive, that industrial growth which has taken place has not generated much employment. In these capital-poor states, agriculture provides much of the employment, but is generally in need of rationalisation, modernisation and investment. The inability of capital-poor government and private sectors to expand productive employment has swelled the informal sector. This has been stimulated by rural to urban migration which has led to overcrowding in cities throughout the capital-poor states, sometimes with low living standards.

All this is in sharp contrast to capital-rich states. Indeed the paths of development of the capital-rich and the capital-poor could hardly be more different. The distinctions are made startlingly evident by their close geographical proximity. While the capital-rich states are planning economic development on exotic levels, planners in the capital-poor states hope merely to maintain *per capita* income. Under these bleak circumstances, international migration for employment has seemed at times the only alternative to unemployment for many of the peoples of the capital-poor states. They flocked to avail themselves of the oppor- tunities manifest in the oil-exporting states, ostensibly relieving the pressure of unemployment in their home states. This movement of labour has now reached such a scale that it has come to comprise yet another constraint to economic growth in these struggling states.

### (d) Pseudo-Capital-Rich States

It is the pattern of development that Oman, Bahrain and Algeria are following which means that they are aptly named pseudo-capital-rich. Their path of economic growth resembles closely that of the capital-rich states proper in all but outright scale and the financial capacity of the governments to pay for their planned programmes.

Thus the Sultanate of Oman, despite its declining oil exports and weak financial position,[13] has adopted development strategy and planning objectives more suited to a country with much higher oil receipts. Rather than concentrating on developing her agriculture, which has great potential, Oman has embarked upon a programme of industrial development. It is most unlikely that the optimistic and misdirected development plan targets will be met. Slightly different is Bahrain, which was the first oil producer in the Gulf. The country followed a gentle path of development, resulting by the early 1970s in a mature economy not suffering an inordinate reliance upon expatriate labour. However, since 1973 Bahrain has been swept along by the momentum of her Gulf neighbours, following a more rapid rate of expansion which bears many of the hallmarks of economic development in the major oil exporters. It is not clear to what extent Bahrain can sustain this rate of growth, and whether or not the broader consequences of it will be deleterious to Bahrain in the medium term. Just how hard it is to effect rapid industrial growth without massive financial strength is illustrated by Algeria, where development along industrial lines is proving elusive, despite some careful decision-making. In the event of a sharp peak of revenues from gas in the mid-1980s, Algerian planners will have to solve the problem of subsidising an inefficient heavy industrial sector in the face of falling government income. At the same time, it is likely that the agricultural sector will also be in decline. In short, it appears that Algeria's income from loans and gas revenues might well prove insufficient for such an ambitious strategy of development.

## 8 Conclusions

The analysis has distinguished between three groups of Arab states: the capital-rich, capital-poor and intermediate pseudo-capital-rich. The style of economic development exhibited by each of these groups is different, and the extremes could hardly be more contrasting. However, in each pattern of economic development, human resources are a critical factor.

The capital-rich states are starved of indigenous human capital; in them, development has only been made possible by the assistance of large numbers of migrant workers. In the capital-poor, population growth has combined with a limited endowment of financial and mineral resources to result in a low level of income *per capita*. Human capital exists in the capital-poor, but of totally the wrong type to be utilised in economic development. Furthermore, the selective process of international migration has led to the effective draining from the capital-poor states of the few skilled and able workers most suitable for facilitating modern economic development. The effect of this out-migration on the economies of the capital-poor states has been, in many cases, harmful. Thus, indirectly, the wealth of the capital-rich has, through the process and nature of international migration, added to the problems of the capital-poor states. This has aggravated the widening gap between capital-rich and capital-poor states.[14]

In the case of some of the pseudo-capital-rich states, inappropriate and misguided policies of economic development give an illusory picture of development. As oil revenues or grants inevitably dry up in the medium term, the costs of this mistaken development will be revealed, for neither human nor economic capital will have been created.

Under any conditions, the task of human resources development is difficult. On the one hand, in capital-rich states, economic growth seems capable of a pace far in excess of that attainable in the field of human resources development. This creates a dependence in the short run on migrant labour which distorts the domestic labour market. There are signs that this short-term dependence on expatriate man-power leads inevitably to a long-term dependence; attempts to accelerate the development of indigenous human resources in these capital-rich states have proved unsuccessful.

On the other hand, in the capital-poor states, development of any kind has been uphill work, and population growth has repeatedly threatened to annihilate those slender achievements that have been made. As a result, unemployment at most levels of educational attainment has been pervasive in these capital-poor states. In Egypt, where educational expansion has been significant, there were 3 million more illiterates in 1976 than in 1960. International migration for employment initially served as a useful escape valve for some of these unemployed. However, in practice, those who departed from the capital-poor states were not the unemployed and unskilled, but those who held roles essential to the development of the labour-supplying states. These departures heralded yet more difficulties in human resource development in the capital-poor states: allocation of scarce investment funds between social services and employment-creating development projects is made especially difficult when the more educated and skilled tend to depart abroad. To what purpose should human resources development be directed in this context?

The entry of large amounts of non-Arab labour into the Middle East labour market has added new dimensions to the labour markets of both capital-rich and capital-poor states. Associated with these changing labour market conditions are new problems for human resource development in all states throughout the Arab world. The pattern of economic development in the 1970s was dependent mainly upon a physical resource — oil; by contrast, in the 1980s the pattern and nature of economic change will be increasingly governed by human resources.

The issues broadly outlined in this introduction are now dealt with on a country-by-country basis, the analysis beginning with Kuwait, the country with the highest GNP *per capita* in the world.

### Notes

1. See J.S. Birks and C.A. Sinclair, *International Migration and Development in the Arab Region* (ILO, Geneva, 1980) for a similar discussion of economic growth in the 1970s in the Arab world.

2. R.E. Mabro, 'Employment, Choice of Technology and Sectoral Priorities', *Manpower and Employment in Arab Countries, Some Critical Issues* (ILO, Geneva, 1975).

3. $250 *per capita* is the figure given in the World Bank source quoted. If remittances were fully added into this figure, GNP *per capita* would rise. The figure quoted in the table serves to illustrate the groupings made, however.

4. R.E. Mabro, *The Egyptian Economy, 1955-1972* (Oxford University Press, London, 1974); *MEED*, 13 November 1978, p. 15.

5. A.R. Hill, 'The Demography of the Population of Kuwait', *Population Bulletin, 13* (Beirut, July 1977), pp. 42-55.

6. For problems of defining 'economically active' in the Middle East, see J.G.C. Blacker, 'A Critique of the International Definitions of Economic Activity and Employment Status and their Applicability in Population Censuses in Africa and the Middle East', *Population Bulletin, 14* (Beirut, June 1978), pp. 47-56.

7. Figures based upon the *Demographic Fact Sheet* (United Nations Economic Commission for Western Asia, Beirut, 1979).

8. J.S. Birks and S.E. Letts, 'Women in Rural Saudi Arabia: Old Roles and New in the Sultanate of Oman', *Journal of Gulf and Arabian Peninsular Studies, III*, 10 (Kuwait, April 1977), pp. 49-65 (in Arabic); C. Makhlouf-Obermeyer, *Changing Veils: A Study of Women in South Arabia* (Croom Helm, London, 1978); N.H. Youssef, *Women and Work in Developing Countries* (Connecticut, 1977); F. Heard-Bey, 'Social Changes in the Gulf States and Oman', *Asian Affairs, 59*, 3 (October 1972), pp. 309-16, F. Heard-Bey, 'Arab Women in the United Arab Emirates', *Arab Women* (London, December 1975), Report No. 27 of the Minority Rights Group, p. 12.

9. See C.A. Sinclair, 'Education in Kuwait, Bahrain and Qatar: An Economic Assessment', unpublished PhD thesis, (Durham University, 1977); J.S. Szyliowicz, *Education and Modernisation in the Middle East* (Cornell, New York, 1973).

10. For example, H. Askari and J.G. Cummings, *Middle East Economies in the 1970s: A Comparative Approach* (Praeger Special Studies, New York, 1976); Y.A. Sayigh, *The Economies of the Arab World* (Croom Helm, London, 1978); M.H. Fouad, 'Petrodollars and Economic Development in the Middle East', *Middle East Journal, 32*, 3 (1978), pp. 307-21; World Bank, *World Development Report 1978* (Washington, DC, August 1978); D.G. Edens, *Oil and Development in the Middle East* (Praeger Special Studies, New York, 1979).

11. See for more details K.G. Fenelon, *The United Arab Emirates, an Economic and Social Survey* (Longman, London, 1976); A.K. al Kuwari, *Oil Revenues in the Gulf Emirates* (Bowkers, London, 1978); J.E. Hazelton, 'Gold Rush Economies: Development Planning in the Persian/Arabian Gulf', *Studies in Comparative International Development, 13*, 2 (New York, 1978), pp. 3-22.

12. J.S. Birks and C.A. Sinclair, *The Nature and Process of Labour Importing: The Arabian Gulf States of Kuwait, Bahrain, Qatar and the United Arab Emirates* World Employment Programme Working Paper (ILO, Geneva, 1978).

13. Recent Omani oil discoveries do not remove the basis of this argument.

14. J.S. Birks and C.A. Sinclair, *International Migration and Development in the Arab Region* (ILO, Geneva, 1980).

# PART II: THE CAPITAL-RICH STATES

# 2 THE STATE OF KUWAIT

## 1 Introduction

Kuwait is found at the head of the Arabian Gulf. Amongst Gulf states, she has the largest population and greatest oil reserves. Oil was discovered in the 1930s, but not extracted until 1947.[1] Bahrain preceded Kuwait in developing oil resources, but Kuwait's production of crude oil is on a quite different scale.

With a population of about 1 million persons, Kuwait probably enjoys the highest level of gross national product *per capita* in the world. The figures quoted vary slightly, as different measures of population and national income are used. A recent estimate for GNP *per capita* is $11,600.[2] Despite such a high average level of income, the distribution of income is very uneven, even amongst the half million Kuwaiti nationals who receive the bulk of the distributed oil wealth. High inflation rates and astronomically high house rents have had a noticeable effect on 'middle-class' Kuwaitis and, more dramatically, upon non-Kuwaitis.

In terms of oil reserves and production, Kuwait ranks fourth in the Middle East after Saudi Arabia, Iran and Iraq.[3] Kuwait's position in these 'league tables' tends to change quite often as constraints are placed on oil production and as new oil reserves are discovered. Oil production has been limited in recent years both for political and economic reasons. It is now thought in Kuwait that a slower rate of extraction which preserves the life of the remaining reserves would encourage a more efficient allocation of resources.

New sources of income unrelated to oil have been sought in recent years, leading to the development of a significant banking and finance centre, and the establishment of an industrial sector. Most of Kuwait's industry is manned by expatriates, and in a sense Kuwait has exchanged one kind of dependence (on oil) for another (on expatriates). Doubts are increasingly being voiced over the wisdom of the policy of industrialisation, which stem largely from the problem of dependence on expatriates. Non-Kuwaitis slightly outnumber Kuwaitis in the population, and by two to one in the work-force.

In the past seven years Kuwait has experienced a spectacular rate of economic growth, and is now embarking on a five-year development plan comprising a total of $15 billion.[4] Despite the outward appearance of prosperity and confidence, there are many social, economic and political tensions in Kuwait which surface occasionally, as they did in August 1976. The coming decade is crucial; in it Kuwait will establish the economic base for the remainder of this century and thereby the nature of Kuwaiti society.

## 2 The Supply of Labour

### (a) Population

Since 1945 Kuwait's population has grown very rapidly. At the time of the first census in 1957, the total number of persons enumerated was 206,470. In 1975 Kuwait's population of 995,000 included 523,000 'non-Kuwaitis'. Discussion of Kuwait's population and work-force returns repeatedly to this duality. Kuwaitis are a relatively well defined homogeneous group linked by a common culture, similar interests and a common ethnic background. The second group, 'non-Kuwaitis', are an ill-defined conglomerate of many different nationalities who have different backgrounds, languages, cultures, interests and religions (though most are Muslims). It is impossible to discuss population, economic development or the labour market in Kuwait or any other capital-rich state in the Arab region without reference to this distinction between nationals and non-nationals.

The rate of population increase amongst both Kuwaitis and non-Kuwaitis from 1965 to 1970 was 9.6 per cent per annum, and from 1970 to 1975 was again very similar, 6.2 per cent per annum respectively. These rates are higher than natural increase alone would permit. The natural rate of increase of Kuwaitis is high, about 3 per cent per annum, but in addition the Kuwaiti population has expanded because of the progressive inclusion of bedouin as Kuwaitis and, to a small extent, through 'naturalisations' (mainly of women from other countries who have married Kuwaitis).[5] In contrast, the non-Kuwaiti population has increased mainly through the arrivals of migrant workers in Kuwait.

The exploitation of oil has had a considerable impact on the demographic characteristics of the Kuwaiti population. Improvements in medical facilities, water supply and medical information led to a rapid increase in population from the mid-1950s onwards, together with increased life expectancy. This was largely achieved by the decline of infant mortality which 'modern' medical facilities effected. Official statistics show the crude birth rate of Kuwaiti nationals to be approximately 55 per 1,000 people and the crude death rate to be 7 per

Table 2.1: Kuwait: Population by Sex and Nationality, 1965, 1970 and 1975

|  | 1965 | Growth Rate (per annum) | 1970 | Growth Rate (per annum) | 1975 |
|---|---|---|---|---|---|
| Kuwaiti |  |  |  |  |  |
| Men | 112,570 |  | 175,510 |  | 236,600 |
| Women | 107,490 |  | 171,885 |  | 235,490 |
| Total | 220,060 | 9.6 | 347,395 | 6.2 | 472,090 |
| Per cent | 47.0 |  | 47.0 |  | 74.4 |
| Non-Kuwaiti |  |  |  |  |  |
| Men | 173,470 |  | 244,370 |  | 307,170 |
| Women | 73,540 |  | 146,900 |  | 215,580 |
| Total | 247,010 | 9.6 | 391,270 | 6.0 | 522,750 |
| Per cent | 53.0 |  | 53.0 |  | 52.6 |
| Grant total | 467,340 |  | 738,665 |  | 994,840 |
| Per cent | 100.0 |  | 100.0 |  | 100.0 |

Sources: Planning Board, *Census, 1965, 1970* (Kuwait); Ministry of Planning, *Census, 1975* (Kuwait) (Arabic).

1,000 (1974). The combined effect of these two indices is to produce a rapid population increase. As a result of a high rate of population increase over several years, the age distribution of the Kuwaiti population is very 'young'. In 1975, 49 per cent of the total population were aged less than 15 years.

The crude activity rate (number of active persons divided by total population) amongst Kuwaitis was 18.8 per cent in 1970, and 19.4 per cent in 1975. This improvement has been brought about by an additional number of economically active Kuwaiti women, together with the ageing of the population. A very high proportion of adult males were already economically active in 1970, and the figure remains high in 1976. The low overall figure for crude activity rate is the consequence of the youthful nature of the Kuwaiti population, and the limited number of economically active women.

*(b) Educational Characteristics of the Population*

Formal schooling in Kuwait began in the 1930s, but only in 1952 was primary school education universally available. Educational expansion has been rapid since; as the social demand for education has grown, so has the country's ability to provide educational facilities. Today more than 100,000 Kuwaitis are attending school, more than one-fifth of their population. Table 2.2 shows the distribution of these pupils between educational levels in 1975/6.

Table 2.2: Kuwait: Enrolment in Schools by Level and Nationality, and
Pupil-Teacher Ratios 1975/6

| Level | Kuwaiti | Non-Kuwaiti | Total | Pupils/ Teacher |
|---|---|---|---|---|
| Primary | 45,910 | 46,330 | 92,240 | 16.9 |
| Intermediate | 39,700 | 20,070 | 59,770 | 12.7 |
| Secondary | 17,060 | 12,900 | 29,960 | 9.1 |

Source: Ministry of Planning, *Statistical Abstract 1976* (Kuwait, 1977), Tables
203 and 204, pp. 300-1.

Table 2.2 also shows the large number of non-Kuwaiti children in
government schools. At the primary level they outnumber Kuwaitis.
Despite considerable efforts to train teachers, the proportion of Kuwaiti teachers is falling except at secondary level, where it is constant,
but only at approximately 10 per cent. In 1966 the University of Kuwait enrolled its first students and, in 1975/6, 2,800 Kuwaitis were
reading for degrees.

Despite the rapid development of education, the general level of
educational attainment amongst adults is low, as Table 2.3 shows. A
majority (59 per cent) of adult Kuwaitis have *not* experienced six years
of education. This reflects the relatively brief period for which modern
education has been available in Kuwait. Non-Kuwaitis are in general
better educated than Kuwaitis. However, the age/sex composition of
the expatriate community in Kuwait is so different from nationals that
straightforward comparisons are somewhat meaningless.

## 3 The Demand for Labour

### (a) Recent Economic Development[6]

Since the early 1950s, when oil revenues became sizeable, three phases
of Kuwait's economic development can be distinguished. First, from
the early fifties to the time of complete political independence (1962),
Kuwait developed infrastructure and social services. The supply of
fresh water and electricity was established on a national scale; roads,
schools, hospitals and government offices were built. Secondly, from
1962 to 1973, a modest degree of diversification was accomplished. A
banking sector was established, and some manufacturing begun, mainly
to substitute for imports. In this period the larger industries were in
the 'mixed sector', owned jointly by government and private interests.

The third phase of Kuwait's recent economic development began in
1973. The comparatively modest levels of oil revenue until 1973 had

Table 2.3: Kuwait: Educational Status of Kuwaitis and Non-Kuwaitis Ten Years Old or More in 1975

| Nationality | Educational Status | | | | | | |
| --- | --- | --- | --- | --- | --- | --- | --- |
| | Illiterate | Literate | Primary Certificate | Intermediate Certificate | Secondary Completion or Post-Secondary Education | University Degree | Total |
| Kuwaiti | 133,614 | 43,940 | 66,188 | 35,415 | 16,603 | 3,979 | 299,739 |
| (per cent) | 44.6 | 14.2 | 22.1 | 11.8 | 5.5 | 1.3 | 100.0 |
| Non-Kuwaiti | 104,860 | 77,875 | 68,472 | 44,851 | 43,295 | 23,267 | 362,620 |
| (per cent) | 28.9 | 21.5 | 18.9 | 12.4 | 11.9 | 6.4 | 100.0 |

Source: Ministry of Planning, *Statistical Abstract, 1976* (Kuwait, 1977), Table 20, p. 36.

limited the rate at which further industrialisation could proceed, as several other sectors of the economy, including social services, had pressing claims on Kuwait's financial resources. The spectacular increases in oil revenue after 1973 led to a heightened domestic concern and ability to create sources of income not related to the sale of oil, and an international 'recycling' problem. Both these factors served to encourage ambitious plans to develop a new scale of industrial sector in Kuwait.

### (b) Gross Domestic Product

Data for gross domestic product by economic sector (1973/4) are not very up to date, nor accurate. However, the mining and quarrying sector which consists almost exclusively of the extraction and sale of oil quite clearly dominates all other sectors. To gain a more accurate picture of national income, oil production and oil revenue are considered.

Table 2.4: Kuwait: Gross Domestic Product by Economic Sector, 1973/4 ($ million)

| Economic Sector | Gross Domestic Product ($ million) | Per cent |
| --- | --- | --- |
| Agriculture, hunting, forestry and fishing | 14 | 0.2 |
| Mining and quarrying | 5,007 | 68.6 |
| Manufacturing | 260 | 3.5 |
| Electricity, gas and water | 149 | 2.0 |
| Construction | 73 | 1.0 |
| Wholesale and retail trade | 391 | 5.4 |
| Transport, storage and communication | 228 | 3.1 |
| Finance, insurance and real estate | 464 | 6.3 |
| Other services | 720 | 9.9 |
| Gross domestic product (market prices) | 7,306 | 100.0 |

Source: Ministry of Planning, *Statistical Abstract, 1976* (Kuwait, 1977), Table 119, p. 167.

### (c) Oil Production and Revenue

Table 2.5 shows that, while oil production grew steadily to 1972/3, it subsequently declined. However, on account of an improving 'take-per-barrel' from 1971 onwards, revenues rose sharply. Even with output in 1975/6 at a lower level than in 1965/6, oil revenue was seven times higher (in money terms).

Table 2.5: Kuwait: Oil Revenue, Production and Take per Barrel
1965/6 to 1975/6 ($ million)

|  | Oil Revenues ($ million) | Oil Production (thousand barrels) | Take per Barrel ($) |
|---|---|---|---|
| 1965/6 | 0.62 | 861,260 | 0.7 |
| 1966/7 | 0.64 | 906,240 | 0.7 |
| 1967/8 | 0.73 | 912,090 | 0.8 |
| 1968/9 | 0.67 | 956,140 | 0.7 |
| 1969/70 | 0.79 | 1,011,780 | 0.8 |
| 1970/1 | 0.82 | 1,090,610 | 0.7 |
| 1971/2 | 0.98 | 1,166,360 | 0.8 |
| 1972/3 | 1.53 | 1,201,600 | 1.3 |
| 1973/4 | 1.88 | 1,102,460 | 1.7 |
| 1974/5 | 7.09 | 929,340 | 7.6 |
| 1975/6 | 4.7 | 760,730 | 6.2 |

Source: Ministry of Planning, *Statistical Abstract 1976* (Kuwait, 1977), Tables 36 and 70.

The decline in oil production from 1972/3 onwards was the result of three factors; the government's decision to limit output for conservation reasons; the oil embargo which followed the 1973 war; and more recently, a decline in demand for oil.

## (d) Government Expenditure

Oil revenues are paid directly to the government, and their disbursement has determined the path of economic development. Table 2.6 shows that until very recently current expenditure has absorbed a share of all expenditure many times greater than capital expenditure. The increase in capital expenditure in 1975 reflects the government's intention to create new sources of income unrelated to oil.[7]

## (e) Government Revenue and Expenditure

Consideration of Table 2.7 shows that in recent years there have been, relative to previous periods, large surpluses of government revenue over expenditure. However, the concern of the government remains that expenditure will continue to increase rapidly while revenue does not. The level of government revenue does indeed seem likely to remain approximately constant as oil output is held to about 3 million barrels per day; the price of oil stabilises in real terms; and current investments may not show positive returns for several years to come.

It is these growing demands upon government income, despite the current financial wealth, which underlie the planners' desires to generate alternative sources of income through industrialisation. Having a

Table 2.6: Kuwait: Distribution of Government Expenditure, 1960 to 1975 ($ million)

| Year | Total ($ m) | Type of Expenditure (per cent) | | | |
|------|------|------|------|------|------|
| | | Capital | Current | Ruling Family | Land Purchase |
| 1960 | 38 | 19.1 | 48.1 | 1.9 | 30.9 |
| 1961 | 44 | 16.2 | 55.2 | 2.2 | 26.4 |
| 1962 | 45 | 16.2 | 53.7 | 2.0 | 28.1 |
| 1963 | 49 | 20.8 | 55.5 | 5.6 | 18.1 |
| 1964 | 51 | 15.3 | 54.6 | 5.4 | 24.7 |
| 1965 | 67 | 8.6 | 54.6 | 4.1 | 32.7 |
| 1966 | 79 | 16.4 | 47.8 | 2.7 | 33.1 |
| 1967 | 89 | 16.3 | 62.2 | 2.4 | 19.1 |
| 1968 | 73 | 13.8 | 76.8 | 3.0 | 6.4 |
| 1969 | 79 | 18.1 | 75.8 | 2.8 | 3.3 |
| 1970 | 84 | 15.7 | 73.8 | 2.6 | 7.9 |
| 1971 | 96 | 14.6 | 77.3 | 2.3 | 5.8 |
| 1972 | 110 | 15.2 | 76.7 | 2.3 | 5.8 |
| 1973 | 180 | 13.6 | 80.3 | 1.4 | 4.7 |
| 1974 | 290 | 12.3 | 83.7 | 0.9 | 3.1 |
| 1975[a] | 250 | 27.4 | 66.3 | 0.8 | 5.5 |

Note: a. 1975 (estimate).
Sources: 1960-70: Al-Kuwari, 'Oil Revenues of the Arabian Gulf Emirates; Pattern of Allocation and Impact on Economic Development' (PhD thesis (Durham University, 1974), p. 310; 1971-5: Central Bank *Annual Report, 1974/75* (Kuwait, 1976), Table 17, p. 52.

Table 2.7: Kuwait: Government Expenditure and Revenue, 1964/5 to 1975/6 ($ million)

| Year | Public Expenditure | Revenue ($ million) | Surplus ($ million) |
|------|------|------|------|
| 1964/5 | 50.6 | 61.7 | + 11.1 |
| 1965/6 | 66.9 | 68.1 | + 1.2 |
| 1966/7 | 79.4 | 69.7 | − 9.7 |
| 1967/8 | 90.0 | 86.7 | − 3.3 |
| 1968/9 | 73.0 | 74.4 | + 1.1 |
| 1969/70 | 79.2 | 85.0 | + 5.8 |
| 1970/1 | 88.6 | 106.1 | + 17.5 |
| 1971/2 | 96.1 | 148.1 | + 52.0 |
| 1972/3 | 123.9 | 190.6 | + 66.7 |
| 1973/4 | 185.5 | 247.4 | + 61.9 |
| 1974/5 | 523.9 | 951.2 | + 627.3 |
| 1975/6[a] | 249.4 | 626.4 | + 377.0 |

Note: a. Estimate of Central Bank.
Sources: 1964/5 to 1969/70: Ministry of Oi, and Finance, *General Budget Report to Parliament, 1971/72* (Kuwait, 1971) (Arabic), p. 47; 1970/1 to 1975/6: Central Bank, *Annual Report 1974/75* (Kuwait, 1976), Table 17, p. 52.

relatively cheap source of energy and a relative abundance of capital, the development of capital-intensive industries which use energy-intensive techniques has been seen as a logical development.

## (f) The Industrial Sector

Kuwait's industrial sector is divided between the private, the mixed and the oil sector. The mixed sector tends to include larger-scale enterprises, with government owning some 50 per cent of the equity shareholding.

The pace of industrial development from 1973 onwards has been dramatic. In 1973 the Industrial Development Bank was established with capital of $35 million. Its purpose was to encourage industrial development in the private sector, and subsequently its capital was increased to $340 million. The industrial area at Shuaiba was extended to cope with the increased demand for industrial sites. The Ministry of Commerce and Industry approved 27 projects in 1973 alone. These generated over 1,000 new jobs. In 1974 the same Ministry produced plans for the development of 'consumer-orientated products' requiring an investment of $349 million and generating 5,500 new jobs. Other 'export-orientated projects' required investment of $986 million and generated 4,000 new jobs directly. These latter projects included a liquid petroleum gas plant, an ethylene plant and further fertiliser plants.[8] These projects, which come before the Licensing Committee of the Ministry of Commerce, are all in the'manufacturing' sector but do not comprise the totality of new ventures; they are only those applying for certain tax and tariff protection privileges. A planned steel smelter and rolling mill was cancelled in 1975, even though design plans were well advanced. The government spokesman gave as the reason for this decision 'the excessive number of foreign workers' which the project would require,[9] a point to which this analysis returns.

The rationale behind the development of an industrial sector to secure an income which is not reliant upon oil revenues is clear. However, industrial development in Kuwait faces a number of constraints. First, having no non-oil mineral resources, all raw materials will have to be shipped and off-loaded into Kuwait. New facilities are required for this. Secondly, while Kuwait is well placed to export to Asia and Africa, these markets may not have the foreign exchange available to purchase Kuwait's industrial exports, particularly as the increased price of oil affects their balance of payments. Thirdly, Kuwait does not have an indigenous supply of labour available to man industrial enterprises. Hence it will be necessary to recruit yet more labour from outside Kuwait. This may involve a number of costs which might outweigh the potential benefits of industrial development. Fourthly, Kuwait's planned industrial development resembles quite closely, albeit on a smaller scale, that of her neighbours in the peninsula. Duplication of effort and wasteful competition between the capital-rich states will be a serious problem in future years. In the recruitment of expatriate labour for manufacturing establishments, Kuwait is already competing with her neighbours. Exactly the same will be true of the markets for industrial products. Although such problems might eventually be less significant than is here suggested, nevertheless they imply a need for caution in development planning which is not always present in the capital-rich states.

It may be that a consideration of these points has led the government to an occasional appearance of hesitancy over the appropriateness of a policy of industrial development. In November 1976, Ali Khalifah al-Sabah, Under-Secretary of the Ministry of Finance said:

Politicians everywhere put a high premium on industrialisation per se. But the underdeveloped countries — such as Egypt, India, etc. have gone through a very bad experience in this field because the projects in question were not studied sufficiently carefully and there was an overriding drive towards industrialisation as such. The oil exporting countries have been under the same pressure ever since the oil price increases of 1973/74 . . . I can't imagine that Saudi Arabia, Kuwait or any other oil producing country in a similar situation would undertake industrial projects merely for the sake of providing employment. The truth is that every additional job provided by a project will have to go to a non-national, and this will in turn entail considerable added investment in services and infrastructure . . . I would hate to see a series of white elephants draining the economies of the oil exporting countries under the guise of industrialisation.[10]

Despite these reservations, the 1976 to 1981 five-year plan gives high priority to 'manufacturing', allocating $3,080 million to it. This represents 21 per cent of the total, and places it with the second-largest share after 'housing', as Table 2.8 shows.

Of all the countries in the area developing industry, Kuwait is probably most aware of the associated risks and difficulties. Yet for either economic or political reasons, industrialisation appears inevitable in Kuwait as in the other peninsula states. The political will and financial muscle of countries like Kuwait to develop industry is currently little questioned. Yet industrialisation will bring profound and irreversible

Table 2.8: Kuwait: Development Plan Allocation 1976 to 1981
($ million)

| Item | Amount ($ million) | Per cent |
|---|---|---|
| Agriculture | 112 | 0.7 |
| Mining | 302 | 2.0 |
| Manufacturing | 3,081 | 20.6 |
| Land transport | 1,057 | 7.0 |
| Sea transport | 1,133 | 7.6 |
| Air transport | 336 | 0.6 |
| Communications | 182 | 1.2 |
| Transport contingency | 170 | 1.1 |
| Trade and finance | 111 | 0.7 |
| Electricity and water | 1,827 | 12.1 |
| Housing | 4,748 | 31.6 |
| Education | 934 | 6.2 |
| Health | 452 | 3.0 |
| Social welfare | 233 | 1.5 |
| Religion | 56 | 0.4 |
| Internal security | 115 | 0.8 |
| Information | 87 | 0.6 |
| Public buildings and utilities | 353 | 2.3 |
| Total | 15,289 | 100.0 |

Source: *The Times*, 'Focus on Kuwait', 12 July 1977, p. 11.

changes to the demographic and social fabric of these societies. These changes are already apparent in the labour market.

## 4 The Labour Market

*(a) The Structure of Employment*

Rather as the overall Kuwaiti economy depends upon oil as a source of income, so it depends considerably on expatriate labour. Non-Kuwaitis comprised 70 per cent of the labour force in 1975. From 1965 to 1975 their number rose from 141,000 to 213,000. This is what underlies the duality between 'Kuwaiti' and 'non-Kuwaiti' populations in the country.

In most Arabian peninsular states few women work in 'modern-sector' employment, and Kuwait is no exception.[11] In 1975 women accounted for 11.5 per cent of all employment. Interestingly, the number of active Kuwaiti women rose almost fourfold from 1970 to 1975, from 2,060 to 7,480 (Table 2.9).

Total employment rose by 63,000 between 1970 and 1975, at an annual rate of 4.7 per cent. The majority of all jobs are found in the

Table 2.9: Kuwait: Employment by Sex and Nationality, 1965, 1970 and 1975

|  | 1965 | Growth Rate (per annum) (per cent) | 1970 | Growth Rate (per annum) (per cent) | 1975 |
|---|---|---|---|---|---|
| Kuwaitis |  |  |  |  |  |
| Men | 41,960 |  | 63,310 |  | 84,370 |
| Women | 1,090 |  | 2,060 |  | 7,480 |
| Total | 43,050 | 8.5 | 65,370 | 7.0 | 91,850 |
| Non-Kuwaitis |  |  |  |  |  |
| Men | 133,600 |  | 162,290 |  | 185,010 |
| Women | 7,680 |  | 14,540 |  | 27,730 |
| Total | 141,280 | 4.5 | 176,830 | 3.7 | 212,740 |
| Grand total | 184,330 | 5.6 | 242,200 | 4.7 | 304,590 |

Source: Ministry of Planning, *Statistical Abstract 1970* (Kuwait, 1971), Table 29, p. 49.

community and personal services sector, which consists mainly of government employment. This sector alone accounted for 56 per cent of all employment in 1975. The next-largest sector is wholesale and retail trade accounting for 13 per cent, followed by construction with 11 per cent.

Examination of employment figures for Kuwaitis in 1970 and 1975 shows that over the period they moved out of jobs in manufacturing, construction and wholesale and retail trade, and into jobs in agriculture and fishing and in community and personal services. The five-year period under discussion was one in which inflation was very high and Kuwaiti government employees enjoyed substantial privileges and allowances which protected them from its worst effects. Moreover, conditions of employment in industry and construction compare poorly with those of government employment. Since all Kuwaiti nationals are entitled to a post in government by law, it was logical for Kuwaitis to leave the private sector and to enter government service.

Table 2.10 also shows the share of employment which Kuwaitis and non-Kuwaitis absorbed in each economic sector in 1975. The overall Kuwaiti proportion of employment is 29 per cent. There is a significant divergence from this share in only three sectors: agriculture and fishing, (53 per cent Kuwaiti); manufacturing (9 per cent); and construction (5.5 per cent). Agriculture and fishing is only a small sector, but the other two account for 19 per cent of all employment. Therefore, in these two significant components of the labour market, Kuwait relies

Table 2.10: Kuwait: Employment by Nationality and Economic Sector, 1975

| Economic Sector | Kuwaiti | | Non-Kuwaiti | | Total | |
|---|---|---|---|---|---|---|
| | Number | Per cent | Number | Per cent | Number | Per cent |
| Agriculture and fishing | 3,983 | 53.1 | 3,531 | 46.9 | 7,514 | 2.5 |
| Mining and quarrying | 1,779 | 36.6 | 3,080 | 63.4 | 4,859 | 1.6 |
| Manufacturing | 2,258 | 9.4 | 22,209 | 90.6 | 24,467 | 8.2 |
| Construction | 1,756 | 5.5 | 30,500 | 94.5 | 32,256 | 10.8 |
| Electricity, gas and water | 2,034 | 28.0 | 5,237 | 72.0 | 7,271 | 2.4 |
| Wholesale and retail trade | 6,327 | 16.0 | 33,232 | 84.0 | 39,559 | 13.3 |
| Transport, storage and communication | 4,567 | 29.2 | 11,118 | 70.8 | 15,685 | 5.3 |
| Community and personal services | 64,265 | 38.6 | 102,537 | 61.4 | 166,802 | 55.9 |
| Activities not adequately defined | 2 | – | – | – | 2 | – |
| Total | 86,970 | 29.2 | 211,444 | 70.8 | 298,415 | 100.0 |

Source: Ministry of Planning, *Census, 1975* (Kuwait, 1976), Table 14, p. 39 (Arabic).

Table 2.11: Kuwait: Distribution of Kuwaiti and Non-Kuwaiti Employment by Economic Activity, 1975

| Economic Activity | Kuwaiti (per cent) | Non-Kuwaiti (per cent) |
|---|---|---|
| Agriculture and fishing | 4.6 | 1.7 |
| Mining and quarrying | 2.0 | 1.5 |
| Manufacturing | 2.6 | 10.5 |
| Construction | 2.0 | 14.4 |
| Electricity, gas and water | 2.3 | 2.5 |
| Wholesale and retail trade | 7.3 | 15.7 |
| Transport, storage and communication | 5.2 | 5.2 |
| Community and personal services | 73.9 | 48.5 |
| Total | 100.0 | 100.0 |
| Total number | 86,970 | 211,440 |

Source: Ministry of Planning, *Census, 1975* (Kuwait, 1976), Table 14, p. 39 (Arabic).

almost totally on expatriate workers.

Most Kuwaitis (74 per cent) work in community and personal services, i.e. for the government (Table 2.11). About 6,000 Kuwaitis work in the wholesale or retail trade, representing 7 per cent of all employment. The distribution of non-Kuwaiti employment is somewhat different, though again, community and personal services account for the largest single share, 49 per cent. The manufacturing, construction and wholesale and retail sectors account for 41 per cent of all non-Kuwaiti employment.

### (b) Occupational Divisions

The 'International Standard Classification of Occupations' (ISCO) is the most commonly used framework of occupational analysis in censuses. The Kuwaiti Central Statistical Office used this classification in 1965, 1970, and again in 1975. However, the ISCO is not a particularly useful classification for analysis of the work-force because occupations are grouped according to 'type of work' and no distinction between different levels of education or training is made. This analysis therefore uses, where possible, an alternative grouping of occupations based on educational and training requirements of jobs. This was first used by Parnes in the Mediterranean Regional Project, and was subsequently developed for use in the Middle East by the Jordanian Statistical Office and the Ford Foundation in Bahrain.

Before proceeding with an analysis of the work-force by a modified Parnesian occupational classification the results of the 1975 census are shown by the conventional classification (Table 2.12). A high proportion of all active Kuwaitis are service workers (38 per cent). In contrast, a relatively large proportion of active non-Kuwaitis are production workers and labourers (43 per cent). However both these groups cover a wide range of skill levels.

Using the alternative method of classification, Table 2.13 shows that of all Kuwaitis who work as professionals, 85 per cent work in jobs which usually require an arts-based university degree (A-2). Only 15 per cent are in jobs wich usually require a science- or mathematics-based university degree (A-1). About 45 per cent of all Kuwaitis work in unskilled occupations which require no special education or training (D). Another bias in Kuwaiti employment is shown by the fact that about twice as many Kuwaitis work in skilled and semi-skilled office and clerical occupations (C-1) as work in skilled and semi-skilled manual occupations (C-2). Approximately 12 per cent of all active Kuwaitis work in sub-professional and technician occupations (B). Half of these are teachers.

Table 2.13 also shows non-Kuwaitis, about whom the following

Table 2.12: Kuwait: Employment by Occupational Category and Nationality, 1975

| Major List Heading | Kuwaiti (per cent) | Non-Kuwaiti (per cent) |
|---|---|---|
| Professional and technical workers | 11.2 | 15.2 |
| Administrative and managerial workers | 1.2 | 0.8 |
| Clerical and related workers | 20.5 | 9.5 |
| Sales workers | 7.1 | 8.5 |
| Service workers | 37.9 | 21.5 |
| Agricultural and husbandry workers | 4.5 | 1.8 |
| Production workers and labourers | 17.6 | 42.7 |
| Total | 100.0 | 100.0 |
| Total number | 86,970 | 211,440 |

Source: Ministry of Planning, *Census, 1975* (Kuwait, 1976), Tables 57 and 58, pp. 214 to 216 (Arabic).

Table 2.13: Kuwait: Distribution of Employment by Occupational Group and Nationality, 1975

| Occupational Group | Kuwaiti | | Non-Kuwaiti | | Share of All Employment (per cent) |
|---|---|---|---|---|---|
| | Number | Per cent | Number | Per cent | |
| A1: Professional jobs usually requiring a science- or maths-based university degree | 1,050 | 1.2 | 9,011 | 4.3 | 98.6 |
| A2: Professional and sub-professional jobs usually requiring a university arts degree | 5,114 | 5.9 | 4,571 | 2.1 | 46.1 |
| B: Technicians and other jobs which usually require one to three years of post-secondary education/training | 10.239 | 11.8 | 25,522 | 12.1 | 71.4 |
| C1: Skilled and semi-skilled office and clerical occupations | 21,204 | 24.5 | 38,284 | 18.1 | 64.4 |
| C2: Skilled and semi-skilled manual occupations | 10,412 | 12.0 | 62,027 | 29.4 | 85.6 |
| D: Unskilled occupations | 38,602 | 44.6 | 71,694 | 34.0 | 65.0 |
| Total | 86,621 | 100.0 | 211,109 | 100.0 | 70.9 |

Source: Ministry of Planning, *Census 1975* (Kuwait, 1976), Tables 57 and 58, pp. 214-16 (Arabic).

points emerge. In contrast to Kuwaiti nationals, there are twice as many non-Kuwaitis working in professional occupations which usually re-quire a science- or mathematics-based university degree (A-1) as there are working in professional occupations which normally require an arts-based university degree (A-2). Moreover, there are also twice as many non-Kuwaitis working in skilled and semi-skilled manual occupations (C-1) as in skilled and semi-skilled office and clerical occupations (C-2).

Some 12 per cent of all active non-Kuwaitis work in sub-professional and technician occupations (B); 72 per cent of these are teachers.

The 29 per cent Kuwaiti share of all employment alters significantly in three cases (Table 2.13). Kuwaitis are over-represented in the A-2 category (professional occupations usually requiring an arts-based uni-versity degree), where their share is 54 per cent. Kuwaitis are under-represented in A-1 professional and technical occupations, usually re-quiring a science- or maths-based university degree. Kuwaitis are slightly under-represented in skilled and semi-skilled occupations (C-2). The converse obviously holds for non-Kuwaitis.

From whatever perspective the labour market of Kuwait is exam-ined, the country's dependence on migrant labour both quantitatively and qualitatively is obvious. As long as total employment grows faster than about 3 per cent per annum, the quantitative dependence will grow. Qualitative dependence need not be so inexorably determined, and could diminish with appropriate education and training pro-grammes and, importantly, employment policies which encourage nationals to work in all sectors of the economy. At present, govern-ment employment policy is not consistent with this objective. In part-icular, civil service employment is open to any Kuwaiti national on terms which are better than those found in the private sector. Wages are not set according to productivity with the result that Kuwaitis, partic-ularly boys, tend to lack motivation. This problem will have to be tackled if Kuwait is to reduce her qualitative dependence on migrant labour. As will be shown, this problem occurs in every capital-rich state, and therefore its solution would be of general application and interest.

## 5 Foreign Workers in Kuwait

The non-Kuwaiti community of 523,000 persons, accounting for more than half of the total population (1975), includes Arabs, Iranians, Asians, Europeans and Americans. In 1975, most non-Kuwaitis were from other Arab lands (80 per cent). Iranians accounted for 8 per cent and Asians 10.5 per cent of the total (Table 2.14). Within the group of 'Arab non-Kuwaitis' the largest community is that of the Jordanians and Palestinians who, in 1975, represented 39 per cent of all non-Kuwaitis. The Egyptian, Iraqi, Syrian and Lebanese communities combined accounted for approximately 33 per cent of all non-Kuwaitis. These six nationalities constitute the bulk of the Arab non-Kuwaiti community, and are nationalities of considerable importance within government circles.

Table 2.14 also permits an analysis of the development of different communities from 1965 to 1975. The Palestinian and Jordanian, Syrian and Egyptian communities have grown in size and overall share during that period. The Iraqi and Lebanese communities have increased in size, but not their share of the total. The only group to reduce in size over the period is the Muscati and Omani community. The development of Oman and a more liberal political regime has induced some return migration.

The different expatriate communities have distinct demographic, social and economic characteristics. For instance, the individual communities have different age/sex profiles. The Iranian community consists almost entirely of single men – the classic migrant community. In contrast, an almost normal age/sex profile is exhibited by the Palestinian and Jordanian community. Between these two extremes lie the Syrian and Egyptian communities. There is a positive association between the extent to which the age/sex distribution of a community is normal, and the degree to which the community is affluent, well educated and occupies the better jobs.

Unfortunately data for educational attainment by nationality do not exist for 1975, but Table 2.15 shows the educational status of particular non-Kuwaiti communities in 1970. Arguably, either the Jordanian and Palestinian or the Lebanese community is the better educated. The trend from groups with more normally distributed populations to those with less evenly distributed ones is clear. In general, the non-Kuwaiti community is better educated than the Kuwaiti population. However, the aggregation of all data on non-Kuwaitis hides the fact that particular communities are very highly educated, namely Palestinians and Jordanians, Lebanese and, possibly, the Egyptians.

Data on the occupations of non-Kuwaitis by nationality are shown on Table 2.16, which divides occupations between the revised occupational groups and ranks nationalities according to average skill level. The latter is measured by the proportion of the total employment of each community found in 'professional' occupations. By this criterion,

Table 2.14: Kuwait: Composition of the Expatriate Community by Nationalit
1965, 1970 and 1975

|  | 1965 | | 1970 | | 1975 | |
|---|---|---|---|---|---|---|
|  | Number | Per cent | Number | Per cent | Number | Per c |
| Jordanian and Palestinian | 77,712 | 31.4 | 147,696 | 37.7 | 204,178 | 3ξ |
| Iraqi | 25,897 | 10.5 | 39,066 | 10.0 | 45,070 | ε |
| Saudi Arabian | 4,632 | 1.9 | 10.897 | 2.8 | 12,572 | Ζ |
| Lebanese | 20,877 | 8.4 | 25,387 | 6.5 | 24,776 | 4 |
| Syrian | 16,849 | 6.8 | 27,217 | 6.9 | 40,962 | 7 |
| Egyptian | 11,021 | 4.4 | 30,421 | 7.8 | 60,534 | 11 |
| Sudanese | 418 | 0.2 | 773 | 0.2 | 1,553 | C |
| Yemeni (PDRY) | 2,635 | 1.1 | 8,604 | 2.2 | 12,332 | 2 |
| Yemeni (YAR) | 144 | – | 2,363 | 0.6 | 4,831 | 0 |
| Arab Gulf nationals | 2,011 | 0.8 | 5,518 | 1.4 | 4,056 | 0 |
| Muscati, Omani | 19,584 | 7.9 | 14,670 | 3.7 | 7,313 | 1 |
| Other Arab | 6,143 | 2.5 | 237 | 0.1 | 1,055 | 0 |
| (All non-Kuwaiti Arab nationals) | (187,923) | (75.9) | (312,849) | (79.9) | (419,232) | (80 |
| Iranian | 30,790 | 12.4 | 39,129 | 10.0 | 40,842 | 7 |
| Indian | 11,699 | 4.7 | 17,336 | 4.4 | 32,105 | 6 |
| Pakistani | 11,735 | 4.7 | 14,712 | 3.8 | 23,016 | 4 |
| Other | 5,133 | 2.1 | 7,240 | 1.8 | 7,599 | 1 |
| (Total non-Arab nationals) | (59,357) | (24.1) | (78,417) | (20.0) | (103,562) | (19 |
| Grand total | 247,280 | 100.0 | 391,266 | 100.0 | 522,749 | 100 |

Source: Ministry of Planning, *Statistical Abstract, 1976* (Kuwait, 1977), Table 17, p. 31.

Table 2.15: Kuwait: The Educational Status of Selected Non-Kuwaiti Communities in 1970 (aged ten years or more)

| Educational Status (per cent) Nationality | Illiterate | Literate | Primary | Intermediate | Secondary | University | Total | Per cent of all Non-Kuwaitis |
|---|---|---|---|---|---|---|---|---|
| Iranian | 70.1 | 24.9 | 3.1 | 1.0 | 0.4 | 0.1 | 36,052 | 13.1 |
| Omani | 57.8 | 31.2 | 7.1 | 2.4 | 0.6 | 0.2 | 12,471 | 4.5 |
| Iraqi | 56.4 | 21.2 | 11.3 | 5.6 | 3.0 | 1.9 | 28,730 | 10.4 |
| Saudi Arabian | 48.4 | 30.9 | 12.0 | 5.7 | 2.1 | 0.6 | 6,677 | 2.4 |
| Syrian | 24.6 | 38.2 | 20.0 | 9.0 | 5.5 | 2.1 | 19,570 | 7.1 |
| Egyptian | 23.4 | 19.2 | 8.5 | 8.7 | 16.4 | 21.1 | 24,599 | 8.9 |
| Jordanian and Palestinian | 16.9 | 26.8 | 20.9 | 15.2 | 15.2 | 3.9 | 85,316 | 31.1 |
| Lebanese | 13.0 | 35.8 | 22.1 | 14.0 | 11.4 | 3.0 | 16,122 | 5.8 |

Source: Planning Board, *1970 Census* (Kuwait, 1971), Table 48, p. 367 (Arabic).

Table 2.16: Kuwait: Distribution of Employment among Occupational Groups for Selected Expatriate Communities, 1975

| Occupation | Palestinian | Egyptian | Jordanian | Lebanese | Indian | Syrian | Iraqi | Pakistani | Yemen (YAR) | Yemen (PDRY) | Iranian |
|---|---|---|---|---|---|---|---|---|---|---|---|
| | | | | | (Per cent) | | | | | | |
| A1: Professional jobs usually requiring a science- or maths-based university degree | 10.8 | 7.2 | 6.5 | 4.0 | 3.6 | 1.7 | 1.9 | 2.1 | 0.3 | 0.2 | 0.1 |
| A2: Professional and sub-professional jobs usually requiring a university arts degree | 3.3 | 3.3 | 2.8 | 3.8 | 1.0 | 1.6 | 1.2 | 1.0 | 1.3 | 0.5 | 0.2 |
| B: Technicians and other jobs which usually require one to three years of post-secondary education/training | 35.9 | 21.1 | 17.7 | 17.5 | 9.0 | 8.8 | 4.1 | 5.5 | 1.3 | 0.7 | 2.7 |
| C1: Skilled and semi-skilled office and clerical occupations | 22.6 | 7.9 | 26.1 | 26.5 | 21.6 | 21.7 | 12.7 | 11.7 | 16.2 | 40.9 | 13.9 |
| C2: Skilled and semi-skilled manual occupations | 14.2 | 25.6 | 25.8 | 27.8 | 12.9 | 39.7 | 40.8 | 59.5 | 12.6 | 4.7 | 48.3 |
| D: Unskilled occupations | 13.1 | 34.9 | 21.2 | 20.4 | 51.8 | 27.1 | 39.3 | 20.2 | 68.2 | 53.0 | 34.8 |
| Total number | 100.0 8,167 | 100.0 37,464 | 100.0 38,935 | 100.0 7,197 | 100.0 21,448 | 100.0 16,519 | 100.0 17,807 | 100.0 11,019 | 100.0 2,749 | 100.0 8,639 | 100.0 27,530 |

Source: Compiled from Ministry of Planning, Census, 1975 (Kuwait, 1976) Table 95, p. 105 (Arabic).

the most 'skilful' community appears to be the Palestinian, followed by the Egyptian, the Jordanian, the Lebanese, the Indian and finally the Syrian community.

There is no question that without the assistance of migrants Kuwait would still have a largely undeveloped economy. Their contribution is now essential in the national economy. What is harder to define is their future place in Kuwaiti society. There are two alternative paths for Kuwait to follow. One is to distinguish increasingly between Kuwaitis and non-Kuwaitis in political and economic terms, and to attempt to ensure that non-nationals regard Kuwait as a temporary residence. Alternatively, the differentiation between Kuwaiti and long-term non-Kuwaiti Arab residents may blur, as a wider range of privileges are extended to certain groups in Kuwait's society. Liberalisation of Kuwait's nationality laws and the extension of political representation would be steps on the second path. The dangers and contradictions of the first 'isolationist' path are understood in Kuwait, but the risks of the second alternative are seen as very high. Kuwaitis feel that they might quickly lose control of their country if power fell into the wrong hands.

Kuwait is experiencing this dilemma long before it occurs in Qatar, the United Arab Emirates or Saudi Arabia because her immigrant community has a maturity unique in the region: the immigrants are mainly Arab, and Kuwait is a small closely knit city. However, when the Emirates or Qatar come to face this problem their options will be significantly less open than are those of Kuwait today. At least Kuwait can boast an indigenous population of 500,000 and an overall share in the community of about one-half. This, as will be shown, is certainly not the case in the Emirates and Qatar.

It is difficult to see the Kuwaiti government sustaining its present stance indefinitely. As long as it hesitates, tension in Kuwait will persist and grow.

## 6 Conclusion

The population living in Kuwait is split clearly into two: Kuwaiti nationals and non-Kuwaitis. The Kuwaiti population is small relative to the country's wealth, homogeneous and closely knit. The non-Kuwaiti community is a conglomerate of several different nationalities with a wide variety of backgrounds, who initially had little in common except for the purpose of their stay in Kuwait: employment. As time passes, however, the length of their residence in Kuwait and weakened ties with their country of origin have given non-Kuwaitis a growing if indistinct common identity. Just how this identity will grow remains to be seen. Its existence is of growing concern to the government of Kuwait.

The rapid economic growth which Kuwait has experienced in recent years and the enhanced oil revenues have created a series of economic, social and political problems. On the economic front a tension exists between the need to develop a source of income unrelated to oil, and the implications of achieving this through industrial development, which are that still more non-Kuwaitis will be imported to man these enterprises. In addition to this major problem there are ancillary problems which include determining the optimal rate of extraction of oil and delimiting appropriate areas either to invest government budget surpluses or to stem the increasing costs of providing social services whilst determining the appropriate trade-off between the rate of economic development and inflation.

The answers to all these questions have labour market implications, which returns the government to the fundamental social problem: that within its boundaries are two communities. One is the Kuwaiti community which can claim a legitimate right to the first call on government revenues. The other community is non-Kuwaiti, but its members believe that it is they who have largely developed Kuwait. The non-Kuwaitis claim that they support the facilities which provide the high standard of living enjoyed by sections of the Kuwaiti national community; therefore, it is claimed, non-Kuwaitis should have some say in Kuwaiti affairs and have reasonable access to health, education, social services and housing.

Political problems which the government faces stem largely from the tensions which exist within the economic and social spheres, and these seem likely to persist for some time to come. These tensions have yet to crystallise in Qatar, but the ingredients for a more serious crisis are present in that smaller country, where many of the issues facing Kuwait are drawn more starkly.

## Notes

1. For a history of Kuwait's development of her oil see Ministry of Finance and Oil, *The Oil of Kuwait, Facts and Figures* (Kuwait, 1970).

2. *The Times*, 'Focus on Kuwait', 12 July 1977.

3. British Petroleum Company Limited, *B.P. Statistical Review of the World Oil Industry* (London, 1977), p. 6.

4. *The Times*, 'Focus on Kuwait', 12 July 1977.

5. See A.G. Hill, 'The Demography of the Kuwaiti Population of Kuwait',

*Demography, 12*, 3 (August 1975).

6. For analyses of Kuwait's economic development see: International Bank for Reconstruction and Development, *The Economic Development of Kuwait* (Johns Hopkins, Baltimore, 1965); R. Mallakh, *Economic Development and Regional Co-operation: Kuwait*, Center for Middle Eastern Studies, No. 3 (Chicago, 1968). For a more recent analysis see C.A. Sinclair, 'Education in Kuwait, Bahrain and Qatar: An Economic Assessment' (unpublished PhD thesis, Durham University, 1977). See also M.W. Khouja and P.G. Sadler, *The Economy of Kuwait* (Macmillan, London, 1979).

7. Government revenues and expenditure are analysed in greater detail up to 1970 in A. Al-Kuwari, *Oil Revenues of the Arabian Gulf Emirates: Pattern of Allocation and Impact on Economic Development* (Bowkers, London, 1976).

8. See *Arab Economist* (May 1974).

9. See *MEED*, 'Kuwait' (July 1975).

10. *MEED, 20*, 4 (November 1976).

11. J.S. Birks and S.E. Letts, 'Women in Rural Arab Society: Old Roles and New in the Sultanate of Oman', *Journal of the Gulf and Arabian Peninsular Studies, III*, 10 (April 1977), pp. 101-12; A. Rassam, 'National Development and the Arab Woman: Contradictions and Accommodations', paper prepared for the Symposium of Centre for Arab Gulf Studies (Basrah, March 1979).

# 3 THE STATE OF QATAR

## 1 Introduction

The population of Qatar will shortly reach 220,000 persons if it has not done so already (1979). Nationals account for less than half of this total. The state's endowment of oil is small compared with her neighbours, Saudi Arabia and Abu Dhabi. But relative to her population, it is substantial. At present levels of production her reserves will last for approximately 25 years.

Economic and social development in Qatar has been particularly rapid, and the development plan is ambitious.[1] As in Kuwait, an industrial development programme is under way which is designed to create a source of income not related to oil. By 1980 the planned industrial zone, Umm Said, will be one of the Gulf's major industrial centres. In 1970 a large majority of the work-force was non-national. Today the number of these workers is correspondingly greater. As the industrialisation programme proceeds, yet more non-nationals will be employed.

As yet, the large number of non-nationals relative to the nationals has not been seen as a major problem, in spite of the fact that non-nationals represent a far larger proportion of the total population and employment than do expatriates in Kuwait, where they are already regarded with concern by the Kuwaiti government. The non-national community in Qatar is of relatively short duration, and is not politically articulate. The proportion of Arabs in the expatriate community in Qatar is lower than in Kuwait; the limited interest of the majority of migrants, who are non-Arab, in matters outside their work is in contrast with the ambitions of migrants in Kuwait. As the expatriate community evolves, it will adopt a new character. In this event, it is unlikely that the Qataris will view their reliance upon immigrant workers with the same confidence. In the meantime, more migrants arrive to effect the development plan.

## 2 The Supply of Labour

### (a) Population

The state of Qatar, which lies 350 miles to the south of Kuwait in the Arabian Gulf, is a peninsula which projects northwards for about 100 miles with a width of approximately 55 miles.[2] The original inhabitants lived in and around the scattered oases to the north of the country. A community settled in Doha, the port on the eastern coast of Qatar, where the main activities were fishing and pearling. Before the development of the Japanese 'cultured' pearl, Qatar's pearling fleet of 400 dhows accounted for one-third of the entire Gulf fleet.[3] With the widespread collapse of the pearling industry in the early 1920s, Qatar experienced a general economic depression which was shared by Kuwait and Bahrain. Oil was first discovered in 1937, but it was not until 1949 that it was actually exported from Qatar.[4]

Prior to 1970, records of population consist of personal estimates; one estimate of population made in 1950 placed it as 'some 25,000'.[5] Since 1950 the population has increased very rapidly, and the census taken in April 1970 showed a total of 111,133 persons. Some 45,000 (40.5 per cent) of the total were Qataris. The reported participation rate of the national community was low, at 18 per cent. This is a reflection of a 'young population', and an almost totally inactive female population: 52 per cent of the Qatari population is aged less than 15. The actual number of active Qataris was approximately 8,200. Of these only 284 were female.[6]

The country has excellent health facilities, and the population now consists largely of urban dwellers. Hence access to the health service is high. Cases which cannot be dealt with in Qatar are typically sent to Europe at the government's expense. In view of the age/sex profile of the Qatari population and the degree of health care, there is a high natural growth rate, probably in the region of 3.5 per cent per annum.

By 1975 the Qatari national population numbered approximately 60,000, having increased since 1970 at 6 per cent each year. This high rate of increase was produced by the naturalisation of some 7,000 persons over the period. In future years a more normal rate of population increase is expected amongst Qataris.

A series of estimates of total population in 1975 have been made which suggest a figure of 158,000.[7] Therefore the non-national community in that year was some 98,000 persons (Table 3.1). In 1970 Qataris accounted for 40 per cent of the population; by 1975 this share had fallen to 38 per cent. In the future the proportion that non-nationals account for will rise further. There are several reasons for this: as Qatar embarks on her programme of industrial expansion, the rate of increase of indigenous Qataris is bound to decrease from its present level, as both the birth rate falls and the rate of naturalisation declines.

Table 3.1: Qatar: Population by Nationality, 1975

|  | 1970 | | 1975 | | Annual Increase 1970 to 1975 (per cent) |
|  | Number | Per cent | Number | Per cent |  |
|---|---|---|---|---|---|
| Nationals | 45,000 | 40.5 | 60,300 | 38.1 | 6.0 |
| Non-nationals | 66,000 | 59.5 | 97,700 | 61.9 | 8.1 |
| Total | 111,000 | 100.0 | 158,000 | 100.0 | 7.3 |

Sources: 1970: Ministry of Information, *1970 Census* (Qatar, 1970), Table 1; 1975: J.S. Birks and C.A. Sinclair, *Country Case Study: Qatar*, International Migration Project Working Paper (Durham, 1978).

*(b) Educational Characteristics of the Population*

The only data available for the entire population are relevant to 1970. At that time Qatar was a community with relatively little formal education. It had only begun in 1951 for boys and in 1955 for girls.[8] Table 3.2 shows a very high incidence of illiteracy amongst both Qataris and non-Qataris.

Table 3.2: Qatar: Illiteracy by Age and Nationality, 1970

| Age Cohort | Qatari (per cent) | Non-Qatari (per cent) |
|---|---|---|
| 15-19 | 21.8 | 59.2 |
| 20-29 | 57.4 | 64.5 |
| 30-39 | 81.0 | 65.1 |
| 40-49 | 86.0 | 66.0 |
| 50-59 | 85.2 | 72.6 |
| 60-74 | 90.6 | 83.6 |

Source: Ministry of Information, *1970 Census* (Qatar, 1970), Table 9.

Since the early days of formal education in Qatar, schools and training institutions have rapidly expanded. The current school enrolment is shown in Table 3.3.

There are almost as many girls in school as boys and, at the preparatory level, more. Not shown on this table are the non-Qatari students who represent about 30 per cent of the total at the primary stage, and rather more at higher levels.

The small number of Qataris in absolute terms is evident; there are only 275 boys in the third grade of secondary education. Even if the entire enrolment in boys' preparatory and secondary schools successfully graduates from secondary school, their number over the next six years will be only about 3,000 in total. This is happening in a period when perhaps as many as 20,000 job opportunities will occur in Umm Said, the industrial zone. As many new jobs again will be generated around Doha.

Table 3.3: Qatar: Enrolment of Nationals in Schools, 1976/7

|  | | Boys | Girls | Total |
|---|---|---|---|---|
| Primary | 1 | 1,665 | 1,510 | 3,175 |
| | 2 | 1,439 | 1,387 | 2,826 |
| | 3 | 1,270 | 1,271 | 2,541 |
| | 4 | 1,362 | 1,380 | 2,742 |
| | 5 | 1,304 | 1,300 | 2,604 |
| | 6 | 1,126 | 799 | 1,925 |
| Total primary | | 8,166 | 7,647 | 15,813 |
| Preparatory | 1 | 816 | 843 | 1,659 |
| (general) | 2 | 632 | 667 | 1,299 |
| | 3 | 467 | 542 | 1,009 |
| Total preparatory | | 1,915 | 2,052 | 3,967 |
| Secondary 1 (General) | | 503 | 503 | 1,006 |
| (general) | 2 (Arts) | 130 | 210 | 340 |
| | 3 (Arts) | 134 | 127 | 261 |
| | 2 (Science) | 188 | 86 | 274 |
| | 3 (Science) | 141 | 81 | 222 |
| Total secondary | | 1,096 | 1,007 | 2,103 |

Source: Ministry of Education, *Annual Report, 1976/77* (Doha, 1978) (Arabic).

Besides the formal school system, there are a series of alternative vocational training centres, including the Regional Training Centre, which train for skilled and semi-skilled manual jobs, a technical school, and a teacher training college.[9]

In September of 1977 the teacher training college officially became Qatar University. The number of Qataris enrolled there together with the number on courses in universities abroad is shown in Tables 3.4 and 3.5.

The combined total is now in the region of 1,500, a quarter of whom can be expected to graduate in any one year. Inspection of Tables 3.4 and 3.5 reveals that arts courses are heavily favoured compared to science. These figures suggest that the majority of technical staff required by Qatar's economic development will have to come from abroad.

The development of the educational system has been rapid, and it is

Table 3.4: Qatar: Enrolment of Nationals in Qatar University, 1976/7

|  | Specialisation | | |
|  | Arts | Science | Total |
|---|---|---|---|
| Grade 1 | 174 | 24 | 198 |
| Grade 2 | 68 | 18 | 86 |
| Grade 3 | 89 | 16 | 105 |
| Grade 4 | 97 | 15 | 112 |
| Total | 428 (85.4%) | 73 (14.6%) | 501 |

Source: Ministry of Education, *Annual Report, 1976/77* Doha 1978), pp. 189-94 (Arabic).

Table 3.5: Qatar: Enrolment of Nationals in Universities Abroad, 1971/2 to 1974/5

|  | Year | | | |
| Specialisation | 1971/2 | 1972/3 | 1973/4 | 1974/5 |
|---|---|---|---|---|
| Arts | 251 | 405 | 445 | 516 |
| Science | 109 | 133 | 160 | 206 |
| Total[a] | 360 | 538 | 605 | 722 |

Note: a. Typically women account for 20 per cent of the total. Figures include both full-time and part-time enrolees.
Source: Ministry of Education, *Annual Report, 1976/77* Doha, 1975).

this pace of change, both within the education system of the country and in the economy that has led to a series of problems. These latter are typified by the shortage of Qatari teachers. At present enrolment in the secondary teacher training institute is dwindling, and very few of the graduates of the College of Education (now the University) enter the teaching profession. Given the exciting opportunities outside the teaching profession, the rigours of classroom teaching are hardly likely to be attractive. The problem, in short, is that there are a small number of Qataris, and a plethora of job opportunities.

The position amongst Qatari women teachers is somewhat different. In their case teaching is one of the very few jobs in which it is acceptable for them to work. Table 3.6 shows the nationality of teachers by level; it is evident that male Qatari teachers account for 30 per cent of their group at the primary level, and only 3 per cent at the preparatory and secondary level.

The majority of expatriate teachers are 'northern Arabs' or Egyptians. This is a pattern commonly found in the Gulf. It reflects the longer period of education in those sending countries and the relatively greater supply of teachers there. It is, of course, essential that teachers be Arabs, so Asian countries are not potential alternative sources of supply of teachers. Indeed, those countries presently exporting large numbers of teachers, namely Egypt, Jordan, Syria and Sudan, will be increasingly called upon for still more teachers.

Table 3.6: Qater: Teachers by Nationality and Level, 1976/7

| Nationality | Primary | | Preparatory and Secondary | | Total | |
|---|---|---|---|---|---|---|
| | Men | Women | Men | Women | Men | Women |
| Qatari | 175 | 348 | 15 | 24 | 190 | 372 |
| Egyptian | 99 | 59 | 177 | 218 | 276 | 277 |
| Jordanian | 129 | 140 | 120 | 66 | 249 | 206 |
| Palestinian | 119 | 149 | 107 | 40 | 226 | 189 |
| Syrian | 12 | 9 | 12 | 8 | 24 | 17 |
| Sudanese | 16 | 2 | 43 | 17 | 59 | 19 |
| Lebanese | 5 | 2 | – | 2 | 5 | 4 |
| Saudi Arabian | 1 | – | – | – | 1 | – |
| Gulf Nationals and Yemeni | 15 | 7 | – | 2 | 15 | 9 |
| Other nationalities | 8 | 3 | 13 | 10 | 21 | 13 |
| Total | 579 | 719 | 487 | 387 | 1,066 | 1,106 |

Source: Ministry of Education, *Annual Report, 1976/77* (Doha, 1978), p. 81 (Arabic).

Table 3.3 shows that in the coming years Qatar will see an increasing number of schoolchildren at the primary level; also large numbers of students at that level will move into higher schools. Inevitably, this will lead to employment of a substantially greater number of expatriate teachers.

The problem of recruiting good expatriate teachers is well known in the Gulf, and to a considerable extent Gulf states and Saudi Arabia are competitors in the same market. The consequences of severe competition between peninsula states for teachers bear speculation. It might be that a higher wage rate brings forward a sufficient supply from those countries which presently provide many teachers. However, it is equally possible that either the supply of teachers proves inadequate or that teachers of an inferior quality are employed. Either way there is a cost; the output of schools is reduced, or the quality of graduates is diminished.

Recruitment of suitable teachers reappears as essentially the same problem in each Gulf state. So far, by a series of domestic compromises on quality and output, and the importation of quite large numbers of expatriate teachers, *ad hoc* solutions have been found. But as time passes the demand for teachers will increase, as will competition for their services.

The education and training of indigenes have become of even greater significance to the government as the demands placed on the national work-force grow. Qatar's problems in this field resemble closely those of Kuwait's.[10] The opportunity to learn from the mistakes of others could be profitable for Qatar at this time.

### 3 The Demand for Labour

#### (a) Economic Development

Qatar has become rapidly affluent on account of oil and natural gas exports. However, her proven reserves and oil production are not, by Middle East standards, spectacular. Indeed, in terms of present oil production Qatar ranks low on the list (Table 3.7).

Table 3.7: Qatar: Petroleum Production of Selected Producers in the Middle East, 1975 to 1977

| Country | Year (thousands of barrels per day) | | |
|---|---|---|---|
| | 1975 | 1976 | 1977 (half year) |
| Kuwait | 2,085 | 2,150 | 1,807 |
| Saudi Arabia | 7,077 | 8,579 | 9,353 |
| Iran | 5,385 | 5,979 | 5,640 |
| Iraq | 2,248 | 2,280 | 2,214 |
| Libya | 1,510 | 1,914 | 2,077 |
| Abu Dhabi | 1,403 | 1,592 | 1,699 |
| Qatar | 439 | 487 | 413 |
| Oman | 340 | 385 | 353 |

Source: 'Oil in the Middle East', *Quarterly Economic Review* (4th Quarter, 1977) (EIU, London, 1978).

By a different measure of relative affluence, oil production *per capita*, Qatar has the highest level on a 'total population' basis and second highest on a 'nationals only' basis. In other words, while Qatar does not have the colossal reserves of, say Saudi Arabia, she does have, relative to her population, a very considerable endowment of oil.

Qatar's oil reserves were estimated in 1977 at 4,560 million barrels; production and revenues are shown on Table 3.9. In a year of uninterrupted production, minimum output is about 475,000 barrels per day (bd). For political and conservation reasons, the maximum production would be about 550,000 bd. Oil reserves will therefore last for be-

Table 3.8: Qatar: *per capita* Oil Production of Selected Countries, 1977

| Country | Barrels per day per head of Population | |
| --- | --- | --- |
| | Nationals only | Total Population |
| UAE | 7.0 | 2.5 |
| Qatar | 6.4 | 2.8 |
| Kuwait | 4.2 | 2.1 |
| Saudi Arabia | 2.0 | 1.0 |
| Oman | 0.7 | 0.7 |

Source: Authors' estimates based on J.S. Birks and C.A. Sinclair, *Country Case Study: Qatar*, International Migration Project Working Paper (Durham, 1978).

tween 23 and 26 years. Obviously a higher rate of extraction will reduce the life of the reserves.

Table 3.9: Qatar: Oil Production and Revenue, 1970 to 1977 ($ million)

| Year | Oil Production (bd) | Oil Revenue ($ million) |
| --- | --- | --- |
| 1970 | 345,140 | 102 |
| 1971 | 404,020 | 166 |
| 1972 | 465,240 | 259 |
| 1973 | 546,000 | 470 |
| 1974 | 504,000 | 1,417 |
| 1975 | 440,000 | 1,789 |
| 1976 | 487,000 | 2,091 (provisional) |
| 1977 | 406,600[a] | 2,060 (budget estimate) |

Note: a. Annual estimate based on first three quarters of 1977.
Sources: C.A. Sinclair, 'Education in Kuwait, Bahrain and Qatar: An Economic Assessment' (unpublished PhD thesis, Durham University, 1977), Table 4.36, p. 173; *Middle East Annual Review, 1976/77*, Qatar; *MEED, Special Report.: Qatar 1977*; 'Oil in the Middle East' *Quarterly Economic Review* (4th Quarter, 1977) (EIU, London, 1978).

There are hopes of finding more oil and already there is evidence of a large reservoir of natural gas offshore. However, gas reserves are not so readily convertible into revenue, and require transformation into a transportable form. It may be that Qatar's gas reserves are of primary value as a cheap source of energy in future years.

*(b) Revenue and Expenditure*

Since 1973 the government's revenues have risen dramatically from $480 million in 1973 to $2,270 million in 1977, a fivefold increase.

However, over the same period expenditure has increased sevenfold (Table 3.10). Expenditure increased at almost exactly 64 per cent per annum between 1973 and 1977. Between 1975 and 1977, expenditure increased at 33 per cent per annum and revenue at 12 per cent per annum.

Table 3.10: Qatar: Revenue and Expenditure, 1973 to 1977 ($ million)

|  | 1973 | 1974 | 1975 | 1976[a] | 1977[b] |
|---|---|---|---|---|---|
| Revenue | 482 | 1,876 | 1,928 | 2,231 | 2,265 |
| Oil | 453 | 1,808 | 1,790 | 2,092 | 2,060 |
| Other | 29 | 68 | 138 | 139 | 205 |
| Expenditure | 430 | 888 | 1,676 | 2,032 | 2,795 |
| Foreign grants | 104 | 134 | 241 | 77 | 109 |
| Other | 275 | 498 | 957 | 1,415 | 1,744 |
| Net lending and equity participation | 51 | 256 | 478 | 540 | 942 |
| Surplus + or deficit − | + 52 | + 988 | + 252 | + 199 | −530 |

Notes: a. Provisional figures.
       b. Budget figures.
Source: Abstracted from *MEED*, 16 September 1977, p. 38.

A closer inspection of expenditure shows that 'capital' expenditures have in recent years absorbed an ever increasing proportion of total expenditure (Table 3.11). In 1977, part of 'capital' expenditure is accounted for by Qatar's industrial programme. The incidence of capital expenditures will diminish as the nation's infrastructure and industrial base are established. A consideration of the net balance of Qatar's budget (Table 3.10) shows that she will be in a deficit position for some years to come.

Table 3.11: Qatar: Current and Capital Expenditure, 1973 to 1977[a] ($ million)

| Year | Current | Expenditure Per cent | Capital | Per cent | Total |
|---|---|---|---|---|---|
| 1973 | 309 | 81.5 | 70 | 18.5 | 379 |
| 1974 | 458 | 72.5 | 173 | 27.5 | 631 |
| 1975 | 806 | 67.3 | 392 | 32.7 | 1,198 |
| 1976 | 862 | 58.5 | 609 | 41.5 | 1,471 |
| 1977 | 996 | 38.1 | 1,616 | 61.9 | 2,612 |

Note a. This table presents the bulk of government expenditure, but not its entirety.
Source: Ministry of Finance and Petroleum, internal memorandum, (Doha, n.d.).

The development of Qatar's current expenditure has also been rapid; between 1973 and 1977 it has expanded at an annual rate of 37 per cent. One does not have to look far to find reasons for this rapid increase. The population grew over the period at an annual rate of approximately 7 per cent. Moreover, the desires and aspirations for social services of Qatar's population were increasing both in a quantitative and a qualitative sense. For example, not only were more secondary schools required, but also a higher standard of education in general, to the point where a university was felt to be appropriate. Finally, Qatar's inflation rate was high between 1973 and 1977, affecting the size of the budget in money terms.

Table 3.12: Qatar: Domestic Inflation Rate, 1973 to 1977

| Reference Period | | Per Annum Rate of Inflation | |
|---|---|---|---|
| | | All Items (per cent) | Food (per cent) |
| August 1973 | — September 1974 | 21.5 | 23.6 |
| September 1974— | October 1975 | 15.1 | 11.8 |
| October 1975 | — September 1976 | 22.7 | 21.2 |
| September 1976— | September 1977 | 12.7 | 14.9 |
| August 1973 | — September 1977 | 17.7 | 17.6 |

Source: Compiled from Qatar Petroleum Producing Authority (QPPA) (Offshore), *Cost of Living Analysis August 1973 to September 1977* (Doha, mimeograph, n.d.).

Table 3.12 shows the inflation rate for 'all items' and 'food' from August 1973 to September 1977. It has never fallen below 10 per cent per annum in that period, and 'food' items increased by 24 per cent between August 1973 and September 1974. The annual rate of increase over the entire period was about 18 per cent for 'all items' and for 'food'. The expenditure of the Ministry of Education presents a good example of the financial implications of extending a service. Table 3.13 shows the education budget between 1965 and 1976.

Between 1972 and 1976, the budget rose by 41 per cent per annum, and between 1974 and 1976, at a rate of 58 per cent per annum. This growth in expenditure is almost exponential. Inevitably part of this rapid expansion is due to capital and therefore non-recurrent expenditures, but equally it reflects a rapidly growing commitment to provide education for the school-age population of Qatar.

The educational sector presents itself as one in a period of transition. The question facing Qatar is whether to continue the provision of education in the same way as before, and to accept the cost as an inte-

Table 3.13: Qatar: Ministry of Education Budget, 1965 to 1976 ($ million)

| Year | Total Expenditure ($ million) |
|------|-------------------------------|
| 1965 | 7.4 |
| 1966 | 7.1 |
| 1967 | 6.6 |
| 1968 | 7.4 |
| 1969 | 8.9 |
| 1970 | 9.4 |
| 1971 | 10.7 |
| 1972 | 15.5 |
| 1973 | 26.6 |
| 1974 | 27.9 |
| 1975 | 50.1 |
| 1976 | 68.8 |

Source: Ministry of Education, *Annual Report, 1976/77* (Doha, 1978), p. 24 (Arabic).

gral part of modern statehood, or to place limits on the educational budget and ration school places. The educational sector is but one example of questions of this nature now being asked. The answers will determine much of the shape of Qatar's future development.

*(c) Industrial Development*

When Qatar first received income from oil in 1950, there was no institutional framework to facilitate the use of revenues or the development of the country. Until 1972, development was slow: only two significant industrial enterprises existed, a cement factory and a shrimp processing plant. In 1972, Sheikh Khalifa bin Hamad al-Thani assumed power, and within a brief period, a fertiliser plant opened (1973), the flour mill commenced production, and plans to diversify the economy were set in train.

The oil price increase of 1973 gave Qatar the financial capital to develop her infrastructure and to broaden the base of the economy. In 1975, a small refinery came on stream, and a natural gas liquids plant was officially opened. In the same year the Minister for Finance and Petroleum, Sheikh Abdul Azziz Khalifah al-Thani, announced an expenditure of $1,500 million on industrial projects, to broaden the base of the economy.

Qatar's diversification divides between 'heavy industry' and 'light industry'. Under the rubric of 'heavy industry' are found five main projects: an extension to the fertiliser plant; a natural gas liquids plant; a natural gas liquids plant; a petrochemical complex; a steel mill; a second cement plant. Umm Said, in the south of the peninsula, has been designated the 'industrial' area where these units will be located, except for the cement plant (at Umm Bab to the west).

The government has approached these ventures with determination, creating the Industrial Development Technical Centre to supervise the development and partly financing it through a $350 million Eurodollar loan, as well as through supplier credits. The total cost is estimated at around $2,000 million, approximately Qatar's oil revenue for one year. Commitment to the development of heavy industry in Qatar exists at two levels: first, the government sees industrialisation as the prime source of income unrelated to oil; secondly, the total cost of these projects is substantial, and to recover this investment the projects must operate successfully. In addition to the direct cost is the establishment of the infrastructure which the projects require; in particular power-generating plants, water distillation units and expansion of port facilities. Also significant is establishment of the housing and social services which the work-force required for these ventures will use.

The number of workers required is substantial. The Umm Said population is likely to be over 30,000 by 1980, according to official estimates, because of enhanced job opportunities, the movement of certain enterprises from Doha to Umm Said on account of the deeper water in the port there, and the development of related services. In fact, this figure is probably conservative. Providing the essential services for Umm Said will create more employment, and a still larger population.

The majority of the Umm Said 'heavy industries', in petrochemicals and related activities, require cheap energy and capitalise on cheap raw materials and a relative abundance of capital. In theory they require a small work-force. The steel mill is a contrast. It will utilise a cheap source of fuel, but will require raw materials from abroad, and a relatively large work-force.

The second facet of the strategy of industrial development concerns light industries. These are to be based around Doha and will include approximately four from a list of 19 alternatives, including bricks, tiles, paper tissues, paints, detergents, cosmetics, PVC products, batteries, car tyres and glass products.

Qatar is therefore committed to the development of an industrial sector including not only petrochemical and related industries, but also 'non-oil' ventures, such as the steel mill and some light industry. Industrial development will require a significant number of extra workers. These workers will be supplied almost exclusively from outside Qatar, and probably largely from outside the Middle East.

## 4 The Labour Market

Total employment in 1975 was about 66,000, of which some 12,500 (19 per cent) were nationals. The share of employment that nationals account for is likely to diminish further quite rapidly. Data on employment in Qatar are scant, and none are available on educational status or skill level for 1975. However, Qatar's qualitative dependence on migrant labour is as pronounced as her quantitative dependence.

Table 3.14: Qatar: Employment by Nationality, 1970 and 1975

|               | 1970   | Per cent | 1975   | Per cent | Rate of Increase 1970-5 |
|---------------|--------|----------|--------|----------|-------------------------|
| Nationals     | 8,200  | 17.0     | 12,500 | 18.9     | 8.8                     |
| Non-nationals | 40,000 | 83.0     | 53,800 | 81.1     | 6.1                     |
| Total         | 48,200 | 100.0    | 66,300 | 100.0    | 6.6                     |

Sources: 1970: Ministry of Information, *Census 1970* (Doha, 1970); 1975: estimates derived in J.S. Birks and C.A. Sinclair, *Country Case Study: Qatar*, International Migration Project Working Paper (Durham, 1978).

More than half of all employed nationals work for the government, and the proportion in the public sector is probably growing. Migrants work almost exclusively in the private sector, where they comprise 90 per cent of total employment.

Table 3.15: Qatar: Employment by Sector and Nationality, 1975

|               | Public Sector | | Private Sector | | | |
|---------------|--------|----------|--------|----------|--------|----------|
|               | Number | Per cent | Number | Per cent | Total  | Per cent |
| Nationals     | 6,760  | 54.1     | 5,740  | 45.9     | 12,500 | 100.0    |
| Non-nationals | 4,050  | 7.5      | 49,750 | 92.5     | 53,800 | 100.0    |
| Total         | 10,810 | 16.3     | 55,490 | 83.2     | 66,300 | 100.0    |

Source: Cited in J.S. Birks and C.A. Sinclair, *Country Case Study, Qatar*, International Migration Project Working Paper (Durham, 1978).

In reality, two labour markets exist, one for nationals, one for migrants. The conditions of entry, the rewards for effort, the criteria of reward, the type of work done and the intensity of work are different for each group. Labour market conditions are markedly superior for nationals.

The implications of this division for the long-term development of Qatar are serious. An attitude may develop that there are certain sectors and employment which nationals will not accept. Moreover, the traditional incentive to work, the need to earn a living, may not be relevant to Qataris, who often receive an income without working, or without working particularly hard. None of this would matter if Qatar were content to remain a small and stable society managed along much the same lines as in the pre-oil era, but at a much higher standard of living. However, if the country has aspirations to be a modern state and to develop an industrial arm to the economy, and wishes to work towards 'self-sufficiency' in manpower, then this analysis draws attention to crucial problems.

Enumerating a rational development of Qatar's manpower is a relatively simple task, but effecting such a policy in practice is extremely difficult. The task is especially difficult because of the many contradictions in the objectives of Qatari economy and society. For example, self-sufficiency in manpower is an objective held concurrently with the notion of the development of Qatar's industry. Given the small size of Qatar's indigenous population, this is totally impossible. The presence of so many migrants in Qatar is eloquent testimony to this.

### 5 Foreign Workers in Qatar

In 1970, 40,000 migrants worked in Qatar. By 1975 their number reached 54,000. During 1975 and subsequently, the number of migrants increased rapidly. By 1980 there may be as many as 91,000 migrant workers, and a total expatriate population of 175,000.

In 1975 the majority of migrants were from India and Pakistan; only 28 per cent were from the Middle East (Table 3.16). The large number of Asians* working in Qatar is due to the relative ease of access of the Indian subcontinent.

In government employment, expatriate staff are almost always Arabs, mainly from Egypt and the Levant. The demand for the services of this group of migrants is relatively predictable, and is likely to in-

*In this book, the term 'Asians' is used to refer to migrants originating in the Indian subcontinent, including India, Pakistan, Sri Lanka, Nepal and Bangladesh. Migrants to the Arab world from countries to the east of the Indian subcontinent are referred to as 'Far Eastern'. They come in particular from Korea, Thailand, the Philippines and Malaya.

Table 3.16: Qatar: Migrant Workers by Nationality, 1975

| Nationality | Number | Per cent |
|---|---|---|
| Jordanian and Palestinian | 6,000 | 11.2 |
| Egyptian | 2,850 | 5.3 |
| Omani | 1,870 | 3.5 |
| Yemeni (YAR) | 1,250 | 2.3 |
| Yemeni (PDRY) | 1,250 | 2.3 |
| Syria | 750 | 1.4 |
| Lebanon | 500 | 0.9 |
| Sudan | 400 | 0.7 |
| (Total Arab) | (14,870) | (27.6) |
| Pakistani | 16,000 | 29.8 |
| Indian | 16,000 | 29.8 |
| Other Asian | 2,000 | 3.7 |
| (All Asian) | (34,000) | (63.3) |
| Iranian | 4,000 | 7.5 |
| European and American | 846 | 1.6 |
| Total | 53,716 | 100.0 |

Source: Derived from J.S. Birks and C.A. Sinclair, *Migration and Development in the Arab Region* (ILO, Geneva, 1980), various tables.

crease at a moderate pace. However, the public sector is growing only slowly, compared with employment growth in Qatar's industry. It is the public sector where Qataris will tend to work increasingly in the future. Thus the prospects for expatriate Arab labour in Qatar are poor in both the public and the private sector.

## 6 Conclusion

Qatar's economy is certain to grow rapidly in the coming years. Increases in the price of oil have given a renewed confidence to official plans to industrialise. The inevitable corollary of further economic development is a growing reliance on migrant workers. Their growing number and increasing significance in proportional terms has not yet disturbed Qatari planners. However, as time passes, the essential smallness of the indigenous population and work-force will seem more of a problem to government than at present. This will be especially true as migrant workers come increasingly frequently from Asia. Arab migrants will tend to work mainly in the government, while non-Arabs will dominate the private sector and industry, almost to the exclusion of Arab workers.

The nature of the crisis facing Qatar is social, not economic. Her society will become increasingly segmented and demarcated as the divisions between national and non-national, Arab and non-Arab, become of greater significance, sharper in contrast, and associated with particular sectors of the economy.

Maintaining economic development in Qatar, with a society where the participant communities have less in common rather than more as time passes, may prove to be impossible. In the United Arab Emirates the geographical diversity and different resource endowments embodied in individual sheikhdoms hides the fact that exactly the same tensions as described in Qatar are beginning to occur, particularly in Abu Dhabi.

## Notes

1. See H. Graham, *Arabian Time Machine, Self Portrait of an Oil State* (Heinemann, London, 1978). R. Mallakh, *Qatar, the Development of an Oil Economy* (Brill, Leiden, 1979) gives a more detailed assessment. Another general overview is given in J. Moorhead, *In Defiance of the Elements: a Personal View of Qatar* (Quartet Books, London, 1977).

2. Ministry of Information, *Qatar into the Seventies* (Doha, May 1973).

3. J.G. Lorimer, *Geographical and Statistical Gazetteer of the Persian Gulf* (Calcutta, 1908), Vol. 2.

4. Ministry of Information, *Qatar into the Seventies* (Doha, May 1973).

5. The Royal Institute of International Affairs, *The Middle East, A Political and Economic Survey* (London, 1950).

6. Ministry of Information, *1970 Census* (Qatar, 1970), Table 13.

7. See, for example, *The Times*, 3 September 1976, 'Qatar'.

8. Ministry of Education, *Annual Report, 1968/69* (Doha, 1970), p. 73.

9. Interested readers may wish to refer to J. Socknat, *An Inventory and Assessment of Employment Orientated Human Resources Development Programs in the Gulf Area* (Ford Foundation, Bahrain, 1975).

10. See C.A. Sinclair, 'Education in Kuwait, Bahrain and Qatar: an Economic Assessment' (unpublished PhD thesis, Durham University, 1977).

# 4 THE UNITED ARAB EMIRATES

## 1 Introduction

In 1971 the seven lower Gulf states of Abu Dhabi, Dubai, Sharjah, Ras Al Khaimah, Ajman, Umm Al Qaiwan and Fujairah moved from their loose association as the Trucial States to form a close political union, the United Arab Emirates (UAE).[1]

The UAE enjoys very substantial oil reserves. Oil income *per capita* in 1975 was $49,900 for nationals, and $12,000 for the entire population. In fact most of the oil is the preserve of Abu Dhabi; Dubai and Sharjah share the remainder.

Since 1971 the UAE has developed rapidly.[2] The population has grown at an annual rate between 1968 and 1975 of some 18 per cent. This is a high figure even for the Arabian Gulf. The total work-force in 1975 (300,000 persons) was almost equal to that of Kuwait. Considering the much shorter period of development of the Emirates than of Kuwait, this is remarkable, especially since about 90 per cent of all employment is found in Abu Dhabi, Dubai and Sharjah.

The UAE is perhaps the best example of a capital-rich state suffering from severely limited indigenous human resources, but experiencing spectacular economic growth. The development plans of the Emirates are dramatically ambitious on the agricultural, financial and industrial fronts.

The social and demographic transformation of the United Arab Emirates which this industrial programme will entail has been little considered, except perhaps in Abu Dhabi. However, the diverse nature of the Federation makes central planning difficult, particularly when non-economic issues are involved. Planned developments are still unfinished and experience acquired after their completion will bring new perspectives to the leaders of the Federation. As things stand, the Emirates have one of the most rapidly developing economies in the world. This economic growth is carrying virtually all social issues before it.

## 2 The Supply of Labour

### (a) Population

In 1968 the population of the seven Trucial States stood at some 180,000 persons, three-quarters of whom lived in Abu Dhabi, Dubai and Sharjah. Expatriates accounted for 36 per cent of the total. Most expatriates also lived in the same three emirates (Table 4.1).

Table 4.1: United Arab Emirates: Population by Emirate and Nationality, 1968

| Emirate | Total Population | Nationals | Per cent | Non-Nationals | Per cent |
|---|---|---|---|---|---|
| Abu Dhabi | 46,375 | 23,187 | 50 | 23,188 | 50 |
| Dubai | 58,971 | 29,485 | 50 | 29,486 | 50 |
| Sharjah | 31,667 | 23,117 | 73 | 8,550 | 27 |
| Ras Al Khaimah | 24,387 | 22,679 | 73 | 1,708 | 7 |
| Fujairah | 9,735 | 7,580 | 98 | 2,155 | 2 |
| Ajman | 4,246 | 4,203 | 99 | 43 | 1 |
| Umm Al Qaiwan | 3,744 | 3,706 | 99 | 38 | 1 |
| Others | 1,300 | 650 | 50 | 650 | 50 |
| Total | 180,425 | 114,607 | 63.5 | 65,818 | 36.5 |

Source: K.G. Fenelon, *The United Arab Emirates: An Economic and Social Survey* (Longman, London, 1976), p. 7.

Between 1968 and 1975 the population increased from 180,000 to 655,000 at 18 per cent per annum, implying a doubling of the population every four years, a most unusual demographic phenomenon. Even this high overall rate is exceeded by individual emirates, notably Abu Dhabi, Ajman and Umm Al Qaiwan. Abu Dhabi's rate of population increase is the most significant, her population being relatively large in 1968. By 1975, Abu Dhabi was the most populous emirate, having overtaken Dubai (Table 4.2).

Between 1968 and 1975 the natural rate of increase of the indigenous population was probably about 3 per cent per annum. However, between 1968 and 1975 some 55,000 Arab expatriates received citizenship. By 1975 the national population totalled some 200,000. Over the same period, though, the expatriate community increased at almost 30 per cent per annum. By 1975 their community was some 455,940 strong, representing 69 per cent of the total population.

In terms of employment, while the indigenous work-force grew at the respectable rate of 3.8 per cent annually, migrant workers increased at a rate of 28 per cent annually. By 1975 nationals comprised only 15

Table 4.2: United Arab Emirates: Population by Emirate, 1968 and 1975

| Emirate | 1968 (April) Number | Per cent | 1975 (December) Number | Per cent | Growth Rate (per cent) |
|---|---|---|---|---|---|
| Abu Dhabi | 46,375 | 25.7 | 235,662 | 35.9 | 23.6 |
| Dubai | 58,971 | 32.7 | 206,861 | 31.5 | 17.7 |
| Sharjah | 31,668 | 17.6 | 88,188 | 13.4 | 14.3 |
| Ras Al Khaimah | 24,387 | 13.5 | 57,282 | 8.7 | 11.8 |
| Fujairah | 9,735 | 5.4 | 26,498 | 4.0 | 13.9 |
| Ajman | 4,246 | 2.3 | 21,566 | 3.3 | 23.6 |
| Umm Al Qaiwan | 3,744 | 2.1 | 16,879 | 2.6 | 25.6 |
| Nationals abroad | – | – | 2,372 | 0.4 | – |
| Other nationals | 1,100 | 0.7 | 629 | 0.1 | – |
| Total | 180,226 | 100.0 | 655,937 | 100.0 | 18.3 |

Sources: 1968: M.T. Sadik and W.P. Snavely, *Bahrain, Qatar and the United Arab Emirates: Colonial Past, Present Problems and Future Prospects*, (Lexington Books, D.C. Heath and Co., Lexington, Mass., 1972); 1975: K.G. Fenelon, *The United Arab Emirates: An Economic and Social Survey* (Longman, London, 1976).

Table 4.3: United Arab Emirates: Population and Employment by Nationality, 1968 and 1975

| | 1968 Number | Per cent | 1975 Number | Per cent | Growth Rate (per annum) |
|---|---|---|---|---|---|
| Nationals | | | | | |
| Population | 114,610 | 63.4 | 200,000 | 30.5 | 7.5 |
| Employment | 33,800 | 43.3 | 45,000 | 15.2 | 3.8 |
| Crude participation rate (per cent) | 29.5 | | 22.5 | | |
| Non-Nationals | | | | | |
| Population | 65,820 | 36.6 | 455,940 | 69.5 | 28.6 |
| Employment | 44,270 | 56.7 | 251,520 | 84.8 | 25.3 |
| Crude participation rate (per cent) | 67.3 | | 55.2 | | |
| Total | | | | | |
| Population | 180,830 | 100.0 | 655,940 | 100.0 | 18.2 |
| Employment | 78,070 | 100.0 | 296,720 | 100.0 | 18.9 |

Source: J.S. Birks and C.A. Sinclair, *Country Case Study; The United Arab Emirates*, International Migration Project Working Paper (Durham, 1978) Table 4, p.6.

per cent of the entire work-force.

*(b) Educational Characteristics of the Population*

The way in which education developed reflects the relationship between the Emirates and the outside world before oil was found. The Trucial States (as they then were) received assistance from two foreign governments: Kuwait and the United Kingdom which, in 1953, established a school in Sharjah. Kuwait paid for the teachers and materials, the UK for the building. Until oil was found and the Trucial States were able to afford to fund their own education, support continued. Sharjah was chosen as the location for the first school partly because there was a British air force base in Sharjah, which was also a stop-over for Far Eastern flights. Sharjah provided education for women before any other emirate and in 1968 was the first emirate to provide secondary education for girls. Sharjah was also the first emirate to have a trade school .(1958).

Shortly after 1953 schools were built elsewhere in the lower Gulf, until every emirate had at least one school, with the exception of Abu Dhabi, where modern educational development only began in 1960. Previously the conservative policies of Sheikh Shakhbut had constrained Abu Dhabi's development in general.

Table 4.4: United Arab Emirates: Employment by Educational Attainment and Nationality, 1968

| Educational Attainment | Nationals | | Non-Nationals | |
|---|---|---|---|---|
| | Number | Per cent | Number | Per cent |
| None | 29,450 | 87.1 | 30,780 | 69.5 |
| Primary certificate | 3,170 | 9.4 | 6,340 | 14.3 |
| Secondary certificate or technical college | 1,040 | 3.1 | 5,360 | 12.1 |
| University or similar education | 140 | 0.4 | 1,790 | 4.1 |
| Total | 33,800 | 100.0 | 44,270 | 100.0 |

Source: Ministry of Information, *Census 1968* (Abu Dhabi, 1968), form 27.

The limited exposure to modern education meant that only a small proportion of the Emirates' population had experienced formal education in 1968.[3] Table 4.4 shows that only 13 per cent of the indigenous work-force had some formal qualification, whilst 30 per cent of the expatriate work-force were similarly qualified. The development of education was slow initially, but after 1967 expanded at a frenetic pace.

Table 4.5 gives primary school enrolment in three selected years by emirate. Yet other students are sent abroad for education.[4] In 1975/6 the ranking of school enrolment corresponds, not surprisingly, to that

Table 4.5: United Arab Emirates: Primary School Enrolments in
Selected Years

|                | 1965/6 | 1968/9 | 1975/6 |
|----------------|--------|--------|--------|
| Abu Dhabi      | n.a    | 6,390  | 16,169 |
| Dubai          | 2,232  | 3,368  | 11,159 |
| Sharjah        | 2,046  | 2,522  | 8,644  |
| Ajman          | 203    | 532    | 1,972  |
| Umm Al Qaiwan  | 232    | 293    | 833    |
| Fujairah       | 230    | 261    | 1,993  |
| Ras Al Khaimah | 1,589  | 1,413  | 5,743  |

Sources: 1965/6: Ministry of Education, *Annual Report 1965/66* (Kuwait, 1967),
p. 257 (Arabic); 1968/9: Ministry of Education, *Annual Report 1968/69*
(Kuwait, 1970), p. 135 (Arabic); 1975/6: Ministry of Education, *Annual Report
1975/76* (Abu Dhabi, 1977), pp. 84-5; 1968/9: K.G. Fenelon, *The United Arab
Emirates, An Economic and Social Survey* (Longman, London, 1976), Table 25,
p. 149.

of both population and wealth. The implications of the increase in
enrolments for the resources of the Emirates, both in terms of manpower and finance, are very serious. In 1975/6 there were about 5,000
teachers, almost all of whom were expatriates. By 1980/1 this figure
will, on current trends, have reached 10,000. They will be recruited
entirely from abroad.

### 3 The Demand for Labour

*(a) Introduction*

The driving force behind the formation of the UAE was, and still is,
Sheikh Zayyed bin Sultan al Nahayyan, the ruler of Abu Dhabi. While
the indigenous inhabitants of the lower Gulf may appear to an outsider
as enjoying a very similar ethic, cultural and religious background, sharp
distinctions between the indigenous peoples and tribes do exist. The
creation and subsequent development of the UAE has been a remarkable achievement, for which Sheikh Zayyed deserves considerable
credit. The UAE has acted effectively in international affairs, both as a
mediator in inter-Arab disputes and in affecting the policies of OPEC.
However, while internal political unity has been a long-standing aim,
disputes over border demarcations and, on occasion, overall policy, are
not unknown. These differences stem from each emirate's considerable
pride and consciousness of a particular historical development. The concept of sublimation of local political and economic decisions to the
Council of Ministers is a new one in the area.

Although the principal concern here is the economic development of the Emirates, it would be incorrect to think that political relationships are irrelevant. Indeed, to a considerable extent they facilitate an understanding of recent economic development and aid prediction of future development.

To discuss economic development, the Emirates are divided into three groups: (1) Abu Dhabi; (2) Dubai; (3) Sharjah, Ras Al Khaimah, Umm Al Qaiwan, Ajman and Fujairah.

## (b) Economic Development

*Abu Dhabi.* Before oil was discovered, the inhabitants of the area now described as Abu Dhabi lived mostly in three places: the Buraimi oasis to the east; the Liwa oases to the south, and Abu Dhabi island itself. The demise of the pearling trade in the 1920s was particularly serious for this island community, since, besides fishing, little means of livelihood existed, unlike the relatively deep creek and the commercial and trading industry of Dubai. The economic fortunes of the peoples living in Abu Dhabi were at a low ebb when oil was discovered in 1950. The conservative policies of Sheikh Shakhbut constrained the impact of the revenues until 1966, when the present ruler acceded to power. Since 1966 the landscape of Abu Dhabi has been transformed following extensive investment in social services and infrastructure.

Abu Dhabi enjoys more than 80 per cent of the oil revenues of the Emirates. Table 4.6 shows oil production in the UAE since 1974. Since 1973, Abu Dhabi has given considerable thought to a common Gulf problem, developing a 'non-oil' source of income. Establishment of basic infrastructure has absorbed a high proportion of the Abu Dhabi budget, but over time that component will diminish. Government planners, and in particular the directors of Abu Dhabi National Oil Company (ADNOC), have been given the responsibility of industrial development. Ruweis, a site about 200 kilometres to the west of Abu Dhabi city and an oil terminal seaport, is where the heavy industrial projects are to be located.

Contracts have been signed for two gas processing plants, which will provide the feedstock for the industrial units at Ruweis. Amongst other projects, a fertiliser plant, an iron and steel works, a petrochemical plant, a cement factory and a liquid petroleum gas plant are being considered.

A consideration of some of the wider aspects of the Ruweis development may, in time, result in some adaptation of the most ambitious version of it. Particular considerations will be the social implications of

Table 4.6: United Arab Emirates: Oil Production by Emirate, 1974 to 1977 (millions of barrels per day)

| Emirate | 1974 | 1975 | 1976 | 1977 | Per cent in 1977 |
|---------|------|------|------|------|------------------|
| Abu Dhabi | 1.4 | 1.3 | 1.5 | 1.7 | (83.3) |
| Dubai | 0.2 | 0.2 | 0.3 | 0.3 | (14.7) |
| Sharjah | 0.02 | 0.04 | 0.04 | 0.04 | ( 2.0) |
| Total | 1.62 | 1.54 | 1.84 | 2.04 | (100.0) |

Sources: 1974 to 1976: Union Bank of Switzerland Reports, Country Studies, *United Arab Emirates* (Zurich, 1977), p. 2; 1977: *MEED*, 31 March 1978.

Table 4.7: Abu Dhabi: Fiscal Position in 1977 and 1978 ($ million)

| Income and Expenditure | 1977 | 1978 |
|-----------------------|------|------|
| Expenditure[a] | | |
| Contribution to federal budget | 3,384 | 3,333 |
| Abu Dhabi budget | 1,370 | 1,860 |
| Foreign aid | 982 | 982[b] |
| Total | 5,736 | 6,175 |
| Income | | |
| Oil revenue | 8,205 | 8,205[c] |
| | | 6,365[d] |
| Net surplus | +2,469 | +2,030[c] |
| | | + 190[d] |

Notes: a. Excludes net transfers from abroad.
      b. Assumes a level of aid in 1978 comparable with 1977.
      c. Illustration of implications of 1977 rate of production.
      d. Illustration of implications of adhering to the government directive
         limiting production to 1.35 million barrels per day at $13 per barrel.
Sources: *MEED, Special Report on the United Arab Emirates* (London, 1977); *The Times*, 'Report on the United Arab Emirates', 24 April 1978.

hosting an expatriate population at Ruweis of between 80,000 and 100,000 and the adverse effect on federal unity of appearing to compete with Dubai, which has a comparable development at Jebel Ali. Probably the scale of Ruweis will be reduced and the venture limited to natural gas or oil-related activities. Even so, Abu Dhabi will remain the dominant force in the UAE and, because of her financial strength, enjoys remarkable flexibility in matters of economic policy (Table 4.7).

Table 4.7 does not include the income Abu Dhabi receives from investments abroad. In 1972 the foreign reserves of the UAE stood at $1.3 billion (thousand million), almost all of which are the preserve of Abu Dhabi. At an interest rate of 7 per cent these investments would yield $91 million, equivalent to about 1 per cent of oil revenue in 1977. Abu Dhabi's foreign investments would be much higher if her aid payments to the developing countries were not so large.[5] In 1977 these represented 12 per cent of oil revenues.

Whatever is finally decided upon for Ruweis, Abu Dhabi certainly has the financial muscle to effect the current plans. Oil reserves are currently put at 30 billion barrels, and gas reserves at 33 billion barrels (oil equivalent). At 1977 production rates, her oil reserves have a life of 50 years. At the more reduced rate of 1.35 mbd they will last 63 years. In short, even if Abu Dhabi imposes an output limit of 1.35 mbd and continues her 1977 level of aid, she will be able to maintain her support of the federal UAE budget and execute the planned industrial projects with some ease.

*Dubai.* Dubai has been prominent in the Gulf as a commercial and trading centre throughout the twentieth century. Dubai creek has encouraged maritime activities, including re-exporting of many commodities, not least gold. The strong indigenous merchant community and the progressive business attitudes of the ruler, Sheikh Rashid bin Said al Maktoum, have served to create in Dubai an economy which is not directly dependent either on oil or on external support.

The life-blood of the present economy is twofold: the flourishing import-export business and the commercial and banking community. When the headlong rush to develop the Arabian peninsula began in 1973, port capacity in the peninsula was severely limited. By virtue of a propitious port development scheme conceived in 1968 and completed in 1972, Dubai benefited from the undercapacity of her neighbours. In 1973 her port handled 1.8 million tons and in 1976 about 4.0 million tons. At present 22 berths are being added to the existing 15 at Port Rashid and the possibility of extending this by a further 20 berths is included in the present developments. These extensions to Port Rashid are in addition to the creation of a 74-berth port at the Jebel Ali complex. The largest exporter to Dubai is Japan, followed by the United Kingdom. In 1976 the total import bill stood at $2.4 billion, having risen from $1.8 billion in 1975 and $1.2 billion in 1974.

It is interesting to compare the development of Dubai's port with that of Sharjah. Earlier in the 1900s Sharjah was politically stronger than Dubai and enjoyed the benefit of a good port. But as a result of neglecting the channel, Sharjah lost both her port facility and the opportunity to cash in on the import boom of the 1970s.

The banking community of Dubai rivals that of Bahrain, though it is slightly more conventional. Its economic value to Dubai is not only the foreign exchange which it earns directly in commission fees, but also in the foreign exchange which enters Dubai to service the banking community. The most recent addition to Dubai's skyline is the massive Trade Centre. As the highest building in the Gulf (excluding the Post Office Towers in Kuwait) it is symbolic of Dubai's previous success in the commercial world and of her continuing commitment to it.

Dubai produced in 1977 about 0.4 mbd of oil, which earned her $1.3 billion in revenue. Dubai's oil reserves are estimated at about 1.4 billion barrels of recoverable oil. At 1977 rates, this leaves her with approximately eleven years of oil life. Consideration of Table 4.8 shows that in fiscal terms Dubai's position is extremely healthy. Though data are patchy, the overall picture is clear. Even when Dubai's commitments on previous borrowing are taken into account (proposed developments at Jebel Ali have been estimated as costing somewhere in the region of $2.0 billion), Dubai still has sufficient funds, at a conservative estimate, to maintain a healthy budget surplus.

Table 4.8: Dubai: Revenue and Expenditure, 1973 to 1977 ($ million)

|  | 1973 | 1974 | 1975 | 1976 | 1977 |
|---|---|---|---|---|---|
| Revenue |  |  |  |  |  |
| Oil | 108 | 560 | 810 | 1,051 | 1,289 |
| Non-oil | 13 | 25 | 34 | 46 | 50[a] |
| Total | 121 | 585 | 844 | 1,097 | 1,339 |
| Expenditure |  |  |  |  |  |
| Capital | n.a. | n.a. | 110 | 130 | — |
| Current | n.a. | n.a. | 63 | 100 | — |
| Total | — | — | 173 | 230 | — |
| Net surplus (+) or deficit (−) | n.a. | n.a. | + 671 | + 867 | — |

Note: a. Estimate.
Sources: Derived from *Middle East Annual Review, 1978* (London; *MEED*, various reports; *The Times*, Special Reports on the UAE (various); *Gulf Handbook, 1978* (London).

Dubai's industrial plans are ambitious. At Jebel Ali, 30 kilometres west of Dubai, it is proposed to create one of the largest industrial areas in the Arab world. Under consideration are the following projects: an aluminium smelter, a steel mill, a liquid petroleum gas plant, power generation and desalination plants, a 74-berth port complex, and an airport.

Initial estimates of the work-force and attendant population range as high as 400,000 by 1985. There are reports that Jebel Ali will be a 'labour free zone' — an area into which entry is possible without a work or residence permit, but that movement will be confined to the limited area of Jebel Ali.

The Jebel Ali development is now under way, and the next few years will reveal the extent of Dubai's commitment to industrialisation. An interesting aspect of the present arrangements at Jebel Ali is that the contractors for the harbour works have been active for more than a year without a signed contract. Such is the extent of the confidence in the judgement and equity of Sheikh Rashid.

It was recently stated in reference to Abu Dhabi by a government official that 'nothing can go wrong in an economy where any mistake is retrievable.' This attitude also prevails in Dubai. While the statement may be an accurate comment on the limited extent of financial constraints, it is not accurate in respect of other constraints, however. In particular, the problems posed by an expatriate community of 400,000 in an emirate which has about 20,000 indigenous males of working age cannot be ignored. It may be that Dubai's experience of operating her massive dry dock will influence decisions about Jebel Ali.

*Sharjah, Ras Al Khaimah, Ajman, Umm Al Qaiwan and Fujairah.* Since the economic development of these individual emirates is closely linked to Zayyed's aims of a federal entity, it is appropriate to detail further the development of the Federation and its present nature. The creation of a union of all the lower Gulf states made obvious political sense. The increased oil revenues from 1973 enhanced Sheikh Zayyed's capacity to persuade rulers of the other emirates that the union also made economic sense.

Through the expansion of the responsibilities of federal ministries to cover such items as schools, labour administration, defence, communications and by supporting the federal budget to the extent of 98 per cent, Abu Dhabi makes an indirect contribution to the exchequers of the other emirates. More directly, loans and grants are made for particular projects, for example the road from Sharjah to Fujairah. Abu Dhabi also underwrites the external borrowing of other emirates.

Dubai has been the least willing participant in federal union, though Dubai's Sheikh Rashid is now the Prime Minister of the Federation. Besides the natural instinct for independence which characterises every emirate, Dubai also has a relatively strong economy which does not depend on support from Abu Dhabi. It does, though, to a certain extent, depend on a belief that the market forces which have been allowed free rein in the past will continue to dominate the economy. Federal legislation might be seen as limiting the natural growth of Dubai's economy in, for example, the fields of labour recruitment and conditions, company law, and even industrial development.

As a consequence of Dubai's lack of enthusiasm for federation and her relative affluence compared with Sharjah and the 'non-oil' emirates, this latter group has received the majority of Abu Dhabi's financial assistance. These members of the UAE have most to gain from federal unity and the resulting generosity of Sheikh Zayyed. Apart from Sharjah, none has oil, though Ras Al Khaimah has hopes of it and Umm Al Qaiwan is optimistic about natural gas. This latter state has signed an agreement to supply Dubai's Jebel Ali with natural gas.

Some of these emirates have a more conventional form of economic development than Abu Dhabi, though in financial terms they are impoverished. Agriculture and fishing in Ras Al Khaimah and Fujairah continue to be reasonably healthy. Sharjah stands out from these relatively poor emirates, receiving some $200 million oil revenue per year. Sharjah aims to capitalise on her liberal tax and company legislation and her now excellent communications. The banking community is small but growing. However, local bankers think Sharjah might be unable to compete with Dubai effectively, and in the absence of an industrial base, the viability of Sharjah as a second financial centre in the Emirates is questionable.

The infrastructure and industrial achievements of even these poorer emirates towards which Zayyed has helped reads like a Third World ideal of development: Sharjah, several hotels, an airport, a new port, a cement factory; Ras Al Khaimah, a cement factory, a fish processing plant, an international airport, and possibly a refinery run in a joint venture with Kuwait, processing Kuwaiti oil; Fujairah, Ajman and Umm Al Qaiwan, steady improvements in infrastructure and social services.

Overall, the investment potential of these states is considerable. If the United Arab Emirates is to be more than a political entity, the economies and resources of the five smaller states must be developed, and in such a way that they are complementary to each other. These states have more diversified economies, though infinitely more humble ones than Abu Dhabi's. In the long run, it is the development of these smaller emirates which will determine the overall identity of the UAE. By investing in them Sheikh Zayyed is not only being generous, but wise as well.

## 4 The Labour Market

The astonishing growth of employment in the United Arab Emirates has been noted. Since the distribution of population accords with oil income, the distribution of employment is similar, Abu Dhabi absorbing 40 per cent of employment, and Dubai one-third. Together Abu Dhabi, Dubai and Sharjah account for about 90 per cent of the total work-force (Table 4.9).

Table 4.9: United Arab Emirates: Employment by Emirate and Sex, 1975

| Emirate | Male | Female | Total | Distribution (per cent) |
|---|---|---|---|---|
| Abu Dhabi | 121,345 | 3,925 | 125,270 | 42.2 |
| Dubai | 98,528 | 3,800 | 102,328 | 34.5 |
| Sharjah | 34,924 | 1,215 | 36,139 | 12.2 |
| Ras Al Khaimah | 16,050 | 543 | 16,593 | 5.6 |
| Fujairah | 6,196 | 87 | 6,283 | 2.1 |
| Ajman | 6,763 | 243 | 7,006 | 2.4 |
| Umm Ali Qaiwan | 2,749 | 148 | 2,897 | 1.0 |
| Total | 286,555 | 9,961 | 296,516 | 100.0 |

Source: Ministry of Planning, *Census, 1975* (Abu Dhabi, 1976).

Indication of the relative growth of each emirate is given by the 1975 and 1977 Establishment Surveys. These surveys cover only the private-sector work-force and therefore they show growth of the 'non-government' sector. In the UAE the 'public sector' is, in terms of employment, far less significant than in Kuwait or Qatar. Initially, the only recognisable form of civil service consisted of the small group of advisers who surrounded the emirs. With the development of 'ministries' and a federal bureaucracy, the public sector has grown in size. Even so, the public sector will remain small in employment terms for some time to come.

It is remarkable that these oil-rich states, particularly Abu Dhabi and Dubai, are able to distribute such large sums of money and to impose upon economic development a recognisable form, in the virtual absence of a government bureaucracy. The explanation lies in the unusual nature of these societies and the remarkable energy and personalities of Sheikhs Zayyed and Rashid.

It is Dubai, the celebrated commercial and trading centre, which had much the largest private-sector employment in 1975 and 1977 (Table

4.10). Over these two years private-sector employment in Sharjah, though considerably smaller than in Abu Dhabi, grew at 82 per cent annually to 57,000 workers. Overall recorded employment increased at 41 per cent annually. However, government officials believe that the 1975 results probably suffered from under-enumeration, so this growth rate is perhaps a little misleading. Nevertheless, it is certain that in 1975 total employment, excluding 79,000 public-sector employees, was about 217,500. If the 1977 Establishment Survey is correct, then private-sector employment grew between 1975 and 1977 at about 22 per cent per annum. This confirms the pattern of economic development described above; the economy was booming between 1975 and 1977.

Table 4.10: United Arab Emirates: Employment in Private Sector Establishments, 1975 and 1977

| Emirate | 1975 | | 1977 | | Annual Rate of Increase 1975 to 1977 |
|---|---|---|---|---|---|
| | Number | Per cent | Number | Per cent | |
| Abu Dhabi | 63,037 | 39.2 | 97,240 | 30.2 | 24.2 |
| Dubai | 67,109 | 41.8 | 135,632 | 42.1 | 42.1 |
| Sharjah | 17,237 | 10.7 | 57,207 | 17.9 | 82.1 |
| Ras Al Khaimah | 7,855 | 4.9 | 16,007 | 5.0 | 42.7 |
| Fujairah | 2,526 | 1.6 | 4,550 | 1.4 | 34.2 |
| Ajman | 2,143 | 1.3 | 8,215 | 2.5 | 95.8 |
| Umm Al Qaiwan | 765 | 0.5 | 2,946 | 0.9 | 96.2 |
| Total | 160,672 | 100.0 | 321,797 | 100.0 | 41.5 |

Source: Ministry of Planning, *Establishment Survey, 1975 and 1977* (Abu Dhabi, 1978), Tables 5 and 6.

*(a) Employment by Occupation and Economic Activity*

The educational attainment of the work-force in 1975 was low. Table 4.11 shows that 68 per cent of all workers had not completed primary school education. About 6 per cent possessed a university or higher degree. The table suggests that the UAE has imported a large number of unskilled manual workers, with a more limited amount of highly qualified manpower.

Information on occupational divisions confirms this. Of total employment, 9.4 per cent are professional, technical and related workers and administrative and managerial workers, comprising 28,000 persons. Over half of all occupations are described as operators and labourers (Table 4.12).

Table 4.11: United Arab Emirates: Educational Attainment of Employed Persons, 1975

| Educational Status | Number | Per cent |
|---|---|---|
| Illiterate | 119,282 | 41.1 |
| Literate | 79,032 | 27.2 |
| Primary certificate | 19,717 | 6.8 |
| Preparatory certificate | 19,414 | 6.7 |
| Secondary certificate | 31,680 | 10.9 |
| Less than university | 4,219 | 1.4 |
| University degree | 15,722 | 5.4 |
| Post-graduate | 1,097 | 0.4 |
| Not stated | 167 | 0.1 |
| Total | 290,330 | 100.0 |

Source: Ministry of Planning, *Establishment Survey, 1975 and 1977* (Abu Dhabi, 1978), Tables 5 and 6.

Table 4.12: United Arab Emirates: Employment by Occupational Group and Sex, 1975

| Occupational Group | Male | Female | Total | Per cent |
|---|---|---|---|---|
| Professional and technical and related workers | 17,703 | 4,323 | 22,026 | 7.4 |
| Administrative and managerial workers | 5,800 | 40 | 5,840 | 2.0 |
| Clerical and related workers | 29,398 | 1,975 | 31,373 | 10.5 |
| Sales workers | 17,942 | 138 | 18,080 | 6.1 |
| Service workers | 43,788 | 2,900 | 46,688 | 15.8 |
| Agricultural, animal husbandry workers and fishermen | 13,694 | 38 | 13,732 | 4.6 |
| Production and related workers, transport equipment operators and labourers | 154,098 | 115 | 154,213 | 52.1 |
| Activities not adequately defined | 564 | 10 | 574 | 0.2 |
| Unemployed | 3,568 | 422 | 3,990 | 1.3 |
| Total | 286,555 | 9,961 | 296,516 | 100.0 |

Source: Ministry of Planning, *Census, 1975* (Abu Dhabi, 1976), Table 38.

In 1975 there were about 14,000 agricultural workers and fishermen. This group comprises largely UAE nationals, though some Omanis travel to the UAE to fish. In 1975 about one-third of the national work-force was engaged in these traditional activities.[6] Table 4.13 confirms 14,000 persons engaged in agriculture and fishing.[7] As in other peninsula states, mining, quarrying and petroleum extraction employ only a small proportion of the total at 6 per cent. The sector employing most people is construction, accounting for 32 per cent. Almost as large is community social and personal services with 29 per cent of all employment. This is the economic sector in which many nationals work.

This pattern of employment is very common in the Gulf: limited primary-sector employment, with swollen tertiary-sector employment (Table 4.13). The size of manufacturing and construction, the secondary sectors, depends on whether the construction phase of development is past and on the extent to which industry has been established. In 1975 the construction boom was marked in the Emirates, but industrial development was limited.

Table 4.13: United Arab Emirates: Employment by Economic Activity and Sex, 1975

| Economic Activity | Male | Female | Total | Per cent |
|---|---|---|---|---|
| Agriculture and fishing | 13,528 | 41 | 13,569 | 4.6 |
| Mining, quarrying and petroleum extraction | 6,679 | 189 | 6,868 | 2.3 |
| Manufacturing | 17,163 | 102 | 17,265 | 5.8 |
| Electricity, gas and water | 6,242 | 22 | 6,264 | 2.1 |
| Construction | 93,635 | 235 | 93,870 | 31.7 |
| Wholesale and retail trade and restaurants and hotels | 37,280 | 436 | 37,716 | 12.7 |
| Transport storage and communications | 23,283 | 318 | 23,601 | 8.0 |
| Finance, insurance, real estate and business services | 5,459 | 538 | 5,997 | 2.0 |
| Community, social and personal services | 79,142 | 7,646 | 86,788 | 29.3 |
| Activities not adequately defined | 576 | 12 | 588 | 0.2 |
| Unemployed | 3,568 | 422 | 3,990 | 1.3 |
| Total | 286,555 | 9,961 | 296,516 | 100.0 |

Source: Ministry of Planning, *Census, 1975* (Abu Dhabi, 1976), Table 32.

*(b) Future Employment Demand*

In assessing the future demand for labour, distinction must be made between Dubai, and Abu Dhabi with the remaining states. In this latter group of six emirates, the demand for labour depends firstly upon the extent to which Abu Dhabi, and in particular Sheikh Zayyed, proposes to develop the infrastructure of the UAE as a whole and expand the responsibilities and size of the federal Ministries. Secondly, and also relevant, are the chances of fulfilment of the plans for an industrial arm to the economy at Ruweis. This is a more complex prospect to evaluate. To assess the implications of developing Ruweis, the relatively detailed estimates of employment generation at Jebel Ali are used (Table 4.14).

Rather as Sheikh Zayyed takes great personal concern in the development of the UAE, so Sheikh Rashid is involved with the development of Dubai and Jebel Ali. The Jebel Ali development has the psychological support of Rashid and his considerable financial muscle. The industries planned for Ruweis and Jebel Ali are comparable.

Table 4.14: United Arab Emirates: Employment Estimates for Jebel Ali Development, 1981 and 1985

|  | 1981 | 1985 |
|---|---|---|
| Management, professional and technical workers | 4,800 | 10,550 |
| Supervisors, skilled manual workers, foremen and office workers | 14,250 | 29,200 |
| Semi-skilled manual and office workers | 24,450 | 53,850 |
| Total | 43,500 | 93,600 |
| Associated population | 67,600 | 160,100 |

Source: Peddle, Thorp, Chapman and Taylor, *Employment and Population Estimates for Jebel Ali Industrial Complex* (Dubai, 1977).

Employment at Jebel Ali in 1985 is equivalent to the total population of Dubai emirate in 1977. If Jebel Ali and Ruweis were developed at the same time, the population of the UAE would increase by about 400,000. The population is already increasing at about 18 per cent per annum without these developments. If plans go ahead, the population total for the UAE in 1985 would be over 3 million.

Ruweis and Jebel Ali are of major importance to the UAE in economic terms and as investments for their oil surpluses. Equally, they will inevitably engender a continued rapid rate of population increase, and so will be of immense social and political significance too.

## 5 Foreign Workers in the United Arab Emirates

The present main development aims of the UAE, and indeed other peninsula states, are listed below.

(i) They must industrialise rapidly.

(ii) A physical separation must be established between the industrial area and the present urban areas. Examples of this approach are numerous: in Kuwait, Shuaiba is 20 miles to the south of Kuwait; Umm Said is 30 miles from Doha in Qatar; Jubail and Yenbo are small towns, assigned to be the two major industrial areas of Saudi Arabia. Similarly, Jebel Ali and Ruweis are some way from present urban centres.

(iii) As the cost of provision of basic services (water, electricity) and social amenities (housing, health, education) to non-national workers is extremely high, there is a considerable economic incentive to mini-mise these. As a result, there is a swing to the recruitment of single men, rather than of those with families.

(iv) On a more general level, there is a nascent concern over the broader implications of hosting an expatriate population many times greater than the indigenous community. This relates principally to the impact of the expatriate community on the culture and identity of the local people. An aim held concurrently with aims (i) and (ii) is to preserve a distinctive national culture and identity.

Each objective mentioned above argues for establishing industrial development in enclaves. Rapid industrial development which is geo-graphically distant from urban centres can be accomplished by an apposite choice of site and the financial capacity to pay. However, effecting the aims (iii) and (iv) means a 'work camp' approach must be used, but on a permanent basis for the operating life of the industrial area, rather than on the temporary basis which is normally the case.

These aims, taken together, ensure that the planners in the UAE will develop the Jebel Ali and Ruweis industrial areas as enclaves, with the labour forces employed on a work camp basis. It is intended that the work-forces should be almost completely segregated from the existing urban centres of Abu Dhabi and Dubai. By using this approach, com-mentators hope that the UAE and other peninsula states can reconcile two apparently conflicting objectives: rapid economic and industrial development concurrent with the preservation of a distinctive national culture and identity.

So far it has been companies from the Far East that have proved capable of effecting enclave projects in the Arab world. In particular the Koreans, Thais, Filipinos and Malays have been able to provide the labour forces prepared to live and work in these labour camp condi-tions. If Jebel Ali and Ruweis are developed as enclaves, built and subse-quently operated on a permanent work camp basis, the majority of the work-force will be Far Eastern.

Table 4.15 shows that in 1975, the Asian and Far Eastern presence was already considerable, comprising some 65 per cent of all employ-ment. Since then, the Far Eastern contribution to the work-force has increased further. This is a trend which is recurring throughout the Arabian peninsula.

Table 4.15: United Arab Emirates: Migrant Workers by Nationality, 1975

| Nationality | Number | Per cent |
|---|---|---|
| Jordanian and Palestinian | 14,500 | 6.0 |
| Omani | 14,000 | 5.5 |
| Egyptian | 12,500 | 5.0 |
| Lebanese | 4,500 | 1.7 |
| Syrian | 4,500 | 1.7 |
| Yemeni (YAR) | 4,500 | 1.7 |
| Yemeni (PDRY) | 4,500 | 1.7 |
| Sudanese | 1,500 | 0.6 |
| Somali | 1,000 | 0.4 |
| Iraqi | 500 | 0.2 |
| Total Arab | 62,000 | 24.5 |
| Pakistani | 100.000 | 39.8 |
| Indian | 61,500 | 24.4 |
| Other East Asian | 2,000 | 0.8 |
| Total East Asian | 163,500 | 65.0 |
| Iranian | 21,000 | 8.3 |
| European and American | 5,000 | 2.0 |
| Total | 251,500 | 100.0 |

Source: Derived from J.S. Birks and C.A. Sinclair, *International Migration and Development in the Arab Region* (ILO, Geneva, 1980), Table 10.

Indigenous workers in the Emirates were a small minority of the total work-force in 1975 (15 per cent). Even the total Arab work-force (of UAE nationals plus Arab expatriate workers) represented only 36 per cent of the total. Arab participation in the development of the United Arab Emirates is diminishing. The Far Eastern contribution is growing. How far this process will continue without restraint is a political question, but at some point concern that an indigenous or even Arab culture and identity will be lost must affect development planning. Even isolation of non-national work-forces in work camps in enclaves can only delay this reaction. However, one point remains certain: the forces and momentum behind the economic development of the Emirates are strong, and tempering them will prove difficult, if not impossible.

## 6 Conclusion

Taken as a whole, the UAE has a formidable capacity for economic and industrial development. Trends suggest that by the mid-1980s the Emirates will have a larger population than Kuwait. The indigenous population of the UAE is, in common with every other oil-rich state in the peninsula, relatively small. The economic development has only been accomplished with the assistance of a considerable number of foreign workers.

Even without the stupendous developments at Jebel Ali and Ruweis, the UAE will continue to rely increasingly on expatriate labour in the foreseeable future. As a result of the nature of present-day development and an inadequate supply of Arab labour, development in the UAE will increasingly be carried out with labour largely from the Far East.

An enclave approach to industrial projects, using work camps as a pemanent form of labour market organisation, will be used to build and man Ruweis and Jebel Ali. However, there are wider implications to large-scale enclave developments which have not yet been fully considered by government planners. In particular, does the enclave approach remove completely the need to constrain the pace of development to preserve some numerical balance between indigenous labour and migrant workers? From an economic perspective there need not be any limit to the use of migrant labour, but political pressures might serve to constrain enclave development, as they have economic growth at large. From a broad perspective, the real value of such enclaves to the indigenous population is not entirely clear.

## Notes

1. M.M. Abdullah, *The Modern History of the United Arab Emirates* (Ad Orientem, Delhi, 1978); H.M. Al Baharna, *The Arabian Gulf States: Their Legal and Political Status and Their International Problems* (Librairie de Liban, Beirut, 1975).

2. M.S. Otaiba, *Petroleum and the Economy of the United Arab Emirates* (Croom Helm, London, 1977).

3. R.A. Mertz, *Education and Manpower in the Arabian Gulf* (American Friends of the Middle East, Washington, DC, 1972).

4. D.O. Clark and R.A. Mertz, *The Coastal Countries of the Arabian Peninsula: A Guide to the Academic Placement of Students from Kuwait, Bahrain, Qatar, United Arab Emirates, Sultanate of Oman, People's Democratic Republic of Yemen and Yemen Arab Republic in Educational Institutions in the USA* (American Association of Collegiate Registrars, Washington, DC, 1974).

5. M.J. Williams, 'The Aid Programs of OPEC Countries', *Foreign Affairs, 54* (January 1976), pp. 308-24.

6. F. Heard-Bey, 'Development Anomalies in the Beduin Oases of al-Liwa', *Asian Affairs, 61*, 5, 3 (October 1974), pp. 272-86; F. Heard-Bey, 'The Gulf States and Oman in Transition', *Asian Affairs, 59*, 3, 1 (February 1972), pp. 14-22; M.S. Otaiba, *Economy of Abu Dhabi – Past and Present* (Abu Dhabi, 1977).

7. This consistency is typical of the census figures available: there is every indication that the census was carefully executed and reasonably accurate.

# 5 THE KINGDOM OF SAUDI ARABIA

## 1 Introduction

Saudi Arabia, in terms of geographical area, oil reserves and production, population and economy, is on an entirely larger scale than the Gulf states which this analysis has dealt with so far. The Kingdom absorbs a large majority of the area of the Arabian peninsula, though it does not cover the more populous mountain regions in the south-east and south-west. Much of the Kingdom is arid desert which was, before the advent of cheap energy, an inhospitable living environment. It is therefore no surprise that, relative to her geographical size, Saudi Arabia's indigenous population is small, though much larger than her neighbours'. Years of uncertainty and political pressures have invited population estimates of too large an order.

As an oil producer, Saudi Arabia dominates the Organization of Arab Petroleum Exporting Countries and is a principal in the world, with reserves expected to last at least 20 years at current levels of production. So great have oil incomes been that the economy has recently been growing at 12 per cent per annum in real terms. Moreover, unexploited as yet are large-scale mineral reserves; Saudi Arabia's present industrial development plans appear ambitious, but they could be far exceeded by a subsequent phase of economic growth based upon mineral resources other than oil.

Obviously the financial and natural resources of Saudi Arabia imply a massive potential for economic development. The major constraint, perhaps more acutely felt than in any other Arab capital-rich state, is the size and nature of the labour force. Saudi Arabian planners are aware of this, and have given human resources development a high priority in budget allocations. The difficulties they face, however, are immense, and paradoxically are aggravated by the exceptional wealth of the Kingdom. Unfortunately, policies designed to distribute income more equitably and to encourage nationals to participate in the modern economic order have an enervating effect, and thereby diminish the effective supply of national labour.

## 2. The Supply of Labour

### (a) Introduction

The wealth and strategic and political importance of Saudi Arabia have led to conjecture over the size of the national population and number of immigrants living in the country. Therefore, this analysis dwells at some length upon the numbers and characteristics of the population of Saudi Arabia.

### (b) The Population

*Estimates of the Present-Day Population.* It is perhaps surprising that there should be speculation about the Kingdom's population, as an official census was held in 1974. However, the results of this census and circumstances surrounding it give rise to concern over its accuracy. A Japanese report estimates the Saudi Arabian population in early 1975 to be 'approximately 3.9 million including some 600,000 expatriates' – a national Saudi Arabian population of 3.3 million.[1] Hoagland wrote that the Saudi Arabian census recorded a population of 5.6 million.[2] Demographic indicators published by the Economic Commission for West Asia give the 1974 population as 7,013,000.[3] What percentage of this population might be foreign is not indicated.[4]

The disparity of these estimates makes it necessary to re-evaluate them and other data to produce a base from which to assess the official census and analyse the labour market.

*Some Historical Evidence of the Size of the National Population of Saudi Arabia.* Hamza[5] claimed a total of 3 million bedouin and 2,110,000 settled people in Saudi Arabia in 1933. This was, however, based upon hearsay and there are obvious shortcomings such as acceptance of estimates by sheikhs of exaggerated figures. It is significant that the bedouin comprise 59 per cent of Hamza's total of 5.1 million, as this group is most difficult to quantify. Hamza was writing when popular feeling romanticised the bedouin, making them more important, in numerical terms, than they really were. Hamza's estimates for the bedouin are certainly greatly in excess of the real figure.[6]

Yet Hamza's figures have proved markedly influential on other estimates over the years. From them derives the notion of there being more than 3 million people in the country. For instance, Hamza's figures lay behind Filahi's assertion that there were 'about three million bedouin',[7] which brought about official repudiation of the 1962 population census figures (see below). In fact, Hamza's estimate has received

Table 5.1: Saudi Arabia: Alternative Estimates of the Population, Nationals and Non-Nationals, 1974/5

| Source | Saudi National Population | Non-National Population | Total Population | Date |
|---|---|---|---|---|
| 1 | 3,300,000 | 600,000 | 3,900,000 | 1975 (early) |
| 2 | – | – | 5,600,000 | 1974 (late) |
| 3 | – | – | 6,200,000 | 1975 |
| 4 | 3,500,000 | – | – | 1975 |
| 5 | 6,695,000 | – | – | 1974/5 |
| 6 | – | – | 7,227,000 | 1975 |

Sources:
1. Japan Co-operation Centre for the Middle East, *Analysis of Demand and Supply of Manpower in the Arabian Gulf Countries* (Tokyo, 1976), p. 13.
2. J. Hoagland, 'Saudi Arabians Push $100 billion Development Plan', *Washington Post*, 13 April 1975.
3. United States, Bureau of Census, Department of Commerce, *Summary of Census Data* (Washington, DC, n.d.).
4. C.A. Sinclair and J.A. Socknat, *An Estimate of the Population of the Yemen Arab Republic and the Number of Workers Abroad* (Sanaa, 1975).
5. Ministry of Education, Kingdom of Saudi Arabia, *Towards an Appropriate Strategy for Training Skilled and Semi Skilled Workers* (Riyadh, April 1974), Table 12, p. 32.
6. United Nations Economic Commission for Western Asia, *Demographic and Socio-Economic Data Sheets for Countries of the Economic Commission of Western Asia* (Beirut, 1978).

an inordinate amount of attention simply because it is the *only* well known estimate for the period.

More significant is the census result of 1962/3, a total of 3,300,000; only about half of Hamza's estimate of 30 years earlier.[8] Filahi, influenced by Hamza's figures, argued that the bedouin had been omitted, the real population being over 6 million.[9] The Saudi Arabians accepted the suggestion that the census was an underenumeration, perhaps seeing the extra prestige brought by a larger population.

In actual fact though, a careful consideration of the *prima facie* 1962/3 census reports suggest that the figure was an *over-estimate*. When the census was taken, there were substantial numbers of non-Saudi Arabians living within the Kingdom, including political refugees, in particular from the then Muscat and Oman.[10] Yemenis were also arriving as migrant workers.[11] These incomers were difficult to distinguish from Saudi Arabian nationals, especially as many were masquerading as such. The 1962/3 census figure therefore included a number of non-Saudi Arabians, making the real number of nationals lower than the repudiated figure.[12] Moreover, labour force data available for 1963 based both upon the census itself and an establishment survey,[13] demonstrates that there was some double counting in the census, again suggesting the census figure to be too high. The establishment survey enables an estimation of the number of economically active Saudi Arabian men in 1962/3; calculated at 662,000.[14] This is a reliable figure which can be related to a total population. The crude activity rate of nationals in Saudi Arabia in 1963 was about 20 per cent. The value was unlikely to be lower because of the agricultural and nomadic sectors in Saudi Arabia, which serve to raise crude participation rates. Moreover, in 1963, the age distribution of the Saudi Arabian population was not as young as now – hence the crude participation rate of 20 per cent.[15] This crude activity rate of 20 per cent and a labour force of 662,000 results in a gross national population of 3,310,000. This confirms, by an entirely different method, that the population census of 1962/3 was of the correct order.

Table 5.2: Saudi Arabia: Summary Table of National and Non-National Labour Force, 1963

| Sector | Total | National | Non-National |
|---|---|---|---|
| Public sector | 76,950 | 71,950 | 5,000 |
| Agriculture and bedouin | 475,000 | 475,000 | – |
| Private establishments | 170,100 | 105,100-125,100 | 45,000-65,000 |
| Totals | 722,050 | 652,050-672,050 | 50,000-70,000 |

Source: J.S. Birks and C.A. Sinclair, *The Kingdom of Saudi Arabia and the Libyan Arab Jamahirija: The Key Countries of Employment*, World Employment Programme Working Paper (ILO, Geneva, 1979), Table 5, p. 56.

This, despite the official claims that the reported 1962/3 census figure was too small, there is firm evidence suggesting that 3.3 million is probably a slight over-statement.

*The Saudi Arabian National Population of 1974/5.* By 1963, the rate of natural increase of the Saudi Arabian population was probably over 2.5 per cent, and soon to rise higher as modern medical facilities were extended. By 1973 the rate of growth had reached 2.97 per cent.[16] In Table 5.3 the 1962/3 Saudi Arabian national population is projected to 1974/5. These projections give a total of 4.6 million Saudi nationals in 1974/5. Since 1975, the population of Saudi nationals has continued to grow rapidly, at 3.0 per cent or perhaps a little more.

*The Official 1974/5 Population Census.* The publication of a fourteen-

Table 5.3: Saudi Arabia: Projection of the National Population, 1962/3 to 1974/5

| Year | Rate of Growth | Population |
|---|---|---|
| 1962/3 | 2.7 | 3,310,000 |
| 1963/4 | 2.7 | |
| 1964/5 | 2.7 | |
| 1965/6 | 2.7 | |
| 1966/7 | 2.7 | |
| 1967/8 | 2.7 | |
| 1968/9 | 2.7 | 3,883,744 |
| 1969/70 | 2.8 | |
| 1970/1 | 2.8 | |
| 1971/2 | 2.8 | |
| 1972/3 | 2.9 | 4,333,117 |
| 1973/4 | 3.0 | 4,558,777 |
| 1974/5 | | 4,592,540 |

Source: J.S. Birks and C.A. Sinclair, *The Kingdom of Saudi Arabia and the Libyan Arab Jamahiriya: The Key Countries of Employment,* World Employment Programme Working Paper (ILO, Geneva, 1979), Table 6, p. 56.

volume census report including many economic and social parameters would seem to conclude the debate on the population of Saudi Arabia.[17] Yet, from the outset, the census result was a source of speculation. Results were withheld, placed under armed guard, eventually released, but then amended. Close examination of the results suggests that the census is an estimate based upon a large sample — not in fact a complete enumeration.

It appears that problems with the census arose after enumeration (September 1974), when it was found that the enumerators had only recorded a proportion of the population — about 20 per cent. This enumerated proportion was increased by what was thought to be a suitable multiplier. But since the total population and the sampling frame were not known accurately, it proved impossible to multiply up the census without errors. In fact, the sample was increased by an over-large factor, yielding a national population larger than really exists. Thus, significant discrepancies are encompassed in the final result. However, the published census does yield a rich harvest of information and, ironically, also contains the key to estimating the real population of Saudi Arabian nationals.[18]

The official census result is a national population of 5.9 million, and a national work-force of 1.3 million. Correction, based upon the age/sex distribution of the census and educational enrolment figures derived from an independent source, yields a total national population of

4.59 million, and a national work-force of 1,026,400. (The official result has been deflated by a factor of 0.77.) These figures for Saudi Arabia's population and work-force are used throughout this study.

The crude participation rate for Saudi Arabian nationals overall according to the census is 22.3 per cent (close to the estimate above), the result of quite high participation of men and a low rate amongst women. In fact, the real participation rate for Saudi Arabian women is higher than the recorded 2.7 per cent because, once again, large numbers of women economically active in the rural sector have been omitted from the work-force.

Sources outside Saudi Arabia suggest that the number of economically active non-nationals was 773,400 in 1975.[19] This contrasts with the 1974/5 census, which reported a migrant work-force of 391,213. This reported total is, like the census figure for the national population, inaccurate. However, the recorded 391,213 non-nationals do constitute a large sample, and the reported crude participation rate of 49.5 per cent is regarded as relatively reliable. Therefore, taking the figure for active migrants derived from sources outside Saudi Arabia of 773,400, and the crude activity rate recorded by the census, the non-national population is estimated as 1,562,400 in 1974.

Table 5.4: Saudi Arabia: Population and Employment, 1974/5

|  | Population | | Employment | |
|---|---|---|---|---|
|  | Number | Per cent | Number | Per cent |
| Saudi Arabian nationals | 4,592,540 | 74.6 | 1,026,400 | 57.0 |
| Non-nationals | 1,562,400 | 25.4 | 773,400 | 43.0 |
| Total | 6,154,940 | 100.0 | 1,799,800 | 100.0 |

Source: J.S. Birks and C.A. Sinclair, *The Kingdom of Saudi Arabia and the Libyan Arab Jamahiriya: The Key Countries of Employment*, World Employment Programme Working Paper (ILO, Geneva, 1979), Table 19, p. 61.

*Conclusion.* Both historical and contemporary sources of the population of Saudi Arabia have proved unacceptable at face value, even the 1974/5 census containing major shortcomings. However, best estimates are that the total population of Saudi Arabia in 1974/5 is 6.1 million persons. Some 4.59 million (74.6 per cent) of these are Saudi Arabian nationals, and 1.56 million (25.4 per cent) are non-nationals. The work-force is 1.8 million, of whom 1.03 million are nationals (57.0 per cent) and 773,400 are migrants (43.0 per cent).

*(c) The Educational Status of the Population*

Predictably, the level of educational attainment of Saudi Arabian nationals is low overall, and very low amongst women (Table 5.5). Of the total population, 30 per cent are at least literate, but the differential is such that only 16 per cent of women are so endowed. If the more usual age limit of '15 years or more' had been used, then these rates would be lower.

In consequence, education receives the largest single allocation in the development plan of $21 billion (24 per cent) out of the total for development projects of $88 billion.

Formal school education in Saudi Arabia follows the primary (4 years), intermediate (4 years), secondary (4 years) pattern. At secondary level there is an option of teacher training, agricultural, industrial or commercial studies, some of which lead on to higher technical/vocational courses. The general secondary programme permits graduates to enter a university course, and consequently absorbs the majority of secondary school enrollees. Table 5.6 shows the enrolments in these levels.

While the efforts of the government to harness and improve the quality of its human capital are admirable, the problems involved are immense. The difficulties are compounded by the fact that potential school or training centre enrollees have lucrative opportunities outside the classroom and so have a tendency not to complete courses. Also, the government has the difficulty that in many areas there is little tradition of academic study, and hence the base from which it can work is small.

## 3. The Demand for Labour

*(a) Economic Development[20]*

*Oil Production, Revenue and the Budget.* Saudi Arabia is the most affluent country in the developing world, rivalling America and Russia in oil production, and assuming a pre-eminent position in the Middle East and a substantive place in the world economy. The Kingdom's share of world oil production in 1976 was 14.5 per cent.[21] In 1976 Saudi Arabia's oil output was 8.6 million barrels per day (mbd); maximum capacity is thought to be in excess of 10 mbd. In 1976 proven reserves were estimated conservatively at about 110 billion barrels[22] and probable reserves were put at 177 billion barrels.[23] This suggests that the oil life of Saudi Arabia's reserves is in the region of 30 years. The actual life of the oil supply is well in excess of that figure,

Table 5.5: Saudi Arabia: National Population Aged 10 Years or More by Educational Status and Sex, 1974

| Educational Attainment | Males | | Females | | Total | |
|---|---|---|---|---|---|---|
| | Number | Per cent | Number | Per cent | Number | Per cent |
| Not stated | 4,548 | 0.2 | 11,237 | 0.6 | 15,785 | 0.4 |
| Illiterate | 1,043,711 | 52.4 | 1,496,788 | 81.3 | 2,540,499 | 66.2 |
| Read only | 75,075 | 3.8 | 46,431 | 2.5 | 121,506 | 3.2 |
| Literate | 461,829 | 23.2 | 177,474 | 9.6 | 639,303 | 16.7 |
| Educated | 408,114 | 20.4 | 110,976 | 6.0 | 519,090 | 13.5 |
| Total | 1,993,277 | 100.0 | 1,842,906 | 100.0 | 3,836,183 | 100.0 |

Source: J.S. Birks and C.A. Sinclair, *The Kingdom of Saudi Arabia and the Libyan Arab Jamahiriya: The Key Countries of Employment*, World Employment Programme Working Paper (ILO, Geneva, 1979), Table 20, p. 61.

Table 5.6: Saudi Arabia: Enrolment in Schools by Level, 1975/6

|  | Total | Male | Female |
|---|---|---|---|
| Primary | 686,108 | 439,502 | 246,606 |
| Post-primary | 210,748 | ·145,011 | 65,737 |
| Higher education | 26,437 | 21,127 | 5,310 |
| Technical education | 4,063 | 4,063 | — |

Source: Saudi Arabian Monetary Agency, *Annual Report* (Riyadh, 1978), Table 1, p. 73.

and might be in the region of 80 years, taking into account the likelihood of oil in unexplored regions.

The rate of extraction is obviously a key variable in estimating the duration of oil life. Aramco, the principal company extracting oil in Saudi Arabia, has plans to expand oil output.[24] However, reports of increases in the level of production are seldom accompanied by corresponding estimates of a diminished oil life. There is some flexibility in the minds of the oilmen about Saudi Arabia's oil reserves. Plans for industrial development at Yenbo and Jubail have impact upon oil output, because the natural gas associated with the oil is feedstock for the energy intensive processes envisaged. As industrial development proceeds, so production of crude oil is likely to rise.

Table 5.7: Saudi Arabia: Oil Production 1971 to 1978 (million barrels per day)

| Year | Oil Production (million barrels per day) |
|---|---|
| 1971 | 4.8 |
| 1972 | 6.0 |
| 1973 | 7.6 |
| 1974 | 8.5 |
| 1975 | 7.1 |
| 1976 | 8.6 |
| 1977 | 9.2 |
| 1978 | 6.9 (average of first seven months) |

Source: 1971-7: Saudi Arabian Monetary Agency, *Annual Report 1977*, (Riyadh, 1978), Table 2, p. 17; 1978: various reports.

Conversely, the arguments for conservation of oil reserves are substantial ones. In the past five years income has exceeded domestic expenditure substantially. However, in the medium term, oil production will move mainly in response to the needs of domestic industry for gas and to the relationship between Saudi Arabia and OECD countries. This will tend to increase output.

With oil production increasing at 11 per cent per annum and the price increases of the 1970s, government revenue has soared. Taxes and royalties from oil account for about 90 per cent of government income. In 1974/5 Saudi Arabia's new-found affluence was almost an embarrassment to the government. Economic, financial and political decisions made in the Kingdom began to carry wider implications.

Current economic objectives are embodied in the Second Development Plan, 1975-80.[25] Commentators observed that limited absorptive capacity of the economy was a serious constraint to development as a whole and to effecting the plan in particular. It was argued that Saudi Arabia, with such limited infrastructure, could not absorb the bulk of her oil revenues in the economy for many years. Although in 1974/5 the government spent only 35 per cent ($9,898 million) of her income, by 1976/7 expenditure had risen to $31,416 million, 83 per cent of revenue. In 1978/9, expenditure is planned in excess of revenue by some 11 per cent (Table 5.8).

Saudi Arabia's capacity to absorb oil revenues has been far greater than expected. Not only are oil revenues and oil reserves on an almost incomprehensible scale, but so it seems is the country's capacity to accomplish economic objectives.

*Gross Domestic Product.* Analysis of gross domestic product is bedevilled by the problem of allowing for domestic price inflation and the rapid increase in the price paid for her oil. To present GDP from 1970 to 1978 at constant output prices of 1970 gives a false impression. At the risk of exaggerating her wealth, Table 5.9 presents GDP at current prices. Clearly, domestic inflation was much less than 53 per cent per annum between 1971 and 1975 (though at times it was very high). Saudi Arabia has enjoyed a rapidly growing national income in real terms in recent years.

Table 5.10 shows the large share of GDP for which oil production accounts. This will remain prominent for some time, but will diminish as diversification progresses. Analysis of GDP by economic activity for 1975/6 shows that mining and quarrying (which includes oil production refining) accounts for 72 per cent of the total. Agriculture is responsible for 1.0 per cent of all national income. Inevitably, at this stage in Saudi Arabia's development, 'construction' is prominent in the non-oil activities.

Table 5.8: Saudi Arabia: Government Revenue and Expenditure, 1971/2 to 1978/9 ($ million, current prices and exchange rates)

| Revenue | 1971/2 | 1972/3 | 1973/4 | 1974/5 | 1975/6 | 1976/7 | 1977/8 | 1978/9 |
|---|---|---|---|---|---|---|---|---|
| Oil | n.a. | n.a. | 10,852 | 26,607 | 29,243 | 34,290 | 37,154 | n.a. |
| Other | n.a. | n.a. | 669 | 1,671 | 1,889 | 3,633 | 4,345 | n.a. |
| Total | 2,396 | 3,188 | 11,521 | 28,278 | 31,132 | 37,923 | 41,499 | 37,681 |
| Expenditure | 2,396 | 3,188 | 5,137 | 9,898 | 25,164 | 31,416[a] | 31,558[a] | 42,029[b] |
| Balance | 0 | 0 | + 6,384 | + 18,380 | + 5,968 | + 6,507 | + 9,941 | − 4,348 |

Note: a. Estimate.

   b. Government estimate expects actual expenditure to be only $37,681 million.

Source: Saudi Arabian Monetary Agency, *Annual Reports 1975, 1976, 1977* (Riyadh): *MEED*, various reports, 1978.

Table 5.9: Saudi Arabia: Gross Domestic Production by Economic
Activity in Current Prices 1966/7 to 1975/6 ($ billion)

| Year | Gross Domestic Product in Current Prices ($ billion) |
|---|---|
| 1966/7 | 2.9 |
| 1967/8 | 3.2 |
| 1968/9 | 3.5 |
| 1969/70 | 3.8 |
| 1970/1 | 5.1 |
| 1971/2 | 6.3 |
| 1972/3 | 9.8 |
| 1973/4 | 27.4 |
| 1974/5 | 37.9 |
| 1975/6[a] | 43.7 |

Note: a. Preliminary figures.
Source: *Saudi Economic Survey*, 22 March 1978.

Table 5.10: Saudi Arabia: Gross Domestic Product by Economic
Activity (at Current Prices) 1975/6

| Economic Activity | GDP ($ million) | Per cent |
|---|---|---|
| Agriculture, forestry and fishing | 488 | 1.0 |
| Mining and quarrying | 33,888 | 72.0 |
| Manufacturing | 2,201 | 4.7 |
| Electricity, gas and water | 105 | 0.2 |
| Construction | 3,545 | 7.5 |
| Wholesale and retail trade, restaurants and hotels | 1,428 | 3.0 |
| Transport, storage and communication | 1,777 | 3.8 |
| Finance, insurance, real estate and business services | 923 | 2.0 |
| Community, social and personal services | 219 | 0.5 |
| Public administration and defence | 1,151 | 2.4 |
| Other services | 1,358 | 2.9 |
| GDP (producer values) | 47,083 | 100.0 |

Source: Saudi Arabian Monetary Agency, *Annual Report, 1977* (Riyadh, 1978).

Oil exports have ensured a balance of payments well in surplus. In 1976, this stood at $13.6 billion, roughly equivalent to 'imports' in that year. As a result there has been some concern amongst the Saudi monetary authorities that the Saudi Riyal might become a speculative currency, and the country a recipient of 'hot' money. So far the low Saudi Arabian interest rates and official discouragement have averted this, but it will become harder to resist the ancillary burdens which a strong currency carries.

*The Development Plan, 1975-80.* Written against the backcloth of colossal increases in oil revenue and in a country still underdeveloped by oil states' standards, the development plan provides a detailed campaign for economic and social development. Total expenditure was put at $141.2 billion and, as the plan's authors wrote, 'it is clear that the financial cost of the plan is not the critical measure.' The financial requirements are certainly well within the scope of the economy.

More serious a drawback than the financial cost was the lack of infrastructure and manpower to execute parts of the plan. The aims are: to achieve a high rate of economic growth; to exploit the mineral resources of Saudi Arabia; to achieve independence from oil as a source of national income; to develop the Kingdom's infrastructure; and to develop human resources. The financial allocations between different spheres is shown in Table 5.11. 'Development' projects account for 64 per cent of plan expenditure, physical infrastructure and economic resource development for 41 per cent.

Table 5.11: Saudi Arabia: Second National Plan Allocations, 1975 to 1980 ($ billion)

|  | $ billion | Per cent |
|---|---|---|
| Economic resource development | 26.1 | 18.5 |
| Human resource development | 22.7 | 16.1 |
| Social development | 9.4 | 6.7 |
| Physical infrastructure development | 32.0 | 22.7 |
| Sub-total: Development | 90.2 | 63.9 |
| Administration | 10.8 | 7.7 |
| Defence | 22.1 | 15.7 |
| External assistance emergency funds, food subsidies and reserve | 18.0 | 12.7 |
| Sub-total | 50.9 | 36.1 |
| Total | 141.1 | 100.0 |

Source: Central Planning Organisation, *Development Plan, Kingdom of Saudi Arabia*, Table VIII. 1, p. 600.

According to one commentator,[26] 'flat out development has been going on for three years.' The implementation of plan objectives has resulted in the construction of physical infrastructure and industries at a spectacularly fast rate. The 'multiplier effect' of these activities, together with the limited base from which the country began, inevitably resulted in high rates of inflation, port congestion and a less efficient process of development than a more conservative path would have yielded. The Saudi Arabian brand of economic development between 1975 and 1977 will not be forgotten by those who experienced port delays at Jeddah approaching 12 months, inflation in the cost of accommodation at 50 per cent per annum, chronic labour shortages, cement being unloaded by helicopter and the transport of houses by plane.

It was with some satisfaction that the Saudi Arabian Monetary Authority wrote in its Annual Report of 1977 that '1976/77 ended with major bottlenecks removed . . . port congestion eliminated . . . inflation has begun to decelerate. The Saudi Arabian economy now has a grip over most of the problems that the process of accelerated development has generated.'

Indisputably, real progress was and is being made. GNP rose between 1975 and 1977 at 12 per cent per annum in real terms, exceeding the plan target of 10 per cent. However, the financial price of this achievement has been higher than would have been the case at a slower pace of development. Even so, under Saudi Arabian circumstances, financially costly development could be thought better than frugal but slow development. This is the decision Saudi Arabian planners have taken.

*Industrial Development.* The commitment to a diversified economy is especially evident in plans for industrial development, to which there are three aspects. First is the expansion and development of existing manufacturing and industrial enterprises, such as cement production, the Jeddah steel mill and ancillary investments in desalination units. Second are seven 'industrial sites' near major urban centres, which will accommodate light industry to meet the needs of the Saudi market. They are financed and run mainly by the private sector. The third, most ambitious aspect of Saudi Arabia's industrial plans is the industrial areas at Yenbo in the west, and Jubail near Dammam in the east, where it is planned to develop a hydrocarbons industry which processes the gases associated with oil. The planned investment is vast, $30 billion being allocated for infrastructure and facilities. An aluminium plant, steel mill, fertiliser plant and additional refineries and hydrocarbon plants are also envisaged.

Yenbo and Jubail industrial sites are ambitious in scale, but represent essentially an extension of Saudi Arabia's existing petrochemical refining activities and some industries which will use the relatively cheap source of power afforded by natural gas. The two sites are similar to the Ruweis (Abu Dhabi), Jebel Ali (Dubai) and Umm Said (Qatar) developments, though on a larger scale. Saudi Arabia's industrial development at Yenbo and Jubail is equal to the development of all the other peninsula states collectively.

Unannounced as yet is a new facet of Saudi Arabian development: the exploitation of her mineral reserves of iron, gold, silver, copper, lead, zinc, nickel and phosphate. An appraisal of economic development which includes the major industrial sites, the other manufacturing activities, the cheap source of fuel, a reasonably large population, a central position geographically and non-oil mineral deposits makes Saudi Arabia's economic future look very bright.

At least, this would be so but for recent word of a substantial cutback in allocations to Ministries for the coming financial year (1979/80). This might indicate a new caution tempering Saudi Arabian economic development. In view of the manifest successes in overcoming economic problems over the past two years, any kind of caution at the moment is perhaps surprising. Any such Saudi Arabian doubt does not stem from pure economics, though. Analysis of the labour market demonstrates some possible causes.

### 4 The Labour Market

*(a) Introduction*

Table 5.12 shows the Saudi Arabian national work-force has been increasing at 4.6 per cent per annum and the non-nationals' (migrant) employment at almost 16 per cent.

In Table 5.13, the distribution of employment by economic sector is taken from the 1974/5 population census; figures for *total* employment are drawn from Table 5.12. Over half of nationals work in agriculture and fishing. This is surprising in view of the spectacular economic development discussed above. A further quarter of indigenous workers are employed in community services. As in other capital-rich countries, migrant workers dominate manufacturing and construction. Apart from the large traditional sector, the pattern of employment is typical of all capital-rich states of the peninsula, and could well describe the Kuwaiti or the UnitedArab Emirates' labour market.

*(b) Employment by Economic Activity: Duality of Labour Markets*

*The Traditional Sector.* In 1966 agriculture, fishing, livestock and

Table 5.12: Saudi Arabia: Employment by Nationality in Selected
Years, 1962/3 to 1974/5

| Year | Nationals' Employment | Non-Nationals' Employment | Total Employment |
|---|---|---|---|
| 1962/3 | 662,000 | n.a. | |
| 1966/7 | 712,859 | 240,397 | 953,256 |
| 1974/5 | 1,026,400 | 773,400 | 1,799,800 |

Source: J.S. Birks and C.A. Sinclair, *The Kingdom of Saudi Arabia and the Libyan Arab Jamahiriya: The Key Countries of Employment*, World Employment Programme Working Paper (ILO, Geneva, 1979), Table 31, p. 64.

bedouins accounted for almost half of all employment.[27] This employment was, at that time, best described as providing a 'subsistence' income.[28] That so large a proportion of active Saudi Arabians were engaged in unremunerative, relatively unproductive activities in 1966 is not surprising. It is remarkable, though, that in 1975 more than half of the indigenous work-force were still engaged in that sector, which has changed little in character.

Saudi Arabian development has proceeded along dual economy lines – the modern sector has forged ahead in enclave industries and primate urban centres. The rural, agricultural sector has remained relatively traditional and subsistence-based, but for occasional large-scale agricultural projects.[29] These are only of small overall impact.

These two facets of the economy – the modern, urban sector, and the rural, traditional, largely subsistence sector – are associated with two separate labour markets. A large proportion of the Saudi Arabian national work-force has not participated in modern-sector development, but has remained in the traditional sector. A variety of factors account for this crucially limited role of nationals in modern development.

Of considerable influence in the early establishment of a dual economy, with nationals moribund in the rural areas, are the sheer distance and the erstwhile poor communications between the regions and the expanding urban centres. Despite traditions of population mobility, the long distances and large sparsely populated areas which isolate the centres of modern development have stunted change in the regions. Large-scale investment in transport infrastructure is only now narrowing the differentials between urban and rural (modern and traditional) sectors.

The survival of the rural, traditional way of life also results from the relative recency of rapid large-scale economic development in the Kingdom. Prior to 1973, the industrial sector in Saudi Arabia was much

Table 5.13: Saudi Arabia: Employment of Nationals and Non-Nationals by Economic Sector 1974/5

| Economic Sector | Total | | Nationals | | Non-Nationals | |
|---|---|---|---|---|---|---|
| | Number | Per cent | Number | Per cent | Number | Per cent |
| Agriculture and fishing | 585,550 | 32.5 | 530,650 | 51.7 | 54,900 | 7.1 |
| Mining and petroleum | 27,000 | 1.5 | 15,400 | 1.5 | 11,600 | 1.5 |
| Manufacturing | 115,900 | 6.4 | 21,550 | 2.1 | 94,350 | 12.2 |
| Electricity, gas and water | 20,350 | 1.1 | 7,200 | 0.7 | 13,150 | 1.7 |
| Construction | 239,300 | 13.3 | 35,900 | 3.5 | 203,400 | 26.3 |
| Trade | 192,100 | 10.7 | 60,600 | 5.9 | 131,500 | 17.0 |
| Transport, storage and communication | 103,800 | 5.8 | 72,900 | 7.1 | 30,900 | 4.0 |
| Finance and insurance | 13,100 | 0.7 | 5,100 | 0.5 | 7,000 | 0.9 |
| Community services | 443,050 | 24.6 | 241,200 | 23.5 | 201,850 | 26.1 |
| Miscellaneous | 60,650 | 3.4 | 35,900 | 3.5 | 24,750 | 3.2 |
| Total | 1,800,800 | 100.0 | 1,026,400 | 100.0 | 773,400 | 100.0 |

Source: J.S. Birks and C.A. Sinclair, *The Kingdom of Saudi Arabia and the Libyan Arab Jamahiriya: The Key Countries of Employment*, World Employment Programme Working Paper (ILO, Geneva, 1979), Table 32, p. 65.

smaller and did not carry the same momentum of growth. There were neither the modern-sector opportunities for the mass of the Saudi Arabian population, nor were pressures put upon them to leave their rural employment. As it was, the drift to the towns was creating problems in urban areas, where under- and unemployment of Saudi nationals were extensive.

Paradoxically, attempts to transform small-scale farming in Saudi Arabia by giving loans and grants to farmers to aid their mechanisation and modernisation of farming are crucial in the preservation of the traditional rural sector. Loans and grants are taken by farmers, but not spent as investment income; they are spent on consumption goods. This consumption income is not associated with intensive labour inputs, and so is highly valued by the farmers. Indeed, this cash helps alleviate the need to derive income from the farms, which are allowed to decline further. Even if invested, loan capital remains underutilised, because of mismanagement and want of sufficient labour inputs. Thus, funds directed towards modernisation of small-scale farming often have the contrary impact to that which is intended: they serve to withdraw labour inputs from the land, but ensure that the population remains rurally orientated. In short, the agricultural sector is preserved in its relatively unproductive form.

In further explaining the persistence of the traditional sector it is plausible to invoke 'a bedouin tradition', not in a romantic sense, but as an umbrella term to cover a range of attitudes typical of many Third World farming and nomadic communities. Outstanding amongst these is the high value that the rural Saudi Arabian population places upon leisure. It is almost hackneyed to refer to this, but the disinclination to work, in particular in manually strenuous jobs, is an important explanatory factor behind many Saudi Arabians' reluctance to enter a wide spectrum of employment in the modern sector.[30] Life on the farms and in nomadic camps is not strenuous for the men, not subject to the rigorous disciplines associated with modern-sector employment, and is not ordered by impersonal authorities which tribesmen have little cause or inclination to respect. There is thus a widespread disinclination amongst the rural population to be formally employed.

In particular the men, who can live a very leisurely life in rural Arabia, where the women take an active part in the local rural economies, see many disadvantages associated with formal employment. The high value put upon leisure is compounded by the limited desires and absorptive capacity of these rural, traditionally based communities. This is illustrated by their high propensity to save once a limited range of consumer goods has been purchased.

Non-wage-based incomes to these rural populations are quite high. This diminishes the incentive to gain regular formal employment. One such 'unearned income' has already been noted – the loans and gifts from banks and agricultural development agencies. Other unearned incomes include social security payments, now widespread. Compensation for drought and other government disbursements related to social welfare also contribute substantially to rural incomes. Less formalised but perhaps more substantial incomes result from patronage, traditional obligations and rents from family properties and land. For instance, rent from a single house in one of the major cities comprises substantial income to a family dwelling in a village in rural Saudi Arabia. Such families, owning property in cities, but choosing to remain in rural areas, are not uncommon. These families do not wish to forfeit the income from their property by moving into it themselves. Therefore, despite having a dwelling in the towns, these families consider that 'they cannot afford to move into the towns'.

There is, moreover, a set of valid economic factors militating against members of the rural economy moving into the modern sector. There are some high financial and social costs which have to be met by a family moving into a town. Those families which do not have property of their own in the towns find that rents are high and dwellings difficult to acquire. Indeed, conditions in towns are poor for all but the highest income-earners. Life in substandard, overcrowded dwellings is the lot of many lower- and middle-income-earning Saudi Arabian nationals living in the main cities. These conditions represent real disincentives to those living, not uncomfortably, in the rural sector.

Women are of significance in preventing a larger movement to the towns and cities. Although, ostensibly, women's life in rural areas is arduous, there is a freedom about the scope of their activities which is not available to women in urban areas. Many rural women are, therefore, reluctant to move to the towns where they see that their lives would be more constrained by a variety of criteria. Women, by exerting this influence, preserve traditional rural life.

Moreover, extensive barriers prevent the participation of many Saudi Arabian men in the modern sector. Their educational attainment, work experience and skill level are all very low. This does not endear them to modern-sector employers, for whom the bringing in of highly qualified expatriates is a relatively easily available option. So there is, even if they were to present themselves, only a relatively small demand for the type of manpower that Saudi Arabian rural population is able to provide. Even at an unskilled manual level (at which, as noted, the Saudi Arabian nationals are reluctant to work) more cost-effective foreign labour is easily available.

All this is not to assert, however, that the modern and traditional labour markets are completely independent. The two do interact, but in a particular way. Members of the traditional sector do join the modern, industrial or formally employed labour force, but only in an informal and part-time manner. Rural males have become short-term periodic migrant labourers, making temporary migrations from their villages to the urban areas in search of employment while their families stay at home.

The rewards from these short-term periods of employment sustain the otherwise declining traditional sector. Remittances form the remaining facet of an agricultural economy which is ostensibly subsistence rather than cash-crop orientated.

Whilst this part-time informal employment does ensure that income generated by (or perhaps, more correctly, dispersed through) the modern sector is distributed amongst a larger section of the national population, it has marked disadvantages from the point of view of the development of Saudi Arabia's human resources. Saudi Arabian nationals win a high income from their informal sector employment — they effectively gain a rent from being nationals. They can enter specific pursuits (such as taxi-driving) which are denied to the wider expatriate labour market. It is this high return to labour (divorced from marginal productivity), combined with the low absorptive capacity of these rural communities, that constrains their inputs into the modern sector. Even given their abnormally high returns to labour, the migrants soon see the opportunity cost of leisure and time spent at home as outweighing further cash earnings. Alternatively they are quickly able to reach the 'target' incomes which they had in mind on departing as a migrant.

There is a series of employment opportunities for Saudi Arabian nationals well suited to this attitude towards wage-earning. Apart from driving, the civilian defence forces and other guarding or watchkeeping jobs proliferate. They are particularly popular because of their lack of association with hard labour.

This part-time employment in the modern sector is deleterious in terms of the development of the Saudi Arabian national labour force from several other points of view. The high returns from informal sector (or informal employment in the modern sector) employment militate against many Saudi Arabians staying the length of training programmes and acquiring skills to enlarge their range of possible employment. Moreover, the lack of preparedness for long-term commitment to a particular form of employment limits further their penetration into the modern sector.

Such an evolution of a rural population – from one based upon agriculture to one receiving a 'dual income', partly from the modern sector, partly a 'subsistence income' – is common throughout the Third World. It represents a phase in the evolution of a traditional society towards one which provides a modern industrial labour force. It is especially marked in communities located at a geographic or economic periphery, that is to say, away from the main cores of economic development.

In Saudi Arabia's case, the rapidity of modern economic development from such a small base has resulted in the majority of the country becoming, effectively, a massive periphery to the main central belt of development. Moves towards regional development and a more widespread provision of industry will serve to reduce this in the future, and will diminish the differential between the two presently existing facets of the economy. Continued growth associated with the considerable wealth of the Kingdom will therefore erode the traditional sector with increasing rapidity. Effectively, then, the modern sector will expand to engulf the periphery.

A transformation of the aspirations and motivations of the rural-sector population will both engender and be brought about by this expansion of the modern sector. There are already signs of this occurring; with the wider spread of education, aspirations are rising rapidly, and new attitudes are developing towards employment. Thus, bedouins' children want to be airline pilots, despite the fact that their father will not drive a lorry for more than four days a week, seven months of the year; farmers' children wish to work in embassies, despite the fact that their father is illiterate, and so on.

The duality in the Saudi Arabian labour market and economy – and the contrast is acute – results fundamentally from rapidity of development, which (facilitated by immigrant labour) has left a large proportion of the Saudi Arabian national population behind in the rural sector. Time and continued growth will, however, transform the situation; a fuller participation in the economy of the national population at large will be facilitated. The question faced by planners is, how long will this take, and how many extra migrants will be needed in the meantime.

*The Modern Sector.* The modern sector of the economy employs virtually all of the migrants working in Saudi Arabia, but less than half of the nationals. The orientation of those nationals who are in the modern sector towards service employment has already been mentioned. Consequently their contribution to other activities in the modern sector is limited (Table 5.13). The proportional contribution of non-nationals to employment in the manufacturing and construction sectors was 84 per cent in 1974/5; this considerable reliance on migrants is common in the peninsula. However, given Saudi Arabia's ambitious plans for rapid industrial development, dependence on migrant labour will increase further.

Industrial growth is on such a scale that by 1981 about 90,000 workers will be employed in the two areas of Yenbo and Jubail alone. Since manufacturing employment in 1975 was only 115,000 rapid growth of employment in this sector is assured. Almost all of this extra labour will have to be imported. Even after 1981, indigenous human capital willing and able to be employed in these industries will comprise only a tiny proportion of the necessary labour inputs.

If industrial development in particular and economic growth in general are to continue as envisaged in Saudi Arabia in the short to medium term, then the proportion of employment accounted for by non-national workers will inevitably increase dramatically.

Saudi Arabia's problem is different from that of Qatar or the United Arab Emirates, however. They import labour because they have such small indigenous populations; Saudi Arabia, in contrast, imports labour because her indigenous human capital is lying dormant. Indeed, the very process of importing labour is further accentuating the tendency of the Kingdom's human capital to remain withdrawn from the modern sector.

Thus Saudi Arabian planners face an acute dilemma: if development is to continue rapidly, then it will be at the cost of increased reliance upon migrant labour in the modern sector; development will continue to leave many, possibly the majority of the national population, behind in the traditional sector. There is thus the likelihood of increased strains upon society as concern increases about the under and unemployment of Saudi Arabian nationals contemporaneous with rapidly increasing imports of labour.

In general terms, the modern-sector Saudi Arabian national workforce is bound to remain small for some time because: few women may work; the population is youthful; and the claims of the educational system on potential labour market entrants are considerable, even if many enrolees do not stay the lengths of their chosen courses. If agriculturalists, fishermen and bedouin could be persuaded to enter the modern sector of the economy permanently and formally, and if women were permitted to work outside the home more broadly than in the one or two areas they are confined to at the moment, the Saudi Arabian national work-force would be profoundly augmented.

In time, those Saudi Arabian nationals presently in the traditional sector will be drawn into the modern sector by virtue of continuing expansion of the economic system and social change. What will cause concern is the numbers of non-nationals who will be working in the Kingdom before this occurs. Many expatriates will have become established communities, and will remain in Saudi Arabia even after the national labour force has begun to participate more fully in the modern sector. This underlies the urgency embodied in the task of developing Saudi Arabia's indigenous human resources.

The task of developing the indigenous work-force, with few skills valuable to a modern economy and probably little inclination to exchange rural life for a more traumatic urban one, in order to speed entry into the modern sector is immense. The increasing efforts of the government in the field of human resources development have yet to come to terms with the motives and aspirations of Saudi Arabian individuals and how to change them in the short term. It seems likely that these programmes will be most effective amongst the younger members of society. Their impact might, however, be enhanced if the general level of wealth were somewhat constrained.

## 5 The Immigrant Community

In view of their present importance and growing significance, the analysis turns to discussion of the non-national population of the Kingdom. The expatriate work-force totalled 773,400 persons in 1975, and is estimated to be about 1 million in 1979. Studies of labour-sending countries enable the blend of nationalities of non-nationals in 1975 to be determined.

Table 5.14 shows that Arabs in 1975 accounted for 91 per cent of the total migrant work-force in Saudi Arabia. Within this group Egyptians amounted to 12 per cent of the total, North Yemenis 36 per cent and Jordanians and Palestinians 23 per cent. The Asian and Far Eastern communities accounted for a further 5 per cent, Europeans 2 per cent and Iranians and Africans accounted for an additional 3 per cent.

Since 1975, this pattern has changed markedly. In Saudi Arabia, the labour market trends have skewed acutely in favour of Far Eastern

Table 5.14: Saudi Arabia: Employment of Non-Nationals by
Nationality, 1975

| Nationality | Number | Per cent |
|---|---|---|
| Yemenis (North) | 280,400 | 36.3 |
| Jordanian (including Palestinians) | 175,000 | 22.7 |
| Egyptians | 95,000 | 12.3 |
| Yemenis (South) | 55,000 | 7.1 |
| Sudanese | 35,000 | 4.5 |
| Lebanese | 20,000 | 2.6 |
| Omanis | 17,500 | 2.3 |
| Syrians | 15,000 | 1.9 |
| Somalis | 5,000 | 0.6 |
| Iraqi | 2,000 | 0.3 |
| (Sub-total: Arabs) | (699,900) | (90.6) |
| Pakistanis | 15,000 | 1.9 |
| Indians | 15,000 | 1.9 |
| Other Asian | 8,000 | 1.0 |
| (Sub-total: Asi  ) | (38,000) | (4.8) |
| European and American | 15,000 | 1.9 |
| African and other | 10,000 | 1.3 |
| Iranians | 10,000 | 1.3 |
| Turks | 500 | 0.1 |
| Grand total | 773,400 | 100.0 |

Source: J.S. Birks and C.A. Sinclair, *International Migration and Development
in the Arab Region* (ILO, Geneva, 1980), Table 10.

labour, as has been noted in the case of the Emirates. Yenbo and Jubail
are both being developed as enclaves, with large Asian and Far Eastern
work-forces who are being housed in work-camps. In Saudi Arabia, the
encroachment of Far Eastern labour has proceeded yet further, however, in that Korean and Filipino labour is widely employed outside
enclave projects. Market forces have overriden the original social
reasons behind the employment of Far Easterners in the capital-rich
states – their willingness to remain isolated from the indigenous Arab
populations. Once the cost-effective nature of Far Eastern labour was
established by the executors of development, wider applications were
quickly sought. This is one of many instances of economic forces push-
ing aside political and social considerations of development.

## 6 Conclusion and Future Prospects

The Kingdom betrays symptoms of conflicting objectives perhaps more acutely than the three capital-rich states discussed previously. Migrant workers are ever more necessary to the economy, but contemporaneously fears grow that the immigrant communities will increase and eventually outnumber the Saudi Arabians themselves. Concern is only expressed over the numbers of Indians and Pakistanis present, but, despite a veneer of Arab solidarity, Saudi Arabian nationals feel a detachment from Palestinians, a lack of respect for Yemenis and a mistrust and dislike of Egyptians, all of whom, they feel, are benefiting inordinately from Saudi Arabian development, especially whilst large numbers of the Kingdom's population remain in the traditional sector.

Such stresses lie beneath an undercurrent or return to strict Islamic principles. As development proceeds apace, some aspects of modernity appear increasingly unacceptable to religious leaders. The result is an Islamic resurgence, but one that is perhaps rather brittle. The consequence of these conflicting forces, the one to modernise with foreign assistance, the other to retain a distinctly Saudi Arabian and religious society, results in paradoxical situations. For example, Saudi Arabia is one of the most generous countries in terms of aid *per capita* and yet attempts to prohibit the employment of female secretaries.

These tensions may presently be ignored by entrepreneurs and executors of development, but eventually they will have to be faced. It is possible that the tensions are coming to the fore in the recent budgetary cut-backs. There is no economic reason why there should be second thoughts about increased government spending at this stage in the Kingdom's development. The motives are primarily social; the government is thinking of marking time a little whilst it attempts to develop its indigenous human capital. This is particularly pertinent in view of the potential for another phase of development, subsequent to the present oil-stimulated boom, which would utilise a far broader range of Saudi Arabia's natural resources. However, even if a pause in development were to occur, the foreign element of the work-force would continue to grow rapidly: the forces set in train in the economy are virtually unstoppable. In consequence, the conditions under which immigrants work may become increasingly restrictive. Arab expatriates will come to feature less as they find the Kingdom a less desirable and welcoming environment.

At the same time, strains in Saudi Arabian society will become more pronounced. The social repercussions of development as it has proceeded so far could well appear minor compared to those which are to come: although different in nature, the Shah's experience in Iran is ignored at their peril by the royal family of Saudi Arabia. Similar stresses also occur, but are dealt with quite differently, in Libya.

## Notes

1. Japan Cooperation Centre for the Middle East, *Analysis of Demand and Supply of Manpower in the Arabian Gulf Countries – An Excerpt* (Tokyo, August 1976), p. 13.

2. J. Hoagland, 'Saudis push $100 billion Development Plan', *Washington Post* 13 April 1975.

3. United Nations, Economic Commission for Western Asia, *Demographic and Related Socio-Economic Data Sheets for Countries of the Economic Commission for Western Asia*, No. 2 (Beirut, January 1978).

4. Other estimates published recently include: US Bureau of Census, Department of Commerce, *Summary of Census Data* (Washington, DC, n.d.) – 6,231,000 (1975); C.A. Sinclair and J.A. Socknat, *An Estimate of the Population of the Yemen Arab Republic and the Number of Workers Abroad* (Sanaa, 1975) – 3,500,000; Ministry of Education, Kingdom of Saudi Arabia, *Towards an Appropriate Strategy for Training Skilled and Semi-Skilled Workers* (Riyadh, April 1974), Table 12, p. 32, from which a total population of 5,695,000 can be derived by calculations using a sex ratio of 104.

5. F. Hamza, *The Heart of Arabia* (1933), p. 78.

6. The present authors disagree with al-Saleh, who uses Hamza's figures to establish that numbers of bedouin were much greater in the past. See N. al-Saleh, 'Some Problems and Development Possibilities of the Livestock Sector in Saudi Arabia: A Case Study in Livestock Development in Arab Lands' (unpublished PhD thesis, Durham University, 1976).

7. M. Filahi, *The Sedentarization of Nomadic Populations* (ILO/TAP/Saudi Arabia/R2, 1963).

8. Saudi Arabia, Central Planning Office, *Population and Housing Census 1962/63* (Riyadh, 1963).

9. See note 7.

10. See J.S. Birks and C.A. Sinclair, *Movements of Migrant Labour from the North of the Sultanate of Oman* International Migration Project Topic Paper (Durham, 1977); and C.A. Sinclair and J.A. Socknat *Migration for Employment and its Impact upon the Yemen Arab Republic*, International Migration Project Topic Paper (Durham, 1978).

11. In the early 1960s opportunities were already greater in Saudi Arabia than in, for example, the Yemens. These inflows of people were significant. In 1959, some 23,000 workers arrived in Saudi Arabia, and the numbers rose steadily to over 33,000 in 1963. See note 10 for more details, and also: ILO/UNDP, *Report to the Government of the Kingdom of Saudi Arabia on the Organisation of a Manpower Assessment and Training Programmes* (Geneva, 1968).

12. United Nations, *Population and Vital Statistics Report*, Statistical Papers, Series A (April 1967).

13. Central Planning Organisation, *Economic Report* (Riyadh, 1965).

14. See note 13.

15. For more discussion of this see J.S. Birks and C.A. Sinclair, *The Kingdom of Saudi Arabia and the Libyan Arab Jamahiriya, Key Countries of Employment*, World Employment Programme Research Working Paper (ILO, Geneva, 1979).

16. United Nations Economic Commission for Western Asia, *Social and Economic Data Sheets* (Beirut, 1978).

17. Kingdom of Saudi Arabia, Ministry of Finance and National Economy,

118    The Kingdom of Saudi Arabia

Central Department of Statistics, *Population Census, 1974*, Vols. I–XIV (Dammam, 1977).

18. Birks and Sinclair, *The Kingdom of Saudi Arabia and the Libyan Arab Jamahiriya*, WEP 2-26/WP 35, gives full details of the corrections to the official census result. It is important to note that although the absolute totals in the official census are best viewed as spurious and exaggerated, the internal proportional distributions of the characteristics remain valid and useful. This is true but for the relative proportions of nationals and non-nationals.

19. J.S. Birks and C.A. Sinclair, *International Migration and Development in the Arab Region* (ILO, Geneva, 1980).

20. The number of publications on the economic development of Saudi Arabia is growing. The most significant include: R.H. Nolte, 'From Nomad Society to New Nation: Saudi Arabia' in K.H. Silvert (ed.), *Expectant Peoples: Nationalism and Development* (New York, 1963), pp. 77-95, which is one of the earliest papers pointing towards the challenge of development; R. Braibanti and F.A. al Farsy, 'Saudi Arabia: A Development Perspective', *Journal of South Asian and Middle Eastern Studies, I* (Fall 1977), pp. 3-43, gives an overview of the literature and a general comment about economic development; J.P. Crerton, *Saudi Arabia 2000: a Strategy for Growth* (Croom Helm, London, 1978); D.G. Edens and W.P. Snavely, 'Planning for Economic Development, Saudi Arabia', *Middle East Journal, 24* (1970), pp. 17-30, F.A. al-Farsy, *Saudi Arabia: A Case Study in Development* (Stacy, London, 1978), P. Hobday, *Saudi Arabia Today: an Introduction to the Richest Oil Power* (Ad Orientem, Delhi, 1978); D. Holden and R. Johns, *The House of Saud* (Brill, Leiden, 1979); S.M. Iqbal, *The Emergence of Saudi Arabia* (Ad Orientem, Delhi, 1977); R. Knaverhase, 'Saudi Arabia's Economy at the Beginning of the 1970s', *Middle East Journal, 28* (1974), pp. 126-40; Y.A. Sayigh, 'Problems and Prospects of Development in the Arabian Peninsula' *International Journal of Middle East Studies, 2* (January 1971), pp. 40-58.

21. OPEC as a whole was responsible for 51 per cent of world oil production and Saudi Arabia for 28 per cent of OPEC's output.

22. Saudi Arabia Monetary Agency, *Annual Report, 1977* (Riyadh, 1977), Table 12, p. 125.

23. Aramco, *Annual Report, 1977* (Dammam, 1978).

24. *MEED, Special Report, Saudi Arabia* (August 1978).

25. Ministry of Planning. Kingdom of Saudi Arabia, *Second Development Plan 1395-1400 AH, 1975-1980 AD* (Riyadh, 1975).

26. *MEED*, 'Saudi Arabia' (12 September 1978), p. 35.

27. See note 13.

28. A.H. Helaissi, 'The Bedouins and Tribal Life in Saudi Arabia', *International Social Science Journal, 11* (1959), pp. 532-9; D.P. Cole, *Nomads of the Nomads: The Al Murrah Bedouin of the Empty Quarter* (Aldine, Chicago, 1975).

29. See J.H. Stevens, 'The Role of Major Agricultural Projects in the Economic Development of Arabian Peninsula Countries', *Proceedings of the Seventh Seminar for Arabian Studies* (1973), pp. 140-4; and R.M. Burrell, S. Hoyle, K.S. McLachlan and C. Parker, *The Developing Agriculture of the Middle East – Opportunities and Prospects* (Graham and Trotman, London, 1976), Chapter 5, pp. 55-64.

30. J.S. Birks and C.A. Sinclair, *A Preliminary Assessment of Migrant Labour Movements in the Arab Region: Background, Perspectives and Prospects*, World Employment Programme Working Paper (ILO, Geneva, 1978).

# 6 THE LIBYAN ARAB JAMAHIRIYA

## 1 Introduction

Although prominent in the Arab world, Libya is, in many respects, not an Arab nation ethnically. The area has been successively occupied by the Phoenicians, Greeks, Romans, Vandals, Byzantines, Arabs, Normans, Spaniards, Turks and, most recently, the Italians. On 3 March 1977, the Libyan Arab Republic became the Libyan Arab Jamahiriya, meaning 'State of the Masses', as distinct from a Republic. At this time the Revolutionary Command Council was replaced by the General Secretariat of the General People's Congress, headed by Mu'ammar Gadafi, who was elected Secretary-General.[1] Political power was to be exercised through People's Congresses, as well as workers' bodies and unions.

Libya's transformation of economy and society is continuing rapidly, with concomitant stresses within society. Examination of the Libyan economy shows it to be surprisingly conventional, especially similar in structure and direction to the economy of Saudi Arabia, despite the period of time for which the country has been directed by the Revolutionary Command Council.[2] This similarity extends to the massive scale of problems in the development of human resources that is troubling Saudi Arabian planners. Neither of the widely differing government ideologies seems presently to be able to resolve the dilemma of rapid growth leaving behind a large proportion of the indigenous population in a traditional sector.

## 2 The Supply of Labour

### (a) Population

The 1973 population census preliminary reports give the total population of Libya as 2,257,000.[3] Although detailed breakdowns of this total vary, probably some 2,087,700 were nationals.[4] Non-Libyans numbered 170,000, about 7.5 per cent of the total. Table 6.1 shows the Libyan national population by age and sex.

Estimates of the sex ratio and numerical details of this population vary according to various means of correction to overcome underenumeration. The sex ratio derived from Table 6.1 is 105.6. Corrected

119

Table 6.1: Libya: Age/Sex Distribution of National Population, 1973

| Age by Five-Year Cohort | Population | Males | Females |
|---|---|---|---|
| 0- 4 | 433,200 | 219,800 | 213,400 |
| 5- 9 | 372,700 | 188,500 | 184,200 |
| 10-14 | 267,900 | 139,600 | 128,300 |
| 15-19 | 172,500 | 87,300 | 85,200 |
| 20-24 | 138,500 | 71,700 | 66,800 |
| 25-29 | 123,700 | 61,900 | 61,700 |
| 30-34 | 99,900 | 52,200 | 47,700 |
| 35-39 | 103,500 | 52,100 | 51,300 |
| 40-44 | 84,700 | 45,500 | 39,200 |
| 45-49 | 74,500 | 39,700 | 34,500 |
| 50-54 | 53,900 | 28,600 | 25,300 |
| 55-59 | 38,700 | 21,100 | 17,600 |
| 60-64 | 35,700 | 18,300 | 17,500 |
| 65-69 | 27,400 | 14,400 | 13,000 |
| 70-74 | 24,900 | 12,600 | 12,400 |
| 75+ | 35,700 | 19,000 | 16,700 |
| Not stated | 300 | 200 | 100 |
| Total | 2,087,700 | 1,072,500 | 1,014,900 |

Source: 'Preliminary Estimates of Ministry of Planning and Scientific Research' (Benghazi, mimeograph, 1976).

sex ratios fall nearer 100. Amended totals of population tend to be higher than those shown in Table 6.1. United Nations advisers have calculated a corrected total of 2,146,000 Libyan nationals, of whom 1,101,600 are males. Most correction has been made in the younger age cohorts, as shown in Table 6.2.

Some 40 per cent of the national population is aged less than 15 years. With increasing provision of medical services, the proportion of the population in this age group will increase markedly. The crude birth rate of 48 per thousand, and a relatively low death rate of less than 10 per thousand, give a rapidly increasing population, which is confirmed by the high age-specific fertility rates.

The population has risen from 1.5 million in 1964. Growth rates of over 3 per cent are built into projections for the Libyan national population: in 1975 the population was some 2.32 million. By 1980 it will be over 2.8 million, rising to almost 3.5 million nationals in 1985.

*(b) The Educational Status of the Population*

Traditional education in Libya was based upon Koranic (*kuttab*) schools, and in particular upon the Sanusi system of *zawiyahs*.[5] However, between 1911 and 1943 an Italian colonial education system was

Table 6.2: Libya: Crude and Corrected Populations of Nationals under Five Years Old, 1973

| Age | Uncorrected Population | Corrected Population | Percentage Correction |
|---|---|---|---|
| Under 1 | 96,930 | 102,000 | + 5.2 |
| 1 | 58,210 | 97,800 | +68.0 |
| 2 | 97,050 | 94,250 | + 2.8 |
| 3 | 91,580 | 91,800 | + 0.2 |
| 4 | 89,420 | 89,560 | + 0.2 |
| 5 | 81,880 | 85,100 | + 3.9 |
| Total | 515,070 | 560,510 | 8.8 |

Source: 'Preliminary Estimates of Ministry of Planning and Scientific Research' (Benghazi, mimeograph, 1976).

imposed, and the *zawiyahs* were destroyed. Enrolment of Arabs in the new schools remained low; by 1943, at the end of the Italian colonial period, the number of pupils had risen to 6,630, but only 1,800 were Arabs. The destruction of the *zawiyahs* was not accompanied by the development of an alternative secondary system. Of the 3,540 students enrolled in 1921, only 340 were at secondary level.[6] Education expanded under Anglo-French control so that by 1951, when King Idris I was established as constitutional monarch, there were 194 primary schools and a total enrolment of over 32,000 pupils.[7]

Libya therefore experienced a colonial, rather than an Arab peninsula pattern of educational development prior to independence. Despite the emphasis of education being on the primary level, in 1952 over 90 per cent of the Libyan population was illiterate.[8]

Between 1963 and 1968 the five-year plan dominated attempts to improve educational facilities. By 1967, 23 per cent of the national budget was devoted to education.[9] By 1969 enrollees in primary schools numbered over 310,000. The 1973 illiteracy rate of 61 per cent represents further improvement, particularly in view of population growth throughout the 1960s.

The full picture of the educational status of the Libyan national population is shown in Table 6.3. Although there has been a considerable improvement in literacy, less than 18 per cent of the population have obtained their primary certificate or any higher qualification. The increasing enrolment rates are shown in Table 6.4. The average enrolment rate for boys aged 6 to 14 has risen from 51 per cent in 1964 to 87 per cent in 1973. More than 95 per cent of boys aged 9 to 14 are now attending school; these critical age groups have now reached virtually

Table 6.3: Libya: Nationals Aged over 15 Years by Level of
Educational Attainment, 1973

|  | Total Population | | Males | |
| Educational Status | Number | Per cent | Number | Per cent |
| --- | --- | --- | --- | --- |
| Illiterate | 616,900 | 60.8 | 204,630 | 38.6 |
| Literate (reading only) | 8,500 | 0.8 | 6,930 | 1.3 |
| Literate (reading and writing) | 207,900 | 20.6 | 167,740 | 31.8 |
| Primary certificate attained | 97,600 | 9.6 | 79,530 | 15.1 |
| Preparatory certificate attained | 41,400 | 4.1 | 34,210 | 6.5 |
| Secondary certificate | 33,500 | 3.3 | 28,040 | 5.3 |
| University degree | 5,800 | 0.6 | 6,370 | 1.2 |
| Not stated | 1,700 | 0.2 | 840 | 0.2 |
| Totals | 1,013,300 | 100.0 | 528,290 | 100.0 |

Source: Ministry of Planning and Scientific Research, Census and Statistical
Department, *Some Preliminary Results of the 1973 Population Census* (Benghazi,
1975).

complete enrolment.

Girls continue to lag behind boys in school attendance. By 1973, 69
per cent of girls of school age were enrolled, compared to 87 per cent
of boys. Discrimination against women continues in higher levels of
education. Although comprising 45 per cent of students enrolled in
primary schools, females only amount to 28 per cent of those in preparatory.[10] One in five pupils at secondary level is female. Only because
students attending teacher training courses are 56 per cent female do
women account for 43 per cent of those in full-time higher education.

Table 6.4: Libya: Percentage of National Children Attending School,
by Age, 1964 and 1973

|  | Males | | Females | | |
| Age | 1964 | 1973 | 1964 | 1973 | Age |
| --- | --- | --- | --- | --- | --- |
| 6 | 12.6 | 40.3 | 6.8 | 34.3 | 6 |
| 7 | 35.6 | 88.2 | 16.7 | 76.0 | 7 |
| 8 | 46.5 | 94.2 | 19.4 | 80.4 | 8 |
| 9 | 62.6 | 96.6 | 29.8 | 83.2 | 9 |
| 10 | 58.6 | 96.6 | 23.5 | 78.4 | 10 |
| 11 | 71.9 | 97.2 | 31.9 | 78.8 | 11 |
| 12 | 65.6 | 96.8 | 22.3 | 78.7 | 12 |
| 13 | 70.5 | 96.6 | 25.0 | 67.2 | 13 |
| 14 | 67.5 | 95.5 | 21.1 | 57.4 | 14 |
| Average | 50.8 | 87.0 | 20.3 | 69.1 | Average |

Source: Ministry of Planning and Scientific Research, *Some Preliminary Results
of the 1973 Population Census* (Benghazi, 1975).

Despite the fact that the first Arab women entered university in Libya in 1958, by 1975 only about 15 per cent of students were female. Although starting from a quite advanced stance some two decades ago, surprisingly little progress has been made on the educational status of women. This has been significant for the Libyan labour market.

Also important is the Libyan educational system's marked bias away from technical and applied subjects. Whilst some 20,000 are involved in taking teacher training courses, less than 3,000 are attending higher and ordinary technical courses.

Table 6.5: Libya: Numbers of Students in Various Levels of Education, in Public and Private Schools, by Sex, 1974/5

| Level of Education | Male | Female | Total | Percentage of Female Students |
|---|---|---|---|---|
| Primary | 285,390 | 237,090 | 522,480 | 45.4 |
| Preparatory | 65,470 | 25,710 | 91,180 | 28.2 |
| Secondary | 11,970 | 3,060 | 15,030 | 20.0 |
| Technical (ordinary and higher) | 2,880 | – | 2,880 | 0.0 |
| Teacher training | 8,580 | 10,970 | 19,550 | 56.1 |
| Cultural centres | 640 | 150 | 790 | 18.8 |
| Total | 374,930 | 276,980 | 651,910 | 42.5 |

Source: Ministry of Education, *Educational Statistics* (Tripoli, 1977) (Arabic).

Thus, despite the longish tradition of education Libya has experienced, and the high investments made in education, the system betrays several of the shortcomings of many other Arab states' educational structures, in particular the bias towards the arts and general education. This has occurred despite the high demand for technical labour experienced in Libya over the past few years. More recently, in 1977, 650 Libyans were receiving technical education abroad. This represents a real attempt to redress the imbalance at the upper levels of the ladder.

Ironically, some 17 per cent of the students at Libyan university are foreign. These are, in large part, Arab students from neighbouring Egypt, Tunisia and, to a lesser extent, the Sudan. Other smaller numbers derive from countries that are recipients of Libyan aid payments.

Overall, it is surprising that the educational status of Libyan nationals

Table 6.6: Libya: Numbers of Students in Universities by Faculty and Sex, 1974/5

| Faculty | Male | Female | Total | Percentage |
|---|---|---|---|---|
| Arts | 2,000 | 710 | 2,710 | 22.6 |
| Economics and commerce | 1,440 | 200 | 1,640 | 13.7 |
| Law | 1,760 | 60 | 1,820 | 15.2 |
| Medicine | 480 | 110 | 590 | 5.0 |
| Arabic and Islamic studies | 900 | 20 | 920 | 7.6 |
| Education | 1,020 | 400 | 1,420 | 11.8 |
| Science | 550 | 190 | 740 | 6.2 |
| Engineering | 950 | 100 | 1,050 | 8.7 |
| Dentistry | 30 | 10 | 40 | 0.3 |
| Agriculture | 640 | 80 | 720 | 6.0 |
| Engineering, petroleum | 350 | 2 | 352 | 2.9 |
| Total | 10,120 | 1,882 | 12,002 | 100.0 |

Source: Ministry of Planning and Scientific Research, *Thirteenth Statistical Abstract (1976)* (Tripoli, 1977), pp. 103 and 104.

is so low, and that the system displays so many shortcomings. The low educational attainment results from the nature of the colonially imposed system, which did not attract the national population to a very extensive degree. This, with a long delayed adult literacy campaign, resulted in the continued high illiteracy level. Another colonial heritage is the present ill-directed pattern of education. The high level of government income has enabled a progressive change of emphasis – there has recently been a marked expansion in technical and science subjects in higher education; oil wealth therefore means that Libya is not as trapped by shortcomings in the structure of the inherited education system as is, for example, the Sudan. Such progress is illustrated by the opening of a Department of Chemistry at Al Fateh University (Tripoli).[11] By 1977, 4,900 students were enrolled domestically on technical courses, a number planned to rise to 8,150 by 1980. The 440 teachers of technical subjects presently employed will rise to 1,000 by 1980.

At lower levels of education, expansion is evidenced by 1,700 classrooms built in the first six months of 1977, with a further 5,800 now under construction. However, population growth makes such expansion essential: numbers in the 15-17 age group will increase by 45.0 per cent, between 1975 and 1980. Investment will have to cover increases in population before making headway with improved quality or higher enrolment ratios.

## 3 The Demand for Labour

### (a) Introduction

Prior to the discovery of oil, the Libyan economy was one of the poorest in the world,[12] dependent for foreign exchange primarily upon aid and upon payments for military base rights. Exports of scrap metal from World War II wrecks and the esparto grass trade were also significant, so low were other foreign exchange earning capacities.

Oil was discovered in 1959. By 1961 the first exports of crude were shipped. The very rapid rise in production that followed is shown in Table 6.7. In 1968 – seven years after the beginnings of exports – Libyan oil exports had risen to 6.7 per cent of the world's total, a level of production which it had taken Iran 40 years to reach.[13] Throughout the 1960s, the geographical proximity of Libya to Europe and the high quality of her oil encouraged rapid expansion of production. Between 1963 and 1968, *per capita* GDP increased at an annual average of 56 per cent.[14] The steep rise in oil production involved many small independents in the Libyan oil industry. This was to become significant in the 1970s when the Libyan government negotiated to raise oil revenues.

Table 6.7: Libya: Oil Production and Revenue, 1961 to 1977

| Year | Oil Production (barrels per day) | Oil Revenues ($ million) |
|------|------|------|
| 1961 | 20,000 | 3 |
| 1962 | 185,000 | 40 |
| 1963 | 465,000 | 10 |
| 1964 | 860,000 | 200 |
| 1965 | 1,220,000 | 370 |
| 1966 | 1,505,000 | 480 |
| 1967 | 1,745,000 | 630 |
| 1968 | 2,605,000 | 950 |
| 1969 | 3,110,000 | 1,130 |
| 1970 | 3,320,000 | 1,300 |
| 1971 | 2,765,000 | 1,770 |
| 1972 | 2,240,000 | 1,600 |
| 1973 | 2,180,000 | 2,300 |
| 1974 | 1,525,000 | 4,490 |
| 1975 | 1,480,000 | 5,670 |
| 1976 | 1,930,000 | 7,500 |
| 1977 | 2,080,000[a] | 9,290[a] |

Note: a. Provisional.
Sources: *British Petroleum Statistical Review of the World Oil Industry* (BP, London, 1976); Economist Intelligence Unit, *Oil in the Middle East* (EIU, London, 1977); International Monetary Fund, *International Financial Statistics* (Washington, DC, 1978)

Under King Idris I, development funded by oil revenues was directed towards transport networks, urban reconstruction and housing.[15] Arms purchases and the cost of defence also grew markedly, as did the conspicuous consumption of a powerful minority. Despite obvious growth, there were cogent arguments for asserting that funds were being misdirected, and that income-spreading was not effective enough. These reservations, together with a growing feeling that Libya was, mistakenly, being drawn away from the Arab world, led to the *coup* of 1 September 1969, and the establishment of the Revolutionary Command Council under Mu'ammar Gadafi.[16]

This opened a new era in which Libya led the Arab oil producers in international negotiations over the price of oil, the success of which is well known. In 1974, Libya was enjoying four times the oil receipts of 1970, although the volume of exports had halved to 1.5 million barrels per day.[17]

These increased revenues were redirected within the domestic economy according to the aims of the Revolutionary Command Council; a new emphasis on planning favoured industrial and agricultural self-sufficiency within a political structure of 'Islamic Socialism'. The new development effort favoured agricultural schemes, factories, oil refineries, harbour extensions, dams, hospitals and schools, with increased direction of funds towards rural areas.

### (b) Government Revenue

Government revenue rose to $9,274 million by 1977. Even so, from time to time, Libya has suffered apparent cash-flow problems. In 1975, a fall in output to less than 1.5 million barrels, combined with a static take per barrel, put pressure on the Libyan balance of payments.[18] Some oil prices were reduced to expand output. Since 1975, the government's financial position has improved. Production reached 2.4 million barrels in 1978, though less is planned for 1980.[19] Present price trends mean that worries about Libya's financial position will be allayed for a period; delays in payments by government to the private sector are thought more likely a symptom of bureaucratic inefficiency than a genuine cash flow problem.

In general, there is not a great deal of concern externally about Libyan government revenues in the short term, despite the relatively modest reserves (published reserves were 26,100 million barrels in 1976, and 26,500 million in January of 1977) by Middle Eastern standards. The post-1970 policy of reducing oil liftings contemporaneously with securing an increased take per barrel has been a marked success.

The government's income has been able to finance domestic growth on as rapid and sustained a scale as the country could reasonably have maintained, yet at the same time oil output was reducing steadily between 1970 and 1976.

## (c) Planning and Recent Economic Development

The evolution and origins of the Libyan GDP are common in pattern to other capital-rich Arab states: agriculture contributes a progressively smaller proportion of GDP, but real diversification of the economy remains limited, mining and quarrying dominating. Only a construction boom and growth in service provision in 1973 lower the proportion deriving from oil in that year. Manufacturing declined, in relative terms, between 1973 and 1974, despite an absolute increase in contribution of nearly 50 per cent. After 1974 oil production rose only slowly and without a greatly increased take per barrel, together with real increases in manufacturing capacity, the contribution of the secondary sectors rose considerably.

Table 6.8: Libya: Industrial Origin of Gross Domestic Product at Current Factor Cost, 1964, 1973 and 1974 ($ thousand)

| Sector | 1964 | Per cent | 1973 | Per cent | 1974 | Per cent |
|---|---|---|---|---|---|---|
| Agriculture | 42.1 | 4.0 | 214.3 | 2.7 | 231.1 | 1.6 |
| Mining and quarrying | 515.8 | 54.0 | 4,060.0 | 52.1 | 10,337.1 | 61.2 |
| Manufacturing | 29.0 | 3.0 | 181.4 | 2.3 | 266.1 | 1.9 |
| Construction | 57.9 | 6.0 | 932.9 | 12.0 | 5,122.5 | 10.3 |
| Electricity, gas and water | 2.6 | — | 38.6 | 0.5 | 44.3 | 0.3 |
| Transport, storage and communications | 39.5 | 4.0 | 461.8 | 5.9 | 688.9 | 4.9 |
| Wholesale and retail trade | 52.6 | 6.0 | 445.7 | 5.7 | 657.9 | 4.7 |
| Public administration and other government services | 68.4 | 7.0 | 1,235.0 | 15.9 | 1,766.8 | 12.7 |
| Services | 147.4 | 16.0 | 224.2 | 2.9 | 335.4 | 2.4 |
| Total | 955.3 | 100.0 | 7,793.9 | 100.0 | 19,450.1 | 100.0 |

Source: Ministry of Planning and Scientific Research, *National Income Accounts* (Tripoli, 1975) (Arabic).

Despite the fact that spending on imports rose by 23 per cent between 1976 and 1977, and on services by 26 per cent over the same period, investment income was the highest for two years at $255 million. Development expenditure amounted to $18,620 million between

1970 and 1978 compared with only $1,380 million over the previous eight years. Although the current account is increasing markedly, the proportion of income directed to investment expenditure is significantly higher than most other capital-rich states of the Arab world.

Libya's three-year development plan, which ended in 1975, encompassed several optimistic growth targets which were exceeded.[20] The 17.5 per cent planned growth rate in non-oil production between 1973 and 1975 was beaten by 2 per cent. Only in agriculture did the actual expenditures fall significantly below the target figures. This plan, which made the Libyan economy one of the most rapidly growing in the world, led the Libyans to embark upon an even more optimistic development plan from 1976 to 1980. This new set of guidelines, 'the economic and social transformation plan', envisages an annual increase of

Table 6.9: Libya: Allocations by Sector of the Economic and Social Transformation Plan, 1976 to 1980 ($ thousand)

| Development Sector | Total Allocations 1976 to 1980[a] | Per cent |
|---|---|---|
| Agriculture and agrarian reform | 1,374,230 | 5.5 |
| Internal agricultural development | 2,859,200 | 11.4 |
| Dams and water resources | 285,800 | 1.1 |
| Nutrition and maritime wealth | 163,870 | 0.7 |
| Industry and mineral wealth | 3,831,400 | 15.3 |
| Oil and gas exploitation | 2,233,330 | 8.9 |
| Electricity | 2,277,330 | 9.1 |
| Education | 1,638,850 | 6.5 |
| Information and culture | 330,560 | 1.3 |
| Manpower | 186,670 | 0.7 |
| Public health | 658,850 | 2.5 |
| Social affairs and social security | 43,860 | 0.2 |
| Youth and sports | 173,400 | 8.7 |
| Housing | 2,647,450 | 10.6 |
| Security services | 116,670 | 0.5 |
| Municipalities | 1,883,690 | 7.4 |
| Transport and communications | 2,199,510 | 8.8 |
| Maritime transport | 1,245,000 | 5.0 |
| Trade and marketing | 122,430 | 0.5 |
| Planning and scientific research | 43,480 | 0.2 |
| Reserves for projects | 766,560 | 3.1 |
| Total | 25,082,140 | 100.0 |

Note: a. As amended in December 1976.
Sources: Ministry of Planning and Scientific Research, *Economic and Social Transformation Plan (1976 to 1980)* (Tripoli, 1976); Tripoli Chamber of Commerce, *Quarterly Bulletin* (Autumn 1977).

GNP of 10 per cent in real terms. The annual increase in *per capita* income is planned to be 5.6 per cent annually, raising *per capita* income to well over $6,000 per annum. Total development expenditure to effect the plan is $25 billion.[21]

As with all other oil exporters' development plans, the general aim is to lessen dependence upon the oil industry by diversification of production and exports. In particular, the intention is to establish heavy industry, and to achieve self-sufficiency in food production. Ancillary aims will be to increase productivity of manpower – an acknowledgement of manpower shortages. Also featured are attempts to engender a more equitable distribution of income throughout all sections of the population, most significant in view of the later part of this analysis.

To achieve this restructuring, a real annual growth rate of 14 per cent in the non-oil branches of the economy is envisaged. Exports are planned to rise at some 8 per cent per annum, outstripping imports. Table 6.9 summarises the allocations of the current plan to the various branches of the economy. Subsequent increases in the development expenditure allotted to the plan have not altered the general pattern.[22]

*Agriculture.* Agriculture is given especial priority, receiving almost 17 per cent of investment, the largest allocation given to any sector. This reflects government concern at its decline. Although Libya is large in area (at 176 million hectares), only some 2.6 million ha (2.1 per cent of this area) are cultivated.[23]

In the late 1960s, the *per capita* growth rate of agriculture was only 1 per cent per annum, since when the deterioration of the sector has continued. The falling *per capita* production of food has, of course, led to an increasing import dependence. In 1974 the government recorded imports of $330 *per capita* of foodstuffs, a figure which is estimated as doubling by 1975/6.

It is in agriculture that the previous plan was least successful. The three-year plan favoured large-scale schemes which have been relatively ineffective because of a lack of rural infrastructure.[24] They have been unjustifiably water-intensive, with decreasing returns to scale. Techniques such as water purification and sewage recycling have been adopted to overcome shortages of irrigation supplies, and mechanisation to offset supposed labour shortages.

Whether or not targets are achieved in agriculture, care must be taken that water resources are not being squandered. A decline in agriculture in two or three decades' time (when population will have increased) brought about by a present-day mining of hydrological resources would be much more critical than the present day's malaise in the sector. Nor is it clear from the broader perspective of human resource utilisation that this investment is well directed, a point to which this analysis returns.

*Manufacturing and Industry.* It is harder to challenge Libyan planning in establishing the beginnings of an industrial sector. Industry established under the last plan was mainly import-substituting and primary processing. Though successful, it was necessarily relatively small-scale and not able to benefit from economies of scale.

The present economic and social transformation plan seeks to alter this by changing the stress of growth from light to heavy industry. The rapid growth of industry continues. Industrial production in 1977 totalled $245 million, an increase of 34 per cent over 1976.[25] This is in line with a declared aim of a 30 per cent annual growth rate in industrial activity. The change of emphasis to heavier industry is most obviously exhibited by the development of the iron and steel industry at Misurata. This, to cost some $1,000 million, is a typical example of an oil exporter trying to diversify and obtain a foreign exchange earning capacity. Local natural gas will be used. Also under development is a $515 million chemical complex, and a second refinery is to be built in the east. Another example of investment in foreign exchange earners is the cement plant, with a planned output of 7 million tons annually by 1980, allowing for exports of some 3 million tons once the domestic market is provided for. Aluminium production is also planned, the plant to be run by a joint company established with Yugoslavia, from where alumina will be imported.[26]

Contemporaneously, creation of infrastructure continues. Major contracts awarded for road construction exemplify the problem of overcoming the size of the country. Investment in housing, health facilities and other services also runs high but Libya, partly because of the strong central control kept upon the economy, has not yet experienced the explosion in current account expenditures on services common in other capital-rich countries, such as Kuwait.

To set against this low current account spending are purchases of arms and grants of foreign aid which continue to drain upon the Libyan budget. Libya has given two squadrons of fighter planes and 500 tanks to Syria, as well as aid to a wide variety of countries in the Middle East, Africa and elsewhere in the world.

The costly construction of infrastructure, military and aid payments are not the only constraints on the Libyan plan, however. The rising price of imported machinery and of construction materials are amounting to a severe inflationary pressure on financial resources.[27] Despite this, Libya has managed to maintain a trade surplus.[28] In the short term, rapid economic progress will continue to be made.

## 4 The Labour Market

### (a) The Structure of the Labour Force

In 1964, there were 96,700 economically active persons in Libya. By 1969 this had almost doubled to 182,000. In 1974 the total employed had risen to 540,000. It is expected that the labour force will increase to some 930,000 in 1980.[29] Of course, it is impossible for such a large increase in the labour force to be met from the indigenous population of Libya; the number of Libyans in employment is planned to rise from 454,000 in 1975 to 545,000 in 1980. This is very optimistic; the number of Libyans in the labour force will probably rise by less than the planned 20 per cent, the balance being made up by increased labour imports; the non-national element of the labour force will rise higher than the presently planned 41 per cent for 1980, immigrant workers numbering in excess of the planned 400,000.

Table 6.10 shows the evolution of the work-force by sector of employment. In 1964, employment in agriculture amounted to almost 40 per cent of the total. By 1973, before the recent rapid spurt of growth was under way, it had fallen to almost a quarter of the total, and reduced further to less than one-fifth by 1975.

Further reduction of manpower on the land is envisaged. However, this decline in the numbers recorded in agriculture is largely illusory, and does not represent an equivalent intake of Libyan manpower into the non-agricultural sectors of the economy, as will be shown.

Employment in manufacturing remains low (about 10 per cent), but represents not inconsiderable diversification of the economy. Table 6.11 shows the degree to which diversification has depended upon food processing and import-substitution industries. Despite the rapid overall increase in employment, the proportion in construction has increased. It will continue to do so, the development boom continuing.

The relative lack of employment in services of various kinds is notable, though whether this is simply a result of the 'immature' state of the economy or a consequence of the firm central planning remains to be seen. None the less, tertiary-sector growth in employment is not inconsiderable: the sector accounted for 39 per cent of workers in 1964, and 48 per cent in 1975.

Table 6.10: Libya: Labour Force by Sector of Employment, 1973 to 1980 (thousands)

| Sector | 1973 Number | 1973 Per cent | 1975 Number | 1975 Per cent | 1980 Number | 1980 Per cent |
|---|---|---|---|---|---|---|
| Agriculture | 129.0 | 24.0 | 133.1 | 19.6 | 157.8 | 17.0 |
| Oil and gas | 10.2 | 1.9 | 10.7 | 1.6 | 12.5 | 1.3 |
| Mining | 5.1 | 0.9 | 6.9 | 1.0 | 10.0 | 1.1 |
| Other manufacturing | 25.9 | 4.8 | 32.9 | 4.9 | 55.9 | 6.0 |
| Electricity, gas and water | 10.2 | 1.9 | 13.0 | 1.9 | 18.0 | 1.9 |
| Construction | 90.4 | 16.8 | 152.6 | 22.5 | 225.6 | 24.3 |
| Trade, hotels | 39.3 | 7.3 | 48.5 | 7.2 | 60.0 | 6.5 |
| Transport, storage and communications | 45.0 | 8.4 | 53.4 | 7.9 | 74.8 | 8.1 |
| Banking and insurance | 6.5 | 1.2 | 7.7 | 1.1 | 10.4 | 1.1 |
| Public administration and defence | 63.6 | 11.8 | 71.1 | 10.5 | 82.8 | 8.9 |
| Education | 45.8 | 8.5 | 58.0 | 8.6 | 91.0 | 9.8 |
| Health | 23.5 | 4.4 | 30.5 | 4.5 | 43.6 | 4.7 |
| Other services | 43.6 | 8.1 | 58.7 | 8.7 | 86.4 | 9.3 |
| Total | 538.1 | 100.0 | 677.1 | 100.0 | 928.8 | 100.0 |

Sources: Ministry of Planning and Scientific Research, *Preliminary Results of the 1973 Population Census* (Tripoli, 1976); Ministry of Planning and Scientific Research, *Economic and Social Transformation Plan (1976 to 1980)* (Tripoli, 1976); Ministry of Labour, *Labour Force Statistics, 1974* (Benghazi, n.d.); Secretariat of Planning, *Note on Manpower in the Economic and Social Transformation Plan* (Tripoli, typescript, n.d.).

Table 6.11: Libya: Employment in Non-Oil Industries, in Establishments Employing over 500 People, 1975

| | Labour Force |
|---|---|
| Food and manufacturing | 2,037 |
| Cement and related | 1,651 |
| Beverages | 1,328 |
| Tobacco manufacturing | 1,267 |
| Wood production | 886 |
| Rubber and plastics | 859 |
| Chemical industries | 736 |
| Total | 8,764 |

Source: Ministry of Labour, 'Labour Force Statistics (1975)' (Tripoli, typescript, n.d.).

Census returns show a fall in the crude economic activity rate of Libyan nationals from 25 per cent in 1964 to 21 per cent in 1973. This is caused by the widening base of the Libyan population pyramid, and is associated with an increasing dependency ratio, from 3.0 in 1964 to 3.8 in 1973. Although the overall activity rates have fallen, and although absolute numbers of economically active women are small, women have become relatively more prominent in the labour force. The expansion in the numbers of Libyans entering the labour force has been slower than overall population growth (1.6 per cent per annum compared with 3.6 per cent respectively). The relatively high participation rate for men of economically active age groups means that there are no prospects for rapid expansion of the national element of the labour force apart from an increase in the role of women.

Table 6.12: Libya: Employment of National Women, 1973

| Occupational Group | Number | Percentage |
|---|---|---|
| Teachers | 4,320 | 14.5 |
| Nurses and other health personnel | 1,970 | 6.6 |
| Other professional, technical and related workers | 140 | 0.5 |
| Clerical and related workers | 590 | 2.0 |
| Sales workers | 130 | 0.4 |
| Service workers | 6,550 | 21.9 |
| Agricultural workers | 13,750 | 46.1 |
| Production and related workers | 2,370 | 8.0 |
| Total employment | 29,820 | 100.0 |

Source: Ministry of Planning and Scientific Research, *Preliminary Results of the 1973 Population Census* (Benghazi, 1976).

The participation rate of women in the economy is only as high as it is because of the relatively large number of women agricultural workers: 46 per cent of the total of economically active women (Table 6.12). In fact, there are more than 14,000 Libyan women economically active in agriculture. This does not, however, detract from the assertion that the role of women in the modern sector is very limited. Women are only significant as teachers, and in some aspects of service provision. Few have professional qualifications, or are recorded under the professional, clerical and sales workers heads. However, as women's educational status improves, so will their participation increase: only 5 per cent of illiterate women were recorded as economically active in 1973, compared to 34 per cent of those who have completed secondary education.

*(b) Non-Nationals in the Libyan Labour Force*

In 1977, some 400,000 expatriates were employed in Libya.[30] Some 78 per cent of labour in construction is non-Libyan, as is over 40 per cent of that in manufacturing (Table 6.13). Only public administration, in which employment is specifically reserved for Libyans, transport and storage, in which Libyans are employed informally, and agriculture are less than 15 per cent expatriate. Reliance upon non-Libyan labour is better demonstrated if the non-agricultural (essentially modern) sector alone is considered. Here non-Libyan labour amounts to 38 per cent of the total.

Table 6.13: Libya: Distribution of Total and Non-Libyan Employment by Sector, 1975

| Economic Activity | Total Employment | | Non-Libyan Employment | | |
|---|---|---|---|---|---|
| | Number (thousands) | Per cent | Number (thousands) | Per cent | Per cent of Total Employment |
| Agriculture | 133.1 | 19.7 | 17.6 | 7.9 | 13.2 |
| Petroleum and gas | 10.7 | 1.6 | 2.7 | 1.2 | 25.2 |
| Mining and quarrying | 6.9 | 1.0 | 2.8 | 1.3 | 40.6 |
| Manufacturing | 32.9 | 4.9 | 13.8 | 6.2 | 41.9 |
| Electricity, gas and water | 13.0 | 1.9 | 3.6 | 1.6 | 27.7 |
| Construction | 152.6 | 22.5 | 118.0 | 53.0 | 77.5 |
| Trade, restaurants and hotels | 48.5 | 7.2 | 7.7 | 3.5 | 15.9 |
| Transport, storage and communications | 53.4 | 7.9 | 6.2 | 2.8 | 11.6 |
| Finance, insurance and real estate | 7.7 | 1.1 | 1.6 | 0.7 | 20.8 |
| Public administration | 71.1 | 10.5 | 5.2 | 2.3 | 7.3 |
| Educational services | 58.0 | 8.6 | 14.1 | 6.0 | 24.3 |
| Health services | 30.5 | 4.5 | 9.8 | 4.7 | 32.1 |
| Other | 58.7 | 8.6 | 19.6 | 8.8 | 33.4 |
| Total | 677.1 | 100.0 | 222.7 | 100.0 | 32.9 |

Source: Ministry of Labour, Demographic and Manpower Section, *Employment Statistics* (Tripoli, 1977).

Other facets of Libya's dependence upon expatriate workers are demonstrated in Table 6.14. Some 58 per cent of professional and managerial manpower is non-national, as are over one-third of technicians and supervisors. Only in the case of clerical workers does the expatriate element fall below one-quarter. Moreover, in 1975, 41 per cent of unskilled labour was non-Libyan. This amounted to over 85,000 unskilled workers, more than double the imports of unskilled labourers of two years earlier, and was due to rise further. In fact, there were already well over 85,000 unskilled non-nationals employed in Libya in 1975. Large numbers of clandestine immigrants, mainly unskilled, pass unrecorded and are excluded from the table.

Table 6.14: Libya: Employment by Occupational Status, Libyans and Non-Libyans, 1975

|  | Total Employment | | Non-Libyan Employment | | |
|  |  |  |  |  | Per cent of |
|  | Number | | Number | | Total |
|  | (thousands) | Per cent | (thousands) | Per cent | Employment |
|---|---|---|---|---|---|
| Professional and managerial | 27.7 | 4.1 | 16.1 | 7.2 | 58.1 |
| Technicians and supervisors | 58.1 | 8.6 | 20.4 | 9.1 | 35.1 |
| Clerical workers | 37.5 | 5.5 | 6.2 | 2.7 | 16.5 |
| Skilled and semi-skilled | 346.6 | 51.2 | 95.2 | 42.7 | 27.5 |
| Unskilled workers | 207.2 | 30.6 | 85.1 | 38.3 | 41.1 |
| Total | 677.1 | 100.0 | 223.0 | 100.0 | 32.9 |

Source: Ministry of Planning and Scientific Research, Census and Statistical Department, *Yearbook 1976* (Tripoli, 1977).

According to official figures produced by the Secretariat of the Interior, some 57 per cent of expatriates were Egyptian (148,000) in 1975. A further 15 per cent were Tunisian (38,000) and some 2 per cent (4,000) Sudanese (Table 6.15). The high levels of clandestine migration mean that these figures for Egyptian, Tunisian and Sudanese are significantly understated. More realistic estimates of workers of these nationalities are: Egyptians, 230,000, Tunisians, 38,000 and Sudanese, 7,000.[31] Since 1975, numbers of workers of these nationalities have increased further in Libya, totalling some 470,00 in 1979.

The extent of clandestine migration from Tunisia can be illustrated by the fact that, in 1971, for 2,984 Tunisians who entered Libya legally, some 41,000 were prevented by the Tunisian authorities from crossing the border because they did not have the necessary documentation.[32] In 1976, Libya expelled some 13,700 Tunisians who were clandestine immigrants.

Other non-national Arab groups are also present in Libya in much larger numbers than official data acknowledge. Together they comprised an immigrant Arab community of up to 480,000 in 1975.

The numbers of non-Arab expatriates are also rising rapidly, though clandestine movements are less important. For example, the 3,600

Table 6.15: Libya: Numbers of Expatriate Workers by Country of
Origin, December 1975

| Country of Origin | Number | Per cent |
|---|---|---|
| Egypt | 148,070 | 56.7 |
| Tunisia | 34,670 | 13.3 |
| Syria | 12,610 | 4.8 |
| Jordan | 6,900 | 2.6 |
| Palestine | 6,570 | 2.5 |
| Lebanon | 5,560 | 2.1 |
| Sudan | 4,250 | 1.6 |
| Morocco | 4,950 | 1.9 |
| | (223,580) | (85.5) |
| Pakistan | 4,540 | 1.7 |
| Yugoslavia | 7,640 | 2.9 |
| UK | 3,630 | 1.4 |
| Rumania | 2,210 | |
| USA | 2,170 | |
| Italy | 2,090 | |
| Bulgaria | 2,070 | Less than 1 per cent |
| Turkey | 1,920 | |
| France | 1,880 | |
| Germany | 1,380 | |
| Greece | 1,090 | |
| Other | 7,050 | |
| Total | 261,250 | 100.0 |

Source: Ministry of Planning and Scientific Research, *Work Permit Statistics*
(Tripoli, 1976, mimeograph).

United Kingdom expatriates in Libya in 1975 had risen to over 7,000
by 1977. In March 1978 the Koreans were negotiating contracts involv-
ing over 1,000 workers. Numbers of Turks, Pakistanis and Eastern
European workers have also increased rapidly. For example, Libya has
asked Turkey for 100,000 workers.[33] It has been claimed that Libya has
vacancies for 250,000 foreign workers. In short, in 1975 and still more
so in 1979, expatriates play a much larger part in the work-force than
the official data in Tables 6.13 and 6.14 imply. Libyan dependence
upon expatriate labour is bound to increase further, especially if the
rapid rate of growth continues as it is set to do.

*(c) The Dual Labour Market*

These large-scale imports of unskilled labour are of profound significance in terms of the development of indigenous Libyan human resources.[34] In Saudi Arabia, the large-scale immigrant work-force has
enabled the withdrawal of the national labour force from modern-

sector development. In Libya this has also occurred. Evidence suggests that another process is at work in the Libyan labour market, however – the large numbers of unskilled non-national workers appear not only to enable the withdrawal of Libyan workers from the modern sector, but in some cases actually to displace them from the modern-sector labour force.

This problem is especially associated with the high levels of clandestine migration into Libya, which means a lack of control of new influxes on to the labour market. It is likely that large numbers of immigrants are given opportunities in wage employment in preference to Libyan nationals. This is because the non-Libyans are willing to work for lower rewards than the Libyan nationals will accept and which are, indeed, less than the legal minimum.

The employment of non-nationals in preference to Libyans is an especially acute problem because the skill levels and educational attributes of many Arab migrants – both clandestine and legal – are the same as of the mass of the Libyan population: they are of low educational attainment, frequently illiterate, of limited modern-sector work experience, and tend to be unskilled or semi-skilled. Thus the large number of unskilled immigrants, especially illegal immigrants whose entry into the labour market is uncontrolled, are displacing Libyans from many positions open to this type of labour in the modern sector.

As in Saudi Arabia, the large numbers of non-national migrants have allowed Libyans to move out of productive occupations into those which they consider more desirable, namely service occupations in the government. Here the same trend that is so developed in Kuwait is beginning to appear in Libya. This transfer of national labour has been made without the economy having suffered overtly, because of the large reservoir of non-national labour. There are insufficient 'desirable' service posts to absorb all Libyans, however, so as numbers of Libyans shun the undesirable jobs which they relinquish to non-nationals, they are opting out of the modern sector altogether.

As they opt out of or do not enter the modern sector, especially the productive modern sector where non-national labour is so important, Libyans prejudice their country's economic development. Consequently, Libya's reliance upon immigrant labour in key occupations is inordinately large. As time passes, certain modern-sector occupations are becoming increasingly associated with non-national labour, and it is difficult to recruit Libyan nationals to work in them. The process is to some extent self-reinforcing: it becomes increasingly difficult to persuade Libyans to work in these productive (but 'undesirable') modern-sector occupations for normal remuneration related to marginal product. Yet because of their limited educational attainment and work experience, these are the very occupations in which Libyans should be gaining modern-sector experience.

As long as non-Libyans are prepared to work in these occupations for the legal minimum wage or less, the numbers of Libyans displaced from these positions will remain high. However, the under- and unemployment remaining so extensively and pervasively in Tunisia, Egypt and the Sudan will ensure a stream of clandestine migrants from these countries into Libya, even if legal migration were banned completely. Libya's long open borders with these neighbouring states mean that it is practically impossible to prevent illegal immigration.

Whilst remaining outside the modern sector, Libyans do not engage in large numbers in modern productive agriculture. Many Libyans dwelling in rural areas remain in the traditional sector, virtually cut off from modern-sector development. Sheer distance, as in Saudi Arabia, is significant in this economic isolation. Thus Libyans in rural areas represent the traditional side of a dual economy which is becoming increasingly acutely drawn. They produce, as do their equivalents in Saudi Arabia, only small amounts of cash crops on their farms, using the land for subsistence crops which, crucially, need only low labour inputs.

Even within agriculture, the dual economy model is sustained. Relatively few Libyans are involved in the modern large-scale projects. It is in these schemes that the immigrants who are employed in the agricultural sector (Table 6.13) find work.

The incomes of the Libyan rural population derive in part from their farms (especially as subsistence income) but are largely from other non-wage sources, such as social security payments, similar to the Saudi Arabian example. They do, too, augment this income by periodic, part-time participation in the modern sector.

Official employment figures for non-nationals are misleading. The employment figures for Libyan nationals are also illusory, but for a different reason. The number of Libyans participating *full-time* in the modern sector is much more limited than Table 6.13 implies. In fact, numbers of Libyans in agriculture are yet more numerous than the 133,000 recorded (Table 6.13). Moreover, many of the men recorded as being in agricultural employment are, as in many of the capital-poor states, in reality underemployed. Libya is markedly more dependent upon non-national labour than official sources suggest.

## 5 Conclusion: The Planners' Dilemma

In essence, Libyan manpower planners are faced with the same problem as their counterparts in Saudi Arabia. Although the scale of the dilemma might be smaller, the time scale is shorter, and Libya's resources more limited. Moreover, the particular problem making labour market control more difficult in the Libyan case is the immediate proximity of large sources of illegal labour market entrants in Egypt, Tunisia and the Sudan. In view of the bleak employment prospects in these three capital-poor states, they might come to comprise increasingly unwelcome neighbours as their labour forces continue to spill over into Libya in search of work.

Yet a certain amount of immigrant labour, including some unskilled workers, is essential to fulfil Libyan development aims, and would be so even if all indigenous human capital were fully involved in modern economic progress. However, economic development will continue to attract illegal migrants for employment from Libya's neighbours. There will always be private-sector executors of development willing to employ these workers, because of their cheapness and limited non-wage demands.

This will serve to aggravate the isolation of many Libyans from their own modern-sector development. The task of development of Libya's own indigenous human capital, with its low level of educational attainment, is anyway an immense and, in view of Libya's relatively limited oil reserves, a pressing task. As expected, the Libyan government is making moves to establish modern-sector enclave development, utilising Far Eastern labour. This is a less complete answer than in the cases of the other capital-rich states, however. The Libyan planners will have to divert yet more funds and effort to the development of human resources, and into transport infrastructure and agriculture in order to break down the dual economy if they are to include more Libyans in the modern sector. Failure to do so will engender yet more stresses in society as Libyan nationals desire increasing rewards from the development of their country on a progressively less realistic basis.

## Notes

1. This is documented in, for example, *MEED*, 11 March 1977, p. 30; see also R. First, *Libya: the Elusive Revolution* (Penguin Books, Baltimore, 1974), and Omar I. El Farhaly, Monte Palmer and Richard Chackerian, *Political Development and Bureaucracy in Libya* (Lexington Books, Toronto, 1977).

2. R. Farley, *Planning for Development in Libya: The Exceptional Economy in the Developing World* (Praeger, New York, Washington, 1971); R. al Mallakh, 'The Economics of Rapid Growth: Libya', *Middle East Journal* (Summer 1969), p. 308.

3. Libyan Arab Republic, 'Preliminary Results of the 1973 Population Census' (Ministry of Planning, Tripoli, typescript, 1975?).

4. A.M. Farrag, for example, took a 1972 estimate of the Libyan national population as 2,084,000 to include 114,000 non-Libyans. See 'Migration between Arab Countries' in *Manpower and Employment in Arab Countries. Some Critical Issues* (ILO, Geneva, 1976), pp. 84-109.

5. For a detailed discussion of the development of the Libyan educational system, see A.M. Zarrugh, 'The Development of Public Education in Libya, 1951-1970, with special reference to University Education' (unpublished PhD Durham University, 1973).

6. Ministry of Education, *Libyan Educational Statistics* (Tripoli).

7. Ministry of Information, *Oil and Planning* (Tripoli, 1968), p. 89.

8. UNESCO, *Report of the Mission to Libya* (Paris, 1952).

9. Ministry of Information, *Oil and Planning* (Tripoli, 1968).

10. The Libyan Arab Republic, like most other Arab states, has adopted a 6-3-3 yearly enrolment scheme.

11. See *MEED*, 22 September 1977.

12. It was ranked as the poorest country in the world by the World Bank in 1954.

13. See *Middle East Annual Review*, 1977, 'Libya'.

14. United Nations Industrial Development Organization, *Comparative Study of Plan of Arab States* (New York, 1976), p. 161.

15. J. Wright, *Libya* (London, 1969).

16. G.H. Blake, 'Libya and the Arab World', *Bulletin of the Faculty of Arts, University of Benghazi, IV* (Benghazi, 1972).

17. *MEED*, 12 January 1978, p. 25.

18. See J.S. Birks and C.A. Sinclair, *Country Case Study: Libya*, International Migration Project Working Paper (Durham, 1978).

19. Libyan National Oil Corporation, cited in *MEED*, 2 January 1978, p. 25.

20. For a comment on the Three Year Development Plan see, A. Sultan, 'Libya', *MEED Special Report*, 18 February 1977.

21. See again Sultan, 'Libya', for more detail on the current plan.

22. *MEED*, 4 January 1977, p. 33.

23. J.A. Allan, K. McLachlan and E.T. Penrose, *Libya. Agriculture and Economic Development* (Frank Cass, London, 1973).

24. R.I. Lawless, *New Agricultural Projects in the Libyan Arab Republic: A Survey* (Durham, 1975).

25. Centre for Statistics, Industry Secretariat, Central Institute for Planning, cited in *MEED*, 31 March 1976, p. 28.

26. See A. Sultan, 'The Three Year Development Plan', *MEED Special Report, Libya*, 18 February 1977.

27. H. Mahdary, 'The Patterns and Problems of Economic Development in Rentier States: The Case of Iran' in M.A. Cook, *Studies in the Economic History of the Middle East from the Rise of Islam to the Present Day* (Oxford University Press, Oxford, 1970), pp. 428-67.

28. N. Cummings-Bruce, 'Rise in 1977 Payments Surplus May Ease Cash Flow Worries', *MEED*, 28 April 1978, p. 4.

29. Ministry of Social and Economic Planning, 'Assessment of the Three Year Plan' (Tripoli, typescript, n.d.).

30. J.S. Birks and C.A. Sinclair, *Migration and Development in the Arab*

*Region* (ILO, Geneva, 1980).

31. J.S. Birks and C.A. Sinclair, *The Kingdom of Saudi Arabia and the Libyan Arab Jamahiriya: the Key Countries of Employment*, World Employment Programme Research Working Paper (ILO, Geneva, 1980).

32. A. Findlay, *Country Case Study: Tunisia*, International Migration Project Working Paper (Durham, 1978).

33. Turkey's Deputy Under-Secretary of Labour in Ankara, March 1977, reported in *MEED*, 25 May 1977, p. 23.

34. For a summary of some aspects of the broader social accounting of the costs and benefits of hosting immigrant workers see M.G. Gupta, *Non-Libyans' Employment and its Costs and Benefits in the Socio-Economic Development of the Country* (Department of Social and Economic Planning, Demography and Manpower Planning Section, Tripoli, 1976).

# 7 THE REPUBLIC OF IRAQ

## 1 Introduction

Iraq is a large country, occupying a central position in the Middle East and bordering six states: Kuwait, Saudi Arabia, Jordan, Syria, Turkey and Iran. The country comprises three main physiographic regions: the mountains adjacent to Turkey in the north-east, the desert to the south-west shared with Saudi Arabia, and the central fertile basin either side of the Tigris and Euphrates. The supply of water afforded by these rivers, particularly the Tigris, gives Iraq a considerable asset in the form of potentially cultivable land. At present only half of Iraq's cultivable land is actually farmed, and that only on an intermittent basis. While the country has a population of 12 million people (1977), population density is low, and many of the agricultural areas are sparsely populated.

Iraq has four assets: people, water, cultivable land and oil. The country has substantial reserves of oil, and is about to overtake Kuwait as the second-largest Arab oil producer after Saudi Arabia. It has been oil revenues which have enabled the government to undertake a massive development programme in the past five years, principally in the fields of industrial development, infrastructure and agriculture.

Iraq's GNP *per capita* was $1,150 in 1977, placing her within the 'capital-rich' group. The bulk of her income is from oil extraction and sale, though the economy is rapidly being diversified, primarily into industry.

Iraq's economy is firmly directed by central government, whose objective is to expand the 'socialist sector' to encompass eventually the entire economy. Since the revolution of July 1968, a path of socialist development has been rigidly adhered to, not without cost at times to various minority groups and often with little regard to humanitarian and social issues. Despite the buoyant state of the economy, soaring revenues and rapid economic development, not to mention the invaluable asset of a large population and more than sufficient cultivable land area, Iraq lives with a number of deep-rooted problems, some of which are political, some economic.

Iraq's port is felt to be precariously close to Iran, which until very recently explicitly maintained a careful eye on Gulf affairs. Fao port was, and is, highly vulnerable to military intervention from Iran. An agreement was made in 1975 between the two countries to respect each other's territorial sovereignty, which superficially appeared to hold. However, this, like many such agreements, has dissolved with the change of administration in Iran.

The Iranian link is also relevant to the problem of Iraq's plurality. Two groups in Iraq cause the central government concern. The first is the Kurds, who live in the oil-rich region to the east, and the second are the Shia Arabs, who live in the south. Events in Iran have encouraged diverse groups in Iraq to express and establish their identity. In the case of the Kurds, there is a continuing saga of conflict which subsided, albeit temporarily, in March 1975, when Iranian support for the Iraqi Kurds ended. The emergence of powerful Shia leaders in Iran has encouraged the Shia of Iraq to assert their independence. These internal political problems are highly relevant to the attainment of Iraq's economic development objectives, since a serious conflict with either group would bring into question the entire programme.

The *rapprochement* between Iraq and Syria in 1979 enabled Iraq to re-open her railway links with Europe and the oil pipeline to the west. The dispute with Syria, which led to the closure of the border in November 1977, disrupted railway traffic to Iraq and ended Iraq's supply of oil to the Banias refinery in Syria. Serious as both these aspects were, a nascent fear in Baghdad was that Syria might attempt to use still more water for irrigation purposes from the Euphrates than she already did. Syria's unannounced disruption of the flow of water in the Euphrates in 1975 caused the failure of Iraq's rice crop in that year.

The longer the dispute with Syria lasted, the more damaging the consequences were becoming. In order to overcome the problem of oil outlets, an oil pipeline through Turkey was built, and a railway line contemplated. The pipeline threatened to be an economic disaster, since Turkey was not able to pay fully for the oil she drew off from the pipeline, and with falling tanker freight rates, pumping via Turkey at the rates agreed was becoming marginally more expensive than tranporting oil by ship from Fao.

Effecting economic development and avoiding international disagreement or domestic inter-communal strife presents the government with a serious challenge. Besides the political problems just mentioned, there are some economic ones. In particular, the agriculture sector has suffered from a depopulation of rural area and considerable instability as land reforms have been instituted. Agricultural output has oscillated from one year to the next, and is now only comparable with the level of the early sixties, despite substantial investments in mechanisation.

Iraq faces immense challenges in development of her resources; the opportunity she now has is unparalleled in the twentieth century. However, in a country like Iraq, economic development is not purely a matter of sound economic planning.

## 2 The Supply of Labour

### (a) Population

The preliminary results of the 1977 population census give a *de facto* population of 12.1 million in 1977. The Ministry of Planning estimates that the annual population increase has been some 3.4 per cent between 1965 and 1977 (Table 7.1).

Table 7.1: Iraq: Population in 1965 and 1977

|  | 1965 | | 1977 | | Growth Rate |
|  | Number | Per cent | Number | Per cent | per annum |
|---|---|---|---|---|---|
| Total population | 8,097,320 | 100.0 | 12,171,460 | 100.0 | 3.4 |
| Citizens abroad | 49,800 | – | 141,700 | – | 9.1 |
| Urban population | 4,112,300 | 51.1 | 7,640,670 | 63.5 | 5.3 |
| Rural population | 3,935,120 | 48.9 | 4,389,090 | 36.5 | 0.9 |

Source: Ministry of Planning, *Man: The Object of Revolution* (Baghdad, 1978), Table 1, p. 11.

Since natural increase could only account for about 3.2 per cent per annum, either Iraq's population has increased in part as a consequence of her naturalisation policy, or the estimate for 1965 is incorrectly low. Iraq has for a number of years given citizenship to any Arab who wishes to live in the country. It is known that a large number of Egyptian farmers have settled in Iraq, but on what legal basis is not clear. Presumably they will be treated according to the official regulations, and given citizenship if they so wish. This point is of more than academic interest, since the Ministry of Planning estimates their number at 600,000, though non-official estimates suggest the Egyptian migrants are fewer than this.

The most dramatic demographic transformation in Iraq has been pervasive outmigration from villages to cities. Whilst the figures on Table 7.1 show a national population growth rate of 3.4 per cent per annum, urban areas grew at 5.3 per cent per annum, and rural areas' population only at 0.9 per cent per annum. This suggests that between 1965 and 1977 1.5 million people left rural areas for towns and cities, many of whom were males aged twenty to thirty-five. Agricultural employ-ment fell dramatically (as Table 7.6 shows) although output was static.

Urbanisation is widely recognised as a problem by the government, and the establishment of urban infrastructure is absorbing large sums. Despite massive spending in towns, or, perhaps partly because of it, there is a serious risk that the process of urbanisation may proceed at a more rapid rate than government can cope with.

### (b) The Educational Status of the Population

In 1977 a very high proportion of the population was illiterate; amongst persons aged ten years or more, 56 per cent were illiterate. In rural areas the rate was higher, at 77 per cent, while in urban areas it was 44 per cent.[1] These rates are very high for the region, but are not surpris-ing when one considers the wide area over which the population is dis-tributed and the absence, until recently, of communications with many parts of the country.

The advent of oil wealth has enabled government to expand and im-prove communications infrastructure and to provide both more schools and higher levels of education. Recently a major literacy campaign was launched which had a significant impact over the whole country. The campaign enrolled some 150,000 illiterates in temporary class-rooms; these temporary pupils were expected to achieve literacy in a comparatively short period. The campaign was officially judged a suc-cess, but only a beginning was made in terms of eradication of illiteracy in that in 1977, some 4.2 million illiterates remained. Most of these live in remote rural areas — the task of educating them remains immense. Further campaigns over several years will be necessary if illiteracy is to be eradicated. Moreover, the capacity to retain literacy has not yet re-ceived the attention of campaign directors, and this may prove to be a severe headache in follow-up work.

Table 7.2 shows that education has been available mainly in urban areas, and that the population of rural areas is generally illiterate and uneducated. However, enrolment in schools is rising rapidly, and Table 7.3 shows the number in school in 1977/8.

Although most boys of primary school age are in school, only about half of the girls are. By any standards, enrolment in secondary and higher education is impressive. So rapid have enrolments at university level been that a Ministry for Higher Education was created in 1970. There are now four universities in Iraq, located at Baghdad, Mosul, Sulaymaniyah and Basra.[2] Besides the universities, there is a plethora of institutions specialising in various aspects of post-secondary

Table 7.2: Iraq: Educational Attainment by Area of Residence, 1977 (Aged 10 years or more)

| Educational Attainment | All Country | Urban Areas | Rural Areas |
|---|---|---|---|
| Illiterate | 55.9 | 44.5 | 77.0 |
| Literate | 21.7 | 25.8 | 13.9 |
| Primary school certificate | 12.9 | 16.4 | 6.5 |
| Intermediate school certificate | 4.0 | 5.5 | 1.3 |
| Secondary school certificate | 3.2 | 4.6 | 0.7 |
| Higher | 2.3 | 3.2 | 0.6 |
| Total | 100.0 | 100.0 | 100.0 |
| Total number | 7,555,252 | 4,923,407 | 2,631,845 |

Source: Ministry of Planning, Central Statistical Office, *Annual Abstract of Statistics, 1978* (Baghdad, n.d.), Table 2/8, p. 35.

Table 7.3: Iraq: School Enrolment in 1977/8

| Educational Level | Boys | Girls | Total |
|---|---|---|---|
| Primary | 1,283,500 | 765,100 | 2,048,600 |
| Secondary | 468,200 | 196,100 | 664,300 |
| Vocational | 27,300 | 7,900 | 35,200 |
| Teacher training and university | 58,900 | 26,500 | 85,400 |

Source: Ministry of Planning, *Man: The Object of Revolution* (Baghdad, July 1978), Table 7, p. 87.

education.

In the mid-1970s, shortages of skilled manual workers became a critical constraint to economic development, and as a result a considerable change of emphasis is planned at the secondary level. Half of all students at that level will study 'vocational' courses, while the other half will continue, as at present, to study theoretical courses which lead to university.

The Ministry of Education has commissioned hundreds of new schools and vocational training centres.[3] Educating young Iraqis in skills which the economy requires is both expensive and difficult. However, the Ministry of Education has set about the task with vigour and determination, and in a direction more calculated to satisfy the needs of the future labour market rather than the demands of the people. The focus of the Iraqi education system means it might avoid some of the pitfalls noted in the other capital-rich states.

## 3 The Demand for Labour

### (a) Economic Development

Oil has been the key to Iraq's economic growth in the past ten years. After 1971, when the negotiations for the nationalisation of the Iraqi Petroleum Corporation were completed, output and the search for new sources of oil were stepped up. Iraq profited from the rising price of oil and, fortuitously, discovered yet more oil. Production in 1978 was 2.2 million barrels per day, and it is planned that production will reach 3.5 million barrels per day by 1980. The investment in the infra-structure of the oil industry has been enormous.[4]

Iraq's landlocked position means that transporting her oil to markets is harder than it is for, say, Saudi Arabia. Iraq has two alternatives: either to pump the oil westwards through Syria or Turkey, or south to the oil terminal at Fao. Both are technically possible, but Iraq's polit-ical disputes with her neighbours have often meant the use of unsatis-factory routes. For example, at great expense, Iraq built an oil pipe-line which bypassed Syria, running through Turkey. Besides receiving royalty payments, Turkey was entitled to buy from Iraq some of the oil which passed through the pipeline. Unfortunately Turkey was never able to pay in full for the oil she took, and the royalty payments agreed actually proved higher than the alternative freight rates were.[5] The con-tinuing instability of relations with Syria means that this problem is by no means solved, and Iraq's worsening relations with Iran now raises the question of the security of Fao.

Government revenues have exceeded expenditures in the period 1974/5 to 1976, as Table 7.4 shows. This is remarkable when it is re-membered that the period was one of intense development in capital projects and infrastructure. Iraq's reserves have consequently been growing.

In 1976 gross domestic product was $15 billion, to which mining and quarrying was the largest contributing sector (54 per cent), natur-ally enough, since this includes the oil industry. Agriculture and fishing only contribute 8 per cent of GDP, a low figure given that 31 per cent of the population are employed in agriculture. The manufacturing sector is still quite small, though equivalent in terms of GDP to agri-culture. The heavy investment in industry in the Basra region and Mosul will increase the contribution of the sector in the future.

### (b) Agriculture

While the agricultural sector's contribution to national income is low

Table 7.4: Iraq: Government Revenue and Expenditure, 1974/5 to 1976 ($ billion)

| Year | Revenue | Expenditure | Deficit (−) or Surplus (+) |
|---|---|---|---|
| 1974/5 | 4.7 | 3.1 | + 1.6 |
| 1975 | 3.0 | 2.5 | + 0.5 |
| 1976 | 5.2 | 4.6 | + 0.6 |

Source: Ministry of Planning, Central Statistical Office, *Annual Abstract of Statistics, 1977* (Baghdad, n.d.), Table 7/1, p. 133.

Table 7.5: Iraq: Gross Domestic Product at Current Prices, 1976 ($ million)

| Economic Sector | Gross Domestic Product | Per cent |
|---|---|---|
| Agriculture, forestry and fishing | 1,180 | 7.6 |
| Mining and quarrying | 8,390 | 54.0 |
| Manufacturing | 1,098 | 7.1 |
| Water and electricity | 75 | 0.5 |
| Construction | 1,203 | 7.7 |
| Finance and distribution | 1,966 | 12.7 |
| Community and personal services | 1,614 | 10.4 |
| Total | 15,526 | 100.0 |

Source: Ministry of Planning, Central Statistical Office, *Annual Abstract of Statistics, 1977* (Baghdad, n.d.), Table 6/1, p. 127.

(8 per cent) the large proportion of people employed in agriculture (31 per cent) means that great importance is attached to it. However, some of the government's efforts to develop the sector have had mixed results.[6]

Until oil was found, the economy depended on agriculture both as a means of livelihood for the population and as, in a small way, an earner of foreign exchange through the sale of cotton and dates. Since 1972 both the area of land cultivated and production have steadily fallen, as Table 7.6 shows.

There are two reasons for this trend. First, the land reforms instigated by the government, the purpose of which was to distribute land more equitably, served to create uncertainty and to disrupt production. However, despite these problems, the land reforms are still being effected. Secondly, many rural areas are experiencing sharp depopulation, as rural to urban migration has been remarkably rapid and pervasive.

Table 7.6: Iraq: Index Numbers of Agricultural Production and Cultivated Area, 1972 to 1977 (1975 = 100)

| Year | Production | Cultivated Area |
|------|-----------|-----------------|
| 1972 | 181.8 | 134.3 |
| 1973 | 112.7 | 87.7 |
| 1974 | 114.7 | 106.5 |
| 1975 | 100.0 | 100.0 |
| 1976 | 132.1 | 106.5 |
| 1977 | 117.0 | 78.4 |

Source: Ministry of Planning, Central Statistical Office, *Annual Abstract of
Statistics, 1977* (Baghdad, n.d.), Table 3/11, p. 60.

The intensive investment in mechanisation of agriculture and the
innumerable schemes to control the flow of water in the Tigris and
Euphrates will eventually arrest the decline in agricultural production,.but they show no sign of doing so yet. So seriously does the
government view the depopulation of rural areas that it has resorted to
somewhat radical measures, notably the settling of large numbers of
Egyptian farmers in Iraq. The literacy campaign had, amongst others,
the objective of raising productivity in rural areas. As has been noted,
illiteracy is indeed extremely high in rural areas. However, somewhat
ironically, one effect of educating peasants may be to increase the flow
of migrants to cities.

The challenge to the government is that the country has fertile land
in abundance, a supply of irrigation water and a large population. Yet
the agricultural sector is in a state of decline. In income terms this is
not such a problem, but in the broader perspective of Iraq's development, it is most undesirable and is a cause of growing unease amongst
economic planners. It is indeed a different scale of decline than found
in the rural economies of Saudi Arabia and Libya, and has much wider
consequences for the overall pattern of development of Iraq.

*(c) Development Planning*

Development planning in Iraq has two component parts. First, the official 'plan', which provides an overall framework for the direction of
economic development, sets targets for sectors and the overall level of
expenditure. Secondly, the day-to-day administration of economic
development, which is in the hands of the Ministries. The experience of
bottlenecks to development, inadequate infrastructure and shortages of
skilled manpower caused a considerable delay in the release of the 1976
to 1980 plan.[7] Eventually, in mid-1977, details of the plan were re-

leased, 18 months late. This illustrates the point that the official 'plan' is in fact no more than a guide to individual Ministries on overall emphasis and spending levels.

The 1976 to 1980 plan detailed expenditure of $49 billion, 40 per cent of which was allocated to industry.[8] Gross national product was to rise by 17 per cent annually, and by 1980 GNP *per capita* would be $1,800.[9] Clearly these are targets rather than forecasts of future development, but the message is clear: given growing oil revenues, development will continue at breakneck speed. Against this, occasional periods of consolidation are announced, though these typically last only a few months before development returns to its normal pace.

In the two main development centres outside Baghdad, Mosul and Basra, anticipated projects include steel mills, aluminium plants, expanded cement plants, new port berths, railways, roads and continuing development of the barrages on the Tigris and Euphrates.

On the macro-economic level, Iraq's development is impressive, but a closer inspection reveals a number of weaknesses. The combination of socialism and a belief in economic growth produces both paradoxes and an inability to cope with some kinds of development problems. While these tensions may fall away as Iraq's income and standard of living rise over the coming decade, serious failure to manage rural to urban migration or a political problem may compromise the entire effort.

### 4 The Labour Market

In 1977 Iraq's work-force totalled 3.1 million, and the crude participation rate was 42 per cent for men and 9 per cent for women. Overall the rate was 26 per cent.

Table 7.7 shows that employment increased from 1968 to 1977 at about 2.9 per cent. The agricultural sector declined annually at 3 per cent. In proportional terms the share it accounted for fell from 54 per cent to 31 per cent. The demographic impact of the transfer of so many workers out of the agricultural sector into the towns and cities is shown on Table 7.1. Table 7.6 suggests that thereby agricultural output may have been affected. Table 7.7 shows the employment implications of this profound change in Iraqi society from a backward rural community with one large city to a predominantly urban-based society.

Personal and community service is the economic sector where most people in Iraq now work. Included here are all service workers, in both the private and public sectors. Government employment totalled about

620,000 persons, so private sector services employment was around 600,000. Many of these are not employed formally, deriving a living from working in the informal sectors of Baghdad, Basra and Mosul. Although so many persons work in the service sector of the economy, it is the industrial sectors and construction industry that government is most concerned to develop. However, the capital intensity of contemporary investment in manufacturing industry makes it unlikely that significantly higher proportions of the labour force will work in industry, though productivity there will be very high.

Table 7.7: Iraq: Employment by Economic Sector, 1968 and 1977 (thousands)

| Economic Sector | Total Employed | | | |
| | 1968 | | 1977 | |
| | Number | Per cent | Number | Per cent |
| --- | --- | --- | --- | --- |
| Agriculture | 1,254 | 54.0 | 943.9 | 31.5 |
| Industry | 174 | 7.5 | 344.4 | 11.5 |
| Construction | 66 | 2.8 | 321.7 | 10.7 |
| Distribution | 280 | 12.0 | 177.8 | 5.9 |
| Personal and community services | 550 | 23.7 | 1,213.1 | 40.4 |
| Total | 2,324 | 100.0 | 3,000.9 | 100.0 |

Source: Ministry of Planning, *Man: The Object of Revolution* (Baghdad, July 1978), Table 5, p. 68; Ministry of Planning, Central Statistical Office, *Annual Abstract of Statistics, 1978* (Baghdad, n.d.), Table 2/9, p. 37.

From Table 7.8 it is clear that most women work in agriculture, and within the agricultural sector they comprise 37 per cent of all employment. Thus Iraq's agricultural output depends very substantially on the continued presence of women on farms. One point of detail is worth noting here: the accuracy of the 1977 census in enumerating female rural employment. So often women working on the land are under-enumerated (and they may be here slightly) but in the Iraqi census this does not appear to have occurred significantly.

If men continue to migrate to cities at the same rate as they have in the past, then agricultural output will come to depend yet more on women. In 1977, 95 per cent of rural women were illiterate, and it seems logical to suggest that the next literacy campaign should focus mainly on rural women.

A sizeable slice of non-farm female workers are employed by the government (86,000) while almost 9 per cent of their total work in manufacturing. Overall women contribute 17 per cent to the total work-force.

Male employment is more even than is that of women, though community, social and personal services absorbs 34 per cent. Only 23 per cent work in agriculture, forestry and fishing; ten years ago that figure was much higher.

Table 7.8: Iraq: Economically Active by Economic Sector and Sex, 1977

| Economic Sector | Employment | | | | | |
|---|---|---|---|---|---|---|
| | Total | | Men | | Women | |
| | Number | Per cent | Number | Per cent | Number | Per cent |
| Agriculture, forestry and fishing | 943,890 | 30.0 | 591,066 | 22.8 | 352,824 | 64.9 |
| Mining and quarrying | 36,835 | 1.2 | 34,716 | 1.3 | 2,119 | 0.4 |
| Manufacturing | 284,395 | 9.1 | 235,777 | 9.1 | 48,616 | 8.9 |
| Electricity, gas and water | 23,190 | 0.7 | 22,241 | 0.9 | 949 | 0.2 |
| Construction | 321,696 | 10.3 | 316,560 | 12.2 | 5,136 | 0.9 |
| Wholesale and retail trade | 224,104 | 7.1 | 207,949 | 8.0 | 16,155 | 3.0 |
| Restaurants and hotels | | | | | | |
| Transport, storage and communications | 177,799 | 5.7 | 172,814 | 6.7 | 4,985 | 0.9 |
| Financing, insurance real estate and business services | 31,089 | 1.0 | 26,023 | 1.0 | 5,066 | 0.9 |
| Community, social and personal services | 957,979 | 30.6 | 871,879 | 33.7 | 86,100 | 15.8 |
| Not adequately defined | 58,237 | 1.9 | 46,258 | 1.8 | 11,979 | 2.2 |
| Unemployed | 74,725 | 2.4 | 64,278 | 2.5 | 10,447 | 1.9 |
| Economically active | 3,133,939 | 100.0 | 2,589,561 | 100.0 | 544,378 | 100.0 |

Source: Ministry of Planning, Central Statistical Office, *Annual Abstract of Statistics 1978* (Baghdad, n.d.), Table 2/9, p. 37.

Two problems characterise the labour market of Iraq. The first does not appear in official accounts of the labour market, nor is it generally recognised. It is the growing number of persons working informally in the sprawling urban areas of the country. Urban growth has been spectacular in the past decade, and although modern-sector employment has grown quickly, there has not been a sufficient demand for the new arrivals in the suburbs. Most of these are illiterate, not having the skills required by Iraq's developing formal economy. As a result, the urban informal sector has mushroomed.

There is a demand in the economy for skilled manpower which is greater than the presently available supply, and labour shortages have emerged as a constraint to development. Thus the task of labour market managers in the coming decade is to train the manpower presently underutilised in the urban informal sector in skills required by the modern formal economy.

This is related to the second problem, which is the low skill and educational level of the work-force. It is ironic that while Baghdad is one of the oldest educational centres in the Middle East, the bulk of the Iraqi people are illiterate. Mobilising and training an unskilled and illiterate work-force to participate in the modern economy is difficult, expensive and time-consuming.

At one point the government offered a range of incentives to persuade certain groups of Iraqi manpower abroad to return to Iraq. The policy was successful in numerical terms, but created problems within the labour market, and many of the returnees had skills of which Iraq did not require more, for example university professors. Although the active recruitment policy has ended, Iraq offers citizenship to any Arab national who wishes to live in Iraq. This policy is quite unique in the Arab world. However, given the physical resources of the country, it is not so surprising, and underlines the remarkable development potential of the country.

## 5 Conclusion

Of all the capital-rich states in the Arab region, Iraq arguably has the greatest potential for development. She does not have oil wealth on the same scale as Saudi Arabia, but Iraq has sufficient oil income to fund her ambitious development plans. Crucially, Iraq does not have the Achilles heel of Saudi Arabia and Libya – small indigenous populations. Even so, the problems which the government of Iraq faces in developing the country cannot be overlooked. They are both political and economic. In Iraq are several communities whose aspirations to separate identities may conflict with the goals of national development. Managing these groups will be difficult. On the economic front, the decline of agriculture must be arrested, and a better use made of the country's manpower. One problem the government faces continually is that of size and distance. For example, there are more than 4 million illiterate people in Iraq; Mosul to Basra is three days by road. Therefore, detailed planning is very difficult, and tends to lead to global solutions for all problems which have unforeseen consequences when implemented. The land reforms provide an example.

Despite the weaknesses in the economy mentioned and the several problems ahead, Iraq's economic prospects are excellent, and increase with the time scale of evaluation. While Saudi Arabia is the economic giant of the Arab world today, in future years Iraq will replace her in that role.

## Notes

1. Ministry of Planning, Central Statistical Organisation, *Annual Abstract of Statistics, 1978* (Baghdad, n.d.).

2. For a comprehensive account of the development of higher education in Iraq, see A. Al-Qazza, 'Development of Higher Education in Iraq, 1900-1972', *Third International Conference of the Center for Arab Gulf Studies* (Basra, March 1979).

3. Specific targets for development in the education sector are outlined in K.I. Kassab, 'Manpower Development in Iraq 1976-1980', a paper presented to the conference on *Population, Migration and Employment* (Arab Planning Institute/International Labour Office, Kuwait, December 1979).

4. See *MEED, Iraq*, 'Oil, Investment and Planning', 3 June 1978, for further details of Iraq's reserves.

5. *MEED*, 17 February 1979, p. 26.

6. Further details are given in K.S. McLachlan, 'Iraq' in R.M. Burrell *et al., The Developing Agriculture of the Middle East* (Graham and Trotman, London, 1976), pp. 41-53.

7. *MEED*, 'Cautious Economic Strategy Gives Way to Ambitious Plans', 31 December 1978, p. 47.

8. *MEED*, 8 July 1977, p. 24.

9. *MEED*, 10 February 1978, p. 28.

# PART III: THE PSEUDO-CAPITAL-RICH STATES

# 8 THE STATE OF BAHRAIN

## 1 Introduction

Three countries are described as pseudo-capital-rich in this book. The group describes states which do have some oil endowment, but only on a limited scale and whose financial resources are concomitantly finite. In this they contrast sharply with the states in the preceding section of the book. In the pseudo-capital-rich states, financial constraints are a real and frequently felt limit to development planning. They are therefore much more circumscribed in overcoming the deficiencies in their human capital, being unable to import migrant workers on the scale of the countries dealt with previously. These states nevertheless enjoy a degree of flexibility of development beyond that of the true capital-poor states. What is of concern is whether the pseudo-capital-rich states, having overestimated this flexibility, and being influenced by their capital-rich neighbours, have over-extended themselves in their efforts to develop. With limited oil reserves, but a small population, Bahrain falls firmly into the category of pseudo-capital-rich.

Bahrain enjoys a central position in the Arabian Gulf and this has lain behind a tradition of trading and commerce reaching back several thousand years. Today, Manama is a thriving commercial centre, rivalling Beirut and Dubai for leadership in the Arab world in this regard. Yet, compared to her neighbours, Bahrain is poor, with a small and declining oil output. The development of the entrepôt trade, an aluminium industry and dry dock have created sources of income and employment unrelated to oil. In a sense, then, Bahrain is ahead of the true capital-rich states, her relative poverty has obliged planners in Bahrain to take decisions about creating alternative income from a more diversified economy. Bahrain has apparently succeeded in the strategy to which all Arab oil-exporting states aspire, albeit at a level which the capital-rich states might consider humble. Historically, Bahrain has been remarkably successful at exploiting her resources and situation. Her capacity to take advantage of opportunities to create a diversified and partly self-reliant economy was stimulated by declining oil revenues in the late sixties and early seventies. By 1973 the government had made considerable progress towards creating non-oil-reliant income and employment.

Against this background, the upsurge of spending in the Arabian Gulf and peninsula after 1973 is a mixed blessing for Bahrain. She benefited from increased trade and investment in the region, and received considerably larger sums in loans, grants and aid than previously. Prior to 1973, Bahrain's fiscal position had been distinctly weak; it is now much improved. However, the cost of this enhanced pace of economic development has been a substitution of the trend towards self-sufficiency by a growing dependence on external support, both financially and in terms of labour. Migration to Bahrain increased considerably with greater development expenditure.

In recent years Bahrain's booming economy and growing use of migrant labour has given the impression that she is a typical capital-rich state; in reality her resources are quite limited. Sooner or later her relative poverty will reassert itself and the scale of development planning and expenditure will have to be revised or, alternatively, a permanent and pervasive dependence on her more wealthy neighbours will become self-reinforcing.

## 2 The Supply of Labour

### (a) Population

Bahrain is a state composed of thirty islands to the north-west of Qatar, most of which are small and uninhabited.[1] Because of Bahrain's trading tradition, the people are mixed ethnically between Persians, Bahraini Arabs and Asians. The Bahraini Arabs themselves are composed of Shi'ite Arabs of Persian and Iraqi extraction, and more orthodox Sunni Arabs. Some are of African descent, originally associated with the slave trade.[2] The population has grown steadily since oil was found, but not as rapidly as that of Kuwait or Qatar. The 1941 census showed a total population of about 90,000, 16 per cent of whom were non-Bahrainis.[3] In 1971 the total population had risen to 216,078 persons; non-Bahrainis had only risen to 17.5 per cent.

The Bahraini population is extremely young: in 1971, 48.4 per cent of the population was aged less than 15 years. The crude birth rate rose suddenly after World War II as improved medical facilities became of general access.[4] There are no reliable records of births and deaths, but the birth rate is still high. Consideration of the two population censuses of 1965 and 1971 establishes the approximate mortality level of Bahrainis. Using United Nations' life tables, Bahrainis are found to have a mortality level of 82.5, and a life expectancy at birth of 61.8 years at birth in 1971.[5]

Between 1965 and 1971, the Bahraini population increased at a rate of 3.6 per cent per annum. The non-Bahraini community declined slightly, from 38,390 persons in 1965 to 37,880 persons in 1971. Consequently the Bahraini share of the total population rose slightly over the period from 79 per cent in 1965 to 82 per cent in 1971 (Table 8.1).[6] These demographic details show clearly a profound difference between Bahrain and her neighbours, Kuwait and Qatar. The share that expatriates account for is relatively small, and between 1965 and 1971 actually fell, in sharp contrast to the situation in other Gulf states.

Considering more recent population growth, between 1971 and 1976 Bahraini nationals increased at an annual rate of 3.6 per cent. Contemporaneously, however, the number of non-nationals almost doubled, and over this period their share rose from 17 to 24 per cent.[7] This sharp reversal of the trend in the proportional size of the expatriate community was caused by the sudden influx of migrants in 1974 and 1975. The growth of the expatriate community between 1973 and 1976 was substantial.

### (b) Educational Characteristics of the Population

Measures of the educational status of the population date from the 1971 census. Table 8.2 shows that the educational development of Bahrain's population (measured by literacy rates) is, by comparison with its Gulf neighbours, relatively high. Only in Kuwait is a higher proportion of the population literate.

Bahrain experienced modern education long before any other Gulf state and has continued to allocate a large proportion of the budget to education for several decades. Social historians have disagreed over the date when formal education actually began in Bahrain. Rumaihi[8] and Winder[9] have observed that the first modern 'school' in Bahrain, apart from the many *kuttab* schools, was a girls' primary school opened in 1892 by the American Arabian Mission. Other commentators have seen 1919 as the time modern education began in Bahrain, when a school was financed by the merchants of the community.[10] In any event, education made an early start in Bahrain relative to other Gulf states, and between 1919 and 1932 other schools opened, including a girls' school and a special boys' school for members of the 'Shia' sect, who would not enrol in other schools for religious reasons. In 1932 the responsibility and administration of all education in Bahrain was handed over to the government.[11]

The first secondary school to open was the Technical School, in 1938. This was followed by 'Manama College' in 1940, a general sec-

Table 8.1: Bahrain: Population by Nationality, 1965, 1971 and 1976

| Nationality | 1965 | | | | 1971 | | | | | 1976 | | |
|---|---|---|---|---|---|---|---|---|---|---|---|---|
| | Men | Women | Total | Per cent of Total | Men | Women | Total | Per cent of Total | Growth Rate per annum 1965 to 1971 (per cent) | Total | Per cent of Total | Growth Rate per annum 1971 to 1976 (per cent) |
| Bahrainis | 72,370 | 71,450 | 143,820 | 78.9 | 89,770 | 88,420 | 178,190[a] | 82.5 | 3.6 | 224,650 | 76.1 | 3.6 |
| Non-nationals | 27,020 | 11,370 | 38,390 | 21.1 | 26,540 | 11,340 | 37,880 | 17.5 | -0.2 | 70,530 | 23.9 | 13.2 |
| Total | 99,390 | 82,820 | 182,210 | 100.0 | 116,310 | 99,760 | 216,070 | 100.0 | 2.8 | 295,180 | 100.0 | 6.4 |

Note: a. Amended to 188,000 to allow for under-enumeration of babies and small children.

Sources: Ministry of Finance and National Economy Statistical Bureau, *Fourth Population Census of Bahrain* (Manama, 1966), Table 20, p. 11; ibid., *Statistics of the Population Census, 1971* (Manama, n.d.), Form 5, p. 8; ibid., *Statistical Abstract, 1976* (Manama, 1977), Table 21, p. 30; J.S. Birks and C.A. Sinclair, *Nature and Process of Labour Importing: The Arabian Gulf States of Kuwait, Bahrain, Qatar and the United Arab Emirates*, World Employment Programme Working Paper (ILO, Geneva, August 1978), Table 4, p. 47.

Table 8.2: Literacy Rates: Bahrain, Kuwait, Qatar, Saudi Arabia, Oman and the United Arab Emirates in Selected Years by Nationality

| State | Literacy Rate (per cent) | | | Population Sample |
| | Nationals | Non-Nationals | Year | |
| --- | --- | --- | --- | --- |
| Bahrain[1] | 47.1 | 47.0 | 1971 | 10+ |
| Kuwait[2] | 52.7 | 66.4 | 1970 | 10+ |
| | 55.4 | 71.1 | 1975 | 10+ |
| Qatar[3] | 32.8 | 34.9 | 1970 | 14+ |
| Saudi Arabia[4] | 30.2 | n.a. | 1974 | 10+ |
| Oman[5] | 20.0 | n.a. | 1975 | 14+ |
| UAE[6] | 13.6 | 32.3 | 1968 | 14+ |

Sources:
1. Ministry of Finance and National Economy, *Statistical Abstract 1972* (Manama, 1973), Table 14, p. 17.
2. Planning Board, *Population Census, 1970, 1975* (Kuwait), various tables.
3. Ministry of Information, *Population Census, 1970* (Doha, n.d.), Table 9.
4. Ministry of Finance and National Economy *Census of Population in the Kingdom of Saudi Arabia, 1974* (Damman, 1978).
5. G. Fischer and A.M. Muzaffar, 'Some Basic Characteristics of the Labour Force in Bahrain, Qatar, United Arab Emirates and Oman', a paper presented to the Conference on Human Resources Development (Kuwait, Arab Planning Institute, 1975).
6. Ministry of Planning, *Population Census, 1968* (Abu Dhabi, 1968).

ondary school for boys. In 1928 the first Bahrainis enrolled in the American University of Beirut. By 1956, a total of 114 students were studying abroad in some capacity or other. The first students to receive teacher training graduated from the Manama College in 1944, and were sent to Cairo to train there. In 1951 the first secondary schools for girls opened, and in 1956 some of the graduates were sent to the Beirut College for Women to be trained as teachers.

The pattern of schooling in Bahrain has altered slightly several times. The current arrangement is that six years primary is followed by two years at the intermediate level, followed by three years in the secondary level. It is planned to extend the intermediate level by one year, thus providing twelve years' education. In 1960, 23,000 pupils were enrolled in Bahrain's schools. Almost all were in the primary level, with only 2.3 per cent of total enrolment in the secondary level, as Table 8.3 shows. Between 1960 and 1976 a more evenly balanced system developed, and by the later year secondary school enrolment accounted for 14 per cent of the total. Both enrolment and the breadth of distribution increased. In 1976, 14 per cent of all pupils were in secondary schools and their total number overall was 63,000, an annual increase of 6 per cent.

The most remarkable educational development between 1966 to 1976 was the expansion of girls' enrolment in secondary schools to the point where they now outnumber boys at that level. Although rather fewer girls than boys enter primary school, their drop-out rate is lower than boys'. Explanations are obvious: alternative opportunities for boys outside school are more numerous and the incentive for girls to acquire academic qualifications is greater, since these are the essential pre-requisite to employment in the modern sector for Bahraini women. Nevertheless, these changes were not predicted ten years ago. Their implications for the labour market are profound; more Bahraini girls will work or at least enter work in the coming decade than have ever done so before. Many of these will be well educated.

Table 8.3: Bahrain: School Enrolment by Level and Sex in 1960/1 and 1976/7

| Level | 1960/1 | | | | 1976/7 | | | |
| | Male | Female | Total | Per cent | Male | Female | Total | Per cent |
|---|---|---|---|---|---|---|---|---|
| Primary | 13,670 | 7,390 | 21,060 | 92.0 | 24,610 | 19,120 | 43,730 | 69.6 |
| Inter-mediate | 1,070 | 260 | 1,330 | 5.7 | 5,400 | 4,520 | 9,920 | 15.8 |
| Secondary | 430 | 110 | 540 | 2.3 | 4,280 | 4,890 | 9,170 | 14.6 |
| Total | 15,170 | 7,760 | 22,930 | 100.0 | 34,290 | 28,530 | 62,820 | 100.0 |

Sources: Ministry of Education, *Educational Statistics 1961/71* (Manama, 1972); ibid, 'Educational Statistics for the Academic Year 1976/77' (mimeograph, 1977).

Again in contrast to other Gulf states, Bahrain is almost self-suffic-ient in teachers, though the number of boys enrolling in the teacher training college has fallen in recent years. In 1976/7 Bahrain relied on some 770 expatriate teachers, 27 per cent of the total. Recently, an experiment in redisposition of resources has proved very effective: women teachers working in boys' schools at the primary level. So suc-cessful has this experiment been in Bahrain that it has been dupli-cated by Kuwait. Qatar is considering following this example to ease the shortage of teachers. Each of these states enjoys an abundant supply of indigenous women teachers, but a dwindling supply of their male colleagues. Such a redistribution of manpower is a rational res-ponse to this position, and may prove to be a yet more sound policy as more well educated women enter the labour market. It also has many advantageous wider implications.

## 3 The Demand for Labour

### (a) Introduction

Bahrain's income from oil is only a small fraction of that enjoyed by Saudi Arabia, Kuwait or even Qatar. Consequently, Bahraini economic development has the objective of creating wealth and raising the standard of living for her people rather than of distributing oil revenues. In 1975, 77 per cent of all Bahraini households were earning less than $250 per month.[12] The annual oil income *per capita* of *nationals* in 1970 was $195, compared with $3,599 for Kuwait and $6,368 for Qatar.

Bahrain's development strategy aims to utilise domestic factor endowments which centre on the limited amount of oil, substantial reserves of natural gas, substantial work-force by Gulf standards, and a central position in the Arabian Gulf. Three elements can be distinguished in the strategy: to extract, but also to refine indigenous oil; to develop entrepôt activities, associated with a communications and commercial centre; and to create alternative income to oil revenues, particularly through the aluminium smelter and allied industries. Underlying the strategy is a concern to create employment for Bahrainis in a domestic modern sector. This employment should be productive and, preferably, foreign exchange earning.

### (b) Economic Development

As early as 1932, Bahrain's wells produced about 84 barrels per day. By 1940 the average output per day had been raised to 19,380 barrels,[13] and reached a maximum in 1970 of 76,640 barrels per day. Since then well-head pressure has fallen steadily and this, combined with the desire to conserve remaining stocks, has led to a sharp decrease in output, as Table 8.4 shows.

Having the first refinery in the area, Bahrain also benefited from the production of Saudi Arabian oil. Bahrain's oil-based revenue now comes from four sources; local crude oil production, refining activities; the Abu Safah oilfield, which is shared with Saudi Arabia, and natural gas reserves. In 1935 the Bahrain government received $118,000 from Bapco's crude oil production, in 1950 $1,937,500.[14] By 1970 her total oil income was $36.2 million.

The discovery of large reserves of natural gas has come at a crucial time for Bahrain; indigenous reserves of crude oil are thought to have only 20 years of life left at declining rates of production. The significance of the natural gas lies in its potential as a source of cheap energy.

Table 8.4: Bahrain: Crude Oil Production, 1970 to 1977 (barrels per day)

| Year | Oil Production (barrels per day) |
|------|-------------------------------|
| 1970 | 76,640 |
| 1971 | 74,920 |
| 1972 | 69,880 |
| 1973 | 68,350 |
| 1974 | 67,340 |
| 1975 | 61,120 |
| 1976 | 58,320 |
| 1977 | 55,970 |

Source: Ministry of Finance and National Economy, *Statistical Abstract 1977* (Manama, 1978).

Reserves are estimated at between 8,000 and 11,000 billion cubic feet.[15]

*(c) Government Revenue and Expenditure*

After oil was discovered government income increased. Traditional sources of government income (customs duties) accounted for a progressively smaller proportion of revenue from 1935 onwards. Oil produced an increasing share of revenue, especially after the price increases of 1973.

Table 8.5 summarises revenue and expenditure; it is evident that the large share which current expenditure absorbed in the early 1970s has been overtaken by capital expenditures. This reflects the government's concern to create non-oil-related sources of employment for the island's population. The projects prominent under capital expenditures include the dry dock, the increasing government stake in the aluminium plant and infrastructure investments, including the extension to the port.

Overall since 1974, the budget surplus has been decreasing, and reached a deficit position in 1976, despite the much larger oil revenues since 1974 and budget support from abroad. Bahrain has been able to finance the budget only by making transfers from her state reserve fund, which by 1977 stood at $433 million.

In recent years Bahrain's increasing imports have overtaken exports and oil revenues. However, if invisible earnings and loans are included, the position remains in surplus. Bahrain's invisible earnings are already substantial and are planned to increase through the expansion of banking centres and the hotel industry.

Table 8.5: Bahrain: Government Revenue and Expenditure, 1973 to 1977 ($ million)

|  | 1973 | 1974 | 1975 | 1976 | 1977 |
|---|---|---|---|---|---|
| Revenue |  |  |  |  |  |
| Oil | 75 | 262 | 277 | 394 | 379 |
| Non-oil | 40 | 46 | 60 | 87 | 114 |
| Grants | – | 7 | – | 2 | 76 |
| Total | 115 | 315 | 337 | 483 | 569 |
| Expenditure |  |  |  |  |  |
| Current | 88 | 112 | 169 | 223 | 281 |
| Capital | 19 | 85 | 135 | 289 | 325 |
| Total | 107 | 197 | 304 | 512 | 606 |
| Budget deficit (−) or surplus (+) | + 8 | +118 | + 33 | − 29 | − 37 |

Source: Ministry of Finance and National Economy, 'Financial Report, 1977' (Bahrain, mimeograph, n.d.).

A high level of imports in a time of economic expansion and industrial diversification is inevitable. However, it is presumably envisaged that the level of imports will fall in the proximate future, as Bahrain is highly dependent on foreign loans to balance payments at present.

Table 8.6: Bahrain: Balance of Payments, 1972 to 1976 ($ million)

|  | 1972 | 1973 | 1974 | 1975 | 1976 |
|---|---|---|---|---|---|
| Exports |  |  |  |  |  |
| Exports and re-exports | 218 | 382 | 459 | 531 | 875 |
| Government receipts | 125 | 190 | 661 | 702 | 1,002 |
| Total | 343 | 572 | 1,120 | 1,233 | 1,877 |
| Imports | − 507 | − 828 | − 1,126 | − 1,473 | − 2,482 |
| Balance of visible trade | − 166 | − 256 | − 6 | − 240 | − 605 |
| Invisibles and loans | + 142 | + 196 | + 289 | + 553 | + 741 |
| Net balance of payments | − 24 | − 60 | + 283 | + 313 | + 136 |

Source: Ministry of Finance and National Economy, various publications (Manama).

## (d) The Economy

Apart from oil, the entrepôt trade dominated the Bahraini economy until the 1960s. The entrepôt trade is significant not only through the customs duties which augment government income, but also because it generates considerable employment. In 1960, concerned that she would lose the pre-eminent position in the re-trading business, Bahrain expanded the port to handle six vessels of 30-foot draught. In addition a 'free transit area' was created adjacent to the docks. Bahrain has plans to expand the entrepôt trade further by capitalising on harbour facilities and close proximity to Saudi Arabia. A causeway is planned from Bahrain to Saudi Arabia, along which imports to Bahrain will be re-exported quickly by road transport rather than, as presently, by sea.

The principle feature on the industrial scene of the 1970s has been the development of Aluminium Bahrain Ltd (Alba). Formed in 1969, Alba consisted of a consortium of aluminium brokers and the Bahraini government.[16] Bahrain was selected as a suitable location largely on account of its large reserves of (cheap) natural gas and the availability of a reasonably able work-force. In 1972 the aluminium plant reached its planned output of 120,000 tons per annum. As the largest industrial venture presently operating in the Arabian peninsula, it has been remarkably successful. A network of aluminium-related industries is beginning to develop, using Bahrain's cheap natural gas. These include a paint factory, an atomiser and an aluminium extrusion plant (Balexco) which is producing window frames, doors and small structures. Not only do these projects constitute a source of foreign exchange earnings, but, as one Minister is quoted as saying in reference to Alba: 'even if the profit per ton is $0.01, Alba is still feeding 5 per cent of the families on the island.'

Banking activities have expanded and the Bahrain Monetary Authority has created an 'offshore banking centre' which has more than 30 licensed operators. The centre is highly successful, as major international banks have taken out licences, and in 1978 assets stood at $15.7 billion. The expanding offshore banking units represent a growing foreign exchange earner for Bahrain and, of the 2,000 jobs which these banks have created, about 1,500 are held by Bahrainis.[17] Low taxation rates and easy profits have attracted foreign banks to Bahrain.[18] Also a significant encouragement to business is the external communications system of Bahrain, which is unrivalled in the Gulf.

An increasingly complex 'productive' service industry has been developed, which includes the Bahrain Ship Repairing and Engineering Company. This concern has two small slipways, capable of taking ships for repair up to 1,000 tons dead weight. On another scale is the Arab Shipbuilding and Repair Yard Company's (ASRY) new dry dock. The $340 million project was completed in the autumn of 1977 and is now in full operation. It is capable of handling tankers of up to 400,000 tons dead weight. Reports from Bahrain suggest that the dock is used almost to capacity. Other productive and foreign exchange earning services are represented by the expansion of Gulf Air (in which Bahrain has a stake) activities on the island. Bahrain is a calling point for intercontinental flights to east Asia and Australia. Apart from aircraft servicing, there are possibilities of generating a tourist trade. The historical legacy of Bahrain, the reasonable climate for part of the year, and the recent improvements in hotel facilities make tourism a real, if limited, possibility for Bahrain in the future.

### (e) Conclusion

The Bahraini economy is passing through a period of transition, during which time the government is attempting to create the basis for a non-oil-supported future. But such diversification is costly, and the economy is in a deficit position in terms of both her budget and balance of payments if external support is excluded. This can be evaluated in two ways, either as an inevitable step in preparing for an oil-less future, a step during which infrastructure and manufacturing investment are at their height, or as the beginning of a permanent dependence on Saudi Arabia. At the moment, the Kingdom provides Bahrain with financial support in several ways. Bahrain's links with Saudi Arabia will grow, particularly as the causeway has an impact on the Bahraini economy and society.

More optimistically, Bahrain's capital stock does now include a large-scale aluminium plant, a dry dock, plus ancillary industrial facilities, all of which provide a means of livelihood for the Bahraini population, and are a source of foreign exchange. The potential for expanding Bahrain's productive services is good.

In the past Bahrainis have proved well able to manage their relatively limited resources to good effect. Even bearing Bahrain's limited size and oil revenues in mind, she has an established position in the Gulf as a manufacturer and commercial centre. By most standards, the future would appear to be reasonably bright. However, Bahrain's economic objective must be to use the financial wealth she temporarily enjoys to create future income without becoming permanently dependent on her neighbours. If such dependence materialises, it would be arguable that in the 1970s Bahrain's development had regressed.

### 4 The Labour Market

Bahrain's labour market is clear evidence of one facet of her erstwhile economic independence of other countries. In 1971, migrants comprised only 37 per cent of the work-force (numbering 22,000). Moreover, their share of all employment was falling. However, the spurt of economic growth following 1973 drew in a large number of migrants, and by 1976 both their number and their proportional share of all employment had increased (Table 8.7).

The rate of increase in the number of economically active Bahraini men between 1965 and 1971 was 3.0 per cent per annum and of women 11 per cent. The growing incidence of women working is readily seen on the island; from 1971 to 1976 their rate of increase in employment was over 12 per cent per annum. In the 1970s, the rate of increase in employment of Bahraini men (4.1 per cent) is much closer to the normal level. Total Bahraini employment in 1976 was approximately 47,000 persons.

An estimate of non-Bahraini employment in 1976, made by combining arrivals and departures data with the known crude participation rates of 1971, provides a figure of about 30,000 non-Bahrainis in employment in 1976. Since this time the number has risen further (Table 8.8).

### 5 Migrant Workers in Bahrain

In 1971, immigrant Asians accounted for about one-third of the expatriate population and just over a quarter of the non-national workforce. Immigrant Arabs accounted for half the non-national population and work-force. However, between 1971 and 1977 the share of total non-national population absorbed by the Arab community fell from 45 per cent to 15 per cent. The Asian contribution rose from 32 per cent to 67 per cent (Table 8.9). The decline in the Arab share is a result of two factors: first, 10,000 Omanis left Bahrain while only 4,000 extra Egyptians and Yemenis took up residence; secondly, the expatriate community was growing very rapidly over the period. This increase was largely accounted for by the immigrant Asian community, which rose from 12,000 in 1971 to 51,000 by 1977.

In terms of employment there is an equally sharp trend: the Arab share of employment of 54 per cent (1971) falls to 16 per cent (1977), while the Asian share rises from 27 per cent (1971) to 65 per cent (1977) (Table 8.10). Therefore, Asian labour now accounts for a substantial majority of the non-Bahraini population and work-force. This is in sharp contrast to the situation in 1971, when Bahrain's expatriate population was predominantly Arab in nature.

Table 8.7: Bahrain: Employment By Sex and Nationality in 1965, 1971 and 1976

| | | 1965 | | April 1971 | | 1965-71 Annual per cent Increase | January 1976 | | 1971-6 Annual per cent Increase |
|---|---|---|---|---|---|---|---|---|---|
| | | Number | Per cent | Number | Per cent | | Number | Per cent | |
| Bahrainis | Men | 30,240 | — | 36,100 | — | 3.0 | 43,570 | — | 4.0 |
| | Women | 990 | — | 1,850 | — | 10.9 | 3,240 | — | 12.6 |
| | Total | 31.230 | 58.6 | 37,950 | 62.9 | 3.3 | 46,810 | 60.8 | 4.5 |
| Non-Bahrainis | Men | 21,010 | — | 20,950 | — | — | — | — | — |
| | Women | 1,030 | — | 1,400 | — | 5.2 | — | — | — |
| | Total | 22,040 | 41.4 | 22,350 | 37.1 | 0.2 | 30,180 | 39.2 | 6.5 |
| Grand total | | 53,270 | 100.0 | 60,300 | 100.0 | 2.1 | 76,990 | 100.0 | 5.3 |

Note: a. The period April 1971 to January 1976 is taken to be 4.75 years.

Sources: Ministry of Finance and National Economy, Statistical Bureau, *Census, 1965, Census, 1971* (Manama, Bahrain); J.S. Birks and C.A. Sinclair, *Country Case Study: Bahrain,* International Migration Project (Durham, 1978), Table 22.

Table 8.8: Bahrain: Size of Migrant Labour Force and Number of
Work Permits Issued, 1971 to 1977

| Year | (1)<br>Labour Force | (2)<br>Work Permits<br>Issued over Year |
|------|---------------------|------------------------------------------|
| April 1971 | 22,350 | 5,920 |
| 1 January 1972 | 17,350 | 3,790 |
| 1 January 1973 | 17,650 | 5,650 |
| 1 January 1974 | 21,880 | 6,500 |
| 1 January 1975 | 22,000 | 11,450 |
| 1 January 1976 | 30,180 | 14,980 |
| 1 January 1977 | 39,700 | |

Sources:
1. Calculated from information in Ministry of Finance and National Economy,
*Statistical Abstracts 1972 and 1976* (Bahrain, 1977).
2. Ministry of Labour and Social Affairs, Manpower Section, *Work Permits Issued,
1971-1976* Bahrain, December 1976).

Table 8.9: Bahrain: Non-National Population of Working Age by
Nationality, 1971 and 1977

| Nationality | April 1971[1] | | January 1977[2] | |
|-------------|--------|----------|--------|----------|
| | Number | Per cent | Number | Per cent |
| Gulf Arab | 2,290 | 6.0 | 2,690 | 3.6 |
| Omani | 10,780 | 28.6 | 650 | 0.9 |
| Iraqi | 80 | 0.2 | 120 | 0.2 |
| Northern Arab | 1,670 | 4.4 | 1,610 | 2.1 |
| Egyptian | 590 | 1.5 | 3,560 | 4.7 |
| Other Arab | 1,590 | 4.2 | 2,720 | 3.6 |
| (Total Arab) | (17,000) | (44.9) | (11,350) | (15.1) |
| Indian | 6,660 | 17.6 | 23,200 | 30.9 |
| Pakistani | 5,380 | 14.2 | 22,810 | 30.4 |
| Other Asian | 180 | 0.5 | 4,600 | 6.1 |
| (Total Asian) | (12,220) | (32.2) | (50,610) | (67.5) |
| Iranian | 5,100 | 13.4 | 2,960 | 3.9 |
| Others | 3,560 | 9.4 | 10,080 | 13.5 |
| Total | 37,880 | 100.0 | 75,000 | 100.0 |

Sources:
1. Ministry of Finance and National Economy, Statistical Bureau, *Census, 1971*
(Manama, 1971).
2. As in Table 8.1.

As might be expected, this change in the composition of the non-
national work-force has been associated with changing labour market
structures and processes similar to those which have been observed in
the capital-rich states. It is possible to observe the evolution of the

Table 8.10: Bahrain: Migrant Work-Force by Nationality in 1971 and 1977

| Nationality | April 1971 | | June 1977 | |
|---|---|---|---|---|
| | Number | Per cent | Number | Per cent |
| Gulf Arab | 1,120 | 5.0 | 1,200 | 3.0 |
| Omani | 8,640 | 38.7 | 525 | 1.3 |
| Iraqi | 40 | 0.2 | 50 | 0.1 |
| Northern Arab | 700 | 3.1 | 640 | 1.6 |
| Egyptian | 260 | 1.1 | 1,560 | 4.0 |
| Other Arab | 1,370 | 6.1 | 2,350 | 5.9 |
| (Total Arab) | (12,130) | (54.2) | (6,325) | (15.9) |
| Indian | 3,790 | 16.9 | 13,200 | 33.2 |
| Pakistani | 2,170 | 9.7 | 9,220 | 23.2 |
| Other Asian | 130 | 0.6 | 3,340 | 8.6 |
| (Total Asian) | 6,090 | 27.2 | 25,760 | 65.0 |
| Iranian | 2,590 | 11.7 | 1,510 | 3.8 |
| Others | 1,540 | 6.9 | 6,105 | 15.8 |
| Total | 22,350 | 100.0 | 39,700 | 100.0 |

Source: Ministry of Finance and National Economy, Statistical Bureau, *Census, 1971* (Manama, 1971).

Bahraini labour market in some detail. The aluminium plant was built by a labour force integrated into the Bahrain labour market at large. The construction was therefore associated with a rapid expansion in the size of the Bahraini labour market. The growth in the labour market was largely accounted for by immigration of Indians and Pakistanis. Their movement to Bahrain was partly spontaneous, but largely in the hands of agents, who recruited the workers in the Indian subcontinent.

Many of the Indian and Pakistani workers who arrived in Bahrain to build the aluminium plant used the opportunity to establish themselves on the island permanently. It is they and their dependents who represent in large part the increase in the number of immigrant Asians between the late 1960s and early 1970s.

It was because of their experience with the labour force that constructed the Alba plant, and in particular because so many of the immigrants used the Alba contract as a means of establishing themselves permanently as part of the Bahraini community, that a different strategy was adopted for the construction of the dry dock. The Bahraini dry dock represented the pioneering of the enclave, work camp approach to major projects in the Arabian peninsula. A South Korean company provided the entire work-force and expertise for this major contract, which they completed on schedule. During construction the Koreans, who consisted of only single men (or married men employed on a bachelor basis), working twelve-hour shifts, were entirely self-sufficient in housing, which they built themselves as part of the contract. Food and even recreation were flown in from Korea. The host government was asked only to provide a minimal amount of services -- water and power -- and virtually nothing in the way of more general services, such as housing, education or health. Moreover, the enclave approach meant that there was only minimal contact between Koreans and the local Bahrainis, and a minimal disruption of the domestic labour market. It was this that was so attractive to the Bahrainis. During the building of the Alba plant, the Bahraini labour market had suffered considerable distortion. This had been associated with what the Bahrainis considered to be an inordinate amount of social upheaval. Both these disadvantageous facets of large-scale infrastructure provision were overcome by the enclave, work camp nature of the contract. Perhaps most important in the minds of the Bahrainis, though, was the virtually complete departure of the Koreans on the completion of the dry dock contract; this contrasted very favourably with the dallying of so many of those involved in the construction of the Alba contract.

Being an island site, the dry dock construction could be run as an enclave development *par excellence*. The advantages which organisation of this kind bestowed upon the host country in minimising local labour market disruption whilst maximising development were quickly evaluated by the other labour-importing states -- the five capital-rich countries. Thus Bahrain, despite not being a major oil exporter, pioneered the labour market developments now common to all the capital-rich states. Not only is the fabric of Bahrain's economy of a nature towards which the capital-rich states aspire, but Bahrain's means of diversification has also served as a source of inspiration to the major oil exporters.

## 6 Conclusion

By comparison with her immediate neighbours, Bahrain must be thought of as small and poor. Yet Bahrain's economy is the most mature and diversified in the Arabian peninsula with a complex blend of manufacturing and productive service industries. Of significance in labour market terms is the full productive participation of so many Bahraini nationals over a wide spectrum of activities within the economy. Bahrain has never been able to afford expensive expatriate staff on a wide scale, and the number of foreigners has therefore necessarily been limited. Almost paradoxically, then, this relatively humble level of wealth has proved to be advantageous in the development of Bahrain's human capital.

It is not yet clear whether Bahrain's economy will in the medium term regain the independence that has characterised it in the past, and stand on its own without external financial support; at the moment Bahrain is heavily dependent upon her neighbours. The post-1973 oil price increases and the consequent increase in the general wealth of the area have had a positive 'spin-off' benefit for Bahrain, as her own revenues have increased comparably with a higher volume of aid, loans and grants from her Arab neighbours. The combined effect of these has been to set in motion a surge of spending in the economy and, optimistic commentators might regard, growth. However, one side-effect of this has been a sudden demand for migrant labour which the now enriched economy could purchase: the slowly evolving character of the Bahraini labour market has changed sharply. Bahrain is becoming more dependent upon imported labour.

The 1980s will show whether Bahrain's present path of development is one which is creating greater strength within the economy or a perpetual dependence on neighbours for financial contributions and on labour suppliers to the east for an essential component of her workforce.

As a pseudo-capital-rich state Bahrain must avoid the temptation to believe that by behaving like a capital-rich state she will become one. Bahrainis may not be able to see this distinction so clearly, however, and the present style of development and rate of spending may transform their attitudes into expectations of expenditure and wealth on this scale forever. Adjusting to the reality of Bahrain's slender resources in the 1980s may be a traumatic experience.

## Notes

1. For a fuller account of the geography of Bahrain, see J.H.D. Belgrave, *Welcome to Bahrain* (Auguston Press, Beirut, 1970).
2. In M. Rumaihi, *Bahrain: Social and Political Change since the 1st World War* (Bowkers, London, 1978), the author provides a full account of the ethnic origins of the Bahraini people.
3. Statistical Bureau, *Statistical Abstract 1972* (Bahrain, 1973), Table 5, p. 9.
4. I. Yacoub, 'Family Planning in Bahrain', *ECWA First Population Conference* (ECWA, Beirut, 1974).
5. See C.A. Sinclair, 'Education in Kuwait, Bahrain and Qatar: An Economic Assessment (unpublished PhD thesis, Durham University, 1977), p. 80.

6. See Economic Commission for Western Asia, 'An Overview of the Population Situation in Bahrain', *Population Bulletin, 14* (June 1978), pp. 57-69.

7. J.S. Birks and C.A. Sinclair, *The Nature and Process of Labour Importing: The Arabian Gulf States of Kuwait, Bahrain, Qatar and the United Arab Emirates,* World Employment Programme Working Paper (ILO, Geneva, 1978).

8. M. Rumaihi, *Bahrain: Social and Political Change Since the 1st World War* (Bowkers, London, 1978).

9. R.B. Winder, 'Education in Al Bahrayn', *The World of Islam* (London, 1959), p. 310.

10. For example A.M. Al-Hamer, *The Development of Education in Bahrain, 1940-1965* (Oriental Press, Bahrain, 1969), p. 7.

11. An administrator's personal experience of education is given in C. Belgrave, *Personal Column* (London, 1960).

12. Llewelyn-Davies, Weekes, Forestier-Walker, *National Housing Policy Study* (Bahrain, 1974).

13. *Bahrain Petroleum Company, Annual Report, 1973/74* (Bahrain, 1975).

14. A. Al-Kuwari, *Oil Revenues of the Arabian Gulf Emirates: Pattern of Allocation and Impact on Economic Development* (Bowkers, London, 1978).

15. Supplement on Bahrain, *Financial Times*, 10 October 1976, 'Reserves are now reliably estimated between 8,000 and 11,000 billion cubic feet', p. 19.

16. United Nations Inter-Disciplinary Reconnaissance Mission, *Bahrain* (Beirut, 1973), p. 51.

17. A. Fyfe, 'Development Bond Satisfies Main Needs', Supplement on Bahrain, *The Times*, 16 December 1977, p. VII.

18. R. Azzi, 'Bahrain Dinar, a Gulf Currency', *Orient, 12*, 4 (Hamburg, 1971), pp. 3-5.

# 9 THE SULTANATE OF OMAN

## 1 Introduction

Oman, although often considered one of the Gulf states, is in reality quite different from them. The Sultanate is much larger, with an area of some 260,000 square kilometres (in contrast to an average of about 9,290 square kilometres for Kuwait, Bahrain and Qatar), and has a bigger national population than most of the Gulf states. These differences between Oman and the Gulf states are compounded by the relatively small oil reserves of the Sultanate. Ranking about eleventh in the league of Middle Eastern Oil exporters, Oman's rate of extraction is already falling. Recent finds in Dhufar, in the south, will stem this decline only for a while.

Despite this, the Sultanate is embarking upon a pattern of rapid economic development similar to that of the Gulf states. The urban-biased programme of industrial growth and diversification has taken priority over agricultural development, despite the Sultanate's endowment of farmland and irrigation water supplies. Although groundwater for irrigation will prove a more severe constraint upon agricultural development than was thought in the early 1970s, Oman's agricultural potential will be a major asset over the next two decades.

The Sultanate has changed rapidly over the past seven years, but before 1970, when it was called Muscat and Oman, it had stagnated under the reactionary rule of Sultan Said bin Taimur. The influence of the world outside was minimised; even other Arabs found it difficult to enter the Sultanate, and indigenes were forbidden to travel internationally.[1] Under these conditions there was only a minimum of social change and economic growth.

Thus, although the rate and absolute nature of the transformation through which Oman has passed in the 1970s has been extreme even by Middle East standards, the economic base from which Oman began to develop in 1970, when the more liberal Sultan Qabus deposed his father, was particularly small. Oman therefore still lags behind the Gulf states, with which it is so often associated, in terms of virtually all socioeconomic indicators.

The growth of the economy has been hindered by the war in Dhufar, which continues sporadically, absorbing a large proportion of government expenditure. Today, the Sultanate's Air Force (now separate from ground forces) is second in the peninsula only to Saudi Arabia's. The Sultan maintains a strong anti-Communist line, made significant by Oman's strategic location at the Hormuz straits, the neck of the Arabian Gulf.

## 2 The Supply of Labour

### (a) The Size of the National Population

The paucity and inadequacy of Omani statistics are well illustrated by the available demographic data. Considerable disagreement still remains over the size of the population. Recent estimates of the number of Omanis vary from 300,000 to 1,500,000.[2] Politically motivated figures range yet more widely. So little is known about the Sultanate's population that there has been a tendency for it to have been ignored in regional labour market calculations. Thus the labour force estimates and projections of the International Labour Office[3] do not list Oman separately, but aggregate it with other (much smaller) territories in the area.

The lowest estimate of the Omani national population to be commonly quoted is 330,000. The figure stems from a programme of cholera inoculation in 1971, when teams could only find this number of Omanis to inoculate throughout the country.[4] However, detailed field inquiries have since showed that substantial numbers of the population had not been inoculated.[5] Some villagers evaded the medical teams, which did not find all the isolated and mobile households. The population is therefore greater than 330,000. In 1971 the estimate quoted in the National Census Bureau Handbook for 1972 was 450,000 and was probably based upon somewhat tentative military estimates.

The most detailed inquiry was based upon a lengthy field investigation, house-counting and use of aerial photographs. This yielded a figure of 435,000.[6]

Two other estimates have been based upon similar detailed field-work. A population figure was calculated by Italconsult for a transport survey,[7] who felt the 1972 figure of 600,000 quoted by the World Bank to be too high. Italconsult's independent assessment gives a total population of 480,000 (1974/5). Extrapolation of a regional demographic study yielded a figure of 550,000, distributed by region similarly to the Italconsult estimates (Table 9.1).

Although several other studies have evaluated the populations of various regions of the Sultanate, they go little way towards establishing

Table 9.1: Oman: Estimate of Population by Region, 1975

| Region | Number | Per cent |
|---|---|---|
| Muscat/Matra | 44,000 | 8 |
| Batina Coast | 176,000 | 32 |
| Interior | 242,000 | 44 |
| Dhufar | 44,000 | 8 |
| Desert area | 33,000 | 6 |
| Musandum Peninsula | 11,000 | 2 |
| Total | 550,000 | 100 |

Source: J.S. Birks and C.A. Sinclair, *The Sultanate of Oman: Economic Development, The Domestic Labour Market and International Migration* (ILO, Geneva, 1978), pp. 3 to 6.

the national total.[8] They do, however, confirm those national estimates which have included regional assessments. For example, the Human Resources section of the Report on the Water Resources Survey of Northern Oman[9] can be used to confirm that the Italconsult figures are of the correct order. Even the population of the capital area of the Sultanate is not accurately known, estimated as between 35,000 and 50,000.[10] It is therefore particularly unfortunate that a 1975 sample census of the five major towns in Oman has not been published.

In summary, it is unreasonable to use a figure of over 1 million; the return of erstwhile exiles has not been on the scale necessary to inflate the national figure to that level. Furthermore, no detailed survey confirms a figure as high as 800,000. In contrast, the estimates of below 450,000 can also be reasonably discounted. The total of Omani nationals is between 450,000 and 600,000. Circumstantial evidence suggests the total to be nearer 600,000 than 450,000 and a figure of 550,000 is adopted in this book.

Sample surveys suggest a sex ratio of between 104.5 and 105.[11] The slight excess of men over women might seem surprising in a society which has recently suffered tribal warfare and a degree of national disruption, but it might be caused by the high maternal death rate.[12] The population of the Sultanate is a young one with some 46 per cent of the population aged less than 15 years. The numbers about to enter the labour force are considerable.

*(b) The Educational Attainment of the Population*

*The Eclipse of the Traditional Education System.* The government has made great strides in the provision of modern educational facilities. In 1970, most Omani children were only receiving very basic traditional education in the Koran and *sharia* law in village-based *kuttab* schools. To assert that, in terms of economic development, the population was benefiting substantially from these institutions would be wantonly optimistic (see Chapter 1). The shortcomings of these schools caused the government to embark upon the provision of new primary schools, staffed predominantly by expatriate teachers, rather than use the *kuttab* as a basis on which to build modern primary education. Only in villages which are too small to justify the provision of a school has the traditional system been reinforced. In these instances, the payment of the teacher has been taken over by the government.

Before 1970, Muscat and Oman was not entirely without modern education. There were three government primary schools, some secondary teaching in Muscat, Matra and Salala, and an American mission school which provided limited elementary education. These schools together only gave education to some 800 pupils, but those pupils were influential; apart from their having been educated outside the *kuttab* school system, they were also of the leading families.

*The Establishment of a New Educational Order.* The modern school system consists of three levels; a primary level of six years, followed by three years' preparatory, after which there are a further three years' secondary education. The growth from three state schools in 1970 to over 200 institutions by 1976 is a remarkable achievement. Numbers of pupils increased from less than 1,000 in 1969/70 to over 55,000 in the academic year 1975/6, and some 2,230 teachers were employed in 1976. Over a quarter of these teachers are female. Government current expenditure on education has risen from $1.3 million (1971) to over $14.7 million (1975). Moreover, some $6.7 million were spent on development expenditure in education in 1974 and $6.2 million in 1975. The numbers who have progressed to preparatory and secondary level are still small (Table 9.2)

Not all children of school age are as yet receiving formal education; some because of the geographical remoteness of their places of residence. Others live within the catchment areas of schools, but either have not responded to the opportunity of formal education, or have been denied it by some of the schools being too full to take them. Some older children are an essential part of the domestic economy and cannot leave their active economic role for school without disrupting the household. The proportion of school-age children attending school is difficult to determine because of doubts about the absolute population size. If the lower estimate of the Sultanate's population (450,000)

Table 9.2: Oman: Numbers of Pupils by Academic Year and Education Level, 1969/70 to 1975/6

| Schools | 1969/70 | 1970/1 | 1971/2 | 1972/3 | 1973/4 | 1974/5 | 1975/6 |
|---|---|---|---|---|---|---|---|
| No. of pupils | | | | | | | |
| Total | 900 | 6,941 | 15,332 | 24,481 | 35,565 | 49,229 | 55,752 |
| Male | 900 | 5,805 | 13,382 | 20,409 | 27,691 | 36,851 | 40,708 |
| Female | – | 1,136 | 1,950 | 4,072 | 7,874 | 12,378 | 15,044 |
| Primary | 900 | 6,941[a] | 15,332 | 24,335 | 35,225 | 48,576 | 54,457 |
| Male | 900 | 5,805 | 13,382 | 20,303 | 27,430 | 36,351 | 39,640 |
| Female | – | 1,136 | 1,950 | 4,032 | 7,795 | 12,225 | 14,817 |
| Preparatory | | | | 146 | 318 | 571 | 1,095 |
| Male | | | | 106 | 239 | 437 | 925 |
| Female | | | | 40 | 79 | 134 | 170 |
| Secondary | | | | | 22 | 82 | 200 |
| Male | | | | | 22 | 63 | 143 |
| Female | | | | | | 19 | 57 |

Note: a. Includes some pupils of pre-primary age.
Source: Ministry of Planning, *Statistical Yearbook, 1976* (Muscat, 1976), Tables 10 and 11, pp. 14, 15.

is accepted, then 42 per cent of 5- to 9-year-olds would be in school as would 40 per cent of 10- to 14-year-olds.[13] If the larger population estimate of 600,000 is considered, the picture does not, of course, look as good. The proportion of children in full-time education between the ages of 5 and 14 falls from 33 per cent to 25 per cent. The critical 5 to 9 age group drops to 31 per cent enrolled in formal education.

There is also a marked difference between the availability of education to boys and girls. Taking the larger population estimate, almost 37 per cent of boys are enrolled, but only 14 per cent of girls. This differential is declining, a desirable trend because there are specific reasons why the education of Omani women should bring about particular benefits.[14]

There were over 370 Omanis receiving higher education abroad in 1975/6. Apart from 180 students in Oman's own new Technical Institute, others receive trade and technical education in the oil company (Petroleum Development (Oman) Ltd). Unfortunately, only few Omani migrants for employment outside the Sultanate receive formal education.

Migration has increased Oman's stock of human capital, however, by the return migration of previously exiled Omanis. Originating mostly from East Africa and therefore referred to as 'Zanzibaris', though having lived in the Gulf and Saudi Arabia, this group is better educated than Omanis who remained within the Sultanate. Although the immigrants' initial contribution was hampered by their lack of facility in Arabic — they are literate in Swahili and English — they are now taking a larger role.

Whilst the provision of formal education in the Sultanate has made great strides, a great deal of work remains. Care must be taken to monitor the direction in which the system is evolving. There are signs that it is falling — with an arts bias — into the pitfalls observed in other states with more mature systems. This should be avoided in the Omani case, especially in view of the more limited oil endowment. The more limited finance means that the planners will have to define the Sultanate's population realistically if resources within education are to be allotted to best effect.

### 3 The Demand for Labour

*(a) Introduction*

In 1969 the Sultanate's economy was largely agricultural, and mainly subsistence. Barter was common and money circulation very low. Fisheries made an important contribution, and there were some traditional exports of dates, dried limes as well as fish, mainly to Iran, the Gulf and India. By the late 1960s, the trade with East Africa, previously an important aspect of the economy, was merely a relict feature. An important aspect of this otherwise traditional economy was an injection of cash, in the form of remittances from migrant labourers in the Gulf states and Saudi Arabia. These remittances undoubtedly began to alter an economy with so little other cash available.

This traditional state of affairs was little disturbed when exports of oil began in 1967. The limited income from the sales of this oil (21 million barrels) was not injected fully into the economy. Relatively gentle evolution, with limited government expenditure, continued until 1970, when Sultan Qabus transformed government policy into one of less restrained growth.

So began the 'New Oman', the development of which was facilitated in 1973, despite a falling off in the quantity of oil exported, by the rise in crude prices. Table 9.3 shows petroleum exports rising until 1970, when a peak of 121 million barrels was attained. After this, production dropped to a plateau of between 100 and 110 million barrels until 1975, when almost 125 million barrels were exported following the discovery of new fields. Exports have since fallen again. The limited potential to export oil is crucial to an assessment of Oman's future. Despite the new finds in Dhufar, which will yield some 70,000

Table 9.3: Oman: Exports of Petroleum, 1967 to 1975 (millions of barrels)

| Year | Exports |
|------|---------|
| 1967 | 20.9 |
| 1968 | 88.2 |
| 1969 | 119.2 |
| 1970 | 121.3 |
| 1971 | 106.3 |
| 1972 | 103.2 |
| 1973 | 106.9 |
| 1974 | 105.8 |
| 1975 | 124.8 |
| 1976 | 134.4 |
| 1977 | 123.1 |
| 1978 | 114.7 |

Source: Ministry of Planning, *Statistical Yearbooks* (Muscat).

barrels per day in the mid-1980s, the government does not expect output to rise above the peak output of 1976. Indeed, recoverable reserves are still only estimated to be equivalent to 12 years' production at current rates of extraction.[15]

### (b) Government Revenue and Expenditure

Omani government revenue from oil amounted to 96 per cent of all revenue in 1971; 94 per cent in 1974; and 81 per cent in 1975, for example. However, despite the similarity of this with other capital-rich states, the economy of the Sultanate is quite different in character. Since 1972 the Sultanate has been running a budget deficit (Table 9.4). This is the background to Oman's increasing international debt, and in particular her application to the World Bank for a loan to help implement the new national plan.

Despite Oman's not being a true capital-rich state, there are signs that the economy is suffering problems which more usually occur in Gulf states, for example a rapid rise in current expenditure since 1971. Capital expenditure, though increasing in absolute terms, comprises a progressively falling proportion of government expenditure.[16] Such a high level of current expenditure is a dangerous trend which the Sultanate can ill afford. It diverts relatively limited funds from development expenditure, and precipitates the crisis which will occur when, in the face of falling oil incomes, government current expenditure will have to be cut.

Another factor which has drained resources which otherwise might have been devoted to capital formation is the war in Dhufar. In 1975,

Table 9.4: Oman: Government Revenue and Expenditure, 1971 to 1978 ($ million)

| Year | Government Revenue | Current Expenditure | Capital Expenditure | Total Expenditure | Surplus Deficit |
|------|------|------|------|------|------|
| 1971 | 128.5 | 66.7 | 51.3 | 117.9 | + 10.6 |
| 1972 | 135.9 | 106.9 | 76.7 | 183.6 | − 47.7 |
| 1973 | 221.0 | 203.2 | 96.5 | 299.7 | − 78.7 |
| 1974 | 1,074.5 | 648.4 | 616.6 | 1,265.0 | −190.5 |
| 1975 | 1,351.2 | 948.5 | 508.8 | 1,457.6 | −106.7 |
| 1976 | 1,486.5 | 1,134.1 | 573.8 | 1,707.9 | −221.4 |
| 1977 | 1,752.0 | 1,110.9 | 426.6 | 1,537.5 | +214.5 |
| 1978 | 1,380.0 | 1,265.7 | 751.4 | 2,017.1 | −637.0 |

Source: Ministry of Planning, *Statistical Yearbooks* (Muscat).

defence absorbed about 74 per cent of current spending, and 39 per cent of gross capital formation. Development in Dhufar is part of the overall war effort in the south, and has meant that this area has received a disproportionately large amount of government expenditure in terms of the population resident in the area.

Expenditure on defence and growing current expenditure has brought about a deterioration of the financial position of the government. Combined with an increased monetary supply, this has caused rapid inflation, in turn bringing about an import boom; values of imports have risen from $47 million in 1971 to $1,025 million in 1975 and $1,232 million in 1978. Consequently, the balance of payments has been under pressure, and has had to be protected by international loans.

Despite the recent finds of oil, these financial constraints to development will continue to be of significance, and are likely to tighten.

## (c) Gross Domestic Product and Economic Growth

Annual increases in gross domestic product have been of the order of 20 per cent in 1971; 12 per cent in 1972; 235 per cent in 1974. Estimated GDP for 1978 is $2,548 million.

Table 9.5 shows that growth has been related to oil revenue (the mining sector). The proportional contribution to GDP of agriculture and fisheries has fallen from 16 per cent in 1970 (in 1967 it was much larger than this, 80 per cent plus) to 3 per cent in 1974. Manufacturing contributes only from 0.2 per cent to 0.4 per cent. The sector grew in monetary terms from $0.5 million to $6.9 million – a small increase in view of internal inflation in Oman.

Thus over the period of oil exports, although growth of GDP has been great, neither agriculture nor manufacturing has benefited greatly. Oman has as yet made little progress towards diversification on a national accounting level of appraisal. Indeed, in 1977 GDP has fallen in line with reduced oil exports.

The GDP *per capita* puts Omani government revenue in a Middle Eastern perspective. If the smallest population estimate (450,000) is considered, then *per capita* GDP amounts to some $3,590 (1975). If the population were 1,500,000, GDP *per capita* plummets to $1,070 and the most realistic value for 1977 is about $2,930 *per capita.* Upon this figure, and its ranking compared to other nations, depends many aspects of the Sultanate's status in the Middle East and in the world as a whole, particularly in terms of requests for international aid, for example. Aid will become an important aspect of Oman's future policies,

Table 9.5: Oman: Gross Domestic Product by Industrial Origin, 1970 and 1974 ($ million)

|  | 1970 | | 1974 | |
| --- | --- | --- | --- | --- |
| Sector | $ million | Per cent | $ million | Per cent |
| Agriculture and fisheries | 42.6 | 15.8 | 60.0 | 3.1 |
| Mining (oil) | 183.6 | 68.5 | 1,341.4 | 68.3 |
| Manufacturing | 0.5 | 0.2 | 6.9 | 0.4 |
| Construction | 21.8 | 8.2 | 200.0 | 10.2 |
| Transport and communication | 1.8 | 0.7 | 42.4 | 2.2 |
| Electricity and water | 0.3 | 0.1 | 4.1 | 0.2 |
| Trade | 4.1 | 1.5 | 93.8 | 4.8 |
| Banking | 1.5 | 0.5 | 12.0 | 0.6 |
| Ownership of dwellings | 3.8 | 1.4 | 16.6 | 0.8 |
| Public administration and defence | 5.9 | 2.2 | 160.0 | 8.2 |
| Other services | 2.6 | 0.9 | 23.1 | 1.2 |
| Total | 268.5 | 100.0 | 1,960.3 | 100.0 |

Source: Ministry of Planning, *Statistical Yearbook 1975* (Muscat, 1976), Table 88, p. 114.

and a large determinant of her rates of growth.

In Oman, though, national *per capita* income conceals wide disparities between the urban and rural sectors. The Sultanate is developing along dual economy lines — despite the potential importance of the rural sector, it is not receiving high priority in development. The structure of development accounting, which until recently grouped agriculture together with petroleum and minerals, makes it difficult to be precise, but since 1973 the proportion of development expenditure devoted to agriculture has fallen. Unlike Saudi Arabia and Libya, which will be able to expand the modern economy to engulf the rural population presently in the traditional sector, the Sultanate's financial resources may not be sufficient to do so. This is, of course, of considerable significance to the future of the labour market.

### 4 The Labour Market

#### (a) The Growth of the Labour Force

At the end of 1975, the private sector employed about 93,000. In early 1976 the number working in the public sector amounted to 15,000, besides some 15,000 in the armed forces. In total, about 123,000 were employed in the modern sector of the economy where growth has been dramatic. Government employment has risen from 1,100 in 1966, an annual increase of 30 per cent. Private-sector employment was only 35,000 in 1972. The increase to about 90,000 has largely been the result of expansion in the construction industry, which now dominates employment in the private sector (Table 9.6).

Numbers employed in agriculture, fishing and crafts in rural areas are impossible to establish with certainty. The *Statistical Yearbooks* make no estimate, nor does the national plan. This omission is particularly significant because rural activities account for some 26 per cent of the economically active.

## (b) The Contribution of Immigrant Labour

The rapid growth which Oman has undergone since 1970 has been very largely dependent upon immigrant labour that the booming economy has drawn in. Indeed the number of expatriates working in Oman is now one of the outstanding features of the economy. Such dependence upon expatriate labour in the capital-rich states might be expected, but is remarkable in the case of Oman for two reasons. First, the Sultanate is not capital-rich, financial constraints to growth have already been experienced. Secondly, Oman is herself a labour exporter; despite her own shortage of labour at all skill levels, she is an important source of labour for the wealthier states of the Gulf and Arabian peninsula, and in particular for Abu Dhabi.[17]

The 14,000 migrants in the private-sector labour force in 1972 had increased to a recorded 65,000 by 1975/6. In fact, there were more than 65,000 expatriates in Oman in 1975/6, because of the numbers entering Oman illegally. They continue to live without residence or work permits, and so continue unenumerated. Neither stocks nor flows of illegal immigrants can be determined accurately. Certainly, in 1974, several hundreds of Asians and a number of Arabs were deported, all were found to be living in the Sultanate without the necessary permits. However, these were not the total number of unregistered aliens, and subsequently the demand for labour has risen substantially. No corrective factor can be used as a multiplier with confidence. Within all occupational categories except service workers and labourers (where migrants are under-enumerated) they comprise a majority of the labour force. This is highly undesirable in a nation which has such a low *per capita* income. By 1975/6 provisional estimates suggest that the proportion of migrant workers had risen to over 70 per cent of the modern sector. Only in the case of service workers is the dependence upon migrant workers decreasing. The contribution of migrants by sector in 1975 is shown in Table 9.7.

Non-nationals are also important in the public sector and comprised more than a quarter of all employment in 1976/7. In the public sector

Table 9.6: Oman: Employment by Type and Nationality, 1975

| Type of Employment | Nationals | | Non-Nationals | | Total | |
|---|---|---|---|---|---|---|
| | Number | Per cent | Number | Per cent | Number | Per cent |
| Rural | 46,850[a] | 34.2 | 10,000 | 12.3 | 56,850 | 26.0 |
| Private sector | 28,000 | 20.5 | 65,000 | 80.0 | 93,000 | 42.6 |
| Civilian public sector | 11,000 | 8.0 | 4,000 | 4.9 | 15,000 | 6.9 |
| Army | 12,750 | 9.3 | 2,250 | 2.8 | 15,000 | 6.9 |
| Workers abroad | 38,400 | 28.0 | – | – | 38,400 | 17.6 |
| Total | 137,000 | 100.0 | 81,250 | 100.0 | 218,250 | 100.0 |

Note: a. This is an estimated figure which assumes a low rate of participation by women in rural areas.
Sources: Authors' estimates based on J.S. Birks and C.A. Sinclair, *The Sultanate of Oman: Economic Development, The Domestic Labour Market and International Migration* (ILO, Geneva, 1978); and Ministry of Planning, 'The National Economic Development Plan for the Sultanate of Oman' (Muscat, typescript, n.d.) (Arabic).

Table 9.7: Oman: Employment in the Private Sector by Nationality
and by Economic Sector, 1975

| Economic Sector | Total | Nationals | Non-Nationals | |
|---|---|---|---|---|
| | | | Number | Per cent of Total |
| Petroleum and mining | 4,679 | 2,892 | 1,787 | 38.2 |
| Manufacturing | 2,199 | 825 | 1,374 | 62.5 |
| Building and construction | 75,236 | 18,640 | 56,596 | 75.2 |
| Trade | 2,764 | 923 | 1,841 | 66.6 |
| Hotels | 2,614 | 1,420 | 1,194 | 45.7 |
| Transportation | 3,080 | 2,286 | 794 | 25.7 |
| Financial institutions | 1,122 | 668 | 454 | 40.5 |
| Services | 1,302 | 348 | 954 | 73.2 |
| Total | 92,996 | 28,002 | 64,994 | 69.8 |

Source: Ministry of Planning, 'The National Economic Development Plan for the
Sultanate of Oman' (Muscat, typescript, n.d.) (Arabic).

too, the Sultanate has found herself short of labour at all levels of skill
and expertise. The government has even had to employ unskilled Asian
labour on a large scale. At the other end of the scale, there are over 200
special advisers at the most senior level, all of whom are expatriate.

*(c) Omanis Abroad*

In view of the extent to which Oman imports labour, it is surprising
that so many of her national work-force are employed abroad. Of a
sample of males of between 14 and 40 years old, 74 per cent were
absent from home in 1974. Only 12 per cent had not spent at least six
months away from home as a wage earner. In 1975, some 38,000
Omanis were employed outside the Sultanate. Most of these were
drawn from the rural areas and so this migration represents a considerable withdrawal of labour from the agricultural system. Although expansion in the role of women has in part compensated for this, the
result is a marked decline in the rural sector, accentuating the dual
economy.[18]

As long as there is a differential in both opportunities and real incomes between Oman and her more developed neighbours, labourers
will leave rural areas. The equalisation of real wages between Oman and
the Emirates would not be enough to stop migration; only opportunities of employment and career development in Oman comparable to
those in Abu Dhabi would cause spontaneous reduction in the numbers
migrating.

Perhaps more important to many Omanis than the actual differential in incomes are these wider opportunities available abroad. Although

work is undoubtedly available locally within the Sultanate, not only is it less remunerative than work in, for example, Abu Dhabi, but it is less desirable to the Omani. A large number of migrants are driven abroad not to find work, but to find easy work. There is always likely to be a greater number of sinecures in the wealthier Arab countries, so this attitude is likely to cause a continuing movement for some time to come.

The future is not bright. At the present, many indications point to a widening in these differentials between Oman and Abu Dhabi, Saudi Arabia and Dubai. Real incomes, especially of poorer people, are being eroded by persistent high inflation in Oman. In, for example, Abu Dhabi, lower-income groups have been able to keep up with inflation rather more closely than in Oman. Omanis are well able to appreciate this, and many are prepared to act upon the realisation.

Also important is 'the tradition of migration' which is developing within Omani society. Kudos associates with the migrant labourer; those who do not depart to seek work are often thought to be lacking in initiative. In short, migration is now fashionable in Oman.

### (d) The Future of the Labour Market

Despite the development plan containing some optimistic growth forecasts, over the four-year period from 1976 to 1980, total employment in the modern sector is expected to fall by almost 10,000 jobs in 1980. The main reason for this decline is a 35 per cent reduction in construction employment in 1980. GDP from construction is also expected to fall from $220 million to $142 million in 1980. The transport sector is also expected to shed employment. Other sectors are not expected to be able to mop up this unemployment even by the most optimistic assessment. Already there are some problems in employing the growing number of educated Omanis who are returning home from studying abroad.

This fall in employment is a major issue. It is planned that most of the decline be met by reduction in the expatriate labour force – the number of economically active expatriates falling by 32,000, whilst numbers of Omanis in employment should increase by 23,000. It is also planned that Omanis should increase to 65 per cent of modern-sector employment in 1980 from 41 per cent in 1976. For this to occur, some 5,600 Omanis per year will have to enter the modern-sector labour force, 1,900 into the public sector and 3,700 into the private sector. There must, given the conditions noted, be serious doubts about whether this can be achieved.

## 5 Conclusion

The Sultanate of Oman, after 1973, embarked upon a headlong rush of economic development modelled upon the capital-rich states of the Gulf. Indeed, the Sultanate behaved in every way as though it were truly capital-rich, embarking at once upon a large programme of infrastructure provision and diversification of the economy based upon an urban focus. Development was executed by private-sector companies, and the Sultanate claimed to be heading for a diversified free enterprise economy. As in the oil exporters of the Gulf, growth was accompanied by rapid inflation, and the development of a large immigrant worker population.

So rapid was this development effort that, as in the other large rapidly developing states of Saudi Arabia and Libya, an acutely drawn dual economy developed. This was exaggerated by the emigration of Omanis from the rural sector, which precipitated rapid decline in agricultural productivity and infrastructure. The rural decline was effectively ignored by planners who focused on developing the modern-sector economy and social services, such as education.

The Sultanate, however, is not capital-rich. Limited resources combined with the war have already brought financial constraints to bear upon the rate of development. Loans have already proved essential to protect the balance of payments. Future development will have to rely increasingly upon external financing as oil revenues fall in real terms. Recent oil finds have not altered this.

Against this picture, Oman's modern-sector development objectives appear increasingly optimistic. But even these optimistic estimates encompass a contracting labour market as the construction phase is passed.

Thus Omani planners have worked themselves into an awkward position from where they aim to achieve increased Omani participation in the modern sector at a time when the modern-sector labour force is declining and when financial constraints to further growth are becoming more stringent. The declared aim of replacing immigrant labour by Omanis will be difficult to effect. It has been found so in the true capital-rich states, where development expenditure is much less constrained. Under the particular conditions prevailing in Oman, it will be especially awkward.

Planners are attempting to entice Omanis into the domestic modern sector at a time when more attractive opportunities are available in neighbouring states. Moreover, it is not clear whether Omanis are at all well enough qualified to participate more effectively in their domestic economy — many are in sinecures abroad. Certainly the educational base is low, and training facilities limited. Also limited are finances with which to expand technical and scientific education. This contrasts markedly with Saudi Arabia, which proposes effectively to 'buy' her rural population into the modern sector. Oman will never be able to afford this.

Furthermore, in ignoring agriculture, Omani planners have neglected what must be a future mainstay of the economy. With its decline, not only are rural Omanis today disposed against an agricultural livelihood, but the decline of infrastructure means they will be unable to derive one in the future.

In short, the profligate spending of the early part of the decade, when Oman embarked upon a Saudi Arabian style of economic development, has to come to an end. In its wake will be a series of major problems which have been made more acute than if development had been more gentle and better thought out. The position of the rural populations of Oman is likely to become increasingly unsatisfactory as agricultural decline continues, but without subsidies from oil revenues or an industrial sector. These populations will find the range of alternatives opening to them declining, despite some improvement in their educational status. Nevertheless, the modern sector will continue to be staffed largely by expatriates. The Sultanate has unfortunately allowed itself to be drawn into a situation in which its economy is suffering or is about to suffer the more acute disadvantages of both labour exporting and labour importing.

## Notes

1. I. Skeet, *Muscat and Oman:The End of an Era* (London, 1974); J. Townend, *Oman: The Making of a Modern State* (Croom Helm, London, 1977); and J.E. Peterson, *Oman in the Twentieth Century: Political Foundations of an Emerging State* (Croom Helm, London; New York, 1978) all provide good background to the economic development of the Sultanate.

2. J.S. Birks, 'Aspects of Demography Related to Development in the Middle East', *Bull. British Society for Middle Eastern Studies, 2* (1976), pp. 79-87; and J.S. Birks and C.A. Sinclair *Aspects of the Demography of the Sultanate of Oman*, International Migration Project Working Paper (Durham. 1977).

3. International Labour Office, *Labour Force Estimates and Projections* (ILO, Geneva, 1977).

4. See also R.A. Mertz, *Education and Manpower in the Arabian Gulf* (American Friends of the Middle East, Beirut, 1972); J.A.Socknat, *Labour Market Conditions and Prospects in the Gulf States and Saudi Arabia* (Central Planning

Organisation, Amman, 1975).

5. Durham University Oman Research Project reports (unpublished).

6. Whitehead Consulting Group, *Sultanate of Oman: Economic Survey* (London, 1972).

7. Ministry of Communications and Public Services, Italconsult, *Oman Transport Survey, Interim Report* (Rome and Muscat, 1974).

8. See footnote 5.

9. Ministry of Communications, Sir A. Gibb and Partners, Institute of Hydrology, International Land Development Consultants, *Water Resources Survey of Northern Oman* (Muscat, April 1975).

10. Michel Ecochard Planning Office, *Study of the New Capital, Interim Reports* (Paris, 1973).

11. See J.S. Birks and C.A. Sinclair, *Movements of Migrant Labour from the North of the Sultanate of Oman*, International Migration Project Topic Paper (Durham, 1977).

12. See J.S. Birks and C.A. Sinclair, *The Sultanate of Oman: Economic Development, Domestic Labour Market and International Migration*, World Employment Programme Working Paper (ILO, Geneva, 1978).

13. Field inquiry does not support such large proportions of school attenders. This is one of the factors which suggests a population in excess of 500,000

14. J.S. Birks and S.E. Letts, 'The Changing Role of Women in a Rural Arab Society', *Journal of Gulf and Arabian Peninsula Studies, 2* (1977).

15. J. Whelan, 'International Monetary Fund Urges Broader Base for the Omani Economy', *MEED* (15 June 1979), p. 6.

16. In 1974, capital expenditure was boosted by the equity settlement for PD(O) Ltd.

17. J.S. Birks and C.A. Sinclair, *International Migration and Development in the Arab Region* (ILO, Geneva, 1980).

18. See, for example, J.S. Birks and S.E. Letts, 'Dying Oases in Arabia', *Tijdschrift voor Economische en Sociale Geografie, xviii*, 3 (1977), pp. 145-51; J.S. Birks 'Development or Decline of Nomads: the Case of the Bani Qitab', *Arabian Studies, V* (1977).

# 10 THE DEMOCRATIC AND POPULAR REPUBLIC OF ALGERIA

## 1 Introduction

More than any other Arab state Algeria has attempted to plan her economic and social development systematically. This is stimulated, to a great extent, by the limited life of the gas reserves, which makes planners feel that Algerian development has to be effected quickly, before income from gas falls. But planners have found the process of development to be a multifaceted one, not easily susceptible to political will or determination, however strong. Many economic and social problems remain after 18 years of central planning, and in some ways progress appears rather superficial. The accomplishments of Algerian planners in the field of hydrocarbon development are indisputable and impressive. In contrast, the performance of the agricultural sector and the growing volume of unemployed give rise to a questioning of the overall development strategy.

## 2 The Supply of Labour

### (a) Population

The population of Algeria in 1977 was some 16.9 million. It is estimated to be increasing at 3.2 per cent annually.[1] The Algerian population is characterised by a very high birth rate, estimated at 50 per 1,000 in 1969/70 compared with 46 per 1,000 in 1954.[2] Negadi *et al.* suggest that the crude birth rate has been about 40 per 1,000 for the last 50 years. Both men and women marry early in Algeria — the average age at marriage for women is 19 years and for men 24 years.[3] Uneducated women marry on average at 19 years, those completing primary education at 21 years, and those who achieve secondary and higher education at 24 years. In 1970, 81 per cent of Algerian women had received no formal education. However, the expansion of schooling for girls should reinforce this trend towards later marriage. A short-term increase in fertility as a result of the development of medicine and public hygiene could well, therefore, be offset by the growing percentage of girls receiving schooling and consequently marrying later. This suggests a tempering of the high birth rate in the medium term.

The mortality rate has declined from 27 per thousand in 1947 to 16 per thousand in 1970. Average life expectancy has risen from 46 years in 1948 to 53 years in 1970. Nevertheless, infant mortality remains very high. These demographic indices suggest a population of over 20 million by 1985, when 45 per cent of all Algerians will be under 15 years of age and 49 per cent in the active age groups (15-59 years). There will be an active male population of a little over 5 million by 1985. The population is becoming still more youthful. From 1936 to 1977 the proportion of Algerians under 15 years of age increased from 36 per cent to 47 per cent, a heavy burden on those of working age (15-59 years) who have fallen from 58 per cent to 47 per cent of the total population during this period.[4]

## (b) The Educational Status of the Population[5]

The educational status of the Algerian population is low; colonial neglect of education, disruption during the transition of power and the emigration of the more educated are all contributing factors. In 1970 52 per cent of men and 81 per cent of women were illiterate, giving an overall literacy rate of 33 per cent. However, since independence Algeria has set ambitious targets for its educational system which amount to a crash programme. In recent years education and training have received between 20 and 30 per cent of the current expenditure and 18 to 25 per cent of the capital budget. In 1977 these amounted to $840 million and $520 million respectively, representing approximately 9 per cent of the country's gross domestic product (one of the highest percentages of education expenditures in the world). Educational planning since 1962 has been mainly concerned with getting more students through the system. The actual number of children now receiving basic education is impressive, and the universities and technical colleges are turning out large numbers of graduates, technicians and engineers.

In 1976 to 1977 some 2.8 million children (of whom 59 per cent were boys (Table 10.1) enrolled in 8,180 primary schools. This represents an annual increase in enrolment between 1962 and 1977 of 9 per cent. In the same year there were 70,500 primary school teachers giving a pupil-teacher ratio of 39 to 1. In 1977, 73 per cent of all children between 6 and 13 years of age were enrolled in primary school (84 per cent of boys and 60 per cent of the girls). In 1976/7, 612,000 students were in middle and secondary schools. Some 66 per cent of students were boys.

In the same academic year 50,200 students (38,500 men) were en-

Table 10.1: Algeria: School and University Enrolment by Sex, 1976/7

|                     | Boys      | Girls     | Total     |
|---------------------|-----------|-----------|-----------|
| Primary             | 1,653,900 | 1,128,100 | 2,782,000 |
| Middle and secondary| 402,200   | 210,000   | 612,200   |
| University          | 38,500    | 11,700    | 50,200    |

Sources: Ministère de l'Education, *Informations Statistiques*, No. 15 (Algiers, May 1977); Ministère de l'Enseignement Supérieur et de la Recherche Scientifique, *Bulletin Statistique* (Algiers, May 1977), No. 6.

rolled in Algerian universities at undergraduate level and 2,310 at postgraduate level. A further 1,800 were studying in foreign universities, especially in France. The annual increase in university enrolment since 1962, when only 3,700 students were studying in university in Algeria, is impressive at 20 per cent. Apart from the Universities of Algiers, founded in 1909 under the colonial regime, Oran, Annaba and Constantine, a new technical university was opened in Algiers in 1974 and had 6,350 students in 1976 to 1977. Another technical university is being built in Oran. In 1976 to 1977 there were 5,380 university teachers, of whom 44 per cent were Algerian.

Algerian formal education has only just begun to adjust to the developmental needs of the country. The structure of university education has remained substantially intact since independence, reforms in 1971 only superficially altering the French academic orientation. The same is true of the schools. However, the notion that the objectives, content and methods of school and university teaching should be conceived with a specific user and a practical use in mind is increasingly preoccupying Algerian planners and educationalists.

The strong emphasis on science and technology presupposes a fast-growing labour market for technicians, engineers and workers trained in industrial skills. Yet Algerian industry is at present capital- rather than labour-intensive and currently employs only 343,000 workers, less than 10 per cent of the active population. There must be a question mark over how jobs will be found for the university students − who will total 150,000 in 1984/5 − and the 3 million children in primary schools, who will be on the job market in 10 to 15 years' time. The rapid expansion in the number of persons in the 15 to 24 age cohort will continue during the next five years creating the need for continual growth in job opportunities within the Algerian labour market. The number of economically active will grow at over 4.1 per cent during the next five years. The increasing proportion of labour market entrants with at least primary education will stimulate a concomitant increase in demand for modern-sector employment opportunities.

Overall, the quantitative targets achieved since independence are impressive. Presently at least 72 per cent of children receive some primary education. This contrasts favourably with the educational attainment of the currently active population, only 20 per cent of whom had in 1966 received a primary education and only 3.5 per cent training beyond primary level.[6]

This rapid expansion of the education system has produced problems. At the primary level the building of schools has not been able to keep up with the growth in numbers. A shift system has been introduced which gives the typical Algerian primary pupil two hours of schooling in the morning and two in the afternoon. Classes are 60 to 70 strong and discipline a major problem. Primary school teachers, the majority of whom are women, are overworked and absenteeism is a problem. Apart from poor conditions of work, salaries are low, promotion prospects are poor and teachers have little formal training. In short, the dramatic increase in primary and higher education since 1962 has inevitably surrendered quality to quantity.

Yet more serious than the problem of declining standards is the success of educationalists in enrolling school children; as the social demand for ever higher levels of education grows, so it will be harder for graduates of any level to find what they regard as suitable employment. In education, as in so many other spheres, it seems that Algerian planners have made what appear to be the right decisions, often at the price of some sacrifice, only to find that their actions hardly assist development and, on the contrary, are a burden to it. It is now almost inevitable that Algeria will have 'educated unemployeds' on the streets before long.

### 3 The Demand for Labour

#### (a) Political and Economic Background

At independence in 1962, Algeria faced enormous political, economic and social problems. The war had claimed the lives of thousands of Algerians and forced half a million to seek refuge in Morocco and Tunisia. Over 2 million people in rural areas had been uprooted from their homes under the pacification programme.

In June 1965 a Revolutionary Council assumed power headed by Colonel Houari Boumedienne. Boumedienne's government set about changing the basic structure of the Algerian economy by embarking on a programme of rapid industrialisation. Central to this were the so-called 'industrialising industries', huge, capital-intensive projects in-

cluding steelworks, petrochemical complexes, refineries and gas liquefaction plants based on Algeria's own natural resources. They are to
supply in turn the raw materials for the secondary sectors of industry,
producing vehicles, farm machinery, pumps, electrical goods and plas-
tics. At the same time the 'Agrarian Revolution', launched in 1972,
aimed to modernise the traditional agricultural sector, and to raise rural
incomes so that the rural population (50 per cent of the total) can
absorb the products of Algeria's new industries. Rural areas are planned
to provide raw materials for industry and to feed Algeria's growing
urban population. Planners hope that by the 1980s these development
programmes will solve the serious unemployment problem and permit
the reintegration into the economy of Algerian workers presently employed in Europe.

The high rate of investment – one of the highest in the Third World
– needed to implement Algeria's ambitious social and economic
policies has been made possible by oil and gas revenues. Equally,
though, large loans are raised in Europe and America on the strength of
future exports of oil and particularly liquefied natural gas. Although
Algeria's oil production is lower than the major Middle Eastern producers', the country possesses huge reserves of natural gas and hopes to
become the world's biggest exporter by the early 1980s. However, although markets for gas now appear secure, technical difficulties with
liquefaction plants and the heavy debts incurred to finance them have
caused considerable concern. The Algerian people have also had to
make sacrifices in order to maximise productive investment. Living
standards, already low, have been held down by a deliberate policy of
austerity.

In 1976 the World Bank suggested a GNP *per capita* of $900, a
figure, moreover, which conceals wide disparities in income. During the
1970s, real growth in GDP has been appreciable and the modern sector
has grown whilst the agricultural sector has declined in proportional
terms. Job creation in the modern sector has also been impressive, if
inadequate, expanding at over 5 per cent annually between 1973 and
1975. However, in spite of the high rate of investment, growth of industrial output has been slower than expected. Port congestion, inadequacy of transport and telecommunications facilities and shortages of
management, supervisory and skilled labour have impaired efficient
plant utilisation. Although not insurmountable, these difficulties constitute constraints on the productivity of Algerian industry that will
prevent growth from attaining its potential level for some years to
come. In particular the human aspect of industrialisation involves costly

investment and long lead times.

The priority given to industrial investment has aggravated the disparities and pressures existing between the development of industry and other sectors of the economy. Both urban development and agriculture have received inadequate investment resulting in acute shortages of housing and community facilities, stagnant agricultural production and a sizeable increase in imports of foodstuffs.[7] Housing problems have adversely affected recruitment of management and skilled workers to new factories, whilst the low level of investment in agriculture has limited the consumption of industrial goods by that sector. These intersectoral imbalances appear to be one of the most serious factors in Algeria's present economic situation, since they could considerably restrain the overall rate of development and cause serious problems in the industrial sector itself. However, the 1978 investment programme reveals a shift in sectoral allocations. Although hydrocarbons and industry still receive the lion's share of investment expenditure, allocations to education, urban housing, community development and urban modernisation have increased substantially in absolute terms.

All development plans implicitly reflect a compromise between economic and social objectives, investment and consumption. These most recent moves by Algerian planners suggest that in the future the general level of personal income and welfare may be permitted to rise to a higher level than in the past.

*(b) Gross Domestic Product*

Between 1974 and 1975 the economy grew, in real terms, at about 7 per cent. The majority of this growth is accounted for by increased value added in the hydrocarbons sector.

Table 10.2 shows clearly the dominance of industry, and in particular hydrocarbons, which will grow further. Of concern is the poor performance of the agricultural sector, which accounts for 7 per cent of national income, although half of the population is rural.

The price increases of 1974 were accompanied by a reduction in crude oil production. For both technical and commercial reasons, production of crude oil and condensate fell from 51 million tons in 1973 to 45 million tons in 1975. Natural gas production, however, rose rapidly, reaching 7.4 billion cubic metres in 1975 compared with 5.6 billion cubic metres in 1973.[8] Half of the gas output went to the two liquefaction plants for export. By 1985 gas production will have reached 73 billion cubic metres, when Algeria expects to be one of the world's largest exporters of gas.

Table 10.2: Algeria: Gross Domestic Product, 1977 ($ million)

| Economic Activity | $ million | Per cent |
|---|---|---|
| Agriculture | 1,353 | 6.9 |
| Mines and quarries | 78 | 0.4 |
| Industry | 7,631 | 39.0 |
| (of which hydrocarbons) | (5,342) | (27.3) |
| Construction | 2,583 | 13.2 |
| Water, electricity and gas | 231 | 1.2 |
| Private services | 3,966 | 20.2 |
| Government services | 2,545 | 13.0 |
| Import duties and taxes | 1,196 | 6.1 |
| Gross domestic product | 19,583 | 100.0 |

Source: Secrétariat d'Etat au Plan, *Données Globales sur l'Evolution de l'Economie Nationale, Année 1976 et Provisions de Réalisation de l'Année 1977* (Algiers, November 1977).

Oil and natural gas revenues continue to provide the principal source of income for the government, but oil reserves are moderate, about 1.0 million tonnes, equivalent to 20 years of production at present levels. These represent reserves similar to Qatar's. However, more important than oil are huge reserves of natural gas, estimated as 2.9 million million cubic metres. Revenue from oil will diminish but sales of natural gas will produce a maximum income between 1986 and 2000 of about $71 billion at today's prices. The prospect of considerable gas revenues for the government is tempered for two reasons. First, the investment necessary to extract, process and market the gas is formidable and appears to prejudice continually the development of other sectors of the economy. Moreover, little employment results from this investment in hydrocarbons. Secondly, Algeria has borrowed heavily from abroad to finance her hydrocarbon developments. Repayment of these monies will moderate the value of future oil and gas revenues. None the less, Algeria remains a safe borrower in banking terms, future revenues being so secure.

*(c) Development Planning*

The economy has been steered through successive development plans since 1966, the rationale for which has often been political. Examination of 'Development Objectives' in plans reflect the likely path of the economy. The most recent plan is the Second Four Year Development Plan, 1974 to 1977. The government's desire to speed up implementation of long-term development strategy shaped the investment policies of the plan. This decision was based on the results of the 1967 to 1973 planning period and the improved financial prospects of the government resulting from the new prices for oil and gas.

The 1974 to 1977 plan incorporated not only an acceleration of investment but also a rapid growth in private consumption – a marked change from the slow growth of consumption during the previous years. The sectoral composition of investment also changed, industry's planned share of investment being significantly smaller in 1974 to 1977 than in the previous plan: 44 per cent as against 50 per cent. Increased shares were allocated to agriculture, economic infrastructures and the social sectors. Furthermore, in order to avoid continued concentration of development in the cities of the Mediterranean coastlands, the plan 1974 to 1977 provided for increased assistance to rural and inland areas.

The general policy of development of hydrocarbons and industry is certain to continue into the 1980s, but the balance between social needs and economic objectives is becoming less clear-cut. Also, Algeria's agricultural sector, which continues to be a weak link in the economy, will have to receive yet more investment. The most challenging problem facing Algerian planners is the optimal form of economic development for the next decade; is yet more capital-intensive investment necessary, or should light industry be developed and thereby more unemployment mopped up? The decision is difficult and there is always the fear that once a particular path is chosen it may be irreversible, even if it proves unsuccessful.

### (d) Balance of Payments

Algeria's balance of payments since 1973 has been dominated by the revenues from oil and natural gas, a source of foreign exchange which has permitted Algeria to double her imports bill, primarily in respect of capital goods. When the investment phase of Algeria's hydrocarbon development is complete, this item should decline rapidly in significance, allowing more consumer imports. Foodstuffs accounted for 29 per cent of Algeria's import bill in 1977, a sign of the failure to revitalise agriculture.

## 4 The Labour Market

### (a) Employment

The earliest comprehensive information on the Algerian labour market comprises the first population census (1966). A second census was held in February 1977, but results relating to employment are not yet available. Other sources are published by the Secrétariat d'Etat au Plan,

Table 10.3: Algeria: Foreign Trade, 1973 to 1977 ($ million)

|      | Imports | Exports | Surplus (+) or Deficit (−) |
|------|---------|---------|----------------------------|
| 1973 | 2,489   | 1,952   | −  537 |
| 1974 | 4,483   | 4,947   | +  464 |
| 1975 | 6,986   | 5,459   | − 1,527 |
| 1976 | 5,334   | 5,329   | −    5 |
| 1977 | 6,974   | 6,357   | −  617 |

Source: Secrétariat d'Etat au Plan, *Données Globales sur l'Evolution de l'Economie Nationale, Année 1976 et Provisions de Réalisation de l'Année 1977* (Algiers, November 1977).

which provides the official view of labour force statistics, not necessarily an accurate account.

The design of Table 10.4 indicates the approach of Algerian planners. The labour market is seen as being divided between the agricultural sector and the non-agricultural sector, a division approximating to modern and traditional sectors. The non-agricultural sector has enjoyed the majority of government attention and investment, being seen as the provider of productive employment in the 1980s, primarily in industry.

Table 10.4: Algeria: Estimates of Employment by Sector 1973 and 1977

|  | 1973 | | 1977 | |
|  | Number | Per cent | Number | Per cent |
|---|---|---|---|---|
| Non-agricultural Sector |  |  |  |  |
| Employed | 1,410,000 |  | 2,100,000 |  |
| Unemployed | 200,000 |  | 209,000 |  |
| Total | 1,610,000 | 46.0 | 2,309,000 | 52.0 |
| Agricultural Sector |  |  |  |  |
| Regularly employed | 520,000 |  | n.a. |  |
| Part-time employed | 805,000 |  | n.a. |  |
| Seriously underemployed | 125,000 |  | n.a. |  |
| Total | 1,450,000 | 41.4 | 1,693,000 | 38.1 |
| Workers Abroad | 440,000 | 12.6 | 441,000 | 9.9 |
| Grand total | 3,500,000 | 100.0 | 4,443,000 | 100.0 |

Source: Secrétariat d'Etat au Plan, *Données Globales sur l'Evolution Nationale, Année 1976 et Provisions de Réalisation de l'Année 1977* (Algiers, November 1977).

The traditional sector holds about 38 per cent of the work-force, a share which is declining over time. Employment in the modern sector has grown at 9 per cent annually, a rate which is less impressive when set against the high level of investment in the economy during the period under review. Investment in industry in 1974 and 1975 totalled $4,960 million and 44,000 new jobs were created in this sector – an average investment of $112,700 per job. In all, the industrial sector provided about 343,000 jobs in 1977, 16 per cent of all modern-sector employment (Table 10.5).

Table 10.5: Algeria: Non-Agricultural Employment by Economic Sector, 1977

| Economic Sector | Number | Per cent |
| --- | --- | --- |
| Industry | 343,000 | 16.3 |
| Construction | 301,000 | 14.3 |
| Transport | 109,000 | 5.2 |
| Trade | 282,000 | 13.4 |
| Services | 260,000 | 12.4 |
| Handicrafts | 45,000 | 2.1 |
| Administration | 390,000 | 18.7 |
| Students, national service employees and others | 370,000 | 17.6 |
| Total | 2,100,000 | 100.0 |

Source: Secrétariat d'Etat au Plan, *Données Globales sur l'Evolution Nationale, Année 1976 et Provisions de Réalisation de l'Année 1977* (Algiers, November 1977).

Despite the ambitious industrial development schemes, the vast majority of job opportunities will occur outside the industrial sector in future years. The bias in education and training towards technical skills may be less appropriate than educationalists think. The unemployment figures for the non-agricultural sector must also be treated with caution (Table 10.4). The Office National Algérien de Main d'Oeuvre, for example, has criticised the employment strategy of the Secrétariat d'Etat au Plan, and has produced estimates of unemployment which are very much higher than those in the plan.

*(b) Algerians Abroad*

The number of Algerians employed abroad in the Arab world is extremely small.[9] In contrast, estimates suggest that about 900,000 Algerians were resident in Europe in 1976. Some 98 per cent of these lived in France, where about 441,000 Algerians worked, amounting to 10 per cent of the domestic work-force.[10] The skill distribution of this group suggests that generally it is those who are more skilled who have been able to find work abroad. Only 27 per cent of the Algerian work-force in France were 'labourers', while the comparable figure for the domestic work-force is likely to be nearer 50 per cent. The 116,000 'skilled workers' would be of immense value to the industrial sector of Algeria in view of the specific skill shortages hampering industrial growth, if ever they could be persuaded to return. However, by officially ending Algerian migration abroad the government has probably made their return less rather than more likely.


## 5 Conclusion

By the late 1980s between 250,000 and 300,000 young Algerians will be entering the labour market every year. The vast majority will be men who have achieved a higher level of education and have greater aspirations than their predecessors. It seems unlikely that either the non-agricultural sector or Algerian industry will be able to absorb these numbers. Even some qualified Algerians may have difficulty finding jobs in future. Those with little or no qualifications will continue to swell the ranks of the under- and unemployed.

Given its present structure, agriculture offers few opportunities for increased labour absorption. There are already over 1 million part-time workers in the agricultural sector, and if they are joined by yet more underemployed labourers and smallholders the index of underemployment in agriculture must deteriorate further. The suspension of emigration has effectively closed one of the major outlets for the unemployed, and this option is unlikely to be reopened in the future because of the state of the French labour market. Surprisingly, the decision to halt emigration was not accompanied by specific measures to create job oppotunities. One Algerian official is even recorded as stating that this was unnecessary because unemployment was no longer a serious problem.[11] The fact that 115,000 Algerians applied to emigrate during the first six months of 1973 before the government stopped taking applications belies this complacency. Official statistics certainly underestimate the level of unemployment in the economy. In addition to over 1 million underemployed workers in agriculture there are probably at least half a million unemployed workers in the non-agricultural sector – together they represent over a quarter of the active work-force. It is revealing that those Algerian officials who are exclusively concerned with employment clearly wanted emigration to continue in 1973 and doubted the capacity of the Algerian economy to absorb the unemployed in the short term. It remains to be seen whether the new industrial economy which Algeria is building will be capable of creating 200,000 new jobs each year after 1980 — the target set in the plan in order to absorb new workers entering the labour market. In fact, this figure is a minimum value.

Given the regime's commitment to the present development strategy, the crucial question is whether the small modern sector, built on capital-intensive heavy industry and supported until now by large subsidies from the revenues of the hydrocarbon sector, can run profitably and act as an effective 'motor' for the rest of the economic system. Any answer to this question at the present time must be highly speculative. What is certain, however, is that the economic system being created in Algeria, even if successful in strictly economic or technical terms, is unlikely to provide a job for every Algerian in search of employment.

By the 1990s, when Algeria's oil and natural gas revenues are diminishing, her employment problem will be greater in quantitative terms. It will then be possible to appraise the decision to opt for industrial and capital-intensive development in the light of that sector's capacity to earn a replacement income to that of oil and gas revenues and to provide employment. Algeria has invested her oil and gas income with purpose and care. However, it looks increasingly as though these revenues might simply be insufficient to establish an effective industrial non-oil or gas-based economy in the future. Despite the fact that Algeria has directed her hydrocarbons revenues with considerably more circumspection than the Sultanate of Oman, their economic and social problems appear remarkably similar. At a time when oil and gas revenues are finite and not large, both governments are facing a declining agricultural sector, widespread unemployment, and a threatened level of welfare and income suffered by a profoundly frustrated and disillusioned population. Under these circumstances the medium endowment of oil might be seen through a historical perspective as a very mixed blessing, serving rather to have raised aspirations unrealistically, and having created rather more dislocation than development.

## Notes

1. Secrétariat d'Etat au Plan, *Preliminary Results of the 1977 Census* (Algiers, n.d.).

2. Demographic data presented here are largely derived from Commissariat National aux Recensements et Enquête Statistiques, *Etude Statistique Nationale de la Population, 1969/70 2*, 4 (Algiers, April 1974).

3. G. Negadi, D.Tabutin and J.Vallin, 'Situation démographique de l'Algérie', *La Demographie Algérienne* (Algiers, 1972), pp.13-30.

4. Ministère de l'Enseignement Supérieur et de la Recherche Scientifique, *Bulletin Statistique* (Algiers), various issues.

5. This section draws heavily on the following sources. British Council, *Education Profile on Algeria* (London, May 1977); Ministère de l'Education, *Informations Statistiques* (Algiers).

6. Commissariat National aux Recensements et Enquête Statistique, *La Population Active au Recensement de 1966* (Algiers, 1970).

7. The rapid increase in agricultural products deprived other sectors of resources that could have been used for their development. Algeria is currently spending one-third of its oil revenues on food supplies.

8. These figures are drawn largely from MEED, *Special Feature: Algeria*, 'Oil and Gas', 24 November 1978, p.11.

9. See J.S. Birks and C.A. Sinclair, *International Migration and Development in the Arab Region* (ILO, Geneva, 1980), Table 10.

10. Amicale des Algériens en Europe, *Nouvelles Perspectives pour l'Emigration Algérienne*, 8e Assemblée Générale des Cadnes, Nancy, 12-13 Fevrier 1977 (Paris, 1977).

11. S. Adler, *International Migration and Development* (Saxon House, London, 1977).

# PART IV: THE CAPITAL-POOR STATES

# 11 THE LEBANESE REPUBLIC

## 1 Introduction

In 1974 Lebanon appeared to have achieved what many developing countries aim for: an increasing level of GNP *per capita* and an economy in which the modern sector was large and growing rapidly. Indeed, the economy looked well set to benefit further from the surplus oil revenues generated by the 1973 oil price increases, which were bound, it was felt, to engender further financial development. In 1974 estimated GNP *per capita* was $1,189, and rising. Despite certain commentators' assertions about an imbalance within the economy and an admittedly sensitive political situation, the future for the Lebanon was bright.

However, political problems, which began to rise to the surface in 1974, not only prevented this growth from taking place, but also compromised profoundly the economic development which Lebanon had accomplished. Lebanon is classified as capital-poor here; before 1974, this would not have been justifiable. Although it was never really wealthy, in the early 1970s Lebanon displayed few of the features generally associated with the capital-poor states. Today, though, 'capital-poor' is a very fair description of Lebanon, particularly when the trend of development is considered. The country's capital stock is declining; domestic investment is minimal; the productive base is not growing; whilst her dependence on external sources of finance, notably workers' remittances, is increasing. Lebanon, despite her past affluence, is rapidly acquiring the features of her capital-poor neighbours. The longer political unrest lasts, the further along the road of decline she will have gone.

Since 1974 almost no data on the economy or on economic development have appeared. This chapter is therefore a qualitative assessment of the trends of development, rather than, as in the other country chapters, a detailed description of that development.

## 2 The Supply of Labour

### (a) Population

Concern over the ethnic composition and religious affiliations of the Lebanese population have meant that there has been no population census since 1932. Consequently, estimates of the number of inhabitants vary considerably. Officially, the population in 1970 stood at 2.1 million persons of whom 90 per cent were Lebanese. The number of non-nationals was therefore about 198,000 in 1970.[1] This figure excluded some 130,000 Palestinians[2] living in camps. It is likely, though, that, in 1970, the number of expatriates was much higher, possibly about 900,000. Apart from Arabs from the capital-rich states who were then living in Lebanon, the two main groups whose dimensions were unknown were the Palestinians not living in camps and the migrant workers from Syria.

The 1970 figure is also thought to suffer from an under-enumeration of some 10 per cent.[3] If it is presumed that growth in the early part of the decade was about 2.5 per cent, the most likely total for the population living in the Lebanon in 1974/5 is about 2.6 million (again, excluding Palestinians in camps). This compares with an official United Nations estimate of 2.87 million, which includes all Palestinians in Lebanon.[4]

Figures like this do not remove the sensitivity that surrounds the Lebanese population. Before the outbreak of armed conflict, the Lebanese government consisted of a finely balanced representation at each level of the different ethnic and religious groups in the country. It was occasionally argued by certain minority groups, for example the Shia Muslims who lived in the southern part of Lebanon, that they were under-represented in government. None of these arguments was based upon firm empirical foundation, however.

ECWA estimates of the demographic indices suggest that the population is growing at 2.13 per cent, with a birth rate of 34 per thousand, and a death rate of 9 per thousand.[5] A smaller proportion of the total population is aged less than 15 years than in the other capital-poor countries – less than 44 per cent. This reflects the different degree of social and economic development of Lebanon and a more typical capital-poor state. In particular, the life expectancy at birth of 64 years reflects a relatively 'developed society'.

Conventional assessment of such demographic parameters is virtually meaningless in this case, however, because of contemporary circumstances in Lebanon. During five years of intermittent armed conflict, most Syrian migrant workers have left, many Palestinians have moved within the country, and many Lebanese have migrated both internally and to other parts of the Arab world. The conflict itself has caused tens of thousands of deaths. In these circumstances, consideration of demographic indices is highly academic.

In 1972, about 42 per cent of the Lebanese population lived in rural areas. Lebanon is significantly more urban than more conventional capital-poor states. Over half of the Lebanese population live in the immediate vicinity of the capital Beirut. Not only is the population relatively urban, it is highly concentrated in one urban region.

## (b) The Educational Attainment of the Population

The Lebanese population was, in 1974, the most educated of the Arab region, in terms of literacy. According to World Bank figures, 68 per cent of adult Lebanese were literate in 1974. The long tradition of education within Lebanon and of Lebanese travelling abroad for education is reflected by this index. While the high level of education has aided the economy, it has also led to a substantial 'brain drain'. However, the widespread Lebanese diaspora in the Arab world has been a necessary precursor to the cosmopolitan nature of Beirut, which has created the appropriate atmosphere for a financial centre.

Table 11.1: Lebanon: Population (aged 25 years and over) and Labour Force by Level of Educational Attainment, 1970

| Levels of Education | Population 25 Years and Over | | Labour Force | |
|---|---|---|---|---|
| | Number | Per cent | Number | Per cent |
| Illiterate | 158,715 | 29.5 | 381,540 | 45.2 |
| Below primary | 189,780 | 35.2 | 245,085 | 29.1 |
| Primary | 81,990 | 15.2 | 90,180 | 10.7 |
| Intermediate | 50,880 | 9.5 | 59,040 | 7.0 |
| Secondary | 33,975 | 6.3 | 41,085 | 4.9 |
| University | 23,070 | 4.3 | 26,130 | 3.1 |
| Total | 538,410 | 100.0 | 843,060 | 100.0 |

Source: M. Yasin, *A Review of the Manpower Situation in Lebanon* (ILO, Geneva, January 1976), Table 7.

Table 11.1 shows the educational attainment of those aged 25 years and more in the population, and of those who were in employment in 1970. By these definitions, 70 per cent of the population and 60 per cent of the work-force are literate. These levels are extremely high, especially in view of the fact that some 19 per cent of the work-force are in the agricultural sector.

ECWA sources give the illiteracy rate of those aged 15 years and over, a more common measure. In 1975, only 20 per cent of the adult male population were illiterate, and 44 per cent of females. Despite the mature and relatively sophisticated nature of education in Lebanon, a bias against females remains.


### 3 The Demand for Labour

Here again the analysis of data is necessarily retrospective.[6] From Table 11.2 it is clear that in 1970 Lebanon was a well developed and diversified economy. Agriculture accounted for only 19 per cent of employment, and 9 per cent of GDP. Industry comprised a small but significant sector, while commerce and financial services accounted for 44 per cent of GDP and 20 per cent of employment. The tertiary sector as a whole accounted for 62 per cent of GDP and 49 per cent of employment.

Table 11.2: Lebanon: Structure of Employment and GDP by Economic Sector, 1970

|  | Percentages | |
| --- | --- | --- |
| Economic Sector | Employment | GDP |
| Agriculture, animal husbandry and fisheries | 18.9 | 9.2 |
| Industry and handicraft | 17.7 | 13.6 |
| Electricity, gas and water | 1.0 | 2.3 |
| Construction | 6.5 | 4.5 |
| Transport and communication | 7.1 | 8.2 |
| Commerce | 17.0 | 31.4 |
| Financial services, insurance, real estate and business services | 3.4 | 12.2 |
| Community and personal services and activities not defined | 28.4 | 18.6 |
| All sectors | 100.0 | 100.0 |

Source: Direction Centrale de la Statistique, *L'Enquête par sondage sur la population active au Liban, Novembre 1970* (Beirut, 1972), p. 114.

The Lebanese economy is an extremely interesting one in the context of contemporary development in the Arab region. Lebanon's economic strength dates from the demise of Cairo as an international banking centre, which Beirut superseded. In 1970 the economy comprised a small manufacturing sector, but a large and productive services sector because of which the country enjoyed a high level of GDP *per capita*, a favourable balance of trade, and an even stronger balance of payments. The basis of this asset and capability was the country's location in respect of the Arab world and Europe, and a pleasant climate, good communications, her trading traditions, and the efficient banking and commercial services available. No other economy in the Arab region has quite the same blend of economic activities as Lebanon had in 1974, though many now aspire to imitate her. Although no centre in or outside the region can claim to have replaced Beirut as the financial centre of the Middle East, together Dubai, Bahrain and Athens have ensured that Lebanon will never regain so completely her pre-eminent position. Indeed, as time passes, the opportunities open to her decline.

It is important to see that the difference between Lebanon and the new and rising 'commercial centres' of the region is that in Lebanon industrial development was a minor facet of the economy. This is in complete contrast to the capital-rich states which have or plan to develop a substantial industrial sector. In this context, the example of economic development provided by Lebanon is extremely useful, since it illustrates an alternative path of development to that most commonly favoured, industrialisation. The Lebanese style of development avoided the problems attendant on large expatriate work-forces, industrial pollution and commitment of capital. It is an example which capital-rich states would do well to examine, before another round of industrialisation is begun

Having said this, the Lebanese economy did display some signs of weakness – other than the political Achilles heel – in the 1960s and early 1970s. Over-extension of banking services was exemplified by the collapse of the Intra Bank in 1966, and more generally by severe inflation in the early 1970s. It might be asserted that the industrial sector of Lebanon was, in fact, rather too slender, and that the failure to exploit the full potential of manufacturing in the country represented an aspect of fundamental imbalance.

Unfortunately, though, it is for political reasons only that the economic future of the Lebanon is so bleak. Without local and international confidence, the essential foundation of a financial centre, a return to the prosperous days of before 1974 is unlikely, almost regardless of how great and widespread are the increases in wealth elsewhere in the Arab world. Indeed, the Lebanese economy is at best likely to stagnate, rather than grow. Under present circumstances, evidence is mainly of decline. In 1979, exports are still falling, and infrastructure is continuing to fail – water rationing is being extended in Beirut, for example. Other urban services fall increasingly far short of satisfying demand. Aid, essential for the redevelopment of the city, has not been forthcoming on anything approaching the scale promised (in 1979). Even the redevelopment of the port, in which a wide range of countries, from

Syria and Jordan to Kuwait and Saudi Arabia, have an interest through the transit trade, is not going ahead at the pace that was expected. Moreover, in rural areas, agriculture is almost certainly in decline, and there is no sign of a resurgence of private-sector manufacturing. This failure of recovery is from a low base – it has been estimated that in 1974 alone almost 50 per cent of the GNP was lost in the first period of civil unrest.

Typical of a general lack of confidence in the future of Lebanon is the continuing trend of international interests to move out of Beirut. This has recently included plans to shift the UNECWA offices outside Lebanon.

It seems inevitable that the economy will become increasingly dependent upon workers' remittances and aid, so adopting more features characteristic of the capital-poor states which Lebanon borders, and amongst which she was pre-eminent in the early 1970s.

## 4 Lebanese Abroad

Despite the long tradition of Lebanese outmigration,[7] it is difficult to be specific about Lebanese expatriates. The uncertainties regarding the size of the Lebanese population and the very widespread distribution of those abroad make it difficult to comment with accuracy upon Lebanese migrants for employment and refugees.

There is one point of reference, however. In 1975, censuses were held in several of the countries in which Lebanese abroad live. Studies of labour migration based upon these census sources show there are about 50,000 Lebanese working in the capital-rich states, primarily Saudi Arabia, Libya and Kuwait.[8] In 1975, their numbers were increasing rapidly as refugees continued to stream out of Beirut. Apart from these, who moved to the key countries of employment, large numbers left Lebanon for Amman and Damascus. Many with ties outside the Arab world took the opportunity to migrate out of the region to avoid the troubles.

Many of these outmigrants might have left the country permanently, and would therefore be classed as refugees. There are signs of some return migration of Lebanese in the late 1970s, however. Libyan figures record a fall in the numbers of Lebanese expatriates in the country towards the end of 1978.[9] Not all the Lebanese departing from Libya need be going home, though; Libya is proving inhospitable as an employer of Arab migrants, and holds little appeal for many of the more cosmopolitan Lebanese. Some Lebanese migrants used Libya as a staging post on moving away from the troubles, and have proceeded to more permanent positions in other capital-rich states.

Recent estimates suggest that remittance rates have risen to some $1,200 million per annum.[10] This amounts to some $600 *per capita* of the national Lebanese population remaining at home. Such a sum represents over 50 per cent of the 1974 figure for *per capita* GNP. Since 1974, GNP has fallen significantly, so remittances now make a major contribution to the Lebanese economy. Such dependence is yet another aspect of the Lebanese economy's exposure to volatile international trends in the Arab world.[11]


## 5 Conclusion

The Lebanese economy prior to 1974 provides planners in the Arab world with an example of a service economy, a model of a successful non-industrial development in a developing country. What shortcomings there were in the extreme *laissez-faire* policy of the government were buried under the benefits of rapid growth. Thus both social injustices and possible imbalances of the economic structure of the country as a whole were not overt problems.

With the physical destruction of Beirut came other less obvious, but equally significant, damage to international and domestic confidence, and to the human capital of the Lebanon – the pillars of the economic order of the early 1970s. With the virtual political disintegration of the Lebanon came the decline of the country from a centre of relative wealth and expansion to one of much lower income. Although brought about by political, rather than economic factors, it is the now exposed economic as well as political difficulties which will make the re-establishment of Beirut as the financial centre of the Arab world so difficult.

Even today, the vestiges of a banking sector remain. However, over the past four years, continued political uncertainty and armed conflict[12] have progressively eroded the vital confidence upon which future expansion must be based.

The quality of Lebanon's human capital was a primary cause of her success. In time of crisis it was precisely this feature of the work-force and its capacity to work elsewhere that has kept the country economically viable. Remittances now provide a major source of income for those in Lebanon and balance the country's overseas payments. Reversing this situation and recreating the financial centre in Beirut becomes harder as time passes. Not only is Beirut losing pre-eminence in such features as international communications because of developments in the Gulf, in particular in Bahrain, but also the expertise formerly unique to Beirutis has been acquired by other Arab populations. It appears increasingly unlikely that the *laissez-faire* policy upon which the erstwhile success of the Lebanese economy was based will be sufficient to recreate the financial centre of wealth. In the future Lebanese human capital will have to be more organised, whilst at the same time preserving the international image of the country.

## Notes

1. M. Yasin, *A Review of the Manpower Situation of Lebanon* (ILO, Geneva, 1976), Table 1.

2. Centre for Palestinian Research, cited in Y. Courbages and P. Fargues, *La Situation Démographique au Liban* (Centre for Palestinian Research, Beirut, 1974).

3. For a discussion of this see R. Tabbarah, 'Rural Development and Urbanization in Lebanon', *Population Bulletin, 14* (Beirut, June 1978), pp. 3-25.

4. United Nations, *Trends and Prospects in Urban and Rural Population, 1950-2000* (New York, November 1975).

5. United Nations Economic Commission for Western Asia, *Demographic and Related Socio-Economic Data Sheets for Countries of the Economic Commission for Western Asia*, 2 (Beirut, January 1978).

6. For another retrospective analysis of the Lebanese economy see Y.A. Sayigh, *The Economies of the Arab World* (Croom Helm, London, 1978), Chapter 7, pp. 281-316, and S.A. Makdisi, 'An Appraisal of Lebanon's Post-War Economic Development and a Look to the Future', *Middle East Journal, 31*, 3 (1977), pp. 267-80.

7. M.A. Salah Al-Khayat, 'Aspects of Lebanese Labour Movement Post the Labour Law of 1946' (unpublished MBA thesis, Beirut, 1972), p. 41.

8. J.S. Birks and C.A. Sinclair, *International Migration and Development in the Arab Region* (ILO, Geneva, 1980).

9. J.S. Birks and C.A. Sinclair, *The Kingdom of Saudi Arabia and the Libyan Arab Jamahiriya, Key Countries of Employment* World Employment Programme Working Paper (ILO, Geneva, 1979).

10. Herald Tribune, *Banking and Finance in the Arab World* (15 May 1979).

11. Aspects of the undesirability of dependence upon remittances are analysed in J.S. Birks and C.A. Sinclair, *Migration and Development in the Arab Region* (ILO, Geneva, 1980).

12. J. Bulloch, *Death of a Country: the Civil War in Lebanon* (Brill, Leiden, 1977).

# 12 THE ARAB REPUBLIC OF EGYPT

## 1 Introduction

The human resources of Egypt are at once the country's greatest asset in terms of economic development yet also her greatest liability. Egypt, with much the largest national body of people in the Arab world, faces more acutely than even Morocco the crucial impact of population dynamics upon economic growth; rapid demographic growth over the past three decades has all but eroded on a *per capita* basis the real economic progress that has been made. Yet this large national population of some 40 million, with its deep-rooted cultural and educational traditions, means that Egypt remains an important force in the Middle East despite the rapid increases in wealth of the oil producers.

Of the Egyptian population, some 98 per cent live in the Nile Valley, where the population density reaches 2,300 persons per square kilometre. Some 96 per cent of Egypt is desert. Rainfall only reaches 200 mm annual on the Mediterranean coast at Alexandria and temperatures are high — averaging over 32°C from April to October.

Agriculture is the dominant pursuit, engaging over half the population, yet contributing only 24 per cent of gross domestic product. Moreover, the prospects for agriculture are not bright. Planned allocations of funds are not great, whilst the sector suffers from ill-advised government direction. Growth of the economy as a whole has been slow, impeded by the hostilities in the Middle East and the need to maintain a large armed force, defence taking as much as 20 per cent of GDP. As yet, real expansion predicted as a result of the much publicised 'Open Door Policy' has not been significant. In any case, many of the benefits of any such growth might be dissipated by continued population growth.

Slow economic expansion and rapid population growth result in extensive unemployment. Furthermore, underemployment is also believed to be widespread in agriculture, government and public corporations.

The large economically active Egyptian population, frustrated by a sluggish domestic labour market, has responded to increased opportunities in the capital-rich Arab countries, and migration abroad for employment has increased markedly. This has reinforced Egypt's traditional role as an international supplier of skills and educated labour. However, in view of the large number of unemployed in Egypt and the shortages of labour in the capital-rich Arab states, it is remarkable that more Egyptians have not migrated in search of work. Why, in view of social and economic conditions at home, and the possibilities abroad, are there so *few* Egyptian migrant workers?

This low propensity to migrate for employment, together with a lack of occupational mobility in the domestic labour market, limit Egypt's capacity to export labour. Therefore exports of manpower, seen by virtually all Egyptian planners as both alleviating unemployment and, through remittances, easing balance of payments problems, has by no means the potential that has been presumed. This is especially so in view of the trends in employment of non-nationals in the capital-rich states, which are swinging away from Arab labour.

In short, another supposed panacea for the Egyptian economy appears not so effective. Egypt will be thrown heavily on her own resources. If economic growth, believed popularly in Egypt to follow axiomatically from 'peace' in the Middle East, also does not live up to expectations, then the Egyptian future looks bleak. Continued population growth could render Egypt's human resources increasingly redundant, better assessed through an Asian rather than an Arab perspective because of the scale of the problem.

## 2 The Supply of Labour

### (a) The Population

The large Egyptian population has resulted in a tradition of population studies which makes it unnecessary to dwell here upon demographic characteristics.[1] Table 12.1 shows that, by 1976, the number of Egyptians had increased almost fourfold from approaching 10 million in 1897. The rate of growth has been high because the Egyptian population has been experiencing the early stages of the demographic transition; after the Second World War, death rates fell sharply from almost 28 per thousand to less than 20 per thousand,[2] while crude birth rates and fertility remained at high values.

Growth rates peaked at 2.5 per cent in the mid-1960s, and are falling slightly in response to a drop in fertility. Nevertheless, annual growth will not fall below 2 per cent in the near future. Even urbanisation has not retarded population growth.[3] The Egyptian population continues to grow by some 1 million per year, the equivalent of an extra person

Table 12.1: Egypt: Population and Rates of Growth in Census Years

| Census Year | Population (thousands) | Average Annual Inter-Censal Growth Rate (per cent) |
|---|---|---|
| 1897 | 9,715 | — |
| 1907 | 11,287 | 1.51 |
| 1917 | 12,751 | 1.23 |
| 1927 | 14,218 | 1.09 |
| 1937 | 15,933 | 1.15 |
| 1947 | 19,022 | 1.79 |
| 1960 | 26,085 | 2.46 |
| 1966 | 30,076[a] | 2.40 |
| 1976 | 38,228 | 2.31 |

Note: a. Sample census; the remainder were full enumerations.
Sources: Central Agency for Public Mobilization and Statistics, *The Increases of Population in the United Arab Republic* (Cairo, September 1969), p. 26; R. Mabro, *The Egyptian Economy, 1952-1972* (Oxford, 1974), Table 2.1, p. 26; Central Agency for Public Mobilization and Statistics, 'Preliminary Results of the General Population and Housing Census, 22-23 November, 1976' (Cairo, typescript, 1977), Table 6, p. 30.

Table 12.2: Egypt: Age Distribution of the Population, 1960 and 1976

| Census Year | Age Group | | | Total |
|---|---|---|---|---|
| | Less than 12 Years | 12-64 Years | 65 Years and Over | |
| 1960 | 35.5 | 61.0 | 3.5 | 100.0 |
| 1976 | 31.6 | 65.5 | 2.9 | 100.0 |

Source: Central Agency for Public Mobilization and Statistics, 'Preliminary Results of the General Population and Housing Census, 22-23 November, 1976' (Cairo, typescript, 1977), Table 6, p. 30.

born every 41 seconds.[4]

The gently falling birth rate of the past decade or so is reflected in a declining proportion of the population aged under twelve years (Table 12.2). There has been a consequent proportional increase of those in their most productive years. However, even though the ratio of children to adults has declined from 5.5 children to 10 adults in 1960, it still remains high at 4.6. This amounts to 0.99 children per head of the economically active population, and reflects the broad base of the population pyramid.

The future numerical increase is considerable. The National Production and Economic Affairs Committee has predicted a rise to 70 million by the year 2000,[5] whilst in contrast, the Minister of Planning, Abdel

Razzaq Abdel Magid, has said that the population will rise to 59.5 million by 1995.[6] Indisputably, at least another 20 million will have been added by the end of the century, a 50 per cent increase over today's total population.

The sex ratio in 1976 was 104[7] and has been increasing since 1960, as the sex ratio of births is increasing and that of deaths decreasing. In the 1960 census, 37 per cent of the enumerated population was classed as urban, and 44 per cent in 1976.[8] Of the urban population of over 12 million, almost 8 million were living in the 'Urban Governorates of Cairo, Alexandria, Port Said and Suez.'[9] This concentration of people in the towns is both a result of, and a contributory reason behind, considerable stresses within society. The impact of this upon the labour force is not clear, however.

*(b) The Educational Status of the Population*

Egypt's literary traditions stretch back into the past, the country always having been a centre of learning, benefiting from links with Africa, Asia and Europe. Egypt has a large, established modern educational system and has exported to other Arab states educational ideas, systems and teachers in an extraordinarily comprehensive way. It is therefore surprising that the educational attainment of the Egyptian people is so low.[10] In 1960, 70 per cent of the adult population were illiterate. In 1976, 57 per cent were illiterate. However, over this period the number of illiterates actually increased by 2.4 million persons (Table 12.3).

Table 12.3: Egypt: Distribution of Population Aged Ten Years and More by Sex and Educational Status, 1960 and 1976

| Educational Status | 1960 | | | 1976 | | |
|---|---|---|---|---|---|---|
| | Male | Female | Total | Male | Female | Total |
| Illiterates | 56.9 | 84.0 | 70.5 | 43.2 | 71.0 | 56.5 |
| Able to read and write | 32.6 | 12.4 | 22.5 | 33.2 | 16.2 | 25.1 |
| Educational qualifications below degree | 9.0 | 3.4 | 6.2 | 20.4 | 11.6 | 16.2 |
| Higher qualifications | 1.5 | 0.2 | 0.8 | 3.2 | 1.2 | 2.2 |
| Total | 100.0 | 100.0 | 100.0 | 100.0 | 100.0 | 100.0 |

Source: Central Agency for Public Mobilization and Statistics, 'Preliminary Results of the General Population Census, 22-23 November, 1976' (Cairo, typescript, 1977), Table 8, p. 30.

There is, even in Egypt, a considerable differential between male and female rates of literacy, less than half of males are illiterate compared to 71 per cent of females (1976). This differential is widening slightly, more progress having been made in male enrolment since 1960. Between 1960 and 1976, when the number of illiterates increased, the number of people with university degrees rose from 140,000 to 570,000. The differential educational attainment between the sexes widens with higher educational level, though over time it is narrowing. In 1976, over 20 per cent of men had educational qualifications other than degrees, compared to 12 per cent of women. This comprises a doubling of this group since 1960.

The increasing number of illiterates concerns educationalists. Large-scale literacy programmes are planned, but the problem may lie in the quality of education. Table 12.4 shows the large numbers in primary schools, and the growing numbers of persons enrolled above that level. Superficially the picture of primary school enrolment is good. Most boys are in primary school, as are a substantial majority of girls. Why were there more people illiterate in 1976 than in 1960?

Table 12.4: Egypt: Enrolment in School and University in Selected Years and Growth Rates

|  | 1972/3 | 1974/5 | Per cent Growth per annum | 1976/7 | Per cent Growth per annum |
|---|---|---|---|---|---|
| University | 218,899 | 301,170 | 17.2 | 307,500 | 1.0 |
|  | 1969/70 | 1974/5 |  |  |  |
| Secondary | 559,867 | 718,225 | 5.1 | 754,666 | 2.5 |
| Intermediate | 797,895 | 1,199,801 | 8.5 | 1,435,529 | 9.3 |
| Primary | 3,618,750 | 4,074,893 | 2.4 | 4,151,956 | 1.0 |

Sources: Central Agency for Public Mobilization and Statistics, *Statistical Yearbooks, 1952-1975* (Cairo, 1976), p. 177; Ministry of Education, Statistical Division, *Development and Flow of General Education since the Middle of the 20th Century, 1950/51 to 1976/77* (Cairo, 1977).

There are two main causes. One is that the quality of primary school education in rural areas is poor and the retentive capacity of the schools very low. The opportunity cost of remaining at school rises with age, so many pupils only reach the third grade before dropping out in search of employment. Secondly, the absolute increase of population was so great that an improvement in relative terms was not sufficient to reduce the number of illiterates. Literacy is an example of Egypt's population growth eliminating what otherwise would be a substantial improvement in terms of socio-economic development.

The educational pyramid is remarkably broad. There are two university students for every five secondary school pupils, and thirteen children in primary school for each university student. Between 1972/3 and 1974/5 university enrolment expanded at a rate of 17 per cent per annum. In higher education there is a small majority of arts students over scientists, but a remarkably large number of the latter (109,000). In addition to the 268,000 university students (1974/5), there are a further 50,000 students receiving vocational/technical training for technician type occupations, and about 3,000 students abroad, mostly studying the sciences.

Education is now a major industry in Egypt. There are 6 million children in schools, and about 183,000 teachers. Of the many burdens that Egypt carries, educating her people must rank as a substantial one. The rapid expansion of higher education in recent years appears to have been at the expense of quality of primary school education. More resources could otherwise have been spent on vocational education. The current efforts at improving literacy and developing vocational training appear a more apposite policy than that of the 1960s, though only belatedly introduced. The legacy of the 1960s is a substantial commitment to higher education and a growing number of university graduates seeking jobs. This ill-adapted system has a considerable momentum of its own which it will be difficult to alter. It makes the productive employment of Egyptians more problematic.

### 3 The Demand for Labour

#### (a) Introduction

Egypt has a large, complex and intricate economy. The links between economic development and employment are difficult to evaluate, but, at first inspection, Egypt has many familiar features of Third World economies: a high rate of population increase; a low level of GDP *per capita*, a low level of consumption *per capita*; a low level of domestic savings; a low level of domestic capital formation; an uneven pattern of income distribution; widespread underemployment; and past rapid rural to urban internal migration. Egypt's high rate of inflation, her obligations to overseas lenders (a partial legacy of 15 years of defence spending) and her inadequate infrastructure, particularly in the large urban areas, might well be added to this list.[11]

In the preamble to the Five Year Plan the author writes: 'the economic problems of the Egyptian economy are endemic and extensive: crisis is always imminent.'[12] It is the hope of the same author that the plan and the open door policy of President Sadat will make some inroads on this situation.

*(b) Gross Domestic Product*

In 1975 gross domestic product (GDP) was estimated at £E3,484 million. This implies an income of between $US240 *per capita* (official rate)[13] and $US145 *per capita* (market rate).[14] The latter gives a more accurate picture of the standard of living of most of the population and the country as a whole; the distribution of income is very uneven.

*Agriculture.* The contribution of agriculture to GDP is prominent. Sales of cotton earn a high proportion of all foreign exchange. About half the work-force are farmers.

Egypt's land is an important asset, yet over the past ten years has received progressively smaller amounts of government investment. Only 2.5 per cent of Egypt is cultivable, and any increase in agricultural output can only come from land reclamation or improved land use. On a *per capita* basis food production has been falling, because of low level of investment in land reclamation, poor land use and loss of land to urban growth, causing a changed farming pattern.[15]

Table 12.5: Egypt: Gross Domestic Product, 1975 ($ million)

| Economic Sector | Amount ($ million) | Per cent |
|---|---|---|
| Agriculture | 1,323.3 | 24.0 |
| Industry, petroleum and mining | 1,187.8 | 21.5 |
| Construction | 203.0 | 5.7 |
| Transport and communications | 381.3 | 6.9 |
| Trade and finance | 610.7 | 11.1 |
| Other | 1,799.5 | 32.8 |
| Total | 5,505.6 | 100.0 |

Source: Ministry of Planning, 'Estimates of GDP in 1975' (Cairo, mimeograph, n.d.).

The government buys much agricultural produce; prices are kept artifically low, so farmers are left with little surplus for investment and attempt to cultivate products the marketing of which is not controlled by government. This lies behind declining rice production, whilst cultivation of fruits and vegetables, goods that are not subject to government control, has been increasing.

A problem facing Egyptian farmers today is that much cultivated land requires draining. This is largely a result of over-watering, made possible by the Aswan Dam. Typically, investment in infrastructure in Egypt has engendered high hidden costs. Low investment in extension work, new crops or fertilisers all contribute to the poor state of the sector. Rural/urban migration has not been accompanied by increased agricultural productivity and output. On the contrary, output has fallen as Egypt's demand for food has increased. Egypt is increasingly dependent on grain imports.

A sound agricultural development policy could yield substantial returns. The quality of advice given to peasants should be improved, and the land-use pattern be permitted to follow that which will yield the highest social return. Government efforts to maximise revenue deriving from cheap purchases of crops and higher priced sales of the same should be ended.

Previously the rural areas have sent migrants in large numbers to cities, but the flow is now declining. This is because while those presently working in rural areas do have a positive marginal product, the urban alternatives to farming are now seen as less attractive by the rural populations than in the past. Today, a growing volume of employment and income comes from non-farm tertiary sector activities in rural areas.[16] While improvements in Egypt's agriculture are essential if she is to be self-sufficient in food in future years, government planners should bear in mind the employment implications of investment projects; non-farm development of rural areas may come to have a key role in future years.

*Manufacturing*. The manufacturing sector, responsible for a fifth of total GDP, employs about 1.1 million people. Production has been hampered by under-utilisation of capacity with inefficient employment and pricing policies controlled by Ministries until 1975. In the 1960s practically all industry became the responsibilities of Ministries. Some recent attempts have been made to decentralise decision-making, but not on key issues such as investment strategy, labour force and pricing policy. Most industry is import-substituting, and relatively small in scale. However, there are plans to develop industrial areas in the Canal Zone and at Ismailia. USAID is investing $750 million in the Canal Zone.

Despite these plans, Egypt's industrial sector remains unfortunately structured. It caters for the domestic market rather than exports and so is constrained quickly by foreign exchange shortages. Raw materials come from abroad, with the result that shortages of foreign exchange often check expansion. Nevertheless, from 1974 to 1975 the economy is estimated to have grown at approximately 10 per cent in real terms, though expansion of the economy induced a shortfall of foreign exchange and inflation. The consequent erosion of personal incomes contributed to the civil disturbances of January 1977. These were symptomatic of a wide malaise incipient within the economy and society of Egypt.[17]

One result of the expansion of 1975 was a dramatic increase in imports, while exports rose more slowly (Table 12.6). Egypt's adverse trading position is improved by taking into account 'invisible' earnings: the Suez Canal, tourism and workers' remittances, which came to $1,180 million in 1976, and served to enable repayment of overseas debts. Foreign exchange earnings should rise as the tourist industry expands, as the Suez Canal extensions are completed, as the SUMED pipeline is used, and as Egypt's oil production expands. In 1978 they should amount to $3,500 million. However, Egypt's obligations to overseas lenders will remain an onerous burden. Until the fundamental structure of the Egyptian economy changes, scarcely an immediate prospect, her foreign trade account will remain in deficit, and growth will be severely constrained.

Table 12.6: Egypt: Foreign Trade, 1973 to 1976 ($ million)

|         | 1973   | 1974   | 1975   | 1976   |
|---------|--------|--------|--------|--------|
| Imports | 1,664  | 3,475  | 4,329  | 3,465  |
| Exports | 1,003  | 1,674  | 1,568  | 1,605  |
| Balance | − 661  | −1,801 | − 2,761 | −1,860 |

Source: Ministry of Planning, *Foreign Trade Statistics, 1971-1976* (Cairo, 1977) (Arabic), Table 14.

Current expenditure absorbs a large proportion of government revenues, capital expenditures only being made possible by foreign borrowings. Defence and food subsidies accounted for 59 per cent of current expenditure in 1976. An unsuccessful attempt was made in 1977 to end food subsidies, though hopefully the peace agreement will serve to temper defence spending. However, both these items will be a continuing current account commitment, only gradual reductions being possible.

These financial constraints mean that Egypt is obliged to borrow, mostly externally, to finance many activities. In 1976 Egypt's external debt was $12 billion, which is more than the national income.[18] Financial survival is only possible by virtue of international aid and soft loans. Debts will serve to constrain economic development well into the 1980s, unless a donor comes forward with funds on a previously unknown scale. Expanded United States aid consequent upon the Egyptian/Israeli peace settlement does not seem likely to fulfil this role, especially as Arab aid is likely to tail off a little. The Egyptian government will need budget support on a scale of $2 billion to $4 billion; thus, Egypt will continue to be dependent on foreign assistance for some considerable time to come.

In fact, aid to Egypt has been surprisingly limited. The Gulf Organisation for the Development of Egypt (GODE) was her principal donor and loaner; relations between it and the Egyptian government have been adversely affected by political developments in the region. The General Authority for Arab and Foreign Investments and Free Zones, one of the more tangible consequences of the open door policy, had received, by November 1977, only $705 million for its various projects. American aid is running at $1 billion per year and will increase, and OECD funds are anticipated.

While these sums are substantial they are relatively small when put against the cost of developing Egypt, and are much smaller than was anticipated. The present level of aid does not free Egypt from the shackles of its debts, nor make a decisive contribution to economic development.

In short, the Egyptian economy neither produces enough food or consumer goods to meet the need of the population, nor exports sufficient to balance its external trade. Liberalisation of the economy and attempts to engender economic development induce shortages of foreign exchange. Meanwhile, the government's ability to invest in the economy remains minimal. Even if the government were in a healthier financial position, or were the recipient of very large sums of foreign aid, it would be several years before it would be possible to repay all its debt obligations. In this context the government is launching its five-year plan.

*(c) The Five Year Plan, 1978 to 1982*

The plan envisages government investment of $15 billion at market rates and private-sector investment of $2.2 billion. This is three times 1975 GDP, and four times the government revenue of 1977, illustrating the extent to which the plan is an ambitious blueprint for economic development in Egypt. Indeed it assumes growth of national income of 9 to 10 per cent annually in real terms. Private consumption is estimated as increasing annually at 8 per cent. The domestic savings ratio is presumed to rise to 17 per cent by 1982, from less than 1 per cent. Industry and transport and communications absorb 46 per cent of all investment. Agriculture, together with irrigation and drainage, accounts for only 9 per cent (Table 12.7).

Table 12.7: Egypt: Development Plan Investment Estimates, 1978 to 1982 ($ million)

| Sector | 1978 Amount | 1978 to 1982 Amount | Total Per cent |
|---|---|---|---|
| Agriculture | 104.6 | 633.1 | 3.9 |
| Irrigation and drainage | 138.7 | 773.1 | 4.7 |
| Industry | 550.6 | 386.2 | 23.7 |
| Petroleum | 120.0 | 898.8 | 5.5 |
| Electricity | 195.2 | 1,478.4 | 9.1 |
| Construction | 51.6 | 340.8 | 2.1 |
| Transport and communications | 592.8 | 3,691.7 | 22.6 |
| Suez Canal | 190.4 | 759.7 | 4.7 |
| Commerce and finance | 49.1 | 345.3 | 2.2 |
| Housing | 136.0 | 936.0 | 5.8 |
| Utilities | 151.4 | 996.6 | 6.1 |
| Services | 253.6 | 1,564.8 | 9.6 |
| Total | 2,534.0 | 16,278.5 | 100.0 |

Source: Ministry of Planning, *Five Year Plan 1978-1982*, 'The General Strategy for Economic and Social Development' (Cairo, 1977), Vol. I, Table 9, p. 73.

The underlying assumptions of the five-year plan are that the economy will grow rapidly over the plan period, especially towards the end, leading to an improving standard of living of the population and a much higher level of savings. It is also presumed that there will be a continuing supply of foreign aid, sufficient to fund not only the plan commitments, but also to meet Egypt's overseas debt obligations. This implies that Egypt's current 'loans' from friendly states will be cancelled, and other debts will be rescheduled.

In short, the plan presents a highly optimistic picture of Egypt's future economic development. Whilst such developments are conceivable, a less rapid rate of growth is more likely. Egypt's economic malaise is so fundamental that planners cannot expect to correct it in the short term.

## 4 The Labour Market

### (a) The Structure of Employment

In 1976, the participation rate of nationals aged six years or more was 53 per cent for males and 32 per cent for females, the work-force comprising 9.9 million men (85.6 per cent) and 1.7 million women. In addition, official sources estimate 600,000 workers abroad, giving 12.2 million economically active persons.[19]

Table 12.8: Egypt: Estimate of Employment by Sector, 1976

| Sector | Number | Per cent |
|---|---|---|
| Agriculture[1] | 6,490,000 | 50.7 |
| Government[2] | 1,740,000 | 13.6 |
| Public sector[2] | 1,210,000 | 9.4 |
| Private sector[2] | 950,000 | 7.4 |
| Armed forces[3] | 342,500 | 2.7 |
| Workers abroad[4] | 600,000 | 4.7 |
| Unemployed[4] | 1,479,000 | 11.5 |
| Total | 12,811,500 | 100.0 |

Sources:
1. J.S. Birks and C.A. Sinclair, *Human Capital on the Nile: Development and Emigration in the Arab Republic of Egypt and the Democratic Republic of the Sudan,* World Employment Programme Working Paper (ILO, Geneva, 1978).
2. Ministry of Planning, *Five Year Plan, 1978-82* (Cairo, 1977), Vol. I, Table 4, p. 31.
3. International Institute for Strategic Studies, *The Military Balance, 1977-1978* (London, 1978), Table 3, p. 85.
4. Ministry of Planning, *Five Year Plan, 1978-82* (Cairo, 1977), Vol. II, p. 184.

The agricultural sector comprises over half of total employment, but only a relatively small proportion falls within the modern sector. Public and private sectors account for 30 per cent of total employment, of which almost half is government. Over 1.5 million, 11 per cent of the work-force, are unemployed.

Table 12.9 shows urban (modern-sector) employment, including the estimated 1.5 million under- and unemployed, mostly within the services sector. This covers informal-sector workers, many of whom live in Cairo on little more than a subsistence level. Mining and petroleum is in its infancy with correspondingly low employment. Manufacturing takes a 22 per cent share of urban employment, but underemployment in the public sector and the policy of employment of graduates means that many persons recorded here are not economically productive.

Table 12.9: Egypt: Estimate of Urban Employment (Employed and Unemployed), 1976

| Economic Sector | Number | Per cent |
|---|---|---|
| Mining and petroleum | 46,200 | 0.8 |
| Manufacturing | 1,163,300 | 21.5 |
| Electricity | 47,000 | 0.9 |
| Construction | 434,000 | 8.0 |
| Transport, storage and communications | 422,100 | 7.8 |
| Finance, trade and services | 3,291,700 | 61.0 |
| Total[a] | 5,404,300 | 100.0 |

Note: a. This total includes 1,479 million persons unemployed.
Source: Abstracted from Ministry of Planning, *Five Year Plan 1978-1982* (Cairo, 1977), Vol. II, p. 200.

## (b) Future Employment

Population increase means that each year 350,000 new jobs must be created to avoid unemployment. Obviously not all new jobs need be modern sector, or urban, but the educational attainment of new labour market entrants is rising. Between 1978 and 1982 there will be 327,200 university graduates,[20] so it will increasingly be jobs in the modern sector that are sought. The picture of rapid expansion of educational facilities in urban areas, and urban unemployment, especially of the well educated, is familiar. It would already be more obvious in Cairo but for the policy of hiring every university graduate in the public sector. However, widespread underemployment in government service has resulted.

It is widely believed that marked underemployment also exists in agriculture, and even that marginal productivity of labour is zero. This is an accepted truth which has not been rigorously examined, and is not accepted here. However, it remains true that the land will not provide job opportunities for those leaving school. While the modern sector must attempt to expand rapidly enough to provide jobs for the majority of educated school-leavers, increasing attention should be given to informal-sector activities in rural areas, which will grow inexorably.

The Ministry of Planning estimates that between 1976 and 1986, 5 million new job opportunities will occur, an annual rate of increase of 4.3 per cent. This assumes that the targets of the five-year plan will be met. This is very optimistic, and postulates that the number of unemployed will fall to 500,000 by 1986 (Table 12.10). Contemporaneously, the number of workers abroad is projected to rise to approximately 1 million by 1986. The falling total of unemployment does not take into sufficient account the manpower policy of the five-year plan.[21]

Table 12.10: Egypt: Official Estimate of Disposition of Labour Force in 1976 and 1986 (thousand)

|  | 1976 | 1986 | Annual Per cent Increase |
|---|---|---|---|
| Total population | 38,228 | 47,334 | 2.16 |
| Economically active | 11,707 | 16,071 | 3.1 |
| Crude participation rate | 32.65% | 29.45% | |
| Demand for labour from abroad | 600 | 975 | |
| Net domestic supply of labour | 11,107 | 15,104 | 3.1 |
| Net domestic demand for labour | 9,628 | 14,617 | 4.3 |
| Number of unemployed | 1,479 | 487 | − 10.5 |
| Per cent of total work-force | 12.6 | 3.0 | |

Source: Ministry of Planning, *Five Year Plan 1978-82* (Cairo, 1977), Vol. II, p. 184.

The plan states that:

> The wage structure in the government and the public sector will be re-evaluated. Wages will reflect productivity and not academic qualifications.
>
> The present policy of employing all graduates will be re-considered, and in the future they will be hired only when an actual job opportunity exists.
>
> University enrolment will be limited and vocational training expanded.
>
> Centres for vocational training and technical education will be created whose aim is to train graduates to work abroad in African and Arab countries.
>
> Under-employment will be eliminated.

If these measures were enforced rigorously and quickly, the streets of Cairo would be full of unemployed graduates. The fourth aim presumes that migration abroad for employment is a positive benefit, and can be of great value in alleviating unemployment. This is a questionable assumption, and of great significance to future unemployment in Egypt.

### (c) Migration for Employment and the Domestic Labour Market

In fact, there were not 600,000 economically active Egyptians abroad in 1975/6.[22] The real number was more like 400,000, or 3 per cent of the work-force.[23] Why, given her large population and experience of migration, has Egypt not exported more than 3 per cent of her work-force? There is another facet to this apparent paradox. Despite the small exports of labour there are acute shortages of certain types of manpower – in particular tradesmen and craftsmen, especially in Cairo.[24] In view of slow domestic expansion of the economy and the falling number in the army, these shortages are due to migration abroad for employment. Yet how does such a relatively small-scale emigration of labour bring about such obvious shortages?

Egypt's labour market appears highly compartmentalised, with very little occupational mobility. It is characterised by extraordinary immobility between even relatively similar occupations. This lack of occupational mobility between similar occupations is of considerable significance: the result of this limited occupational mobility is little internal readjustment within the labour market to compensate for the exports of certain types of manpower. Thus the skills exported from Egypt are not replaced quickly by nationals moving into the vacancies created by their departure. For example, exports of Egypt's skilled craftsmen and tradesmen are substantial, but there is little movement of labour up the occupational scale as replacements. Consequently, there are shortages of this type of labour, despite the small overall proportion of the labour force which has migrated.

The lack of upward occupational mobility to compensate for exports of labour appears true of all levels of the labour market. Indeed, today there is even relatively little transfer of labour from the traditional to the modern sector in the short to medium term. In particular, the construction industry has been demonstrated to be short of all types of labour.[25]

Some 75 per cent of the labour market comprises those in public employment who are occupationally immobile. Some migrant workers are government secondees but their number is small. The secure income, with annual increments, that government employment provides, means that a public-sector employee maximises long-term economic returns by remaining in the post, and so is neither a potential migrant, nor occupationally mobile within the domestic labour market.

Non-agricultural private sector employment amounts to only 3,000,000 persons. These are the potential migrants for employment, and replacements of those who have migrated. Not only is this group small, but it is of low educational attainment, frequently illiterate, lacking in employment experience and, often, unemployed. They are, therefore, not demanded as migrants, nor can they move easily to higher levels of occupational status.

Thus Egypt's potential as a labour exporter is limited by the inability of the labour market to provide readily labour of the qualities demanded in the capital-rich states. Therefore there is unlikely to be a *substantial* expansion in the numbers of Egyptians migrating for employment. Egyptians with the skills demanded overseas, who are prepared to migrate, are more limited in number than is commonly envisaged.

It is doubtful that planners in Egypt are wise in notionally setting many extra departures of migrant workers against anticipated unemployment. If the government desires to export larger numbers of workers, it must take a series of active steps to encourage this. In this, Egyptian planners must face three major problems encountered in expanding the numbers of Egyptians overseas. First, the market for Arab migrant labourers in the capital-rich states is not expanding rapidly. It is therefore an especially bad time to be attempting to increase Egyptian penetration of the market.

Secondly, the demand for Arab migrant labour is falling most quickly in respect of unskilled workers, those which the Egyptian planners are most interested in having migrate for employment.

Thirdly, it is in these less qualified and skilled categories of labour where the Egyptians are competing most directly with South-East Asian labour. Egyptian labour of this type is particularly disadvantaged because of the lack of Egyptian large-scale enterprises able to effect major 'enclave projects' in the capital-rich states. It is on these large projects that South-East Asian companies have proved particularly attractive to the Arab countries of employment.

However, there are opportunities abroad for Egyptian labour. At the moment the Egyptian education system is not directed towards the production of school-leavers or graduates with the technical and trade qualifications demanded abroad. It would be too long-term a process to attempt to redirect the education system; therefore, Ministries and government agencies who command so much of the labour market should instigate short-term training courses. These would produce numbers of workers of a type desired in the capital-rich states, of known quality, who can be supplied in known numbers to meet predicted demand. Perhaps some remittances might be utilised to pay for these training schemes. The training of craftsmen and low-grade technicians would have the incidental effect of decreasing some of the acute shortages of labour of this type in Cairo. Efforts must then be made to market this labour internationally and institutional constraints to their migration minimised.[26]

In short, it is possible for Egypt to enlarge her role as an exporter of labour but it will take effort, investment and some marketing flair. Greatly increased numbers of Egyptians will not migrate spontaneously.

## 5 Conclusion

It is highly unlikely that the numbers of Egyptians working abroad will reach 1 million by 1985. It is also unlikely that other manpower targets in the five-year plan will be met because of the constraints to the expansion of the economy dwelt upon above.

The future of the Egyptian labour market is, therefore, bleak. Despite some improvements in economic performance, unemployment will rise, perhaps startlingly. It is hard to see effective policies that could offset this. Population limitation policies cannot act quickly enough, and even if Egypt were to receive aid of an unprecedented scale (an increasingly unlikely prospect in view of the way in which Egypt is drifting away from the core of the Arab world), it is hard to see how economic growth could mop up unemployment of the scale envisaged. Whether Egypt's economic, social and political framework is strong enough to bear the weight of a number of unemployed approaching 3 million will remain to be seen. This is the prospect that Egyptian planners should be contemplating, though. Hiding behind over-optimistic targets of employment creation and exports of manpower to other Arab states engenders false aspirations and bad planning decisions. The country's economic and employment prospects are bad — so bad that the sooner Egypt and the Arab world face them the better.

## Notes

1. For example, G.I.Dorance, 'Population Growth in Egypt, 1800-2000: An Essay in the Quantification of Trends' (unpublished MA thesis, Durham University, 1975); J.Waterbury, *Egypt: Burdens of the Past, Options for the Future* (American Universities Field Staff Report, Cairo, 1978); Abd el Aal Wassim,

'Spatial Patterns of Population Dynamics in Egypt: 1947-1970' (unpublished PhD thesis, Durham University, 1977).

2. See also R. Mabro, *The Egyptian Economy 1952-72* (Oxford University Press, 1974), p.25.

3. Central Agency for Public Mobilization and Statistics (CAPMAS), *The Increase of Population in the United Arab Republic* (Cairo, 1969).

4. CAPMAS, 'Preliminary Results of the General Population and Housing Census, 22nd-23rd November, 1976' (Cairo, typescript, 1977).

5. National Production and Economic Affairs Committee Report, cited in *MEED*, 15 July 1977, p. 18.

6. As reported in *MEED*, 23 October 1977, p. 19.

7. CAPMAS, 'Preliminary Results', Table 9.

8. A.F. Nassef, 'Internal Migration and Urbanisation in Egypt', *Urbanization and Migration in some Arab and African Countries*, Cairo Demographic Centre, Research Monograph Series (Cairo, 1973), pp. 171-265.

9. CAPMAS, *Preliminary Results* (1976), Table 12, p. 36.

10. G.D.M. Hyde, *Education in Modern Egypt; Ideals and Realities* (Brill, Leiden, 1978).

11. For more background, see B. Hansen and G.A. Marzouk, *Development and Economic Policy in the UAR (Egypt)* (McGraw Hill, Amsterdam, 1965); D.C. Mead, *Growth and Structural Change in the Egyptian Economy* (Illinois, 1967).

12. Ministry of Planning, *Five Year Plan; 1978-1982* (Egypt, August 1977).

13. The official rate in 1975 was £E1 = $US2.6.

14. The market rate in 1975 was approximately £E1 = $US1.58. The current market rate is used in all conversions in this chapter.

15. E. Lee and S. Radwan, *The Anatomy of Rural Poverty: Egypt, 1977* (ILO, Geneva, 1980).

16. Lee and Radwan, *Anatomy of Rural Poverty*.

17. See R. Mabro, 'Increased Opportunities in Wake of Strife', Supplement on Egypt, *The Times*, 7 December 1977; Ministry of Planning, *Five Year Plan*, Vol. I (Egypt, August 1977).

18. Ministry of Planning, *Five Year Plan*, Vol. I (Egypt, August 1977), p. 5.

19. Table 12.8 gives a slightly higher total, which is a consequence of a different assessment of agricultural employment, details of which are given in J.S. Birks and C.A. Sinclair, *Human Capital on the Nile: Development and Emigration in the Arab Republic of Egypt and the Republic of the Sudan*, World Employment Programme Working Paper (ILO, Geneva, 1979).

20. Ministry of Education, Department of Higher Education, *The Development of Higher Education in Egypt* (Egypt, 1978).

21. Ministry of Planning, *Five Year Plan, 1978-82*, Vol. I (Egypt, August 1977), pp. 47-8.

22. J.S. Birks and C.A. Sinclair, *Migration and Development in the Arab Region* (ILO, Geneva, 1980).

23. J.S. Birks and C.A. Sinclair, 'International Labour Migration in the Arab Middle East', *Third World Quarterly*, 1, 2 (April 1979), pp. 87-99.

24. N. Choucri, *Labour Transfers in the Arab World: Growing Interdependence of the Construction Sector*, paper presented to the Seminar on Population, Employment and Migration in the Gulf Countries, Arab Planning Institute (Kuwait, 1978).

25. P. Shaw, *Migration and Employment in the Arab World: Construction as a Key Policy Variable*, paper presented to the Seminar on Population, Employment and Migration in the Gulf Countries, Arab Planning Institute (Kuwait, 1978).

26. Birks and Sinclair, *International Migration and Development in the Arab Region*.

# 13 THE KINGDOM OF MOROCCO

## 1 Introduction

Morocco is a poor country located at the periphery of the Maghreb and the Arab world. Income *per capita* in 1976 was estimated at $540.[1] The Moroccan population of some 18 million persons in 1977 is second only to Egypt in the Arab world in size. The vast majority of Moroccans are illiterate.

In 1956, when Morocco gained independence, unlike other Maghreb countries, she had considerable financial reserves with which to initiate development. However, economic progress has been limited, and much of her resources have been allocated to relatively unproductive activities such as the expansion of government and public works. Only in 1973 did a programme of industrial development begin seriously.

The departure of the French in 1956 did not alter Morocco's reliance on Europe and France, to which the country is orientated rather than to the Arab world. Many teachers and other professional workers are French,[2] and a large proportion of Moroccan trade is with France. Moreover, a large number of Moroccans have migrated to France for employment. However, as Moroccans are amongst the least skilled of all migrants, the declining demand for migrant workers in Europe since 1974 has affected them particularly. The government views the prospect of the return of her migrants with considerable concern, as there are already half a million unemployed.

## 2 Supply of Labour

### (a) Population

The population of Morocco more than doubled between 1935 and 1971. By 1977 it had risen to 18.4 million persons (Table 13.1). Its present annual rate of increase is approximately 3.5 per cent. By the end of this century the population will be 40 millions, the present size of Egypt. The crude death rate is presently 14 per thousand[3] while the crude birth rate was estimated at 49 per thousand between 1971 and 1975. Morocco is experiencing a population explosion which will undoubtedly have serious repercussions for economic development five or ten years hence.

Table 13.1: Morocco: Population in Selected Years, 1935 to 1977

| Year | Population |
|------|-----------|
| 1935 | 7,040,000 |
| 1952 | 9,342,000 |
| 1960 | 11,626,000 |
| 1971 | 15,153,800 |
| 1977 | 18,400,000 |

Source: Adapted from S. Cherkaoui, 'Human Resources as a Factor in the Development of Morocco' (unpublished MPhil thesis, Cairo University, 1975).

Although a family planning programme was introduced in 1966, its seems probable that the population will continue to grow at a rapid rate in the immediate future. Although the average number of children per family is 4.5 in urban areas and 7.0 in rural areas, it does not appear that rural to urban migration will check population growth more than marginally.

Some 45 per cent of the population are below the age of 15,[4] contributing to the high dependency ratio.[5] This scale of dependency, when coupled with the low level of female participation in the modern sector of the economy, indicates the considerable burden which is placed upon the actively employed population.

*(b) The Educational Status of the Population*

Although enrolments remain low in relation to the number of children and young adults of school age, the government's efforts in improving educational opportunities have not been entirely in vain. Since independence the numbers enrolled in primary schools have risen from 487,000 (1956) to 1,547,000 (1977) and in secondary schools from 27,000 to 486,000 over the same period.[6] Increased investment in education is also reflected in a gradual rise in the national literacy rate. However, only 12 per cent of the rural population was literate in 1970, compared with a national average of 24 per cent.[7]

The structure of the education system involves two years' attendance at Koranic schools prior to enrolment at age 7 years in state education. School attendance is voluntary, and in view of the limited range of educational facilities available, it is unlikely to become obligatory in the near future. Employment of children (particularly of girls) in the carpet and other industries is a practice which further discourages enrolment.

The percentage of primary pupils completing their schooling has risen progressively over the last decade, and 36 per cent advance to secondary levels of instruction. Nevertheless, investment in secondary education has perhaps been disproportionate to the numbers benefiting from the system, and money might have been better used in expansion of primary education. Exactly the same point could be made in regard of higher education: in 1976/7, 44,000 students were enrolled at that level of education, which has been very costly to provide in Morocco.

It is a sad fact that the efforts of government to pass the benefits of modern education to an ever growing number will lead to widespread unemployment amongst those newly educated. As in most capital-poor states, new entrants to the labour market have ever improving qualifications, but the number of modern-sector job opportunities is small, and increases only slowly with economic growth. It is difficult to avoid the conclusion that imparting literacy to the 76 per cent of the adult population who cannot read or write should receive a higher priority than further expansion of modern education, especially at more advanced levels. Yet the expansion of modern education accomplished thus far makes a change of strategy difficult; the social demand for education is already well established, and will grow.

## 3 The Demand for Labour: Economic Development

The inheritance of the colonial period in Morocco is clearly expressed in the country's dualistic economy. Twenty years after independence, the urban service sector and modern agricultural enterprises established by the colonists still contrast sharply with the generally traditional form of agriculture.

Economic growth since independence has been hampered by a number of problems, including low and variable agricultural productivity, rapid population growth, limited foreign and domestic markets for manufactured goods, and growing disparities between rural and urban areas in terms of incomes, infrastructure and employment opportunities. Economic growth during the 1960s was so low that the level of GDP *per capita* scarcely changed throughout the decade.

In recent years GDP has oscillated with fluctuations in the agricultural and mining sectors (Table 13.2). While over 50 per cent of the population are employed in the agricultural sector, agriculture contributes only 24 per cent of GDP.[8] The low levels of labour productivity and high levels of underemployment amongst the rural labour force reflect the traditional nature of most of Moroccan agriculture: 87 per cent of all agricultural households possess less than four acres. Al-

Table 13.2: Morocco: Gross Domestic Product by Economic Sector, 1970 to 1976 (at 1960 prices, $ million)

| | 1970 | 1971 | 1972 | 1973 | 1974 | 1975 | 1976 | Annual Growth Rate 1974-6 |
|---|---|---|---|---|---|---|---|---|
| Agriculture | 735 | 781 | 890 | 889 | 954 | 893 | 1,009 | 2.8 |
| Energy | 69 | 73 | 94 | 117 | 120 | 136 | 144 | 9.5 |
| Mining | 122 | 124 | 165 | 212 | 227 | 178 | 188 | – 9.0 |
| Manufacturing | 335 | 351 | 401 | 493 | 483 | 544 | 576 | 9.2 |
| Construction | 138 | 148 | 161 | 173 | 191 | 339 | 439 | 51.6 |
| Transport | 432 | 454 | 520 | 612 | 612 | 683 | 726 | 8.9 |
| Commerce | 539 | 561 | 642 | 769 | 780 | 875 | 941 | 9.8 |
| Total | 2,370 | 2,492 | 2,873 | 3,265 | 3,367 | 3,648 | 4,023 | 4.0 |

Source: Banque du Maroc, *Exercise 1976* (Rabat, 1977).

though the 1973 to 1977 plan allocated considerable investment to irrigation and dam projects ($387 million), the cereal lands, where the majority of the peasantry live, have received much less assistance. It remains doubtful whether investment in irrigated agriculture will in the long term yield higher returns than equivalent investment in the areas of traditional rain-fed cultivation.[9]

Inefficiency in the agricultural sector is highlighted by the recent trend in trade, in which food imports have grown to exceed food exports (Table 13.3).

Table 13.3: Morocco: International Trade in Food, 1970, 1972, 1974 and 1976 ($ million)

|                          | 1970  | 1972  | 1974  | 1976  |
|--------------------------|-------|-------|-------|-------|
| Exports                  | 246   | 301   | 379   | 439   |
| Imports                  | 115   | 136   | 422   | 481   |
| Surplus (+) or Deficit (−) | + 131 | + 165 | − 43  | − 42  |

Source: Banque du Maroc, *Exercise 1976* (Rabat, 1977).

The phosphate mining industry accounted for 8.6 per cent of GDP in 1975. Typical of its turbulent history are the large fluctuations in output. For example, between January and December 1972, the tonnage mined grew 21 per cent. In contrast, in 1975, it declined by 27 per cent over the year. Moroccan exports account for one-third of all phosphate traded on the international market. Moroccan phosphate sales increased rapidly between 1972 and 1974, production rising to 20 million tons in 1974 (Table 13.4), but revenues increased at an even greater rate: the price of phosphates soared from $14 per ton in 1973 to $68 per ton in 1975, though subsequent economic recession on the the world market, coupled with continued high prices, led to a fall in demand in 1975. Sales recovered again in 1976. It is planned to open a new phosphate mine to raise production to 30 million tons per annum.

Manufacturing occurs only on a very limited scale. As has been noted,[10] during the early colonial period, the French did not encourage industrial activities on a very wide front. Industrial employment continues to be dominated by those industries fostered by the French in the last decade of the colonial period, such as textiles, chemicals, food processing and sugar refining.

A deteriorating economic situation in the early 1970s greatly influenced the goals of the national plan (1973 to 1977). The plan had dual

Table 13.4: Morocco: Production of Phosphate 1972 to 1977 (thousand tons)

| Year | Output |
|------|--------|
| 1972 | 15,100 |
| 1973 | 17,080 |
| 1974 | 19,750 |
| 1975 | 14,120 |
| 1976 | 15,660 |
| 1977 | 15,700 |

Source: Banque du Maroc, *Exercise 1977* (Rabat, 1978).

aims: maximisation of economic growth; and a more equitable social and geographical distribution of growth. This second goal was a direct response to the increasing social and regional inequalities which had emerged in the late 1960s and early 1970s.[11]

The most recent developments suggest that heavy industry is being accorded high priority. A one million ton per annum steel mill is planned, and a petrochemical complex is to be established, in co-operation with Abu Dhabi. The capacity of the cement industry is being expanded to meet increasing demands for construction materials. With the exception of the further development of food processing industries, the plan favours continued investment in capital-intensive units rather than in labour-absorptive activities. This is surprising in view of the avowed policy of nurturing those industries offering the greatest scope for job creation.[12]

## 4 The Labour Market

The most recent source of comprehensive labour market information is the census of 1971. The 1973 to 1977 plan included projections of anticipated employment in 1977, but these were of a highly speculative nature. Although current detailed information on employment in Morocco is lacking, the main features of the labour market are known. The total labour force in 1977 was estimated as some 4.4 millions, giving a crude participation rate of 24 per cent. This figure does not include women who work on the land who, when included, raise the crude participation rate to 30 per cent. About half the recorded work-force are employed in agriculture (Table 13.5). Again, in reality, this proportion would also rise significantly with the inclusion of working women. The construction sector employed an estimated 8 per cent of the work-force in 1977, and is thought to be growing annually at 16 per cent in terms of employment.

Table 13.5: Morocco: Estimate of Employment by Economic Sector, 1977[a]

| Economic Sector | Number | Per cent |
|---|---|---|
| Agriculture and fishing | 2,135,000 | 48.0 |
| Mining and energy | 80,000 | 1.8 |
| Manufacturing | 600,000 | 13.5 |
| Construction | 370,000 | 8.3 |
| Commerce | 345,000 | 7.7 |
| Transport and private services | 580,000 | 13.1 |
| Government services | 340,000 | 7.6 |
| Total | 4,450,000 | 100.0 |

Note: a. This table includes a number of unemployed persons estimated to be in the region of 450,000.
Source: Secrétariat d'Etat au Plan, *Plan de Développement Economique at Social 1973-1977* (Rabat, 1973), pp. 119-21.

### (a) Unemployment

The 1971 census recorded a 9 per cent unemployment rate. However, enumeration was carried out during the summer months, a period of high employment in both the agricultural and service sectors. This resulted in a marked underestimation of true levels of unemployment. The census also recorded some underemployment as full employment. Even so, a measure of underemployment, based on the number of months worked in the previous year, showed 22 per cent of the labour force to be underemployed in addition to the unemployed. A more recent estimate suggests that in 1976/7 there were about 450,000 unemployed.[13]

In broad terms, Morocco's unemployed and underemployed are an inevitable result of a large population and a relatively small economic base. However, two particular factors have contributed towards the problem. First, the programme adopted by the government to combat unemployment through public works and job creation schemes has not been effective. It proved to be only a temporary palliative rather than a permanent solution to the problem of unemployment. The programme was designed to absorb surplus labour in rural areas, in government sponsored projects such as reafforestation schemes, soil restoration and housing provision, for example. The essentially temporary nature of the programme has served to leave the overall situation unchanged. In any event, at its peak, the programme provided only 50,000 jobs, a small proportion of the estimated unemployed.

Secondly, changes in the European labour market have reduced the annual flow of Moroccan migrants to Europe to a tenth of its previous extent. The number of Moroccans leaving the country to work in Europe slumped dramatically in 1974. In 1973, 30,000 migrants left the country, but by 1975 the number had fallen to 3,000 (Table 13.6). Outmigration had previously comprised an important aspect of the labour market.

Table 13.6: Morocco: Number of Migrants Leaving for Europe, 1973 to 1977

|  | 1973 | 1974 | Year 1975 | 1976 | 1977 |
|---|---|---|---|---|---|
| Number of Migrants | 29,700 | 14,100 | 2,900 | 1,800 | 1,300 |

Sources: Secrétariat d'Etat au Plan, *Plan de Développement, 1973-1977* (Rabat, 1977), p. 122; Office National D'Immigration, *Statistiques de l'immigration, Année 1976, 1977* (Paris).

*(b) Moroccans Abroad*

Outmigration from Morocco to Europe has occurred extensively throughout the 1960s and early 1970s. Consequently, government economic and employment plans now include reference to the likely volume of outmigration. The unpredictability of external demand for Moroccan migrants makes this a risky task. The number of Moroccan workers in Europe is not known exactly. Estimates for 1974[14] suggest a figure in excess of 200,000 workers. Since then, the number of Moroccans abroad has plummeted. Not only have Moroccan migrant workers had to return home from Europe, but an unfortunate consequence of the dispute between Morocco and Algeria over the western Sahara was the forced repatriation of some 30,000 Moroccans between December 1975 and January 1976.[15] Thus yet another door has closed for unemployed Moroccans, whilst the returnees have increased further the pressure upon the government to create more employment.

Remittances from migrants abroad had come to be an important source of foreign exchange for the economy. Table 13.7 shows the income from remittances and their contribution relative to that of phosphate exports. In fact Table 13.7 is not comparing like with like, since the phosphate 'earnings' are at the disposal of the government, while remittances are not, being private transfers. None the less, remittances are a welcome source of foreign exchange, the decline of which, with the net return of the workers from France, will prejudice adversely the Moroccan balance of payments.

Table 13.7: Morocco: Remittances of Migrant Workers and Foreign
Exchange Derived from Phosphate Sales, 1966 to 1975 ($ million)

| Year | Remittances | Foreign Exchange from Phosphate Sales |
|------|-------------|---------------------------------------|
| 1966 | 31 | 105 |
| 1967 | 41 | 108 |
| 1968 | 39 | 107 |
| 1969 | 60 | 109 |
| 1970 | 62 | 113 |
| 1972 | 95 | 116 |
| 1972 | 139 | 146 |
| 1973 | 249 | 192 |
| 1974 | 358 | 937 |
| 1975 | 526 | 691 |

Source: Banque du Maroc, *Exercise 1976* (Rabat, 1977).

Official estimates based on bank figures shown in the table of remittances are inevitably underestimates. Money is also transferred by postal services and by migrants returning on vacation. It is difficult to find data permitting a direct comparison of wages in France and Morocco. Most figures suggest that a Moroccan worker in France can return between $97 and $122 per month, whilst the average worker in Morocco would earn between $49 and $73 per month.[16] The reward for working outside Morocco was therefore considerable, and will be sadly missed.

Whilst the number of migrants departing compared to the total work-force has not been large compared, for example, to Jordan, the opportunities of working in Europe presented Moroccans with an alternative to the domestic labour market. Thus unemployment levels, as long as migration was possible, were eased by the absence of migrant workers. This tempering effect of labour exports upon the Moroccan labour market has now been lost.

It was in an attempt to redress this that an agreement was signed between Morocco and Saudi Arabia in September 1976 for the transfer of between 50,000 and 100,000 Moroccan workers. So far, it is clear that by no means this number have departed. Indeed, 8,500 Moroccan workers were reported to have found employment in Libya and Saudi Arabia in 1977.[17] However, international migration to the Arab world will certainly not be the new pattern for the future: Moroccans have neither the skills nor the institutional framework required by Arab labour importers.

## 5 Conclusion

Demographic, economic, locational and political factors have combined to constrain the strategies open to Moroccan manpower planners. In post-war years surplus Moroccan labour has left to work abroad, especially in France. However, this has proved unsatisfactory as a long-term policy of reducing unemployment. With the imminent return of yet more migrants from France, labour exporting now appears to have been no more than a method of accumulating labour management problems for the future. Not only have Moroccan employment policies since independence assumed the continued ability of European economies to absorb large numbers of the Moroccan unemployed, but they have also come to view labour absorption by emigration as a substitute for employment creation within Morocco.

The government now faces a crisis. Population growth adds daily to the demands on social services and an ever increasing number of youths enters the labour market each year. Many of these are highly educated, but the vast majority of the population are illiterate. The economy is small, dependent on France and the price of phosphates. No scheme of economic development can hope to absorb the estimated 500,000 Moroccans presently unemployed; even employing the new labour market entrants annually will be difficult. Meanwhile avenues of worker migration are foreclosing; Morocco is being thrown ever more completely on her own resources. Although Morocco's problems are not as advanced as those of Egypt's, they are in nature similar, and potentially of the same scale.

### Notes

1. World Bank, *Development Report, 1978* (Washington, DC, 1978), Table 1.
2. Ministry of Education, Statistical Department, *Annual Report, 1976/77* (Rabat, 1977).
3. United Nations Statistical Council, *Demographic Yearbook, 1976* (New York, 1977).
4. Secrétariat d'Etat au Plan, *Recensement général de la population et de l'habitat, 1971* (Rabat, 1971). 5, E.
5. S. Cherkaoui, 'Human Resources as a Factor in the Development of Morocco' (unpublished MPhil thesis, Cairo University, 1975), p. 22.
6. Ministry of Education, Statistical Department, *Annual Report, 1976/77* (Rabat, 1977).
7. A. Motassime, 'La politique de l'enseignement au Maroc de 1957 a 1977', *Maghreb-Machrek, 79* (1978) p. 40.
8. Economist Intelligence Unit, *Quarterly Economic Review*, Annual Supple-

ment, Morocco (London, 1977), p. 7.

9. A. Benhadi, 'La politique Marocaine de barrages', *Annuaire de l'Afrique du Nord* (Paris, 1976), p. 284.

10. R.I. Lawless, 'Industrialisation in the Maghreb: Progress, Problems and Prospects', *Maghreb Review, 1*, 3 (London 1976), p. 11.

11. P. De Mas, 'The Place of Peripheral Regions in Moroccan Planning, *Tijdschrift vor Economische en Sociale Geografie, 69* (Summer 1978), p. 80.

12. Secrétariat d'Etat au Plan, *Plan de Développement Economique et Social, 1973-1977* (Rabat), p. 123.

13. *MEED*, 14 January 1977, p. 14.

14. A. Findlay, A. Findlay and R. Lawless, *Country Case Study: The Kingdom of Morocco*, International Migration Project Working Paper (Durham, 1978), Table 35, p. 37.

15. S. Dialto, 'Les explusions en Afrique', *Jeune Afrique, 79* (1975), p. 17.

16. OCDE, *Migrations et transferts de technologie: étude de cas Algerie, Maroc, Tunisie et France* (Paris, 1975), p. 68.

17. Economist Intelligence Unit, *Quarterly Economic Review*, 4 (Moroceo, 1976), p. 1.

# 14 THE YEMEN ARAB REPUBLIC (YAR)

## 1 Introduction

The Yemen Arab Republic (YAR) is located in the south-west of the Arabian peninsula, north of the People's Democratic Republic of Yemen. The terrain is largely rugged and mountainous. Internal communications are consequently difficult and, until recently were very limited. The first census of the country, taken in 1975, enumerated about 4,700,000 inhabitants. The country is generally acknowledged as poor: by World Bank standards, it is one of the 25 least developed countries in the world enjoying a *per capita* income of $250 (1976).[1] Most of the population gain a living from traditional means, mainly agriculture; the modern sector is small, and provides only limited employment. As a result of poverty and, by peninsula standards, a relatively large population, the YAR has been for some years, and continues to be, a major supplier of labour to Saudi Arabia and the other Gulf states. Some 330,000 persons were recorded as being temporarily abroad at the time of the census, representing some 6 per cent of the population, and 20 per cent of the work-force.

The government is dependent to a considerable extent on financial grants and aid from donor agencies and neighbouring governments, notably Saudi Arabia. Yemen's endowment of resources, or rather lack of them, makes her a truly capital-poor state. Despite this, the Yemen's (YAR) present style of development has more than a little in common with capital-rich states.

## 2 The Supply of Labour

### (a) Population

The first reliable and comprehensive source of information on the population of the Yemen (YAR) is the census of 1975. After adjustments have been made for various familiar types of census inaccuracies, such as the under-enumeration of small children, the total *de facto* (inhabitant) population for 1975 is 4,705,300, with a sex ratio of 91 malesto 100 females. In addition, various estimates were made of the numbers outside the country during the census reference period.

While there has been widespread acceptance amongst commentators of the number of *de facto* residents, considerable debate has surrounded the figure of those temporarily abroad. The first point to make is the distinction between those Yemenis (YAR) temporarily abroad, with or without families, mostly working in Saudi Arabia, and those Yemenis abroad who are long-term emigrants, having left the country on a semi-permanent basis. Steffan describes this latter group as those abroad for longer than five years, who have lost contact with their relatives in Yemen (YAR).[2] He estimates their number in 1975 as about 250,000, of whom 40 per cent were living in other Arab countries, 20 per cent in Ethiopia and Eritrea and 16 per cent in Europe and North America. This group is not included in the *de jure* population of Yemen (YAR).

Initially, before the census was fully analysed, an official estimate of the number of Yemenis (YAR) abroad was made of 1,234,000.[3] It was unfortunate that this estimate, based on the personal opinions of various advisers to the government, should have been so high. Since that estimate, several others have been made, some based on the census, others on a variety of economic and social data. Estimates derived from the census have been made by Allman and Hill,[4] who calculated a figure of 348,000 temporarily absent Yemenis (YAR) on census night, and by Steffan, who estimated 350,000 short-term emigrants on census night.[5]

Prior to the release of the full results of the census, Sinclair and Socknat,[6] using economic and social data such as border crossings remittances and data on employment in capital-rich countries in 1975, estimated a maximum figure of 600,000 Yemenis (YAR) abroad on census night. After the preliminary census was released, this figure was revised downwards, and the same authors estimated that in 1977, 541,000 Yemeni (YAR) migrant workers were abroad.[7]

All these approaches tackle the problem of the number of Yemeni (YAR) migrants by trying to construct a picture consistent with extant Yemeni data sources. Yet another approach is to utilise the part of the matrix of all migrant workers by country of origin and country of employment in the Middle East for 1975 constructed by Birks and Sinclair.[8] This source suggests that in 1975, 290,000 Yemeni workers were abroad, a number which is certainly compatible with the demographic estimates made earlier since, assuming a crude activity rate of 83 per cent, the total Yemeni (YAR) migrant community would be approximately 350,000.

There is, therefore, a consensus of opinion amongst technicians that about 350,000 Yemenis were absent on census night. This figure is much lower than the oft-quoted figure of 1,200,000, which has no basis in observable evidence. Here a figure produced by Steffan, based on the census of 331,650 short-term emigrants on census night is accepted. By combining the *de facto* inhabitants with these short term emigrants, a total *de jure* population of 5,037,000 is obtained.

According to census figures, Yemen's (YAR) crude birth rate is about 47 per 1000, and crude death rate 29 per thousand. Thus net population increase is in the region of 1.8 per cent per annum. These figures confirm an overall impression of an underdeveloped society, and one which has not yet experienced a population explosion. That, how-ever, appears imminent, given the likely impact of development on child mortality rates, and hence the overall death rate. The pervasive outmigration of males tends to depress fertility rates, but the high cash incomes accruing to those households with absent males partly amelior-ates this depressive effect on population growth, as nutritional levels are raised, and access to medical care becomes greater.

In 1975 only 11 per cent of the population was living in urban areas, on the basis of the rather dubious definition of 'settlements comprising over 2,000 inhabitants'. Slightly over half of this urban population is accounted for by three cities: Sanaa (138,620 inhabitants), Hodeida (82,720 inhabitants), and Taiz (81,000 inhabitants).[9]

## (b) The Educational Attainment of the Population

The level of educational attainment in Yemen (YAR) is low. The 1975 census showed that the literacy rate for those aged over 10 years was 13 per cent for both sexes, and as low as 2 per cent for women (Table 14.1). The numbers of the population holding a school certificate is low: only 1.5 per cent of the population hold such a certificate. Most certificate holders live in the governorates in which the three main cities are situated.

Modern education began to succeed the traditional *kuttab* system in 1962, but expansion was slow until the end of the civil war. The modern education system established in the Yemen (YAR) follows the six years of primary, three years of preparatory and three years of sec-ondary pattern common in the Arab world. At the preparatory and secondary levels students may select teacher training or general studies. In addition, boys may select a commercial specialisation at the secon-dary level. A 'technical institute' in Sanaa is operated by a Chinese technical assistance mission. The institute takes entrants after comple-tion of primary school. Part of the five-year curriculum is taught in the Chinese language. Enrolments in the academic year 1974/5 for the

Table 14.1: Yemen (YAR): Literacy by Age Cohort, 1975

| Age Cohort | Males) (per cent) | Females (per cent) | Total (per cent) |
|---|---|---|---|
| 10-19 | 29.4 | 5.3 | 17.6 |
| (10-14) | (30.0) | (6.4) | (18.9) |
| (15-19) | (28.8) | (4.0) | (15.4) |
| 20-29 | 29.2 | 2.1 | 12.8 |
| 30-39 | 23.4 | 1.0 | 10.5 |
| 40-49 | 21.7 | 0.7 | 10.4 |
| 50-59 | 23.9 | 0.7 | 11.4 |
| 60+ | 19.7 | 0.7 | 9.6 |
| Total 10+ | 25.6 | 2.4 | 13.0 |

Source: Central Planning Office, *Population Statistics of the Yemen Arab Republic* (Sanaa, 1976), Table 7 (Arabic).

Table 14.2: Yemen (YAR): School Enrolment by Educational Level and Sex, 1974/5

| Educational Level | Boys | Girls | Total | Ratio |
|---|---|---|---|---|
| Primary | 209,996 | 22,788 | 232,784 | 45.8 |
| Preparatory | 11,765 | 1,263 | 13,028 | 2.6 |
| (of whom in teacher training) | (222) | (336) | (558) | |
| (of whom in technical institute) | (222) | ( — ) | (222) | |
| Secondary | 4,703 | 376 | 5,079 | 1.0 |
| (of whom in teacher training) | (108) | (180) | (288) | |
| (of whom in commerce) | (215) | ( — ) | (215) | |
| (of whom in technical institute) | (115) | ( — ) | (115) | |

Source: C.A. Sinclair and J. Socknat, *Assessment of Manpower Development and Policy and Programme Suggestions for the Yemen Republic, 1976,* Report to ILO, UNDP and Government of the Yemen Arab Republic (Sanaa, January, 1976), pp. 3. 27-3.37.

three levels are shown in Table 14.2.

The difficulties experienced in developing the education system have been substantial. A combination of low teacher salaries and general un-availability of qualified teachers has presented a major problem. In the 1974/5 academic year approximately 15 per cent of teachers in the pri-mary level were employed on a 'contract' or part-time basis; many of these teachers had themselves dropped out of primary school. The alter-native of importing qualified and graduate teachers from abroad is too expensive for the Ministry of Education to undertake on a large scale. As might be expected under these circumstances, drop-out and re-peater rates have been high throughout the system.[10]

Despite the obstacles faced by the government in providing basic education, Sanaa Higher College (since renamed Sanaa University) was opened in 1970. In 1974/5, 1,200 Yemeni (YAR) students and 1,500 foreign students enrolled in the university, the large majority of whom read either arts or commerce (76 per cent).

Other formal training institutes and programmes include a health manpower and nursing institute; a motor vehicle mechanics training centre operated by the highway authority; a police college, a training programme operated by the Yemen (YAR) Electricity Corporation for its staff involved in maintenance of electricity generation equipment; and an Institute of Public Administration with language, secretarial and various courses, some of which are tailor-made for the requirements of individual Ministries.

The most recent five-year plan, 1976/7 to 1980/1,[11] outlines a rapid expansion of primary education and a diversification of education at the preparatory and secondary levels. Despite these latter efforts, it seems that the bulk of education resources will be devoted to formal education. With so small a modern sector it seems likely that the majority of school-leavers will be obliged to remain outside the formal 'wage sector' of the labour market. In future years there may be a growing imbalance between the aspirations and qualifications of labour market entrants and the jobs open to them.

### 3 The Demand for Labour

*(a) Recent Economic Development*

In the early 1970s, the traditional subsistence agriculture base of the Yemeni (YAR) economy began to lose its overwhelming dominance. Government especially, and to a lesser extent other sectors, began to develop under the new-found stability and with increasing external financial assistance. The task of transforming this traditional economy into a modern one has been approached with energy, and GNP *per capita* has increased quickly since 1973. This is not to say that development has been as rapid, though change certainly has.

Yemen's (YAR) development is, in some respects, paradoxical: it is a poor country, yet receives more aid than she can spend; her population is large, yet labour shortages compromise her development plans; her visible trade balance is in the red, while the current account is in surplus.

*(b) Sectoral Origin of Gross Domestic Product*

In 1976/7 Yemen's (YAR) GNP *per capita* was estimated as $390.[12]

Since then this figure has increased substantially, principally as a result of increasing workers' remittances. Gross domestic product has also risen over the past few years; between 1972/3 and 1975/6 it grew at 5.9 per cent in real terms, suggesting a rise in GNP *per capita* of some 4 per cent per annum.

The economy is based on agriculture, much of which is conducted at a subsistence level. Table 14.3 shows that agriculture accounted for 44 per cent of GDP in 1975/6. Some 1.5 million hectares of land are usually cultivated. As much as another 2.0 million hectares are occasionally farmed in years of especially plentiful rainfall.[13] Of the normally cultivated 1.5 million hectares, approximately 85 per cent is rainfed. Only the remainder is irrigated. Yields therefore vary widely.

Table 14.3: Yemen (YAR): Gross Domestic Product by Sector, 1975/6 ($ million)

| Economic Sector | Gross Domestic Product | |
|---|---|---|
| | Amount | Per cent |
| Agriculture, fishing and forestry | 542 | 44.5 |
| Industry, mining and electricity | 71 | 5.8 |
| Construction | 53 | 4.4 |
| Trade | 287 | 23.5 |
| Finance and banking | 33 | 2.6 |
| Transport and communications | 35 | 2.9 |
| Government | 120 | 9.9 |
| Housing | 47 | 3.9 |
| Other services | 30 | 2.5 |
| Gross domestic product | 1,218 | 100.0 |

Source: World Bank, *Yemen Arab Republic: Development of a Traditional Arab Economy* (Washington, DC, January 1979), Table 2.1, p. 223.

Agricultural self-sufficiency for the Yemen (YAR) does not seem imminent, despite the aims and efforts of the planners. Although declining as a share of total imports, in absolute terms the value of food imports had risen by early 1977 to nearly six times its 1970 level (current prices).

After agriculture, trade and government are the next most important sectors. This pattern will change only slowly, as the stock of infrastructure is so low that neither the manufacturing sector nor transport and communications are in a position to make much contribution to the national accounts. The construction sector will probably grow quite rapidly, as development proceeds, through the construction phase.

*(c) Balance of Payments*

Yemen (YAR) is in considerable deficit on her visible account, but more than compensates with her invisibles, principally workers' remittances. Exports represent only 2 per cent of imports. This is itself a clear illustration of how little real development has proceeded in Yemen (YAR). If workers' remittances were to decline to more moderate levels, then the country would suffer severe economic difficulties and the population a much reduced standard of living.

Table 14.4: Yemen (YAR): Balance of Payments, 1975/6 to 1976/7 ($ million)

|  | 1975/6 | 1976/7 |
| --- | --- | --- |
| Trade balance | − 392 | − 704 |
| Exports | 13 | 18 |
| Imports | − 405 | − 722 |
| Service balance | 46 | 43 |
| Private transfers | 484 | 833 |
| Receipts | 556 | 1,002 |
| Payments | − 72 | − 169 |
| Current account balance | 138 | 172 |

Source: World Bank, *Yemen Arab Republic: Development of a Traditional Economy* (Washington, DC, January 1979), Table 3.1, p. 227.

Workers' remittances increased dramatically from 1974/5 to 1976/7, increasing almost five times in this two-year period. Whilst the number of workers in the oil-rich states was increasing over that period, wage rates were also rising very rapidly. The character of Yemeni (YAR) migration may also have been altering in such a way as to increase the volume of remittances. Private capital transfers are also included in the figures on Table 14.5. Normally these would be small, but in 1976 Saudi Arabia terminated all non-nationally owned businesses. Many Yemeni traders remitted their capital from Saudi Arabia either then or subsequently, swelling the recorded private transfers and remittances. Therefore, some of the increase in transfer payments in and just after 1976 has to be seen as a 'once and for all' kind. Leaving that problem aside, remittances increased at the steadier level of about 10 per cent per annum from 1977/8 to 1978/9. Discounting for inflation leaves remittances more or less constant in real terms.

Despite the aura of stability and steady growth conveyed by Table 14.5, the predictions made in Chapter 20 are that the demand for Yemeni migrants in Saudi Arabia will decline. This will inevitably lead

Table 14.5: Yemen (YAR): Private Transfers, 1971/2 to 1978/9
($ million)

| Fiscal Year | Private Transfers ($ million) |
|---|---|
| 1971/2 | 65 |
| 1972/3 | 111 |
| 1973/4 | 119 |
| 1974/5 | 216 |
| 1975/6 | 556 |
| 1976/7 | 1,005 |
| 1977/8 | 1,300 |
| 1978/9 | 1,454 |

Source: Central Bank of Yemen, Foreign Exchange Department, unpublished typescripts (1973, 1978 and 1979).

to a reduced flow of remittances, with the serious consequences spelt out above.

*(d) Conclusion*

Yemen (YAR) is currently enjoying the financial benefits of the goodwill of her oil-rich neighbours and the concern of a wide range of international and bilateral donor agencies. The Yemeni (YAR) economy is also experiencing the uncertain benefit of very high levels of workers' remittances. The economy has a small productive base, and expanding it is bound to be slow and difficult. Even so, Yemen (YAR) has flexibility enough on the foreign exchange front, and sufficient financial resources through international aid to make substantial progress in the coming five to ten years provided these financial resources are sensibly harnessed. Compared to many developing countries, the Yemen (YAR) must be considered exceptionally privileged.

## 4 The Labour Market

A large majority of economically active Yemenis are farmers. Table 14.6 shows that, out of the total work-force of some 1.4 million persons in 1975, 69 per cent were working as farmers or in informal employment. The modern sector of the work-force is extremely small, employing only 6 per cent of the total. This provides confirmation of the impression gained from GDP figures: the Yemeni economy is still traditional and orientated towards agriculture, with a small modern base. Of the 90,000 persons working in the modern sector, government employees account for 37,470 persons, some 42 per cent. Thus the non-government private sector is very small indeed.

Furthermore, the modern-sector employing establishments in the country are small in scale and of minimal organisational complexity. In 1975, some 14,400 private establishments were located in the five main urban areas of the country: Sanaa (39 per cent), Taiz (27 per cent), Hodeida (20 per cent), Dhamar (88 per cent) and Ibb (6 per cent). Of all employees in these establishments, 70 per cent were engaged in firms with less than five workers. The remaining employees worked in 740 establishments, the vast majority of which are operated as sole proprie- torships. Thus the basis upon which further modern-sector development can be built is very small indeed. In the census, some 64,000 persons were reported as unemployed. These represent some 4.5 per cent of the total work-force. Apart from those recorded as unemployed, there are large numbers of underemployed in rural areas (despite the outmigra- tion) and a growing volume of informal employment in the larger settle- ments.

Men account for the large majority of employment, 91 per cent, and the large majority of the 129,600 active women in 1975 worked on the farms. The pervasive outmigration of Yemeni (YAR) men has led to an increased participation of women in the rural economy, which now depends on female labour in a substantially greater way than pre- viously.

Table 14.6: Yemen (YAR): Disposition of Labour Force, 1975

| Sector | Number | Per cent |
|---|---|---|
| Farmers and informal sector | 982,000 | 68.9 |
| Modern sector | 90,200 | 6.3 |
| Unemployed | 63,600 | 4.5 |
| Workers abroad | 290,100 | 20.3 |
| Total | 1,425,900 | 100.0 |

Source: Derived from J.S. Birks, C.A. Sinclair and J.A. Socknat, *Country Case Study: The Yemen Arab Republic*, International Migration Project Working Paper (Durham, 1978).

## 5 Yemeni (YAR) Workers Abroad

Traditionally, Yemenis have been highly mobile geographically. The existence of Yemeni communities in the Far East, Europe and America bears witness to this. However, from the perspective of contemporary economic development, it is the movement of migrants to Saudi Arabia for employment which has become of particular significance.

The number of migrants for employment abroad on a short-term basis grew quickly from the mid-1960s, when it stood at around 130,000, to a figure of about 290,000 in 1975. The distribution of these Yemeni (YAR) workers is shown on Table 14.7. The vast majority, 97 per cent, are found in Saudi Arabia. In 1975 these 290,000 migrants represented about 20 per cent of the entire Yemeni (YAR) work force. However, this proportion understates the wider significance of the impact of migration, which has not yet been fully evaluated. For example, the loss of Yemeni workers from agriculture may have affected domestic output and, crucially, the maintenance of rural infrastructure. Domestic wage rates have risen with the departure of migrants, as has the cost of living. Migrants who work abroad return with a different perspective and approach to life, which in some ways may be beneficial to the economy and in some ways harmful. Evaluating comprehensively Yemen's (YAR) experience of supplying labour to the oil-rich states is not yet possible, since we are still in a period of change. It seems appropriate to observe that the very pervasive type of outmigration Yemen (YAR) has experienced may carry with it some nominal advantages, such as a high level of remittances, but equally some substantial costs, which at present are little appreciated or understood.

Table 14.7: Yemen (YAR). Migrant Workers Abroad, 1975

| Country of Employment | Number | Per cent |
|---|---|---|
| Saudi Arabia | 280,400 | 96.6 |
| United Arab Emirates | 4,500 | 1.6 |
| Kuwait | 2,757 | 1.0 |
| Qatar | 1,250 | 0.4 |
| Bahrain | 1,121 | 0.4 |
| Oman | 100 | — |
| Total | 290,128 | 100.0 |

Source: J.S. Birks and C.A. Sinclair, *International Migration and Development in the Arab Region* (ILO, Geneva, 1980), Table 10.

## 6 Conclusion

Despite immense challenges to Yemeni (YAR) development, the past decade is generally considered, in economic, political and social terms, to have been one of success and improvement. Yemen (YAR) has so far tended not to suffer the disadvantages of international migration but rather to benefit from it, chiefly through remittances which have increased GNP *per capita*. Moreover, Yemen's (YAR) internal political problems died down in the late sixties, just as remittances began to boost GNP and bilateral and international donor agencies were becoming more concerned about the economic plight of the world's poorest nations, a category into which Yemen (YAR) aptly fell. Furthermore, as an Arab nation, Yemen also qualified for her share of the sudden wealth of OAPEC countries.

To the casual observer, economic development appears to have been frenzied after 1975, as migrants' remittances poured into the economy, port congestion emerged as a serious problem, imported cars and trucks proliferated, and as aid donors actually appeared to compete to assist the government. However, the more discerning eye is less impressed by the rising tide of consumer imports, the rate of inflation, and the trend of switching from labour-intensive to capital-intensive technology in rural areas. Behind a superficial appearance of development, it is not clear what has been accomplished that will outlast the largesse of donor agencies and the demand for labour in Saudi Arabia. The answer is, of course, not 'nothing', but much less has been achieved than appears at first sight. There has been very little progress in enlarging the productive base of the economy, or in engendering self-sustaining economic development with a domestic momentum, rather than a reliance upon external funding.

Perhaps still more importantly it appears that the government-led style of economic development which has been enforced upon the Yemen (YAR) is engendering a pattern of attitudes and aspirations amongst the work-force which is more often found in the urban work-forces of the capital-rich states. With the extra developmental constraints faced by the Yemen (YAR), any such 'capital-rich type' aspirations and the reluctance to participate realistically in the modern sector of the economy will be a profound drawback to real economic growth. Perhaps more than in any other country in the peninsula, the Yemen's (YAR) population must be one of her prime assets in development, particularly in view of her lack of physical resources. If the value of Yemeni (YAR) human resources to the developing economy is reduced because of unrealistic attitudes and aspirations gained through migration to capital-rich states, then the task of improving Yemeni standards of living will be yet more difficult. Great attention must be focused upon the utilisation and nurturing of Yemeni (YAR) human resources.

Finally, and more broadly, the question might be posed: given that

Yemen (YAR) came late to the field of modern development, has her development effort and the advice given her shown signs of learning from past mistakes? Donor agencies and technical advisers surely cannot plead lack of experience in this field, yet in so many ways the same problems based upon unsound decision-making are beginning to emerge.

## Notes

1. See World Bank, *World Development Report, 1978* (Washington, DC, 1978), Table 1, p. 76. But estimates of this figure can vary considerably, depending on what figure is taken for remittances.

2. H. Steffan, 'Population Movement' (mimeograph, n.d.), Fig. 2-23, p. 1-91.

3. Yemen Arab Republic, Central Planning Organisation, *The Housing and Population Census, Preliminary Results* (Sanaa, 1976), p. 31.

4. J. Allman and A.G. Hill, 'Fertility, Mortality, Migration and Family Planning in the Yemen Arab Republic' (mimeograph, March 1977), p. 10.

5. H. Steffan, *et al., Final Report on the Airphoto Interpretation Project of the Swiss Technical Co-operation Service, Berne* (Zurich, April 1978), p. 1-92.

6. J.A. Socknat and C.A. Sinclair, *An Estimate of Yemen's Total Population and Workers Abroad in 1975* (Sanaa, November 1975), p. 31.

7. J.A. Socknat and C.A. Sinclair, *Migration for Employment Abroad and its Impact on Development in the Yemen Arab Republic,* International Migration Project Working Paper (Durham, July 1978), Table 35, p. 46.

8. J.S. Birks and C.A. Sinclair, *A Summary of Provisional Findings: Empirical Patterns, Past Trends and Future Development,* International Migration Project Working Paper (Durham, November 1978), Table 4, p. 12.

9. H. Steffan, *Preliminary Report No. 5, Data Bank of Yemen's Population and Housing Census* (Zurich, May 1977), pp. 80-1.

10. C.A. Sinclair and J. Socknat, *Assessment of Manpower Development in the Yemen Arab Republic* (Sanaa, 1976), pp. 3.27-3.37.

11. Central Planning Office, *Five Year Development Plan, 1976/77 to 1980/81* (Sanaa, 1976).

12. This more recent estimate than the one mentioned in note 1 was also made by the World Bank, in *Yemen Arab Republic: Development of a Traditional Economy* (Washington, DC, 1979).

13. Central Planning Organisation, Statistical Department, *Statistical Yearbook, 1974/75* (Sanaa, 1976), Table 22, p. 55.

# 15 THE PEOPLE'S DEMOCRATIC REPUBLIC OF YEMEN (PDRY)

## 1 Introduction

The People's Democratic Republic of Yemen is located at the south-west corner of the Arabian peninsula. Political independence came in 1967, and with it two profound setbacks to the economy. In most of the capital-poor states, limited economic growth appears to be achieved despite the continual challenge of population growth, the sudden shock of labour outmigration and periodic economic crises. However, occasionally countries suffer a quantum setback in economic development, which lowers the GNP by a considerable proportion. Such devastating blows tend to be of political, rather than economic, origin. For example, Jordan's GNP fell by some 32 per cent when the West Bank was lost in 1967. Similarly, the Lebanese civil war all but completely destroyed the country's economy, at a full cost yet to be calculated.

The setback suffered by Yemen (PDRY) falls into this category. In 1967 the British colonial authority withdrew abruptly and completely and at the same time the Suez Canal was closed.

The British presence in Yemen (PDRY) was a major support to the economy. Not only were the British major employers, tenants and consumers, but they also contributed a substantial proportion of the government's budget. The economic loss of the British withdrawal compounded the social disruption. Moreover, during the period of British administration, the Suez Canal had ensured a flow of ships through the Gulf of Aden, some of which had used the services of the deep-water port of Aden. The effective cessation of this productive service industry brought about a marked loss in Yemen's (PDRY) foreign exchange earning capacity.

The combined effect of these two economic reversals was to reduce GNP by between 20 and 30 per cent. The standard of living of the urban population was lowered considerably.

The government, the National Liberation Front, has tackled the country's development problems with a socialistic perspective. Income distribution has been a major preoccupation since 1967, in which time the level of social services and the proportion of the population having access to water and electricity have improved continuously.

256

The resource endowment of the country is severely limited. Only 0.2 per cent of land area is cultivable, mainly rain-fed wadis which yield unpredictably. Much of the country is mountainous, and communications are poor, particularly to the east. No mineral deposits have been found, though the search for oil continues.

Since 1973 Yemen's (PDRY) economic fortunes have improved. Rather as in the case of Yemen (YAR), the government has begun to receive substantial sums in grants and as aid from Arab, bilateral and international agencies. The reopening of the Suez Canal in 1973 also gave a major boost to the economy. Most recently, workers' remittances have risen sharply. Thus, since about 1973, the government's financial position has improved considerably, and as a result, GNP *per capita* has risen by about 3 per cent in real terms over the past six years. This is a remarkable achievement.

## 2 The Supply of Labour

### *(a) Population*

The last census was held in 1973 when the total population amounted to 1.59 million persons. Of these, one-third lived in urban areas, 57 per cent dwelt in rural areas, and 10 per cent were recorded as 'nomads'. The formal, structured aspects of Yemen's (PDRY) modern development have scarcely touched this group, who live mostly in the north-eastern areas bordering Oman and Saudi Arabia.[1]

The birth and death rates of the Yemeni (PDRY) national population are not known with accuracy, but commentators estimate that the overall growth rate is somewhere between 2.5 and 3.0 per cent. Relatively high fertility levels ensure that population increase will continue, though efforts at birth control look like having a significant impact in the medium term.

One respect in which the census is incomplete is the number of Yemenis abroad on census night. Yemen's (PDRY) tradition of out-migration and employment statistics in neighbouring states both confirm that large numbers of Yemenis were outside PDRY in 1973.

International migration for employment of Yemenis from PDRY was officially stopped in 1973, though it is certain that outmigration has continued on a more limited level since then. The main concern here is to establish the relative scale of the number of workers abroad, and the size of the domestic labour market in Yemen (PDRY). Table 15.1 gives an estimate of this for 1976. The figures are based partly on Ministry of Planning estimates, and also on research into migrant communities of the region carried out in the host countries of Yemeni (PDRY) workers abroad.[2]

Table 15.1: Yemen (PDRY): Population and Work-force at Home and Abroad, 1976

|  | Yemen (PDRY) | Abroad | Total |
|---|---|---|---|
| Labour force | 399,000 | 80,000 | 479,000 |
| Unemployed | 17,000 | – | 17,000 |
| Total | 416,000 | 80,000 | 496,000 |
| Population | 1,680,000 | 183,000 | 1,863,000 |

Source: Ministry of Planning, unpublished materials (Aden); and authors' estimates.

The crude participation rate for the entire community at home and abroad is 27.5 per cent. This figure is consistent with that of similar countries in the region. The extra participation in the economy of females, which has been encouraged by the Yemeni (PDRY) government, does not show in these figures. None the less, the country is certainly one of the most forward in expanding its formal work-force by the emancipation of women.

*(b) Educational Attainment of the Population*

As a result of the political upheavals of the 1960s, culminating in independence in 1967, and the meagre resources available for expansion of the social services after 1967, the educational level of the population is low. In 1973 only 28 per cent of the population aged ten years or more were literate (Table 15.2).

Table 15.2: Yemen (PDRY): Literacy Rates (population aged 10 years or more), 1973

|  | Men | | Women | | Total | |
|---|---|---|---|---|---|---|
|  | Number | Per cent | Number | Per cent | Number | Per cent |
| Illiterate | 254,180 | 51.2 | 482,050 | 91.3 | 736,230 | 71.9 |
| Literate | 242,450 | 48.8 | 45,720 | 8.7 | 288,170 | 28.1 |
| Total | 496,630 | 100.0 | 527,770 | 100.0 | 1,024,400 | 100.0 |

Source: Central Statistical Organisation, 'Preliminary Results of the 1973 Census' (Aden, mimeograph, n.d.).

If the measure used more commonly in this context, 'those aged 15 years or more', were adopted, then this rate would fall significantly.

The vast majority of women (91 per cent) are illiterate; the traditional bias in education towards boys remains despite the general impression of the emergence of Yemeni women.

This measure of educational attainment implies a very backward people. However, it is misleading to accept the data on Table 15.2 at face value for the following reason: by 1973 a large number of Yemenis had left the country to work abroad. Some went to Taiz in Yemen (YAR), others to Gulf states, and many to Saudi Arabia. These migrants included many of the most able and often the more wealthy members of Aden's urban dwellers. If it were possible to include in Table 15.2 the entire Yemeni community, then the impression given would be of a significantly better-educated population, particularly in the case of the men. This departure of the more qualified elements of her work-force is yet another facet of the setback faced by the Yemeni (PDRY) economy on independence.

Every effort is now being made to enrol children into schools. Table 15.3 shows school enrolments in 1976/7. Although the educational pyramid tapers off quite sharply at preparatory and secondary level, the presently limited number of job opportunities in the country for well educated people suggests that this distribution of school places is appropriate. Efforts must be made to expand technical education, though.

Table 15.3: Yemen (PDRY): School Enrolment, 1976/7

| Level | Boys | Girls | Total |
|---|---|---|---|
| Primary | 134,800 | 71,500 | 206,300 |
| Preparatory | 32,600 | 10,800 | 43,400 |
| Secondary | 8,600 | 2,300 | 10,900 |

Source: Ministry of Education, Department of Statistics (Aden, mimeograph, n.d.).

At the primary level, nearly 90 per cent of all boys of school age are enrolled. The figure for girls remains less than half, however. Thus, overall about 60 per cent of school-age children are in school.

The government has made great strides in the field of quantitative expansion of schooling, but severe inadequacies exist in standards of education. The qualifications of teachers, number of classrooms and teaching materials are all markedly inadequate. The size of classes tends to be large. In tackling these problems the government is continually constrained by its small income and the very high opportunity cost of investment expenditure. Contemporaneous with these efforts in the field of modern education for children are classes for adults in literacy training. Special efforts have also been made to reach the children of nomads, though poor communications and the transient nature of their dwellings make progress slow.

### 3 The Demand for Labour

#### (a) Economic Development

With a *per capita* GNP of $280 in 1976, Yemen (PDRY) ranks as a poor country, with a similar level of income to Yemen (YAR) and Egypt.[3] Her economy has picked up significantly since 1973, mainly for the reasons noted – improved trade and servicing revenues in Aden port following the re-opening of the Suez canal; the contemporaenous increase in soft loans and grants-in-aid; and increased worker remittances from abroad. As a consequence of this improved financial position, imports to Yemen (PDRY) have soared, and have triggered off an import-led economic boom.

Table 15.4 shows that the country's largest single productive sector is agriculture and fishing, contributing 18 per cent to GDP. In recent years the agricultural sector has been reorganised so that land holdings are distributed more equally, and government participation has increased considerably. However, whether for this or other reasons, output has stagnated or even fallen in some parts of the sector. On the other hand, the fishing industry has made considerable progress following substantial state investment in modern boats, often in partnership with other countries.

Although fishing by traditional methods has declined, a modern industry has emerged which provides both employment and, crucially, foreign exchange, as much of the catch is exported.

The largest overall contributor to GDP is government, accounting for about 19 per cent of the total. The mining and quarrying and manufacturing sectors account for about 12 per cent of GDP. Included here is the oil refinery. Although this appears as a major asset, it is presently running at below break-even point, and is therefore a liability in overall terms. The refining and marketing of petroleum is a highly competitive business and the dated technology of the Aden refinery does not bring profitability any closer. This well intentioned development venture provides an interesting comparison to the Egyptian iron and steel plant which also runs at a foreign exchange deficit.

Aden port, one of the best deep-water harbours in the region, makes

Table 15.4: Yemen (PDRY): Gross Domestic Product by Economic Sector (factor costs) ($ million), 1976

| Economic Sector | GDP | Per cent |
|---|---|---|
| Agriculture and fishing | 99.8 | 18.1 |
| Mining and quarrying | 2.7 | 0.5 |
| Manufacturing | 62.8 | 11.4 |
| Electricity, gas and water | 12.5 | 2.3 |
| Construction | 53.3 | 9.7 |
| Trade | 72.3 | 13.1 |
| Restaurants and hotels | 22.6 | 4.1 |
| Transport, storage and communications | 71.9 | 13.0 |
| Finance, insurance and real estate | 28.5 | 5.2 |
| Business and personal services | 17.9 | 3.2 |
| Government services | 107.1 | 19.4 |
| Total | 551.4 | 100.0 |

Source: Ministry of Planning (Aden, mimeograph, n.d.).

a major contribution to the transport, storage and communications sector. The possibility of improving the road link to Yemen (YAR) via Taiz with a view to utilising the Aden port facilities more fully has often been discussed, particularly when waiting time at Hodeida rose to 90 days, as it did in 1977. However, the cost of adequate road construction and the tense political relationship between the two Yemens have so far precluded this option from becoming reality.

*(b) Balance of Payments*

Table 15.5 shows the extent of Yemen's (PDRY) dependence on external sources of income. Visible imports exceed exports by an enormous margin. However, workers' remittances and capital transfers serve to put the overall account in credit. In this respect the two Yemens are remarkably similar, their current surplus of foreign exchange and aid payments has given them both a freedom to undertake development and to import the requisite materials and expertise in a previously unknown way. But it must be remembered that neither workers' remittances nor aid can be assumed to last indefinitely. Development must be rapid if the most is to be made of the present opportunity, and preferably be in areas which will yield foreign exchange in years to come.

Amongst all the increases in invisible earnings, the most rapidly rising component of the balance of payments is workers' remittances. Table 15.6 shows the threefold increase from 1975 to 1977.

Such a relatively and absolutely large increase in remittances over this short period suggests that either the number of migrants increased, or

Table 15.5: Yemen (PDRY): Balance of Payments, 1977 ($ million)

| Item | $ million |
|---|---|
| Trade balance | − 295 |
| Exports | 29 |
| Imports | − 324 |
| Invisibles | 205 |
| Workers' remittances | 180 |
| Other | 25 |
| Balance on goods and services | − 90 |
| Official transfers | 55 |
| Capital transfers | 75 |
| Net balance | 40 |

Source: Central Bank of Yemen, *Annual Report, 1977* (Aden, 1978).

Table 15.6: Yemen (PDRY): Workers' Remittances, 1973 to 1977 ($ million)

| Year | Workers' Remittances ($ million) |
|---|---|
| 1973 | 33 |
| 1974 | 41 |
| 1975 | 56 |
| 1976 | 115 |
| 1977 | 179 |

Source: Bank of Yemen, *Annual Reports* (Aden); and Ministry of Planning (unpublished data, n.d.).

the wage rates in the countries of employment rose, or that the remitting habits of Yemeni (PDRY) migrants changed. In fact, the total of migrants increased only slightly, certainly not on a sufficient scale to account for the increase. Wage rates in countries in which the Yemeni (PDRY) migrants are employed in some cases (Saudi Arabia) rose dramatically, but even so, a combination of these two factors does not explain the tripling of remittances in two years. Data for Yemen (YAR) show a similar leap in remittances at this time. The explanation given in Sanaa for the increase was the remitting of capital sums by Yemeni traders in Saudi Arabia, following legislation prohibiting their businesses. Almost certainly the same explanation applies to the case of Yemen (PDRY). Many Yemenis who left PDRY after 1967 were traders who had worked in Aden. Large numbers departed to Saudi Arabia to re-establish their businesses in a more prosperous environment. This means that the level of 'remittances' will either decline or level off in the immediate future, because Yemeni merchants cannot continue to remit capital sums indefinitely. Therefore, the government cannot expect its present surfeit of foreign exchange to continue to increase, as it has in the recent past. Indeed, it is likely that the government's foreign exchange position will become increasingly tightly constrained.

## 4 The Labour Market

The last census was in 1973, and contemporary data on employment are of limited reliability. However, the overall distribution of employment can be derived (Table 15.7).

Predictably, agriculture and fishing absorb the single greatest share of employment, the majority being in agriculture. Government and personal services account for 27 per cent of all employment, a reflection of the growing importance of government in the process of development, its expanding responsibilities in the field of social services, and its much greater participation in agriculture. Also government employment, as in other capital-poor states in the region, has been used as a means of mopping up some of the urban unemployed.

Table 15.7: Yemen (PDRY): Employment by Economic Activity, 1976

| Economic Activity | Employment | |
|---|---|---|
| | Number | Per cent |
| Agriculture and fishing | 181,000 | 45.4 |
| Industry | 27,000 | 6.8 |
| Construction | 28,000 | 7.0 |
| Trade, restaurants and hotels | 30,000 | 7.5 |
| Transport, storage and communications | 24,000 | 6.0 |
| Finance, insurance and real estate | 2,000 | 0.5 |
| Government and personal services | 107,000 | 26.8 |
| Total | 399,000 | 100.0 |

Source: Estimates obtained from Central Statistical Office, Aden.

The present objective of Yemeni (PDRY) development plans is to increase the significance, in value added and employment terms, of the unequivocally 'productive' sectors of the economy. The efforts of the government in this sphere will influence the pattern of employment in time. Sinecure employment of the erstwhile unemployed must not be allowed to obstruct this progress.

## 5 Yemenis Abroad

Yemenis left the country in large numbers following 1967. In 1973 the official termination of emigration reduced outmigration significantly, but did not stop it completely. The emergence in 1976 of shortages of particular skills, principally in manual occupations, confirm that further outmigration occurred after 1973. Even a small outflow of skilled workers has a noticeable impact on the domestic labour market, since the stock of skilled Yemeni manpower is so limited. In fact, the economic boom meant that the demand for labour began to increase significantly after 1975. This highlighted the shortages that were already nascent because of outmigration to Yemen's (PDRY) wealthier neighbours.

The domestic work-force in 1976 comprised some 433,000 persons. The number of Yemeni (PDRY) migrant workers employed outside the PDRY was 80,000 or so. Thus some 15.6 per cent of the work-force were abroad that year. However, although Yemeni migrants appear to remit as other migrants do, their duration of stay abroad is rather longer than is usual. This results from official disapproval of migration, which serves to discourage present migrants from returning home; they fear it might prove difficult to migrate back to their country of employment in the future. It is probable that most Yemenis who wish to migrate for employment have already done so. (It is this, rather than the government's imposition of negative controls, which are known to be of little impact in other labour-exporting countries, that explains the falling rates of outmigration in the mid-1970s.) Therefore the liberalisation of migration policy might induce return migration in excess of extra departures. This would prove a welcome augmentation of the Yemeni work-force, especially as the returnees are likely to have rather better qualifications than are typical of the present domestic Yemeni (PDRY) work-force.

The majority of Yemeni workers abroad are employed in Saudi Arabia (78 per cent), and most of the remainder are in Kuwait and the United Arab Emirates (Table 15.8). An unknown number are living in Yemen (YAR), mainly in the south of the country, an area which has long-standing connections with Yemen (PDRY). These outmigrants are to some extent political refugees, but they have an important replacement function, too.

Table 15.8: Yemen (PDRY): Migrant Workers Abroad by Country of
Employment, 1975

| Country of Employment | Number | Per cent |
|---|---|---|
| Saudi Arabia | 55,000 | 77.9 |
| Kuwait | 8,658 | 12.2 |
| United Arab Emirates | 4,500 | 6.4 |
| Qatar | 1,250 | 1.8 |
| Bahrain | 1,122 | 1.6 |
| Oman | 100 | 0.1 |
| Total | 70,630 | 100.0 |

Source: J.S. Birks and C.A. Sinclair, *International Migration and Development in
the Arab Region* (ILO, Geneva, 1980), Table 10.

## 6 Conclusion

After the setbacks which followed independence, Yemen (PDRY) has
made serious efforts to develop the country. Since 1973 some real progress has been made, primarily reflected in growth of GNP *per capita*.
Yet the economy has only a small productive base; most of her people
are agriculturalists living on subsistence-based farms; imports dwarf
exports, and a large majority of population and work-force are illiterate. Thus the task of development is enormous. While recent increases
in grants, aid and remittances are most welcome, they are not a permanent source of income and must be invested in order to achieve a genuine foreign exchange earning capacity.

Although Yemen (PDRY) does not have development problems of
the same scale as those of, say, Egypt, they are nevertheless of the same
qualitative order. Yemen (PDRY) is likely to remain one of the poorest
Arab states for some time to come.

## Notes

1. See, for an example of spontaneous change amongst nomads at the periphery, J.S. Birks, 'Development or Decline of Nomads: the Example of the Bani
Qitab', *Arabian Studies*, *V* (1978), pp. 7-28.
2. J.S. Birks and C.A. Sinclair, *International Migration and Development in
the Arab Region* (ILO Geneva, 1980).
3. The World Bank, *World Development Report 1978* (Washington, DC,
1978), Table 1.

# 16 THE REPUBLIC OF TUNISIA

## 1 Introduction

Tunisia, the smallest of the three Maghreb countries both by area and population, became an independent republic in 1956 under President Bourgiba. The economic policies of Bourgiba have sought to correct the imbalances in the economy left by French colonialism. The departure of 200,000 persons, or nearly the entire European population, in the decade following independence left Tunisia with a relatively homogeneous Arab-speaking population.

Since independence the government has had moderate success in achieving economic growth. Continuing dependence on France and the world market for phosphates has meant that the economy has remained vulnerable to swings in commodity prices and to changes in foreign trading policies. The government has sought to decentralise the economy by encouraging the regional development of chemical and textile industries. Statistics for the gross national product and GNP *per capita* indicate that Tunisia is wealthier than some other capital-poor states. In 1976, according to World Bank estimates, Tunisia enjoyed a *per capita* income of $840.[1] However, the distribution of wealth within Tunisia is still very uneven.

The social gains that have been achieved on a national scale since 1956 are significant. In 1971 public capital expenditure on social services represented 11 per cent of the gross domestic product.[2] In 1977, some 167,000 persons — 12 per cent of the population — were unemployed.

The level of underemployment in the rural sector remains difficult to gauge. Perhaps more worrying than the absolute numbers unemployed is the growing imbalance in recent years between the types of jobs desired by school-leavers and Tunisia's present employment structure. Only 3 per cent of first time job-seekers stated their chosen occupation as agriculture, while over half the population is employed in this sector.[3]

The government's policy of encouraging foreign investment in labour-intensive and often export-oriented industries has facilitated an impressive record by developing country standards of employment creation. However, the large number of unemployed and underem-

266

ployed will persist, partly as a consequence of the reduction of employ-ment opportunities in Europe and the vagaries of migration to Libya.

## 2 The Supply of Labour

### (a) Population

The 1975 census indicated that the Tunisian population had reached 5.57 million persons, and of these 46 per cent were under 14 years of age.[4] With a natural growth rate of 2.4 per annum between 1966 and 1975, demographic expansion continues to be rapid. The population has risen from 1.9 million in 1926 to 3.6 million by 1956 and is con-tinuing to increase rapidly to the present time (Table 16.1). A con-siderable decline in the mortality rate has occurred while the birth rate has remained high. The lowered infant mortality rate combined with the increased number of births has caused a considerable broadening of the Tunisian age/sex pyramid with a large increase in the popula-tion aged less than 15. However, several factors have combined to limit the crude fertility rate of the population: the increasing percentage of girls receiving schooling; the trend towards later marriages; the initia-tion of a family planning programme; and finally the labour migration of young men both within Tunisia and also to other countries.

Table 16.1: Tunisia: Population Growth, 1926 to 1975

| Year | Population (thousand) |
|------|-----------------------|
| 1926 | 1,918 |
| 1931 | 2,142 |
| 1936 | 2,325 |
| 1946 | 2,904 |
| 1956 | 3,602 |
| 1966 | 4,463 |
| 1975 | 5,570 |

Source: République Tunisienne, *Recensement général de la population et des logements* (Tunis, May 1975), p. 21.

The smallness of Tunisia's population compared with her land area and her neighbours might be considered an asset from some perspec-tives; Tunisians do not experience poverty of the kind found in Egypt and increasingly in Morocco. Where absolute numbers are smaller, pop-ulation growth is not as likely to destroy achievements in the field of development.

*(b) The Educational Status of the Population*

The national literacy rate was 55 per cent in 1972, a high figure for the Arab region. Universal education has been one of the highest priorities of the Tunisian government since independence, educational facilities having been expanded as rapidly as possible. Within a decade, enrolment in primary schools has doubled and numbers in secondary have quadrupled. Population growth, as well as the government's desire to increase the educational attainment of the population, ensures a continued increase in primary school enrolments in the 1980s. There were 866,000 primary enrolments in 1974/5. Secondary enrolments stood at nearly 20 per cent of this, with 4 per cent enrolling in vocational schools. There were a total of 180,000 students in secondary education and 12,000 in university, corresponding to 19 per cent and 2.5 per cent of the relevant age groups (1973/4). Education has remained free, but not compulsory.

A survey in 1973 suggested that the qualitative output of the primary education system was low, with only 27 per cent of sixth-grade pupils able to understand a French national newspaper, and 38 per cent an Arabic newspaper; only 23 per cent of pupils had a functional facility in arithmetic.

There are two salient features of Tunisian labour supply which will bear on the labour market of the 1980s. First, rapid expansion in the numbers of persons in the 15 to 24 year age cohort will continue during the 1980s, creating a need for continued growth in job opportunities within the Tunisian labour market. The economically active population will grow at 3.3 per cent (while the population as a whole will only increase at 2.6 per cent) per annum up to 1981. Secondly, the labour entering the market over the next decade will be more highly qualified than ever before. The rising percentage of the active population with at least primary education will stimulate a concomitant increase in the demand for skilled and semi-skilled employment opportunities.

The Tunisian government has little scope for manoeuvre; it is not possible to effect a radical change in educational policy that could change the characteristics of labour market entrants and their aspirations.

### 3 The Demand for Labour: Economic Development

Agriculture expanded at an annual rate of 11 per cent between 1970 and 1975, a significant advance in comparison with its poor performance in the previous five years. In 1975, agriculture represented 16 per cent of GDP yet employed 43 per cent of the active population. Manufacturing and mining also progressed over the decade, but phosphates, a vital earner of foreign exchange, suffered from a slump in world prices at the end of 1975.[5] Output and export of phosphates dropped by 50 per cent in 12 months and the production of chemical fertilisers declined by 12 per cent. Such swings cause serious cyclical unemployment amongst the 30,000 or so persons employed in the mining sector.

Table 16.2: Tunisia: Capital Formation by Economic Sector, 1975 ($ million)

| Economic Sector | Investment | Per cent |
|---|---|---|
| Agriculture | 134 | 10.6 |
| Mining | 32 | 2.5 |
| Petroleum | 149 | 11.8 |
| Energy | 93 | 7.4 |
| Manufacturing | 258 | 20.6 |
| Transport | 225 | 17.9 |
| Housing | 181 | 14.4 |
| Tourism | 25 | 2.0 |
| Other services | 14 | 1.1 |
| Infrastructure | 148 | 11.7 |
| Total | 1,259 | 100.0 |

Source: Banque Centrale de Tunisie, *Statistiques Financiers 1977* (Tunis, 1977), No. 45.

Table 16.2 summarises fixed investment by its sectoral distribution. Secondary sectors, including energy generation, absorbed 42 per cent of all investment. However, the ratio of investment to employment creation in these sectors is such that relatively few jobs have been created, though value added per unit of labour is high. By contrast, the construction sector has absorbed a rapidly increasing number of workers. In 1972, 60,000 persons worked in the building sector and in 1975 140,000.[6]

Much investment is financed by foreign companies; short of capital, Tunisia has encouraged foreign firms when the opportunity has arisen.[7] Kuwaiti capital has resulted in the development of the large Sousse-Nord tourist complex, and recently Libya agreed to invest $42 million in further expansion of tourist facilities. In 1975 over 1 million tourists visited Tunisia, and since then numbers have increased because of unrest in other parts of the Mediterranean, notably in Cyprus and Lebanon, which has diverted visitors to Tunisia.

Tunisia is extremely fortunate in her ability to attract commercial investors; many of the poorer Arab states are not able to. Although this latter group, which includes Morocco, Egypt and Syria, do qualify for and receive institutional investment as aid or soft loans, its impact on the economy is relatively slight in the short term, since institutional lending is essentially limited in volume by country and region, and is a strictly finite source of development funds. The merit of private investment is that it is in a sense a windfall gain which does not of itself preclude further institutional lending.

In so far as Tunisia enjoys a stable political environment and maintains her present level of growth, her economic prospects remain favourable. With a small population, the scale of her development problems appears correspondingly limited.

### 4 The Labour Market

*(a) Introduction*

In 1975 the active work-force totalled some 1.9 million persons, of whom 73 per cent (1.4 million) were men. The crude activity rate was 33.5 per cent, a high figure for the Arab region, though not unusual for a country with an agricultural sector. About 500,000 women work, and of whom about 50 per cent are in agriculture; a surprisingly large proportion of women are employed in the modern sector, where they comprise about 22 per cent of all employment. This is an unusual characteristic in the Middle East region, and to a certain extent reflects the stage of Tunisian development.

Officially, unemployment has remained fairly constant from 1966 to 1975 at about 16 per cent of the work-force. While employment has grown at about 2.7 per cent, the relevant age cohorts of the work-force have grown a little faster. This figure of unemployment does not include seasonal workers, who are out of work for a majority of the year. Their inclusion would raise the unemployment rate significantly.

*(b) Employment by Economic Sector*

Tunisia's largest employer of labour is the agriculture and fishing sector, which is relatively more important for women than men. Relatively more women also work in the manufacturing sector, the second largest employer, than do men. This is because the textiles industry tends to employ women. Manufacturing and construction together account for a quarter of all employment. Some 29.5 per cent work in the tertiary sector. Government service only accounts for 160,000 (10 per cent of all employment). This distribution of employment between economic sectors is normal for a developing country. By the end of the twentieth century, the proportion of all jobs accounted for by agriculture will fall. It is not clear, though, whether emigrants from rural areas will be able to move into secondary sector activities or productive tertiary sectors. Almost inevitably many will swell the numbers of the unemployed.

### (c) Employment by Occupational Group

The skill distribution of Tunisians in non-agricultural employment is shown on Table 16.4. The pattern is familiar, with a relatively small proportion of professional workers, and a relatively large number of transport workers and labourers.

An alternative to grouping occupations by skill level is to examine the educational attainment of the work-force. Table 16.5 shows that 57 per cent or 54 per cent of all workers are illiterate, depending on the classification given to those with a *kuttab* education. At any rate, the proportion is more than one half. About 14 per cent have experienced post-primary education. However, formal educational qualifications are not a particularly good judge of the skill level of a work-force, since in many cases skills are acquired 'on the job'. Moreover, these figures do not include migrants, of whom there were more than 200,000 in 1975. Adding them into Table 16.5 would probably improve the picture, as the majority of migrants are skilled, and some highly qualified.

### (d) The Future

Demographic projections show an increase of 567,000 persons in the active age groups (15 to 64 years) by 1981. Assuming the same activity rates as those recorded in the 1975 census (82 per cent for men; 31 per cent for women), this implies the need to create 303,000 jobs between 1977 and 1981.

The expansion of employment described in the fifth plan does not satisfy the demand for employment that will occur. Clemenceau and Hadjadj[8] estimate a shortfall of 71,000 jobs, which will add to the already high levels of unemployment. It seems likely that the only outlet for the surplus labour supply will be foreign labour markets. Exactly where these job opportunities might be are now examined.

Table 16.3: Tunisia: Employment by Economic Sector, 1975

| Economic Activity | Total | | Men | | Women | |
|---|---|---|---|---|---|---|
| | Number | Per cent | Number | Per cent | Number | Per cent |
| Agriculture and fishing | 690,000 | 43.2 | 440,000 | 38.4 | 250,000 | 55.3 |
| Mines and energy | 30,300 | 1.9 | 29,450 | 2.7 | 850 | 0.2 |
| Manufacturing | 267,200 | 16.7 | 134,650 | 11.7 | 132,550 | 29.4 |
| Construction | 140,000 | 8.7 | 139,000 | 12.1 | 1,000 | 0.2 |
| Transport | 53,000 | 3.3 | 51,400 | 4.5 | 1,600 | 0.3 |
| Tourism | 22,000 | 1.4 | 19,100 | 1.7 | 2,900 | 0.6 |
| Commerce, banks, insurance | 99,000 | 6.2 | 92,100 | 8.0 | 6,900 | 1.5 |
| Administration | 160,000 | 10.0 | 134,400 | 11.7 | 25,600 | 5.6 |
| Other services | 76,000 | 4.7 | 51,700 | 4.4 | 24,300 | 5.4 |
| Not stated | 62,000 | 3.9 | 55,000 | 4.8 | 7,000 | 1.5 |
| Total | 1,599,500 | 100.0 | 1,146,800 | 100.0 | 452,700 | 100.0 |
| Unemployed | 267,500 | 14.3 | 213,200 | 15.7 | 54,300 | 10.7 |
| Total work-force | 1,867,000 | 100.0 | 1,360,000 | 100.0 | 507,000 | 100.0 |

Source: P. Clemenceau and B. Hadjadj, *Contribution à l'étude des problèmes de l'emploi et de la formation en Tunisie*, Ministère du Plan (Tunis, 1976), p. 96.

Table 16.4: Tunisia: Non-Agricultural Employment by Occupational Group, 1975

| Occupational Group | Number | Per cent |
|---|---|---|
| Professional, technical and related workers | 72,090 | 7.9 |
| Administrative and managerial workers | 4,700 | 0.5 |
| Clerical and related workers | 85,790 | 9.4 |
| Sales workers | 74,620 | 8.2 |
| Service workers | 93,940 | 10.4 |
| Transport workers, labourers, etc. | 545,980 | 60.0 |
| Not stated | 32,380 | 3.6 |
| Total non-agricultural employment | 909,500 | 100.0 |

Source: République Tunisienne, *Recensement général de la population et des logements* (Tunis, 1975).

## 5 Tunisians Abroad[9]

Tunisia's relationship with France has encouraged labour migration to Europe. During the 1960s a fairly constant stream of migrants left for France, coming to an abrupt halt in 1974. In 1973, 21,000 Tunisian workers migrated to France, but by 1974 only 4,000 are recorded as leaving.

The collapsing demand for Tunisians in Europe had less significance for the domestic labour market than might have been the case but for the almost simultaneous growth of labour demand in Libya. However, the opportunities in Libya were for less skilled and qualified workers than those employed in France. Thus there was not a simple reallocation of the same labour, but a profound change in the labour market. Farm workers in the south-east of the country, those least likely to migrate successfully to France, were able to cross the border into Libya in large numbers, often clandestinely. By 1975 there were about 38,500 Tunisians working in Libya, but this number was increasing rapidly. Very few Tunisians have travelled beyond Libya to other parts of the Arab world, the intervening countries being an effective barrier.

Predicting the likely permanence of employment in Libya for Tunisian or Egyptian migrants is hazardous. Political considerations are relevant to labour demand, and relations have occasionally in the past been strained. In broad terms Tunisians can expect to participate in the Libyan labour market for some time, but the demand for their services will be confined to particular skill levels and economic sectors. Planners must not be over-optimistic about opportunities in Libya. Tunisian

Table 16.5: Tunisia: Educational Status of Employed Persons, 1975

| | | | Educational Status | | | |
|---|---|---|---|---|---|---|
| | Illiterate | Kuttab | Primary | Secondary | Higher Education | Special Education | Total |
| Total | 860,640 | 54,850 | 457,070 | 202,850 | 22,810 | 1,810 | 1,600,030 |
| Per cent | 53.8 | 3.4 | 28.7 | 12.6 | 1.4 | 0.1 | 100.0 |

Source: République Tunisienne, *Recensement général* (Tunis, 1975).

migrants in Libya in 1975 represented only about 2 per cent of the Tunisian work-force. Even if the number of migrants to Libya rose sevenfold, it would only equal the number of unemployed Tunisians in 1975, who totalled 267,500. As the total demand for migrants of all nationalities in Libya in that year was 332,000, Tunisian manpower planners therefore are obliged to create domestic job opportunities rather than seek recourse to labour markets abroad.


## 6 Conclusion

Of the three Maghreb countries, Tunisia is by far the smallest. Yet her endowment of wealth in relation to the population makes possible a less traumatic future than Algeria and certainly than Morocco. If the usual economic indices of development are studied, Tunisia is relatively affluent for a developing country. However, the distribution of income and wealth is very uneven, a large proportion of the community still living and working on the land.

With a relatively rapid rate of population increase and an ever expanding number of school and university graduates, the demand for modern-sector employment seems likely to outstrip the available jobs. The short-term problem for Tunisian manpower planners is to capitalise on the opportunities to reduce labour surpluses offered by the proximity of Libya's labour market, without forfeiting the elements of the domestic labour force which are crucial for further economic development within Tunisia. Unfortunately, opportunities in Libya are likely to be for experienced skilled manual workers and technicians rather than for school and university graduates. It is this latter group that the government would most like to export, at least temporarily.

With the closure of the European labour market, it seems likely that Libya will continue to be the chief destination for Tunisian migrants in the 1980s. However, the proximity of this market presents problems for the Tunisian government, as control of migration to Libya is extremely difficult. If migration fluctuates in the future as wildly as it has in the past, then the Tunisian economy will certainly suffer.

As Tunisians have begun to migrate more frequently to Libya, so Tunisian ties with the Arab world have grown. Tunisia has begun to appear similar to Jordan: small, dependent on her neighbours, a free enterprise economy in a better economic situation than the poorest of the Arab world. Jordan's development has been constrained, to some extent, by the pervasive outmigration of labour. However, in view of the extent of unemployment in Tunisia, and the limited extent of opportunities for her labour in Libya and further afield in the Arab world, this is not a problem which is likely to impinge too sharply upon the Tunisian labour market. Provided that Tunisian manpower planners continue to recognise that migration for employment to Libya is a temporary relief of unemployment, such migration might well be considered advantageous rather than problematical.

## Notes

1. World Bank, *World Development Report, 1978* (Washington, DC, August 1978), Table 1, p. 76.
2. Ministère du Plan, *Cinquième Plan de Développement, 1977-81* (Tunis, 1977).
3. *La Presse*, 24 July 1977.
4. République Tunisienne, *Recensement général de la population et des logements* (Tunis, May 1975).
5. Economist Intelligence Unit, *Quarterly Economic Review, 1976* (London, 1977).
6. Ministère du Plan, *Cinquième Plan de Développement, 1977-81* (Tunis, 1977).
7. Maghreb Selection, *Situation de l'industrie à fin 1976 (Tunisie), 7*, 7 (Paris, 1977), p. 377.
8. P. Clemenceau and B. Hadjadj, *Contribution à l'étude des problèmes de l'emploi et de la formation en Tunisie*, Ministère du Plan (Tunis, 1976), p. 112.
9. See A. Findlay, *Country Case Study, Tunisia*, International Migration Project Working Paper (Durham, March 1978) for a fuller consideration of international migration of Tunisians.

# 17 THE HASHEMITE KINGDOM OF JORDAN

## 1 Introduction

Jordan occupies a strategic position in the Middle East: bordering Israel, she has suffered in Middle East wars and continues to devote large sums to defence. The loss of the West Bank was a profound setback to the economy, from which recovery began in the early 1970s, only to receive another shock in 1973. However, as a 'front line state' Jordan receives substantial aid from friendly Arab states.

This aid, together with workers' remittances and budgetary support, covers Jordan's balance of payment deficit. Being a relatively small country in relation to comparable capital-poor states like Egypt, Sudan, Tunisia or Yemen, Jordan has suffered particularly from the oscillation in demand for her workers in the capital-rich states and the rising level of inflation in the region.

Economic planners have had to cope with problems more often found in very wealthy states — labour shortages, inflation, speculation in land prices. Foreign exchange has not been short, either. But in the coming decade a different pattern will appear.

## 2 The Supply of Labour

### (a) Population

Estimates of the Jordanian population in 1975 vary between the officially quoted figure of 1.9 million[1] and a significantly higher figure of 2.8 million.[2] The difference between these two figures is considerable, and occurs because Jordan:

(i) lost the West Bank in 1967. This means that the 1961 census which covered both 'Banks' cannot be used to predict the 1975 East Bank population accurately;

(ii) has absorbed many Palestinians from the West Bank since 1967.

Thus some Palestinian refugees became 'Jordanian' citizens, whilst others are still living in refugee camps as registered Palestinians in Jordan. Yet others remain in the West Bank. No accurate current data exist on the number of West Bank inhabitants, nor the number of erstwhile West Bankers who have moved to the East Bank, i.e. Jordan.

Recent research on this topic[3] calculates the work-force and population of East Bank Jordanians in 1975 (Table 17.1). This estimate includes all persons living in Jordan whose origins are either the East Bank or the West Bank, i.e. this estimate is of the *de facto* Jordanian population in 1975. It also includes Jordanians living temporarily outside Jordan. From Table 17.1, the Jordanian population stands at 2.6 million persons, of whom about a quarter live outside the country. The majority of these are in the Middle East.

Table 17.1: Jordan: Labour Force and Population of Jordan, 1975

| Labour Force | | Population | | Crude Participation Rate (per cent) |
|---|---|---|---|---|
| Number | Per cent | Number | Per cent | |
| Inside Jordan (East Bank) | | | | |
| 382,800 | | 1,953,000 | 74.6 | 19.6 |
| Outside Jordan | | | | |
| 15,000 | 28.2 | 663,700 | 25.4 | 22.6 |
| All Jordanians | | | | |
| 532,800 | 100.0 | 2,616,700 | 100.0 | 20.4 |

Source: J.S. Birks and C.A. Sinclair, *Country Case Study: The Hashemite Kingdom of Jordan*, International Migration Project Working Paper (Durham, 1978), Table 3.

*(b) Demographic Parameters*

With 15 deaths per thousand persons and 50 births per thousand (1975), Jordan s population growth rate is, according to this source, in the region of 3.5 per cent per annum.[4] The rate of increase has been high for some time and consequently the population has a youthful structure: almost half of the total are aged less than 15 years. Improved medical care, wider access to educational facilities in rural areas and an improving level of literacy have engendered a lower level of infant mortality. Eventually fertility levels will also fall and growth rates decline, but the population will continue to increase rapidly in the medium term.

A low infant mortality rate is an accomplishment that not every developing nation can claim, but the lowering of the average age of the population creates a substantial burden for the economy. The proportion of dependents and social service consumers is high in Jordan, while the proportion of the population in the economically active age groups is low.

Jordanians who migrate to other parts of the Arab world tend, unusually for Arab migrants in the Middle East, to reside abroad with their families. The lavish provision of social services in Gulf states is a major incentive for Jordanians to work there, and the departure of Jordanians in families is in some ways a welcome relief to the Jordanian economy.

## (c) Educational Attainment of the Population

*Literacy.* Jordan is not particularly well endowed in natural resources, but in spite of her relative poverty her people are amongst the best educated in the Arab world. In terms of literacy, in 1974 Jordan enjoyed the high rate of 62 per cent amongst adults, probably second only in the Middle East to that found in Lebanon (Table 17.2). By 1976, 71 per cent of the population were literate, an improvement even on the figure shown in Table 17.2.[5] Some 59 per cent of women are literate and 82 per cent of men. Bias towards male education evidently still persists.

Table 17.2: Jordan: Adult Literacy Rates for Selected Countries in the Middle East, 1974

| Country | Adult Literacy Rate (per cent) |
| --- | --- |
| Lebanon | 68 |
| Jordan | 62 |
| Kuwait | 55 |
| Syria | 53 |
| Iran | 50 |
| Egypt | 40 |
| Algeria | 35 |
| Iraq | 26 |
| Saudi Arabia | 15 |

Source: World Bank, *World Development Report, 1978* (Washington, DC, 1978), Table 18, p. 110.

Development economists have, in recent years, begun to look for alternative measures of economic development to GDP *per capita*, and literacy is seen as a measure of the stock of human capital. By this criterion Jordan is one of the more developed countries in the Middle East, and Saudi Arabia one of the least. This is not an entirely spurious result and is borne out in other measures of development, such as the proportion of the population who gain a livelihood from farming.

*The School System.* The education system is based on six years in primary school, three years in preparatory school, and three years in secondary school. Although most pupils read 'general' secondary studies, about 12 per cent enrol in the commercial, agricultural or technical secondary schools. Jordan's university at Amman enrolled, in 1976/7, about 7,000 students, 36 per cent of whom were women (Table 17.3). A large number of Jordanians also study at foreign universities inside the Middle East, in Europe and in America. Therefore the actual number of university graduates is many times larger than those leaving Amman University. A second university has been established at Yarmouk, which specialises in technical and scientific subjects.

Table 17.3: Jordan: Enrolment in Formal Education, by Level 1976/7

| Level | Boys | Girls | Total |
|---|---|---|---|
| Primary | 214,570 | 187,830 | 402,400 |
| Preparatory | 71,730 | 53,250 | 124,980 |
| Secondary: general | 31,460 | 21,710 | 53,170 |
| vocational | 5,430 | 2,120 | 7,550 |
| Total secondary | 36,890 | 23,830 | 60,720 |
| University | 4,370 | 2,460 | 6,830 |
| Teacher training institutes | 4,280 | 2,720 | 7,000 |
| Vocational | 1,490 | 400 | 1,890 |
| Total higher | 10,140 | 5,580 | 15,720 |
| Grand total | 333,330 | 270,490 | 603,820 |

Source: Ministry of Education, *Education in Jordan in Figures, 1976-1977 (East Bank only)* (Amman, 1977).

The origins of Jordan's modern educational system reach back to before World War I.[6] On the East Bank education was run originally by the Turks, and then by the administration of TransJordan. By 1930, 65 schools existed on the East Bank with two secondary schools and one vocational training school. On the West Bank there were, even in 1914, 500 primary schools, and by 1948 250 intermediate and 20 secondary schools under the British mandate. The continuing investment in human capital throughout the twentieth century have made the Jordanians an educational elite in the region. Throughout the Middle East Jordanians work as teachers, doctors, statisticians, bankers and technocrats. The successful migration of individuals whose skills are in considerable demand outside Jordan is described within Jordan as the 'brain drain' problem. It is difficult to evaluate comprehensively the cost or benefit to Jordan of the 'brain drain', but superficially it does seem that the country invests resources over many years to train its people, only to lose the same to more wealthy neighbours just as individuals reach their prime working age.[7]

### 3 The Demand for Labour

#### (a) Economic Development

Jordan has quite large deposits of phosphates which she has recently begun to exploit. Aqaba port handles both her mineral and manufactured exports, and expansion of the port is under way. Recently the economy has experienced an imports boom, triggered off by workers' remittances, aid payments and the movement of the Lebanese business community and many other Beirutis to Amman. Inflation has been a problem, and in 1977 was thought to be in the region of 33 per cent.

Jordan has a small economy, a highly mobile and well educated population, and often finds herself attempting to cope with immensely strong external factors, which periodically buffet the economy first one way then the other. In this context the five-year plan explicitly aims to reduce Jordan's dependence on external assistance. Whether or not it will be successful in this remains to be seen.

In 1976 Jordan's GNP *per capita* was about $610.[8] Between 1975 and 1977 GNP *per capita* scarcely grew at all, and GDP *per capita* fell at about 5 per cent per annum. Despite so poor a performance in terms of these indicators, the country proceeded with its plans to develop agriculture, its mineral resources and infrastructure. As long as inflation is running at about 33 per cent per annum, little growth can be expected of national income in real terms.

#### (b) Budget

The government has run a deficit budget for the entire period from 1971 to 1977. This has been made possible by a variety of forms of domestic loans in the form of treasury bills, bonds and external borrowing but, most importantly, foreign grants (Table 17.4). Typically, foreign grants have been almost as large as domestic revenues. Jordan's foreign borrowings have also shown an upward trend in recent years.

Jordan devotes a large share of expenditure to defence. Of course, it is because Jordan does so as a 'front line state' that she is the recipient of such large external grants.

#### (c) Structure of the Economy

The Jordanian economy is, by Middle East standards, small and highly susceptible to external influences. For example, changes in the price

Table 17.4: Jordan: Government Revenue and Expenditure, 1971 to 1977 ($ million)

| | 1971 | 1972 | 1973 | 1974 | 1975 | 1976 | 1977 |
|---|---|---|---|---|---|---|---|
| Revenue | 198.6 | 229.2 | 298.7 | 404.8 | 630.5 | 519.4 | 811.5 |
| of which | | | | | | | |
| External grants | 98.8 | 124.0 | 151.3 | 192.6 | 344.1 | 162.6 | 383.3 |
| (per cent of revenue) | (49.7) | (54.0) | (50.6) | (47.6) | (54.6) | (31.3) | (47.2) |
| Expenditures | 231.5 | 295.0 | 367.6 | 500.6 | 696.9 | 735.2 | 951.5 |
| Current | 169.1 | 195.8 | 244.2 | 341.0 | 426.4 | 466.8 | 606.1 |
| of which defence | 107.8 | 124.8 | 152.2 | 164.4 | 190.5 | 207.1 | 237.6 |
| (per cent of current expenditure) | (63.7) | (63.7) | (62.3) | (48.2) | (44.6) | (44.3) | (39.2) |
| Capital | 62.4 | 99.2 | 123.4 | 159.6 | 270.5 | 268.4 | 345.4 |
| (per cent of all expenditure) | (26.9) | (33.6) | (33.5) | (31.9) | (38.8) | (36.5) | (36.3) |
| Net balance | − 32.9 | − 65.8 | − 68.9 | − 95.8 | − 66.4 | 215.8 | −140.0 |
| Financing | | | | | | | |
| of which | | | | | | | |
| Foreign loans | 60.0 | 28.4 | 47.4 | 55.1 | 94.9 | 61.6 | 127.3 |
| Domestic | 50.7 | 36.5 | 49.0 | 17.0 | − 14.9 | 81.6 | 12.7 |

Source: Derived from Central Bank of Jordan, *Monthly Statistical Bulletin* (Amman), *13, 9* various tables.

of phosphates, the level of remittances, the abundance or scarcity of rainfall or the rate of inflation have a profound impact on economic development and GDP.

Between 1975 and 1977 Jordan's GDP rose from $912 million to $1,200 million in market prices, an annual increase of 15 per cent. Adding in workers' remittances and indirect taxes to obtain GNP we find the annual increase of GNP to be 29 per cent. These money increases are deflated into real terms using the Jordan cost of living index, as provided by the central bank, and shown on Table 17.5.

In real terms GDP actually fell by 2.3 per cent annually from 1975 to 1977. GNP, which includes remittances and indirect taxes, rose annually at 4.0 per cent per annum. As the population is increasing at 3.2 per cent per annum, then even GNP *per capita* was only rising by 0.8 per cent annually from 1975 to 1977 in real terms. The impact of inflation on national income could hardly be more pronounced, and provides a vivid demonstration of the vulnerability of the Jordanian economy.

In contrast, prior to 1976 the economy was growing rapidly: 28 per cent per annum in real terms in 1975. The two areas of most rapid growth were the construction sector (25 per cent per annum) and 'net factor income from abroad' − workers' remittances (40 per cent per annum). These latter were equivalent to 42 per cent of GDP in 1976.

The demise of Beirut as the regional service centre in 1975 had given the Jordanian economy a considerable impetus. Land prices and rents rose dramatically, encouraging the construction boom which workers' remittances and the relative liquidity of banks helped to facilitate. The general shortage of labour and consequent high wage rates contributed towards the very high inflation rates prevalent in Jordan in the period 1976 to 1977, which eroded the gains of the previous year. In short, although the product of all sectors grew in 1977 compared with 1976 in money terms, the high rate of domestic inflation annihilated the apparent growth.

Table 17.5: Jordan: Cost of Living Index, 1975 to 1977

| | | | | | | | |
|---|---|---|---|---|---|---|---|
| 1975 | = | 100 | | | | | |
| 1976 | = | 115.3 | 1975 | − | 1976 | = | 15.3 per cent |
| 1977 | = | 154.1 | 1976 | − | 1977 | = | 33.6 per cent |

Source: Central Bank of Jordan, *Monthly Statistical Bulletin* (Amman), *13*, 9 (September 1977).

Turning to the sectoral distribution of GDP, the traditional view of Jordanians as entrepreneurs is born out (Table 17.6). About 65 per cent of GDP originates in the tertiary sector, deriving from services of one sort or another. However, within this sector is 'public administration and defence' amounting to about 18 per cent of the total in 1977, which represents a somewhat different class of service to banking, commerce, insurance and general service activities. In the same year agriculture contributed about 10 per cent of GDP and the secondary sectors, mining and manufacturing and construction, about a quarter of the total.

The agricultural sector output has fluctuated considerably in past years as Table 17.7 shows. Overall the trend in output has been downward. The mining and manufacturing sector overall is affected profoundly by the price of phosphates on the world market. Output between 1971 and 1977 grew at a rate of 22 per cent per annum. However, the sales value of Jordanian phosphate has remained at the same level for several years at about $57 million, on account of a declining price.

### (d) The Development Plan 1976 to 1980

Jordan's five-year development plan has set the economy a formidable growth objective of 12 per cent per annum in real terms.[9] The aims of the plan are as follows: 'to speed up the growth of the economy, reduce the budget and trade deficit, reduce dependence on external financing, increase labour productivity and improve the distribution of income'[10].

Overall spending is set at $2.36 billion, to be financed largely from external sources. Three-quarters of the plan expenditure is allocated to 'economic sectors', i.e. development projects, and 25 per cent to 'social sectors', i.e. income distribution. Amongst the development projects, the lion's share falls to mining and manufacturing, which takes almost 30 per cent of the entire plan expenditure. Development of Jordan's phosphates is seen as a means of achieving a higher level of exports and a reduced level of dependence on external financing from the government. Infrastructure, water and agricultural projects account for much of the remainder.

Jordan's plan targets are indeed targets, and since the plan relies almost entirely on external finance, its success cannot be evaluated on technical grounds alone. The extent to which Jordan can entice friendly governments to provide additional funds will be as relevant to its success as the economic returns of the projects themselves.

Table 17.6: Jordan: Jordan: National Income Accounts by Sector, 1975 to 1977 (at 1975 prices) ($ million).

| Economic Sector | 1975 | | 1976 | | 1977 | | Sectoral Distribution | Annual Growth 1975-6 | Annual Growth 1976-7 | Annual Growth 1975-7 |
|---|---|---|---|---|---|---|---|---|---|---|
| | $ million | per cent | $ million | per cent | $ million | per cent | | | | |
| Agriculture | 88.1 | 9.7 | 104.2 | 11.1 | 81.8 | 10.5 | 10.5% | + 24.2 | − 16.4 | + 1.9 |
| Mining and manufacturing | 165.4 | 18.8 | 170.6 | 18.2 | 137.6 | 17.8 | 24.6% | + 8.4 | − 14.1 | − 3.5 |
| Construction | 54.6 | 6.0 | 65.2 | 6.9 | 53.0 | 6.8 | | + 25.4 | − 13.4 | + 4.2 |
| Electricity and water supply | 10.5 | 1.1 | 10.0 | 1.2 | 8.2 | 1.0 | | + 0.0 | − 12.9 | − 6.7 |
| Transport and communications | 84.4 | 9.3 | 93.9 | 10.0 | 82.4 | 10.6 | | + 16.8 | − 6.5 | + 4.5 |
| Trade (wholesale and retail) | 148.8 | 16.3 | 141.0 | 15.1 | 123.9 | 15.9 | | − 0.4 | − 6.4 | − 3.4 |
| Financial institutions | 14.6 | 1.6 | 14.5 | 1.5 | 13.6 | 1.8 | | + 4.6 | − 0.4 | + 2.2 |
| Ownership of dwellings | 53.2 | 5.8 | 48.4 | 5.1 | 45.2 | 5.8 | 74.9% | − 4.4 | 0.0 | + 2.6 |
| Public administration and defence | 190.2 | 20.9 | 188.1 | 20.0 | 143.3 | 18.4 | | + 3.9 | − 6.6 | − 8.1 |
| Other services | 102.0 | 11.2 | 102.6 | 10.9 | 88.5 | 11.4 | | + 5.6 | − 18.8 | − 1.5 |
| GDP at factor cost | 911.8 | 100.0 | 938.5 | 100.0 | 777.5 | 100.0 | | + 8.1 | − 8.1 | − 2.3 |
| Indirect taxes | 125.4 | | 191.3 | | 147.3 | | | + 60.2 | − 11.8 | + 14.6 |
| Net factor income from abroad | 210.2 | | 391.6 | | 280.9 | | | + 39.9 | − 18.0 | + 22.2 |
| GNP at constant 1975 prices | 1,247.4 | | 1,521.4 | | 1,205.9 | | | + 28.1 | − 23.6 | 4.0 |
| GNP at market prices | 1,247.4 | | 1,755.5 | | 1,860.3 | | | + 47.8 | + 12.8 | 29.1 |

Source: *The Middle East* (September 1978).

Table 17.7: Jordan: Agricultural Production in Jordan, 1972 to 1976 (thousand tons)

| Item | 1972 | 1973 | 1974 | 1975 | 1976 |
|---|---|---|---|---|---|
| Field crops | 278.8 | 66.7 | 334.1 | 74.1 | 100.7 |
| Vegetables | 223.0 | 124.6 | 205.8 | 262.3 | 201.8 |
| Fruits | 152.3 | 104.0 | 156.7 | 91.7 | 83.4 |

Source: Central Bank of Jordan, *Monthly Statistical Bulletin* (Amman), *13*, 9, Table 43.

*(e) Balance of Payments*

The Jordanian economy is suffering a familiar problem of developing countries; attempts to expand the productive base of the economy and hence exports are resulting in a worsening trade balance in the short run.

Since 1973 Jordan's commodities trade balance has worsened from a deficit of $247 million in 1973 to $721 million in 1976. A substantial level of external support, together with workers' remittances, transforms the position into one of credit (Table 17.8).

Table 17.8: Jordan: Balance of Payments, 1973 to 1976 ($ million)

|  | 1973 | 1974 | 1975 | 1976 |
|---|---|---|---|---|
| Exports | 170 | 254 | 380 | 551 |
| Imports | − 417 | − 611 | − 942 | −1,272 |
| Balance | − 247 | − 357 | − 562 | − 721 |
| Interest and investment income | 6 | 21 | 26 | 25 |
| Workers' remittances | 45 | 75 | 167 | 397 |
| Net transfers | 197 | 270 | 438 | 381 |
| Net balance of payments | 1 | 9 | 69 | 82 |

Source: Derived from Central Bank of Jordan, *Monthly Statistical Bulletin* (Amman), *13*, 9.

In 1976 consumer goods accounted for 39 per cent of imports, raw materials 26 per cent and capital goods 34 per cent. Between 1975 and 1976 imports rose overall by 45 per cent, the most rapid increase being recorded by foodstuffs (65 per cent). The influx of Lebanese families to Amman and a poor harvest acted to increase imports of food. The rationale behind the government's efforts to exploit the Jordan Valley more successfully is evident: increased agricultural output would have a significant impact on the balance of payments. Overall, consumer durables absorb only 7 per cent of all imports, but after foodstuffs, are the fastest-growing component of exports.

The net transfer payments, mostly aid or grants, protecting the Jordanian balance of payments have increased steadily since 1973, but declined slightly in 1976. A lack of enthusiasm to contribute further to Jordan's apparent affluence amongst aid donors in the Arab world might be the reason. The increase in workers' remittances is dramatic: $45 million in 1973 to $397 million in 1976. Taken together, net transfers and workers' remittances still more than cover the deficit on the real account. Consequently, the Jordanian dinar has been strong in international markets, appreciating against the dollar recently. Yet Jordan's strength in her balance of payments is somewhat illusory. A change in the perspective of aid donors or in the propensity of Jordanian workers to remit would cripple the economy.

Jordan's dependence on external sources of financing is demonstrated on Table 17.9 in various ways. Expressing her aid payments as a percentage of imports shows that in 1975 they stood at 59 per cent, and in 1976 37 per cent. In 1976 aid *per capita* was $146. Remittances were $162 *per capita* and GDP $484 *per capita*.

Jordan's close relationship with other Arab states is also demonstrated on Table 17.9. Of all aid received in 1976, Arab donors gave 63 per cent. The majority of Jordan's migrant work-force are in peninsula states; their remittances were slightly higher than all aid received in 1976.

Jordan hopes to see in future years the maintenance of aid payments from oil-rich Arab states and an increasing level of workers' remittances, at least until her plan objectives are accomplished. Unfortunately both these factors are beyond the control of the government. Jordan's vulnerable financial position is not enviable.

### (f) Future Economic Prospects

The Jordanian economy can best be described as an 'aid', economy, which contains most features one would expect, together with some surprising ones. The productive base of the economy is small, and some sectors have suffered neglect in recent years, particularly agriculture. The development plan aims to increase the productive components of the economy and thereby achieve a degree of independence from foreign donors. In attempting to effect plan objectives, two problems are faced: still greater sums of aid are required for planned development, and the domestic market is so small that the heightened pace of spending has created a dramatic increase in inflation. While Jordan attempts to correct a fundamental weakness in the economy, so, as a

Table 17.9: Jordan: Balance of Payments Indicators, 1972 to 1976 ($ million)

| Year | Aid Payments | Per cent of Imports | Per cent of GDP Market Price | Proportion Accounted for by: Arab States (per cent) | Proportion Accounted for by: Others (per cent) | Aid per capita (East Bank) | Remittances per capita | GDP per capita |
|------|------|------|------|------|------|------|------|------|
| 1972 | 188.5 | 69.2 | 26.4 | 35.2 | 64.8 | 77.1 | 8.9 | 229.1 |
| 1973 | 195.8 | 56.4 | 22.7 | 38.7 | 61.3 | 79.8 | 19.2 | 351.0 |
| 1974 | 270.2 | 54.2 | 24.8 | 55.1 | 44.9 | 106.7 | 30.3 | 430.6 |
| 1975 | 467.8 | 59.0 | 45.0 | 76.5 | 23.5 | 178.6 | 69.2 | 396.9 |
| 1976 | 396.0 | 36.5 | 30.4 | 63.2 | 36.8 | 146.5 | 162.9 | 483.9 |

Source: Derived from Central Bank of Jordan, *Monthly Statistical Bulletin* (Amman), *13*, 9 (1977), various tables.

result of her underdevelopment, she tends to create a different but equally profound set of problems.

It is difficult to appraise Jordan's development without recourse to the political situation of the region. Defence absorbs much of government expenditures, but is largely offset by aid from sympathetic Arab states. A political settlement in the region would transform Jordan's economy, though not necessarily in a beneficial way in the short run. A large proportion of the work-force is employed by the army, and termination of their employment would inevitably have a depressing effect on the economy. But, with domestic shortages of labour and very high inflation rates, this might not be entirely disadvantageous.

## 4 The Labour Market

### (a) The Structure of Employment

Out of an estimated total population of 2,616,700, Jordan's work-force totalled some 532,800 persons in 1975, of whom about 150,000 (28 per cent) were abroad.[11] The sectoral distribution of employment in Jordan confirms the tertiary sector or services orientation of the economy; about 63 per cent of all employed persons work in one of the tertiary sectors (Table 17.10). Of this group, more than half are employed in the armed forces, and are not 'productive' in an economic sense as are other participants of the service sectors.

Table 17.10: Jordan: Domestic Labour Force by Economic Sector, 1975

| Economic Sector | Number (thousands) | per cent |
|---|---|---|
| Agriculture | 73.0 | 19.4 |
| Mining and quarrying | 3.4 | 0.9 |
| Manufacturing | 24.0 | 6.4 |
| Construction | 40.0 | 10.7 |
| Electricity, gas and water | 2.1 | 0.6 |
| Wholesale and retail trade, restaurants and hotels | 25.2 | 6.7 |
| Transport storage and communications | 19.0 | 5.1 |
| Finance insurance and real estate and business services | 3.3 | 0.9 |
| Community, social and personal services | 57.0 | 15.2 |
| Not identifiable (including army) | 127.8 | 34.1 |
| Total employment | 374.8 | 100.0 |
| No. seeking work | 8.0 | 2.0 |
| Total labour force | 382.8 | 100.0 |

Source: *MEED*, Special Report, *Jordan* (1976).

About 20 per cent of the domestic work-force are engaged in agriculture on a permanent basis. Rather more than this number work on the land at various harvesting times. Agricultural output has suffered in recent years from the disruption caused by war in the region, drought, and recently by substantial rural to urban migration. This situation has developed in the last few years, as many more Jordanians have left to work either in cities or abroad. So critical have the shortages of rural manpower been that since 1977 immigrant workers from Pakistan and Egypt have begun working on farms. More traditionally, Syrians have for many years migrated to Jordan during the harvesting period. Recently their number is thought to have increased in response to the overall manpower shortages in Jordan. Unofficial estimates in Amman made by the Ministry of Labour put the number of Syrians working temporarily in Jordan at about 20,000.[12]

The small size of the other 'productive' sectors of the economy, mining and quarrying, manufacture and construction, in income terms, was noted earlier. The employment these sectors account for is similarly small: 18 per cent of the 1975 total.

### (b) Future Trends in the Labour Market

According to National Planning Council estimates, there are two occupational categories where a shortage of skills will occur: at the technician level and amongst skilled manual workers. These estimates are of more value as indications of government thinking on manpower than as precise predictions of the future. In 1975, 150,000 Jordanians were working abroad in non-farm civilian jobs, and if these were to return there would be, on the basis of official figures, substantial unemployment.

Unemployment has fallen dramatically from about 8 per cent in 1971[13] to 2 per cent in 1975,[14] largely because of the migration of more Jordanians abroad. Moreover, certain groups of workers have left the country in such large numbers that 'manpower shortages' have effectively raised domestic wage rates, thereby contributing to domestic inflation.

### (c) Foreign Workers in Jordan

Egyptian and Pakistani workers began to enter Jordan in 1975, and 2,228 non-nationals have been recorded in the civilian non-farm sector (Table 17.11[15]).

Probably many more immigrants were working in Jordan in 1975 than the number shown on Table 17.11. Estimates of the number of

Table 17.11: Jordan: Immigrant Workers by Nationality, 1975

| Nationality | Number | per cent |
| --- | --- | --- |
| Syrian | 196 | 8.8 |
| Egyptian | 280 | 12.6 |
| Lebanese | 137 | 6.1 |
| Other Arabs | 1,252 | 56.2 |
| Pakistanis | 121 | 5.4 |
| Other foreigners | 242 | 10.9 |
| Total | 2,228 | 100.0 |

Source: National Planning Council, *Manpower Survey, 1975* (Amman, 1975).

Egyptian workers in Jordan made in Cairo for 1975 suggest that some 5,000 Egyptians were in Jordan then.

In March [1977] Egyptian workers were arriving at a monthly rate of 10,000 . . . There are over 60,000 foreign workers in Jordan today and the government is on the point of instituting controls on the import of workers, with more bilateral agreements expected to follow the one already signed with Pakistan.[16]

Today (1979) there are probably more than 40,000 Egyptians working in Jordan.

In January 1978 almost 1,000 work permits were issued to non-Jordanians.[17] However, the estimate of 60,000 foreign workers is without hard statistical foundation, and might err on the 'low' side. None the less it is evident that replacement migration to Jordan exists on a substantial scale, sufficient to cause the government concern. Replacement migration overcomes the problem of absolute shortages of labour which halt economic development, but by its nature it creates a more costly and perhaps a slower rate of development.

### (d) Jordanian Workers Abroad

Table 17.12 shows the distribution of Jordanian and Palestinian workers in the Arab world in 1975, based on information obtained in countries of employment. If the 1977 'official' estimate of 150,000 Jordanians abroad is applied to this total, then the share of Jordanians in the total is 57 per cent and of Palestinians is 43 per cent.

### (e) Jordanians in Kuwait

Considerable detail relates to Jordanians and Palestinians in Kuwait in 1975. In 1975 there were 172,800 Jordanians living in Kuwait and

Table 17.12: Arab Middle East: Distribution of Jordanian and
Palestinian Migrant Workers by Country of Employment, 1975

| Country of Employment | Number of Migrant Workers | Per cent |
|---|---|---|
| Saudi Arabia | 175,000 | 66.1 |
| Kuwait | 47,650 | 18.0 |
| UAE | 14,500 | 5.5 |
| Libya | 14,150 | 5.3 |
| Qatar | 6,000 | 2.3 |
| Iraq | 5,000 | 1.9 |
| Oman | 1,600 | 0.6 |
| Bahrain | 610 | 0.2 |
| Yemen (YAR) | 200 | 0.1 |
| Total | 264,710 | 100.0 |

Source: J.S. Birks and C.A. Sinclair, *A Summary of Provisional Findings:
Empirical Patterns, Past Trends and Future Developments*, International Migration Project Working Paper (Durham, 1978), Table 4, p. 13.

31,400 Palestinians.[18] Together this group comprise 39 per
cent of the total immigrant community in Kuwait. These two communities are best discussed together because the data are often aggregated.

Their sex ratio was 114 (1975)[19] and therefore is not too widely
different from that found in Jordan itself, of 103.[20] This is because
Jordanians and Palestinians in Kuwait frequently live with their
families, a fact related to the considerable time for which there has
been a Jordanian community there. The proportion of Jordanians and
Palestinians presently living in Kuwait who were born there is high: 45
per cent.[21] Correspondingly the average duration of stay is also high: 8
years. The data we have on these Jordanians and Palestinians ever born
in Kuwait and on their duration of stay suggest that within Kuwait this
group is an established community which has a growing permanence.
Indeed, in 1972/3, 22,000[22] Jordanians and Palestinians were enrolled
in government schools, and others are educated at special schools for
Palestinians.

Within the economy Palestinians and Jordanians are an important
group: they account for 16 per cent of all employment and many of
the more skilled jobs. Table 17.13 shows that these groups are amongst
the most educated of any immigrant community in Kuwait; they
occupy a high proportion of the more skilled jobs in the economy.

Palestinians and Jordanians are an influential group in the oil-rich
states on account of their relative size, their coherence as a group, their
technical skills and of course their Arab origin. Kuwait is a good ex-

Table 17.13: Kuwait: Distribution of Employment between Occupational Groups for Selected Expatriate Communities, 1975

| Occupational Category | Palestinian | Egyptian | Jordanian | Lebanese | Indian (per cent) | Syrian | Iraqi | Pakistani | Yemen (YAR) | Yemen (PDRY) | Iranian |
|---|---|---|---|---|---|---|---|---|---|---|---|
| A–1 Professional jobs usually requiring a science- or maths-based university degree | 10.8 | 7.2 | 6.5 | 4.0 | 3.6 | 1.7 | 1.9 | 2.1 | 0.3 | 0.2 | 0.1 |
| A–2 Professional and sub-professional jobs usually requiring a university arts degree | 3.3 | 3.3 | 2.8 | 3.8 | 1.0 | 1.6 | 1.2 | 1.0 | 1.3 | 0.5 | 0.2 |
| B– Technicians and other jobs which usually require one to three years of post-secondary education training | 35.9 | 21.1 | 17.6 | 17.5 | 9.0 | 8.8 | 4.1 | 5.5 | 1.3 | 0.7 | 2.7 |
| C–1 Skilled and semi-skilled office and clerical occupations | 22.7 | 7.9 | 26.1 | 26.5 | 21.6 | 21.1 | 12.7 | 11.7 | 16.2 | 40.9 | 13.9 |
| C–2 Skilled and semi-skilled manual occupations | 14.2 | 25.6 | 25.8 | 27.8 | 12.9 | 39.7 | 40.8 | 59.9 | 12.6 | 4.7 | 48.3 |
| D– Unskilled occupations | 13.1 | 34.9 | 21.2 | 20.4 | 51.8 | 27.1 | 39.3 | 20.2 | 68.2 | 53.0 | 34.8 |
| Total | 100.0 | 100.0 | 100.0 | 100.0 | 100.0 | 100.0 | 100.0 | 100.0 | 100.0 | 100.0 | 100.0 |
| Total number | 8,167 | 37,464 | 38,935 | 7,197 | 2,448 | 16,519 | 17,807 | 11,019 | 2,749 | 8,639 | 27,530 |

Source: Ministry of Planning, Census 1975 (Kuwait, 1976), Table 95, p. 105.

ample of a peninsula state which has relied and which continues to rely on the support and the contribution of all expatriates but particularly that of Jordanians and Palestinians.

In so far as it is possible to discern a pattern or trend of Jordanian and Palestinian migration, it is towards an increasing permanence in countries of employment, particularly amongst more highly qualified migrants, and development of the community in demographic terms is towards an age/sex distribution of the kind that one might find in Jordan itself.

Table 17.14: Kuwait: Employment of Jordanians and Palestinians by Occupational Category, 1975

| Occupational Category | Jordanians and Palestinians | Per cent of All Migrants | All Migrants |
|---|---|---|---|
| A—1 Professional jobs usually requiring a science- or maths- based university degree | 3,429 | 34.1 | 10,061 |
| A—2 Professional and sub- professional jobs usually requiring a university arts degree | 1,351 | 14.2 | 9,485 |
| B— Technicians and other jobs which usually require one to three years of post-secondary education/training | 9,769 | 27.3 | 35,761 |
| C—1 Skilled and semi-skilled office and clerical occupations | 12,004 | 20.2 | 59,488 |
| C—2 Skilled and semi-skilled manual occupations | 11,213 | 15.5 | 72,439 |
| D— Unskilled occupations | 9,336 | 8.5 | 110,296 |
| Total | 47,102 | 15.8 | 297,530 |

Source: Ministry of Planning, *Census 1975* (Kuwait, 1976), Table 95, p. 105.


## 5 Conclusion

Planning economic development in Jordan, or any other small economy in the Middle East, is an extremely difficult task. In Jordan's case, dwarfed by the giants of the Middle East — Saudi Arabia, Kuwait and Libya — and small in comparison with even her poorer neighbours, Syria, Egypt and North Yemen, she is particularly vulnerable to external developments. The rapid departure for Saudi Arabia of a sizeable slice of her domestic labour force after 1974, the sudden entry of Lebanese refugees, the dramatic growth in remittances and the phenomenon of high rates of domestic inflation, all contribute to make her task of development planning difficult.

In the particular field of human resources development, Jordan has three problems: how to survive in the short term as labour shortages hamper development; how to cope with the imminent return of her erstwhile migrants, particularly those who are unskilled; and how to cope with a continuing 'brain drain' problem. The decline in remittances and the return of unskilled migrant workers will place a considerable strain on the eocnomy. It will also signal the return to countries of origin of the replacement migrants in Jordan, assuming that the attitudes and aspirations of Jordan's erstwhile migrants for employment have not changed to the extent that they regard their old jobs as unacceptable.

The Jordanian economy and labour market have experienced several changes of a profound nature in the past twelve years; it is about, yet again, to experience a sharp change in her economic position over which Jordanians have no control. Once more the Jordanian labour market will be characterised by labour surpluses rather than shortages. These surpluses might well be of a new larger dimension, and associated with new social and political stresses.

## Notes

1. Department of Statistics, *Statistical Yearbook 1975* (Amman, 1976), Table 1, p. 1.

2. The World Bank, *World Development Report, 1978* (Washington, DC, August 1978), Table 1, p. 76.

3. See J.S. Birks and C.A. Sinclair, *Country Case Study: The Hashemite Kingdom of Jordan*, International Migration Project Working Paper (Durham, November 1978), pp. 1-9.

4. United Nations Economic Commission for Western Asia, *Population Bulletin, 12* (Beirut, 1977), Table 2, p. 7.

5. Department of Statistics, *The Multi-Purpose Household Survey, January to April, 1976* (Amman, 1970), Table 4, p. 56.

6. See P. Turing, 'Two Universities Crown Educational System', *The Times*, Supplement on Jordan (London, 11 August 1978) for an elaboration of the historical development of Jordan's educational system.

7. See T. Abdel Jaber, *The Brain Drain Problem in the ECWA Countries* (UNECWA, Beirut, 21 July 1978) for an extended discussion of this problem.

8. The World Bank, *World Development Report, 1978* (Washington, DC, August 1978), Table 1, p. 7.

9. National Planning Council, *Five Year Plan 1976-1980* (Amman, 1976), p. 32.

10. *The Middle East* (September 1978), p. 77.

11. J.S. Birks and C.A. Sinclair, *International Migration and Development in the Arab Region* (ILO, Geneva, 1980).

12. *The Middle East* (June 1977), p. 100.

13. National Planning Council, *Sample Survey of Households 1971* (Amman, May 1971), Table 2.

14. Department of Statistics, *The Multi-Purpose Household Survey, January to April, 1976* (Amman, 1976), Table 2, p. 37.

15. National Planning Council, *Preliminary Results of the 1975 Manpower Survey* (Amman, 1975).

16. *The Middle East* (June 1977), p. 100.

17. *MEED*, 31 January 1978.

18. Ministry of Planning, Central Department of Statistics, *Population Census, 1975* (Kuwait, May 1976), Table 96, p. 171.

19. Ministry of Planning, Central Department of Statistics, *Population Census, 1975* (Kuwait, May 1976), Table 97, p. 187.

20. Department of Statistics, *The Multipurpose Household Survey, January to April, 1976* (Amman, 1976), Table 1, p. 1.

21. Ministry of Planning, Central Department of Statistics, *Population Census, 1975* (Kuwait, May 1976), Table 96, p. 171.

22. Planning Board, Statistical Department, *Statistical Abstract, 1973* (Kuwait, August 1973), Table 39, p. 76.

# 18 THE DEMOCRATIC REPUBLIC OF THE SUDAN

## 1 Introduction

Although Arab in political affiliation, and particularly in links with Egypt, the Sudan is usually thought of as African. It is, for example, frequently referred to as 'the largest country in Africa' with its area of almost 1 million square miles. A transect from north to south of this massive area passes from hot arid deserts through grasslands to humid swamp land and tropical forests in the south. The Sudan therefore straddles the Arab Negro boundary which has led to much internal political upheaval, culminating in the acceptance by Khartoum of a virtually autonomous body to run the southern provinces.[1]

The Sudan, whilst not a dual economy, has a high degree of concentration of economic wealth and development. Khartoum, Gezira and Kassala are the provinces which account for virtually all exports, receive a majority of government investment, and have the best developed infrastructure. The remaining areas of the Sudan are typified by rural and traditional economies, and have received little investment, though they do produce some cash crops (groundnuts and millet). Their main role in the economy of the Sudan is supplier of labour to the more developed areas.

Sudanese economic patterns contrast with most of the other Arab states; some 65 per cent of the labour force is in agriculture, and over 60 per cent of the value of exports is accounted for by cotton. Although exploration is under way, the Sudan is not an oil producer, and therefore firmly a capital-poor state.

The Sudan is a typical neo-colonial African country, with high rates of under- and unemployment. Its pattern of economic development has been dominated by the quest for jobs. At least, this was so until the mid-1970s, when the Sudan suddenly became a large-scale exporter of labour. Now shortages of certain skills are considered impediments to economic expansion. There has been a complete change of conditions in the Sudanese labour market.

Whether or not exports of labour are a permanent feature, the Sudan will have to develop a manpower policy covering all aspects of human resources development over the next decade, which will be crucial to her economic development. A positive and consistent line to manpower planning will have to be developed, or yet another obstacle will make economic progress more elusive than ever.

## 2 The Supply of Labour

### (a) The Population

The first population census (1955/6)[2] reported a Sudanese population of 10,263,000. The 1973 census[3] enumerated 14,113,590 people, rather fewer than expected: estimates for 1973 tended to be about 16,000,000,[4] because of the high rates of fertility prevailing in the Sudan. Although under-enumeration has been suggested, the area of virtually zero population growth is in the south. This makes the recording of so little growth more plausible; 17 years of disruption in the region were not conducive to high rates of population growth, and caused large-scale movements of peoples.[5]

Table 18.1: Sudan: Total Population by Age and Sex, 1973

| Age Cohort, Years | Total | Male | Female |
|---|---|---|---|
| Under 1 | 372,285 | 190,089 | 182,196 |
| 1- 4 | 2,067,711 | 1,058,686 | 1,009,025 |
| 5- 9 | 2,464,407 | 1,277,744 | 1,186,663 |
| 10-14 | 1,560,199 | 823,958 | 736,241 |
| 15-19 | 1,217,207 | 603,477 | 613,730 |
| 20-24 | 1,000,440 | 453,394 | 547,046 |
| 25-29 | 1,212,809 | 539,613 | 673,196 |
| 30-34 | 904,277 | 429,502 | 474,775 |
| 35-39 | 919,784 | 471,565 | 448,219 |
| 40-44 | 641,490 | 334,505 | 306,985 |
| 45-49 | 487,525 | 267,451 | 220,074 |
| 50-54 | 393,402 | 208,918 | 184,484 |
| 55-59 | 208,842 | 116,605 | 92,237 |
| 60-64 | 241,552 | 130,663 | 110,889 |
| 65-69 | 126,574 | 71,968 | 54,606 |
| 70+ | 267,982 | 143,874 | 124,108 |
| Not stated | 27,104 | 15,952 | 11,152 |
| Totals | 14,113,590 | 7,137,964 | 6,975,626 |

Source: Department of Statistics, *Preliminary Results of the 1973 Population Census* (Khartoum, 1977), Table 12(a).

Some 46 per cent of the population are below the age of 15. The very high fertility and birth rates are continuing (Table 18.1). The sex ratio is 102.6, suggesting little under-enumeration of young females.[6] Only less than one-fifth of the population is urban (Table 18.2). The sex ratio of this urban population is 113.1, male Sudanese having a greater propensity to migrate to the town than women. Virtually two-thirds of the population are of a 'rural settled' mode of living. It is important to realise the extent to which these and the nomadic population are dispersed. Although some 15 per cent of the Sudan's area is virtually uninhabited, the remaining area only has a density of about 16 persons per square mile.

In the near future, the Sudan will experience continued rapid population growth. There is little to suggest that fertility and the birth rate are about to fall, and every indication that survival rates will increase.

## (b) The Educational Status of the Population

The Sudanese literacy rate is low. In 1966 it was 14 per cent amongst adults, when only 1 per cent of adult females were literate.[7] The low literacy rate, despite a long history of education, is a result of the colonial educational system which the Sudan inherited in which there was no attempt at universal primary school education or adult literacy programmes.[8] Table 18.3 shows the improved literacy rate amongst those aged ten years old and over in 1973. At independence (1958) there were 700,000 literates in the Sudan; by 1973 nearly 3 million people were literate. However, the number of illiterate adults in 1973 was 6 million; the educational task remaining has not become any easier. This is an especially cogent example of population growth making development difficult.

Regional differences in literacy are acute. The literacy rate is 58 per cent in Khartoum province, but less than 4 per cent in Bahr el Ghazal province. The ranking of the five provinces of Khartoum, Northern, Kassala, Red Sea and Blue Nile in the most favourable positions, with the remaining provinces falling well behind and comprising a second, less well-off group, is a recurrent theme in the analysis of socio-economic data in the Sudan.

In 1976, 45 per cent of children of primary school age were enrolled. Moreover, 10 per cent of the relevant age group were at junior secondary schools, 5 per cent in higher secondary schools, and over 2 per cent in higher education.[9]

However, Table 18.4 shows continuing educational disparities between urban and rural areas, which have not altered much since 1973. The regional inequalities of illiteracy are being perpetuated. In terms of enrolment ratios, the three southern and two western provinces lag behind the east, north and centre of the Sudan. Enrolment rates are six times higher in the north than the south. Primary enrolment in some urban centres is now rising to around 90 per cent (of the age group 7 to

Table 18.2: Sudan: Population by Mode of Living and Sex, 1973

| Mode of Living | Total[a] | | Male | | Female | |
|---|---|---|---|---|---|---|
| | Number | Per cent | Number | Per cent | Number | Per cent |
| Urban | 2,605,896 | 18.5 | 1,382,853 | 19.4 | 1,223,043 | 17.5 |
| Rural settled | 9,204,492 | 65.2 | 4,567,418 | 64.0 | 4,637,074 | 66.5 |
| Rural nomadic | 1,629,710 | 11.5 | 834,121 | 11.7 | 795,589 | 11.4 |
| Cotton pickers | 673,492 | 4.8 | 353,572 | 4.9 | 319,920 | 4.6 |
| Total | 14,113,590 | 100.0 | 7,137,964 | 100.0 | 6,975,626 | 100.0 |

Note: a. There are no people classified as nomads in the three southern provinces of Bahr el Ghazal, Equatoria and Upper Nile. Cotton pickers were only enumerated in Blue Nile province. If 5 per cent under-enumeration is presumed, then the total population becomes 14,819,270.
Source: Department of Statistics, *Preliminary Results of the 1973 Population Census* (Khartoum, 1977), Table 9.

Table 18.3: Sudan: Literacy Rate by Sex and Mode of Living (persons aged ten years or more), 1973

| Sex | Total Population | Urban | Rural |
|---|---|---|---|
| Total | 31.3 | 53.4 | 24.6 |
| Male | 44.3 | 65.5 | 37.7 |
| Female | 18.0 | 38.9 | 12.2 |

Source: Department of Statistics, *Preliminary Results of the 1973 Population Census* (Khartoum, 1977), Table 7.

Table 18.4: Sudan: School Attendance by Sex and Mode of Living, Ages 7 to 24 Inclusive, 1973 (percentages)

| Sex | Total Population | Urban | Rural |
|---|---|---|---|
| Total | 31.0 | 48.1 | 25.6 |
| Male | 40.0 | 53.3 | 35.5 |
| Female | 22.0 | 42.4 | 16.0 |

Source: Department of Statistics, *Preliminary Results of the 1973 Population Census* (Khartoum, 1977), Table 7.

12), but the corresponding rural rates are only 30 to 35 per cent. The disparities between town and country in secondary enrolment are even greater.

In 1973, of the 7- to 24-year-olds only 30 per cent were attending school. Drop-out rates are high; only 0.5 per cent of attenders manage to complete more than higher secondary. Only 4 per cent complete higher secondary. There is large wastage through the educational ladder. Higher secondary education, the first level at which specialisms may be taken, is dominated by the general academic disciplines.

Table 18.6 shows the enrolments of Sudanese at university in Khartoum. This illustrates the high (and only slowly declining) proportion of students in the arts and social sciences. This arises not only because of the disposition of school courses, but also because of the existence of the Islamic University of Omdurman and the inability of the Sudanese government to control the intake at the Khartoum branch of the University of Cairo.[10]

Some progress has been made in redirecting higher education, but planners have found themselves constrained not only by the inherent momentum of the old patterns, but also by a lack of funds.[11] Financial constraints are aggravated by the expansion of primary education. In short, the tasks before the government in the field of human resources

Table 18.5: Sudan: Number of Students in Higher Secondary Education by Type of School, 1976/7

| Type of Secondary School | Total | | Boys | | Girls | |
|---|---|---|---|---|---|---|
| | Number | Per cent | Number | Per cent | Number | Per cent |
| Total | 71,200 | 100.0 | 51,200 | 100.0 | 20,000 | 100.0 |
| General academic | 59,090 | 82.9 | 42,040 | 82.1 | 17,050 | 85.2 |
| Technical | 7,400 | 10.4 | 6,470 | 12.6 | 930 | 4.7 |
| Agricultural and other institutes | 4,710 | 6.7 | 2,690 | 5.3 | 2,020 | 10.1 |

Source: Ministry of Education, *Educational Yearbook 1976/77* (Khartoum, 1978), p. 13 (Arabic).

Table 18.6: Sudan: Students Attending Universities in Khartoum by Sex and Faculty, 1974/5

| | Male | Female | Total | Per cent |
|---|---|---|---|---|
| Science | 1,320 | 250 | 1,570 | 8.7 |
| Engineering and architecture | 880 | 30 | 910 | 5.0 |
| Agriculture | 780 | 80 | 860 | 4.8 |
| Veterinary | 340 | 30 | 370 | 2.1 |
| Medicine and dental | 810 | 90 | 900 | 5.0 |
| Pharmacy | 150 | 20 | 170 | 0.9 |
| Arts and general studies | 7,670 | 2,940 | 10,610 | 58.8 |
| Economics | 900 | 180 | 1,080 | 6.0 |
| Law | 1,340 | 220 | 1,560 | 8.7 |
| Total | 14,190 | 3,840 | 18,030 | 100.0 |

Source: Ministry of Education, Department of Statistics, Research and Training Division, *Educational Yearbook 1974/75* (Khartoum, 1976), Tables 6, 7 and 8.

are immense but resources slender.

## 3 The Demand for Labour

### (a) Recent Economic Development

Comprehensive planning began in the Sudan in 1961 with the introduction of the first ten-year plan.[12] Following the *coup* of 1969, a second plan (1970 to 1975) was implemented, but in 1972 dissatisfaction led to its complete revision,[13] which commissioned several large-scale projects aiming at self-sufficiency in agriculture and basic industrial goods.[14] In the most recent plan (1977/8 to 1982/3),[15] the government had adopted a longer-term, more integrated approach.

Today, Sudanese development appears to be about to 'take off'.[16]

But so it has seemed for some time. The overriding constraint has been the poor financial state of the government, its low income only being supplemented by meagre development grants and aid from outside.[17] In general terms it is easy to enumerate factors militating against rapid development.[18] The size of the Sudan and the poor communications network; the political instability suffered by its government, and in particular the southern problem; the poor world markets for cotton; the closure of Suez; together with attendant factors such as low domestic investment and literacy rates, for example. That rather optimistic development plan objectives have not been maintained is hardly surprising.[19]

## (b) Gross Domestic Product

Tabulation of evolution of gross domestic product by origin of economic activity from 1955/6 to 1974/5 shows the contribution of agriculture falling from 58 per cent to less than 40 per cent (Table 18.7). This suggests diversification, but is misleading for much of the growth is in government services and the provision of utilities. Nevertheless, there has been some genuine growth in the manufacturing sector, which now contributes 9 per cent of GDP compared to 4 per cent in 1955/6. However, this industrial growth (and that of GDP as a whole) is, in real terms, not great.[20] GDP actually fell in money, let alone real terms, in the 1960s. Even the improved rate of growth of the 1970s is severely eroded in real *per capita* terms by inflation and increases in population.

Stagnation of the Sudanese economy has made the Sudan's balance of payments position weak. Debt servicing has become an important item, putting further pressure upon the balance of payments. The vagaries of world prices for primary products has increased the financial pressures on the economy. Revenue from cotton fell from $258 million to $157 million at current prices between 1973 and 1974 and resulted in a substantial trade deficit for the latter year, despite an increase of other exports.[21] There has been no major increase in the cultivation of other crops with the possible exception of groundnuts, a cash crop of increasing significance.[22] It is useful to consider the distinction between 'modern' and 'traditional' means of production of national income. Some 45 per cent of GDP is produced by traditional methods (Table 18.8). This means that the apparent diversification of the economy must be looked at with care before any transformation is purported. The table also illustrates how productive the traditional sector can be. Significant, too, is the regional distribution of the traditional sector contribution – the traditional accounts for virtually the whole contribution to GDP of the southern and western provinces.

Table 18.7: Sudan: Gross Domestic Product by Economic Activity at Current Prices, 1955/6 to 1974/5 ($ million)

| Economic Activity | 1955/6 | | 1965/6 | | 1974/5 | |
|---|---|---|---|---|---|---|
| | $ million | Per cent | $ million | Per cent | $ million | Per cent |
| Agriculture, forestry, hunting, livestock and fishing | 493.1 | 57.6 | 579.1 | 41.7 | 1,672.3 | 37.0 |
| Mining and quarrying | 0.6 | 0.1 | 0.9 | 0.1 | 13.1 | 0.3 |
| Manufacturing and handicrafts | 35.7 | 4.2 | 75.1 | 5.4 | 395.1 | 8.7 |
| Electricity and water (including porterage) | 35.7 | 4.2 | 47.4 | 3.4 | 59.7 | 1.3 |
| Construction and public works | 46.3 | 5.4 | 64.3 | 4.6 | 185.7 | 4.1 |
| Commerce, hotels, etc. | 50.3 | 5.9 | 185.7 | 13.4 | 700.6 | 15.5 |
| Transport, storage and communications | 60.8 | 7.1 | 88.6 | 6.4 | 366.5 | 8.1 |
| Finance, insurance, real estate, business services, etc. | 28.0 | 3.3 | 47.4 | 3.4 | 318.3 | 7.0 |
| Government services | 49.1 | 5.7 | 131.4 | 9.5 | 431.7 | 9.5 |
| Others | 56.6 | 6.5 | 168.6 | 12.1 | 385.4 | 8.5 |
| GDP at market prices | 856.2 | 100.0 | 1,388.5 | 100.0 | 4,524.4 | 100.0 |

Source: Ministry of National Planning, *National Income Accounts and Supporting Tables* (Khartoum), various years.

Table 18.8: Sudan: Gross Domestic Product by Economic Activity and
Modern or Traditional Means of Production, 1974/5 ($ million)

| Kind of Economic Activity | | Gross Domestic Product (market price) ($ million) | Per cent |
|---|---|---|---|
| Agricultural (crops) | Total | 752.6 | |
| | Modern | | 55.7 |
| | Traditional | | 45.3 |
| Manufacturing | Total | 395.1 | |
| | Modern | | 82.1 |
| | Traditional | | 17.9 |
| Electricity | Total | 59.7 | |
| | Modern | | 36.4 |
| | Traditional | | 63.6 |
| Construction and public work | Total | 185.7 | |
| | Modern | | 38.3 |
| | Traditional | | 61.7 |
| Real estate | Total | 232.0 | |
| | Modern | | 27.6 |
| | Traditional | | 72.4 |
| Total | Total | 1,625.1 | |
| | Modern | | 51.0 |
| | Traditional | | 49.0 |

Source: Ministry of National Planning, *National Income Accounts and Supporting Tables, 1974/75* (Khartoum, 1976), Annex 3.1, p. 62.

The present six-year development plan is the first stage in a long-term plan which will be completed in 1995. It aims to engender self-sustained growth increasing *per capita* income from a present value of $316 to £890 in 1995. The contribution of agriculture to national income should drop to 33 per cent in 1994/5 from 42 per cent in 1977. Industry's share should rise to 16 per cent.

These aims are to result from growth of 7.5 per cent per annum, with higher rates for industry and mining (10 per cent), and construction (9 per cent). The significance of these substantial growth rates upon the labour market, if they were to be achieved, are dealt with below.[23]

## 4 The Labour Market[24]

### (a) The Characteristics of the Labour Market

The crude activity rate of those over 15 is 55 per cent. This is quite low for an African country, but high for the Middle East, the Sudan falling between the two regions in socio-economic characteristics as it does geographically. The rate for urban areas, at 52 per cent, is lower because of higher education, retired persons, and the fact that fewer women are economically active in towns.

Table 18.9: Sudan: Employment by Economic Sector, 1973

| Economic Sector | Number | Per cent |
|---|---|---|
| Agriculture, fishing, hunting and forestry | 2,253,158 | 65.2 |
| Mining and quarrying | 2,984 | 0.1 |
| Manufacturing | 135,153 | 3.9 |
| Electricity, gas, water | 34,718 | 1.0 |
| Construction | 70,545 | 2.0 |
| Wholesale, retail trade, restaurants, hotels | 185,809 | 5.5 |
| Transport, storage and communications | 128,588 | 3.8 |
| Financing, insurance, real estate, etc. | 4,523 | 0.1 |
| Community, social and personal services | 380,367 | 11.0 |
| Activity not adequately defined | 257,390 | 7.4 |
| Total | 3,453,235 | 100.0 |

Source: Department of Statistics, *Preliminary Results of the 1973 Population Census* (Khartoum, 1977), Table 16.

Agriculture is the dominant pursuit, employing some 65 per cent of the total of economically active despite its falling contribution to GDP. Manufacturing, producing only some 9 per cent of GDP, employs less than 0.1 per cent of the labour force. The government, in planning expansion of the formal modern sector, has to contend with a smaller base from which to start than is generally acknowledged.

The overall labour force in the urban area of Khartoum falls between 313,000 and 370,000 (1974).[25] Of these, some 163,000 were wage earners. If it is presumed that 20 to 30 per cent of non-agriculturally economically active outside the Khartoum area are in the modern sector, then the modern-sector work-force of the Sudan falls between 270,000 and 360,000. Although this is a rough calculation, it does serve to show the scale of the modern-sector labour force, which is small.

Under these circumstances, the past incidence of high unemployment in urban centres appears particularly ironic.[26] So too does the new role of the Sudan as an international supplier of labour.

*(b) Sudanese Workers Abroad*

In 1968, only 900 Sudanese workers left the country. Most of these left for Libya, and Saudi Arabia was the next most important destination. Skilled manual workers featured in this movement, but most were unskilled labourers and some were clerical workers.[27] In view of the unemployment prevailing at the time, this export of labour was only to be expected, and might indeed have been larger. It was certainly not an unhealthy development.

By 1975, however, the number of Sudanese workers abroad had reached 52,000.[28] Whilst this might not seem such a large total in itself, if it is compared to the number of the modern-sector labour force established above to be about 315,000, it appears substantial, amounting to 16 per cent of the total. Such a withdrawal from the modern-sector labour force must be of considerable impact.[29]

A factor aggravating the impact of this labour movement was the rapidity of the workers departing overseas. As Kidd and Thurston noted[30] in 1975, major studies of the education and labour market were still being directed towards the supposed problem of unemployment in the urban labour markets. Such was the speed in the turnabout of the labour market.

In 1975, the number of workers abroad was still increasing. By 1980 it has probably reached 100,000. Presuming the modern-sector labour force to have grown only at 3 per cent per annum, then in 1980 as many as 27 per cent might be working outside the Sudan.[31] In fact, of course, not all the migrants for employment are drawn from the urban and modern-sector labour force. However, most are, and since it is difficult to replace modern-sector workers who have migrated abroad by drawing upon the rural population, the impact of migration on the economy is serious.

The impact on wages and on economic development generally of Sudanese emigration was felt immediately. This is easy to illustrate anecdotally. For example, there are losses in specific technical fields of higher educational teachers of 50 per cent, resulting in an overall reduction of university staff between 1970 and 1975 of some 25 per cent. There have also been large losses of medical personnel. In specific fields of government, the result of migration has been one of virtual paralysis. It has been estimated, for instance, that over 25 per cent of the qualified government statisticians were abroad in 1976. Similarly, the migration of stenographers, typists, punch card operators, bookkeepers, as well as the skilled and semi-skilled manual workers, craftsmen and tradesmen, is an obstacle to efficient progress. There has certainly been a reduced number of skills upon the domestic labour market, resulting in a decline in a quality of work and a rise in wage levels for these inferior standards.

The question of ultimate importance is: does migration of Sudanese for employment and the removal of human resources from home represent a real threat to effecting development? Indeed, in view of the numerous problems which have to be overcome before real growth can be expected, does exporting of labour in this way comprise the final demise of what little development might otherwise have occurred?

*(c) The Future Labour Market and Economic Growth*

The significance of the exports of labour upon development planning is likely to be great because in the plan predictions of a shortfall of labour have already been made (Tables 18.10 and 18.11).

Table 18.10: Sudan: Demand for and Supply of Professionals, 1977/8 to 1982/3

| Profession or Speciality | Graduates from Local Sources | Graduates from Overseas | Total Supply 6 years | Demand 6 years | Surplus/ Deficit |
|---|---|---|---|---|---|
| Agriculture | 1,251 | 1,409 | 2,660 | 5,000 | − 2,340 |
| Veterinary science | 505 | 495 | 1,000 | 2,200 | − 1,200 |
| Medicine | 1,407 | 1,333 | 2,740 | 2,405 | + 335 |
| Dentistry | 105 | − | 105 | 105 | − |
| Pharmacy | 204 | 156 | 360 | 500 | − 140 |
| Engineers | 1,023 | 1,217 | 2,240 | 4,400 | − 2,160 |
| Basic sciences | − | − | 2,000 | 2,900 | − 900 |
| Law | − | − | 1,730 | 495 | + 1,235 |
| Accounting and finance | − | − | 3,000 | 4,700 | − 1,700 |
| Economics and social sciences | − | − | 2,690 | 1,500 | + 1,190 |
| Teachers of higher secondary schools | − | − | 1,640 | 1,700 | − 60 |
| Others | − | − | 3,585 | 200 | + 3,385 |
| Total | 4,495 | 4,610 | 23,750 | 26,105 | − 2,355 |

Source: Higher Grants Commission, *Manpower in Sudan's Six Year Plan for Economic and Social Development, 1977/78 to 1982/83* (Khartoum, n.d.), p. 40.

Kidd and Thurston took the Sudan's own predictions of manpower shortfalls and added to these estimates of further labour deficits caused by migration for employment (Table 18.13). Without migration for employment a shortfall of 9 per cent of professionals and of 40 per cent of technicians was predicted by Sudanese planners, on top of which Kidd and Thurston estimated a loss of some 7,000 professionals and perhaps as many as 14,000 technicians as migrants. If exports of labour increase over the period of the plan, then by 1982/3 a critical shortage

Table 18.11: Sudan: Demand for and Supply of Technicians, 1977/8
to 1982/3

| Speciality | Demand | Supply | Surplus/ Deficit |
|---|---|---|---|
| Agriculture and forestry | 5,000 | 2,150 | − 2,850 |
| Veterinary sciences | 2,000 | 580 | − 1,420 |
| Medical assistants | 2,400 | 1,370 | − 1,030 |
| Mechanics and electricity | 3,500 | 580 | − 2,920 |
| Engineering and architecture | 2,200 | 550 | − 1,650 |
| Surveying and transport | 3,450 | 3,330 | − 120 |
| Chemical engineering | 2,100 | 1,600 | − 500 |
| Accounting, finance and banking | 1,600 | 1,600 | − |
| Librarians | 500 | 500 | − |
| Teachers (general, secondary) | 900 | 900 | − |
| Others | 300 | 530 | + 230 |
| Total | 23,950 | 13,690 | −10,260 |

Source: Higher Grants Commission, *Manpower in Sudan's Six Year Plan for Economic and Social Development 1977/78 to 1982/83* (Khartoum, n.d.).

of qualified manpower would result, demand for technical and professional labour outstripping supply by 25,000. Kidd and Thurston write,

A shortage in the order of magnitude of 25,000 should remove all cause for complacency. It should give rise to an immediate reassessment not only of the projected manpower situation over the period of the six-year plan and thereafter, but also of the economy to absorb capital and of all assumptions resting on the availability of professional and technical manpower.

They advocate a 'positive strategy' of expanded output of the desired personnel, claiming that modest investment in the educational system of the Sudan could produce the numbers of qualified persons.

This positive strategy appears to enable the Sudan to benefit from the opportunities to export skills and yet to produce enough skills to facilitate domestic development. Expanded output of Sudanese professionals and technically qualified manpower are certainly desirable. However, an increase of a scale directed towards making up a shortfall of 25,000 is a dangerous strategy likely to result in yet more educated unemployment.

First, it is not certain that the domestic demand for labour will rise to the plan predictions, let alone beyond it, as postulated by Kidd and Thurston. The goals of past plans have only been met in part. It is un-

Table 18.12: Sudan: Kidd and Thurston's Estimates of Minimum Numbers of Sudanese Working Abroad, 1976

| Country | Total | Professionals | | Technical | | Other | |
|---|---|---|---|---|---|---|---|
| | | Low | High | Low | High | Low | High |
| Saudi Arabia | 20,000 | 2,570 | 4,580 | 5,140 | 9,160 | 6,260 | 12,290 |
| Libya | 8,000 | 1,027 | 1,832 | 2,054 | 3,664 | 2,504 | 6,260 |
| Kuwait | 2,000 | 257 | 458 | 514 | 916 | 626 | 771 |
| United Arab Emirates | 2,000 | 257 | 458 | 514 | 916 | 262 | 771 |
| Total | 32,000 | 4,111 | 7,328 | 8,222 | 14,656 | 9,652 | 20,092 |

Source: C.V. Kidd and J.L. Thurston, *Higher Education and Development in the Sudan* (Institute of Higher Education, New York, 1977), p. 7.

likely that the targets of the present plan will be met in full: the man-power requirements stipulated in the plan will not become an *effective demand*.

Secondly, it is unwise to base future manpower and educational requirements upon presumptions of a continuing international demand for qualified Sudanese manpower in even the short term. Sudanese labour will probably be demanded less in the near future. In view of the commitment that an expansion in educational facilities represents, and of the fact that over-production of educated manpower a decade or so in the future is likely to have dire political consequences, quite apart from being wasteful of resources, Sudanese planners must beware of a future net return of the migrants. To ignore this would increase problems of reabsorption of return migrants in the future.

Thirdly, the Sudan can import labour, and some replacement move-ments are probably already taking place. These underlie the increasing migration of Egyptians into the Sudan. A second source of replacement labour for the Sudan is the west. The populations of Chad, Cameroon and West Africa have in the past responded in large numbers to oppor-tunities in the Sudan. Despite the new wealth and consequent oppor-tunities in Nigeria, it would be surprising if substantial numbers were not attracted to the Sudan in response to high wages and a labour short-age. In short, the market forces causing an outflow of labour with ex-ports from the Sudan will bring about imports of labour if domestic manpower shortages become critical. Although replacement migrants generate social costs to be borne by the host nation and although their productivity is generally lower than that of the migrants whom they are replacing, such a replacement movement would ameliorate crucial shortages of labour in the Sudan.

Manpower shortages are likely to continue to be a constraint upon development; they patently are now. Expanded educational output is indeed essential, but care must be taken over the level of output of trainees. In view of the high financial and opportunity cost of invest-ment in education in the Sudan today, any over-production is econ-omically and politically acutely undesirable.

## 5 Conclusion

The Sudan is placed in a very difficult position from the point of view of manpower planning. The modern sector labour market has passed quickly from surplus to shortage, but there is a real possibility, in the event of a return of migrants, that surpluses will reappear, especially if the Sudan's own development plan has not been especially successful. Any expansion in output to cover present shortages could easily aggravate future unemployment.

The Sudan will have to reassess domestic manpower projections as realistically as possible, and look again at the impact that continued exports of manpower in particular will have upon domestic development. This should not be allowed to obscure the positive benefits accruing to the Sudan from the exports of labour, though. Apart from the wider issues, such as receipt of remittances, the Sudan has been able, in contrast to, for example, Egypt, to export a good deal of unemployment. The Sudanese labour market appears to be responding to exports in a relatively flexible manner, so that modern-sector work experience and training are being acquired by far larger numbers than would have been the case if the Sudanese were not migrating internationally.

This is a present-day tax upon progress and efficiency, but in the Sudan's case the exports and further training of labour abroad might serve to benefit the country's development in the medium term. On their return after spells of work overseas, erstwhile migrants might represent a considerably greater asset to their country in development terms than if they had remained at home. Their extra experience and modified aspirations might be harnessed to further the Sudan's progress. This is particularly the case with some of the more qualified migrants; with the unskilled there is greater probability that their raised aspirations will lead to frustration.

## Notes

1. F.A. Lees and H.C. Brooks, *The Economic and Political Development of the Sudan* (Macmillan, London, 1977); Sir D. Newbold, *The Making of the Modern Sudan* (Greenwood Press, Connecticut, 1974); P.M. Holt, *A Modern History of the Sudan* (Grove Press, New York, 1974).

2. Department of Statistics, *First Population Census of the Sudan, Nine Interim Reports and Two Supplements* (Khartoum, 1956). Other details can be obtained from Department of Statistics, *Household Sample Survey in the Sudan, 1967-68* (Khartoum, 1970).

3. Department of Statistics, 'Second Population Census of the Sudan, 1973' (Khartoum, unpublished).

4. Department of Statistics, *Population Projections* (Khartoum, 1969) and United Nations, *Population Growth and Manpower in the Sudan* (New York, 1964).

5. The question of under-enumeration, if it occurred mainly in the south, is not too important to this analysis.

6. Having said this, the 0-4 cohort might be considered smaller than expected.

7. Ministry of Education, Republic of the Sudan, Bureau of Educational Statistics, *Educational Statistics for the Academic Year 1966-67* (Khartoum, 1968).

8. International Labour Office, *Growth, Employment and Equity, a Comprehensive Strategy for the Sudan* (ILO, Geneva, 1976). Chapter 9 gives useful background on the educational system.

9. For more data on the Sudanese higher education system see F. Bowles *et al., Higher Education in the Sudan* (UNESCO, Paris, 1974).

10. M.O. Beshir, *Educational Policy and the Employment Problem in the Sudan* (Development Studies and Research Centre, Khartoum, May 1977), p. 3.

11. Ministry of Education, Democratic Republic of the Sudan, 'The Six Year Plan, 1977/78 to 1982-83' (Khartoum, mimeograph, n.d.); E. Abdel Rahman, Ali Taha and Mohammed el Hassan Mehaisi, *Higher Education and Development in the Sudan, A Review of New Policy* (Economic and Social Research Council, Khartoum, December 1976), p. 11.

12. See, for example, Dr S. Nimeri, *The Five Year Plan (1970-75): Some Aspects of the Plan and its Performance* Development Studies and Research Centre, Khartoum, May 1977), p. 1.

13. Ministry of Planning, Republic of the Sudan, *The Five Year Plan of Economic and Social Development (1970 to 1975)* (Khartoum, 1970).

14. See Nimeri, *The Five Year Plan,* for more details of this Action Programme.

15. Ministry of Planning, *Six Year Social and Economic Development Plan for the Republic of the Sudan 1977/78 to 1982/83* (Khartoum, 1978) (Arabic).

16. A similar point is made by F. Bowles *et al., Higher Education in the Sudan* (UNESCO, Paris, 1974), p. 2, footnote 9.

17. M.M. Mustafa has noted how relatively and absolutely low are the Sudan's foreign aid receipts; see Table 7 in 'Manpower and Employment Problems in Developing Countries: A Case Study of the Sudan' (unpublished MA thesis, Boston, 1973).

18. See also A.A. Beshai, *Export Performance and Economic Development in Sudan, 1900-1967* (Ithaca Press, London, 1976).

19. See Ahmed Safi el Din, *An Appraisal of the Five Year Plan,* Economic and Social Research Council (Khartoum, 1976), p. 33; W. Keddeman and A.A. Gader Ali, *Employment and Incomes in Rural Sudan,* Economic and Social Research Council (Khartoum, 1978).

20. Mustafa, 'Manpower and Employment Problems'.

21. Bank of Sudan, *Seventeenth Annual Report* (Khartoum, 1976), p. 71, and Beshai, *Export Performance and Economic Development in the Sudan.*

22. Ministry of Agriculture, Department of Agricultural Economics, *Statistics, 1974* (Khartoum, 1975), Table 13, p. 24, and *Current Agricultural Statistics* (Khartoum, June 1976), Table 1, p. 3.

23. For a useful overview of the Sudanese Labour Market, see M. el Mustada Mustafa, *The Sudanese Labour Market. An Overview of its Characteristics and Problems with Special Emphasis on the Urban Labour Market* (International Institute for Labour Studies, Geneva, 1976) and B.C. Sanyal and J. Verslius, *Higher Education, Human Capital and Labour Market Segmentation in the Sudan,* Education and Employment Project Working Paper (ILO, Geneva, 1976).

24. Some of the rural labour force is also, of course, working in the modern sector, both as tradesmen and on agricultural schemes. The most useful studies are: Ministry of Planning, Department of Statistics, *Industrial Survey of Establishments Employing less than 25 workers, 1970-71* (Khartoum, 1976) (Arabic); Ministry of Public Service, *Establishments Survey, 1973* (Khartoum, 1974); MEFIT, *Regional Plan of Khartoum and Master Plan for the Three Towns* (Rome, 1974); ILO/UNDP, *Growth Employment and Equity, 1976,* Technical Papers 9

and 12 (ILO, Geneva, 1977).

25. For details of this, see M.K.M. El Amin, 'A Plan for Increasing Employment in the Sudan' (unpublished thesis, Arab Planning Institute, Kuwait, 1974); T. Mulat, *Educated Unemployment in the Sudan*, Education and Employment Project Working Paper (ILO, Geneva, 1975); B.C. Sanyal and J. Versluis, *Higher Education, Human Capital and Labour Market Segmentation in the Sudan*, World Employment Programme Working Paper (ILO, Geneva, 1976); M.O. Beshir, *Educational Policy and the Employment Problem in the Sudan, 1977* (Economic and Social Research Council, Khartoum, 1978).

26. Ministry of Labour, unpublished statistics, Khartoum.

27. J.S. Birks and C.A. Sinclair, *International Migration and Development in the Arab Region* (ILO, Geneva, 1980).

28. C.V. Kidd and J.L. Thurston, *Higher Education and Development in the Sudan* (Institute of Higher Education, New York, 1977), pp. 3-4. For the background to this, see Chapter 21.

29. A.A. Gadir Ali, *A Note on the Brain Drain in the Sudan* (Economic and Social Research Council, Khartoum, December, 1976); *Report of the Committee for the Study of Staff Affairs, 1975* (University of Khartoum, Khartoum, 1976).

30. Kidd and Thurston, *Higher Education and Development in the Sudan*.

31. For example, L.A. Fabunmi, 'Nigerians on the Nile', *West Africa* (4 August 1956); I.A. Hassoun, 'Western Migration and Settlement in the Gezira', *Sudan Notes and Records, xxxii* (1952), pp. 60-112; D.B. Mather, 'Aspects of Migration in the Anglo Egyptian Sudan' (unpublished PhD thesis, University of London, 1953); A.G. Balamoan, *Migration Policies in the Anglo-Egyptian Sudan 1884-1956 — the first part of a history of human tragedies on the Nile* (Harvard University Press, Cambridge, Mass., 1974); H.R.J. Davies, 'The West African in the Economic Geography of the Sudan', *Geography, 49* (1964); P.F. McLoughlin, 'Economic Development and the Heritage of Slavery in the Sudan', *Africa, 32*, 4 (1962), pp. 355-91.

# 19 SYRIAN ARAB REPUBLIC

## 1 Introduction

By comparison with other developing countries, Syria's economic performance is enviable. Her GNP *per capita* in 1975 was $780[1] and is estimated here as having grown annually in real terms at 7.5 per cent. In terms of development and wealth, Syria lies centrally in the league of 'middle-income countries'. Sixty-four nations are listed by the World Bank as less developed than Syria. Syria's moderate endowment of oil and geographical proximity to both the Mediterranean and the Arab oil states has given her the opportunity of earning foreign exchange through transiting and processing crude oil from the Gulf.

Syria also has a population of average size, some 7.5 millions in 1975, thus she is smaller in these terms than Egypt or Morocco, and yet larger than all of the capital-rich states and her neighbour, Jordan. Although Syria's stock of human capital is lower than government planners wish, it is high compared to other Arab countries. With a literacy rate of 53 per cent (1975) and a long tradition of education, the work-force is in demand by oil-rich states. Despite the many problems experienced by and still facing the Syrian economy, given her resource endowments, her economic prospects are bright by Third World standards.

## 2 The Supply of Labour

### (a) Population

Two full censuses have been taken in Syria since independence in 1946. Table 19.1 shows the total populations and growth rate indicated by these censuses, together with estimates of similar indices for 1976. The growth rates are quite high and are attributable to a high and constant birth rate combined with a relatively low and declining death rate.

### (b) Educational Status of the Population

Although Syria has had an educated elite since the nineteenth-century Ottoman period, at independence the educational system was still overwhelmingly foreign (French) and sectarian in administration, humanistic and theoretical in content, and of very limited access to the general

Table 19.1: Syria: Selected Demographic Indices, 1960, 1970 and 1976

| | | 1960 | Annual per cent Increase 1960 to 1970 | 1970 | Annual per cent Increase 1970 to 1976 | 1976 |
|---|---|---|---|---|---|---|
| De facto population | Males | 2,344,200 | | 3,233,100 | | 3,895,000 |
| | Females | 2,220,900 | | 3,071,600 | | 3,700,000 |
| | Total | 4,565,100 | 3.28 | 6,304,700 | 3.15 | 7,595,000 |
| Crude birth rate (per thousand) | | 47.9 | | 47.8 | | 47.8[a] |
| Crude death rate (per thousand) | | 17.1 | | 15.6 | | 15.1[a] |
| Sex ratio | | 105.6 | | 105.3 | | 105.3 |

Note: a. 1975.
Source: Office of the Prime Minister, Central Bureau of Statistics, *Statistical Abstract 1977* (Damascus, 1978), Tables 2/1, 2/7, 2/10, 2/11, 2/16 and 2/17.

populace. In 1946, formal education was estimated to reach about 5 per cent of the population; only 20 per cent of the 3 million total were literate. Less than a quarter of children aged between six and twelve attended primary school and fewer than 5,000 were enrolled in the 13 public secondary schools (though others of course were privately educated).[2]

In the following two decades to 1966, educational change concentrated on expansion of primary schooling, which was made free and theoretically compulsory, and on attempts to replace the foreign administration and content of education. Only in the third decade after independence, from about the mid-1960s, was the foreign connection felt to have been sufficiently eliminated to enable concentration on adapting the quantity and quality of education to the needs of an independent developing country. The government now controls curriculum at all levels of education. Its annual expenditure on education (including other cultural expenditure and information) amounted to between 8 and 10 per cent of total expenditure from 1975 to 1977. Yet still only 47 per cent of the population aged ten years or more were literate in 1970. However, for the region this is a comparatively high rate. Typical of the Middle East, though, is the disparity between males and females at the primary, secondary/vocational and university levels of educational attainment. In the 1960s for the first time the number of males whose *maximum* attainment was literacy exceeded the number of illiterate males. For females the opposite remained true, and by a very wide margin. Table 19.2 shows that enrolment increased, for both sexes at all levels from primary upwards between 1970 and 1976. However, at each of these levels, enrolment of women was only a fraction of that of men, with the notable exception of teacher training institutions where female enrolment overtook male and, by 1976, had exceeded it by a wide margin.

There are no readily available figures for educational enrolment as a percentage of each relevant age group. An official survey estimated that primary enrolment had not yet reached more than 75 per cent of the primary age group in 1970.[3] Despite the general educational advance made in quantitative terms, there are signs that the quality of education has fallen. It has been argued that increases in the number of classes and number of teachers between 1960 and 1970 did not keep pace with the increase in student numbers at either primary or intermediate and secondary levels, and that a decline in quality ensued.

The picture of education which therefore emerges for the 1970s is one of accelerated expansion, particularly at secondary level. Female

Table 19.2: Syria: Enrolment in School by Level and Sex in 1976 and Growth of Enrolment, 1970 to 1976

| Educational level | Men | | Women | | Total | |
|---|---|---|---|---|---|---|
| | Number | Annual per cent increase 1970 to 1976 | Number | Annual per cent increase 1970 to 1976 | Number | Annual per cent increase 1970 to 1976 |
| Literacy classes | 3,830 | −12.7 | 8,290 | 7.4 | 12,120 | − 1.8 |
| Kindergarten | 18,530 | 4.0 | 14,940 | 4.4 | 33,470 | 4.2 |
| Primary | 769,000 | 5.8 | 504,900 | 9.4 | 1,273,900 | 7.1 |
| Intermediate | 225,800 | 6.8 | 107,900 | 12.1 | 333,700 | 8.3 |
| Secondary | 90,600 | 7.8 | 39,000 | 14.5 | 129,600 | 9.5 |
| Teacher training | 2,880 | 15.4 | 4,400 | 31.3 | 7,280 | 23.2 |
| University | 50,500 | 8.9 | 14,590 | 14.5 | 65,090 | 10.0 |

Source: Office of the Prime Minister, Central Bureau of Statistics, *Statistical Abstract 1977* (Damascus, 1978), Tables 10/33, 10/31, 10/6, 10/14, 10/15, 10/19, 10/21, 10/25.

educational enrolment and attainment is much lower than that of males at all levels except teacher training, but is improving at a faster rate. While overall average educational attainment has risen steadily, it is uncertain whether the quality of education has kept pace. Certainly the development plan (1976 to 1980) suggests it has not. This problem is widespread in the Arab world generally and in the more wealthy states particularly. The dilemma which Syrian planners face is to trade off quality of education against an expansion of education quantitatively. Unfortunately, their freedom of choice is somewhat limited by their past efforts which have effectively created a substantial social demand for education at the post-secondary level: the inevitable ageing of the school population accentuates this.

## 3 The Demand for Labour

### (a) Introduction

Syria has great economic potential. Although the population has a relatively high rate of increase at just over 3 per cent, at 7.5 million it is still very manageable: population density was estimated at 41 persons per square kilometre in 1976.[4] Its fertile agricultural land has in the past supported larger populations and recent decades have seen constant expansion into 'new' or hitherto abandoned territory.[5] Small but useful quantities of oil and of other minerals have been and are still being discovered. Its ports are well placed on the Mediterranean seaboard and the country lies astride the main fertile crescent land routes to the Arabian peninsula and Indian Ocean. Syrians have a long tradition of settled farming, craft industry and commercial entrepreneurship. Although independence in 1946 was followed by a lengthy period of acute political instability, the country has enjoyed, since 1970, a period of unbroken rule by one relatively constructive government. During this time comparative internal harmony has been matched externally by trade, aid and political ties with partners as diverse as Saudi Arabia and Libya, the Soviet Union and the United States of America, the World Bank and the Islamic Development Bank.

Yet the Syrian economy is presently in a precarious position.[6] Its difficulties have largely been generated outside the economy itself. The war with Israel in 1973 resulted in severe economic disruption. A massive inflow of funds from Arab oil states seems to have made good this overt dislocation remarkably rapidly, but in so doing produced pressures which the Syrian economy was ill equipped to withstand. New development projects were commissioned for which neither suitable labour nor raw materials was readily available. The foreign funds fuelled inflation. Yet development on the scale now envisaged depended on a maintained flow of precisely these funds. The Syrian budget has depended for some years on revenues accruing from dues payable by Iraq and Saudi Arabia for oil transiting Syria in pipelines to Mediterranean terminals. A benefit also accrued from a portion of the transit oil sold to Syria at preferential rates for domestic refining and consumption. These sources of income have proved unreliable. Iraq stopped pumping oil across Syria in April 1976 and switched to new alternative pipelines to be independent of Syrian transit at will. Saudi Arabia also pumps less across Syria. Moreover, the post-war subventions from the Arab oil states have drastically reduced. Resumption at anything like their previous level is becoming doubtful.

While the origins of these changes were mainly political (a longstanding dispute with Iraq; Syrian intervention in Lebanon in the summer of 1976), their effects were directly felt in the economy. Syrian revenue from oil transit has plummeted and foreign aid reduced considerably. While this might help stabilise inflation, falling revenue will prejudice the completion of development projects. Furthermore, the continuing Syrian presence in Lebanon is estimated to have cost $2 to $2.5 million a day since June 1976. This represents an immense drain on finances, and accounted for a quarter of total official planned budget expenditure in 1977 and 1978. The medium- and long-term effects on the economy of spending on this scale should not be underestimated, even though some of the necessary finance may be gifted.

On the other hand, a change for the better in Syria's economic fortunes occurred in 1978, when Syria and Iraq were officially reconciled. The most dramatic and immediate result of this *rapprochement* has been the promise of considerable sums in aid. How much will reach Damascus remains to be seen, but the broad implications for the Syrian economy are anyway significant. The resumption of oil transiting through Syria's pipelines would mean a useful further addition to government revenues. In the longer term, the development of economic ties and land communication with the Iraqi market gives Syrian economic prospects a brighter look.[7] However, the change of leadership in Baghdad in August 1979 appears to bring some of these benefits into question.

*(b) Gross Domestic Product*

Table 19.3 shows the growth of gross domestic product since 1960 in real terms. Economic growth, according to these figures, is highly satisfactory, and *per capita* annual growth is very impressive and apparently

Table 19.3: Syria: Gross Domestic Product and Gross Domestic Product *per capita*, 1960, 1970 and 1976 (at 1963 prices, $ million)

| | 1960 (1963 prices) ($ million) | Annual per cent increase 1960 to 1970 | 1976 (1963 prices) ($ million) | 1976 Annual per cent increase 1970 to 1976 | 1976 |
|---|---|---|---|---|---|
| Gross domestic product | 775 | 6.6 | 1,470 | 11.0 | 2,752 |
| Gross domestic product *per capita* ($) | 171 | 3.2 | 235 | 7.4 | 362 |

Source: Office of the Prime Minister, Central Bureau of Statistics, *Statistical Abstract 1977* (Damascus, 1978), Table 17/27.

is double that experienced during the previous decade.

Official statistics indicate a rate of inflation which probably quadrupled from about 3 per cent per annum between 1963 and 1970 to about 12 per cent per annum in the 1970s.[8] Much higher rates have been estimated for 1976 (24 per cent), 1977 (20 per cent) and 1978 (20 per cent plus[9]). These reflect the upheavals of 1976.

*(c) The Development Plan, 1976 to 1980*

Looking at plan objectives, the four sectors in which the government wants growth to be faster than the proposed annual average over 1976 to 1980 are: transport and communications; building and construction; industry, mining and energy; and finance (Table 19.4). The government sees its own sector, general administration, as one of the slower-growing sectors, but aims to make it cheaper and more efficient.[10] The overall economic strategy is to achieve self-sufficiency in energy and in most agricultural products, whilst generating agricultural and mineral surpluses for export. These will pay for the industrial imports which Syria will need for the foreseeable future.[11]

Table 19.4: Syria: Planned Growth of Gross Domestic Product by Economic Sector, 1976 to 1980

| Economic Sector | Annual per cent Increase, 1976 to 1980 |
|---|---|
| Irrigation and agriculture | 8.0 |
| Industry, mining and energy | 15.4 |
| Building and construction | 16.0 |
| Production Sectors | 13.1 |
| Transport and communications | 16.4 |
| Trade | 10.2 |
| Finance | 12.1 |
| Rents | 11.5 |
| General administration | 10.1 |
| Services | 11.2 |
| Other sectors | 11.1 |
| All sectors | 12.0 |

Source: Syrian Arab Republic, *Fourth Five Year Economic and Social Development Plan 1976-80* (Arab Office for Press and Documentation, Damascus, 1977), Documents Series 1127, p. 6.

The overall structure of the economy in and since 1960 is shown in Table 19.5. Of the three largest sectors, agriculture and trade show a gentle decline as a percentage of the total over the decade and a half;

Table 19.5: Syria: Gross Domestic Product by Economic Sector, 1960, 1970 and 1976 (at 1963 prices, $ million)

| Economic Sector | 1960 | | 1970 | | 1976 | |
|---|---|---|---|---|---|---|
| | Amount | Per cent | Amount | Per cent | Amount | Per cent |
| Agriculture, forestry and fishing | 612.1 | 21 | 1,152.7 | 20 | 1,891.3 | 19 |
| Mining, manufacturing, electricity, gas and water | 554.7 | 19 | 1,109.1 | 20 | 2,027.9 | 20 |
| Construction | 119.0 | 4 | 158.7 | 3 | 470.4 | 5 |
| Transport and communications | 304.0 | 10 | 623.4 | 11 | 778.8 | 8 |
| Wholesale and retail trade | 650.0 | 22 | 997.8 | 18 | 1,948.0 | 19 |
| Finance and insurance | 67.5 | 2 | 120.0 | 2 | 207.8 | 2 |
| Ownership of dwellings | 264.0 | 9 | 347.2 | 6 | 432.4 | 4 |
| Government | 203.0 | 7 | 704.3 | 13 | 1,577.7 | 16 |
| Services | 188.0 | 6 | 403.2 | 7 | 768.6 | 7 |
| Total | 2,962.3 | 100 | 5,616.4 | 100 | 10,102.9 | 100 |

Source: Syrian Arab Republic, Office of the Prime Minister, Central Bureau of Statistics, *Statistical Abstract, 1977* (Damascus, 1978), Table 17/15.

mining and manufacturing show an equally gentle but steady increase as a proportion. The greatest changes over the period are ownership of dwellings (more than halved) and government (more than doubled).

The most noticeable trend of the economy from a sectoral point of view is therefore the large increase in the government share of GDP, reflecting the rapid centralisation and socialisation of the 1960s. This trend has continued but decelerated under the present government in the 1970s.

Government economic policy in recent years has been to increase confidence in the future of agriculture after the unsettling land reforms of 1958 to 1966, to modernise it and above all to reduce its dependence on the notoriously unreliable rainfall. Of the many irrigation schemes in Syria the most important are those of the new Euphrates dam at Tabqa. Syrian agricultural strategy is now facing a familiar dilemma: should more land be devoted to high export potential crops, in this case cotton, and less to food, and thereby increase food imports, or vice versa? Despite the relatively low sectoral growth rate accorded in the current plan, agriculture and its associated industries have been the object of substantial investment over recent years and will remain one of the mainstays of the Syrian economy.[12]

Mining and manufacturing, including electricity, gas and water, accounted for about 20 per cent of GDP in 1976 (Table 19.5). Most of the sector's product is petroleum derivatives. It is seen as one of the fastest growing sectors of the current quinquennium (Table 19.4). Syria is not a large producer or exporter of oil by Arab standards (Table 19.6), but her economy has been transformed since 1968 by exploitation of the small quantities of mostly heavy oil which have been discovered so far. Table 19.7 shows the rise in production from 1972 to 1976. The 1977 production is estimated to have been about 200,000 barrels per day, rising to 230,000 in 1978. Syria is already a net exporter of crude oil and since 1974 oil and oil products have joined cotton and cotton products as the most important sources of foreign exchange. At current rates of extraction, the minimum reserves shown in Table 19.6 would last about 35 years. Further prospecting is taking place in several areas. However, the government's policy is clearly to limit the rate of extraction by reference to the long-term needs of the economy.[13]

Expansion of the oil industry downstream and of the associated gas industry is planned so as to achieve self-sufficiency in natural gas and related products. Net export of oil and products and maximal domestic refining and manufacture of both resources are a priority. A new

Table 19.6: Selected Arab States: Oil Production, Reserves and Refined Products, 1975/6

| | Crude Oil Production (thousand barrels per day, 1976) | Refined Products (barrels per day, 1976) | Crude Oil Reserves (million metric tons, 1975) |
|---|---|---|---|
| Saudi Arabia | 8,580 | 703,500 | 15,200 |
| Iraq | 2,470 | n.a. | 4,700 |
| Kuwait | 2,150 | 410,800 | 10,150 |
| United Arab Emirates | 1,950 | 8,200 | 5,560[a] |
| Libya | 1,930 | 51,000 | 3,820 |
| Algeria | 1,010 | 114,200 | 1,280 |
| Qatar | 500 | 5,400 | 700 |
| Egypt | 300 | 199,900 | 210 |
| Syria | 200 | 54,300 | 390 |
| Bahrain | 60 | 212,400 | 40 |

Note: a. Data relate to Abu Dhabi and Dubai only.

Sources: Based on Organization of Arab Petroleum Exporting Countries, *Fourth Statistical Report 1975-76* (Vienna), Tables 1, 5 and 6; and United Nations Organization, Statistical Office, *Statistical Yearbook 1976* (New York), Table 52.

Table 19.7: Syria: Domestic Oil Production, 1972 to 1976 (barrels per day)

|  | 1972 | 1973 | 1974 | 1975 | 1976 |
|---|---|---|---|---|---|
| Production (barrels per day) | 111,500 | 105,400 | 122,200 | 182,000 | 190,900 |

Sources: Office of the Prime Minister, Central Bureau of Statistics, *Statistical Abstract 1977* (Damascus, 1978), Table 5/6; Organization of Arab Petroleum Exporting Countries, *Fourth Statistical Report 1975-76* (Vienna, 1977), Table 107.

refinery should be in production soon (1980). Crude exports should consequently diminish markedly whilst refined exports will expand.

Syria aims at self-sufficiency in energy by 1980. So far as electricity is concerned, Stage II of the Euphrates Dam Project, the Tabqa Hydro-electric Station, is now operational.

As for transport and communications, the idea of recreating old land routes to make Syria the vital, easy link for trade between the Mediterranean and the Indian Ocean is not new, but has received powerful stimulus from a series of political and economic events since 1967. Plans for building or upgrading international highways and railways, particularly in conjunction with Jordan, have therefore been dovetailed with Syria's internal communications strategy. This in any case required improved road and rail communications between the oil-fields and other mineral areas, the ports and the commercial establishments of, in particular, Aleppo, Homs and Damascus. Better telecommunication links and more and better shipping and airline facilities are integral with this role. Syria is no stranger to the vulnerability of transit trade, as her relations with Iraq illustrate.

*(d) Foreign Trade*

The foreign trade figures of Table 19.8 indicate how far the Syrian economy remains from its objectives. Overall and current account deficits are growing. Imports rose faster than exports between 1974 and 1976, partly as a result of domestic development, but also the influx of Lebanese refugees. The cessation of oil transit revenues and the decline of aid also increased the current account deficit. Hence the crucial importance, given the limited quantity of Syrian oil (and assuming no major new oil discoveries), of boosting agricultural production and agriculturally based manufacture. The capital investments made in the agricultural sector over recent years should show returns in the near future which will either generate foreign exchange or save importing goods.

Table 19.8: Syria: Balance of Payments, 1974 to 1976 ($ million)

|                              | 1974      | 1975      | 1976      |
|------------------------------|-----------|-----------|-----------|
| Exports                      | 832.5     | 955.8     | 1,128.4   |
| Imports                      | − 1,193.1 | − 1,582.5 | − 2,004.2 |
| Services and non-monetary gold | 47.8    | −   3.2   | −  423.4  |
| All goods and services       | −  312.8  | − 629.9   | − 1,299.2 |
| Transfer payments            | 489.8     | 725.4     | 481.7     |
| Current account balance      | 177.0     | 95.5      | −  817.5  |

Source: Central Bank of Syria, *Quarterly Bulletin 1974, 1975 and 1976* (Damascus) (various issues).

## (e) Domestic Budget

The extent of dependence on outside subvention is illustrated by successive budget figures (Table 19.9). Domestic revenues have accounted for progressively smaller proportions of all expenditure. Defence has accounted for over 40 per cent in recent years. The 1977 figures are 'budget' estimates and are surprising in that a yet larger deficit is planned. The deficits have hitherto been covered by external grants, made partly because of Syria's 'front line' role in the Middle East conflict, and by foreign borrowings.

Table 19.9: Syria: Government Domestic Revenues and Expenditure, 1974 to 1977 ($ million)

|                    | 1974    | 1975     | 1976     | 1977     |
|--------------------|---------|----------|----------|----------|
| Revenue            |         |          |          |          |
| Domestic           | 1,226   | 1,833    | 1,849    | 1,698    |
| Expenditure        |         |          |          |          |
| Current            | 915     | 1,434    | 1,643    | 1,693    |
| Defence            | 480     | 911      | 990      | 1,054    |
| Capital            | 677     | 1,251    | 1,420    | 2,650    |
| Total expenditure  | 2,072   | 3,596    | 4,053    | 5,397    |
| Net balance        | −  846  | − 1,763  | − 2,204  | − 3,699  |

Source: Ministry of Finance (Damascus mimeograph, n.d.) (Arabic).

The extent to which Syria can continue to rely on external support in what may be an era of peace remains to be seen. At present, improved relations with Iraq might provide a welcome source of financial assistance. However, without budgetary support on a fairly massive scale, Syria's present fiscal policies will lead to another severe bout of inflation.

## 4 The Labour Market

The Syrian crude activity rate remained fairly constant between 1960 and 1975 at relatively low rates between 23 and 25 per cent.[14] The male rate was 41 per cent in 1964, 43 per cent in 1970 and 42 per cent in 1976. The female rate has declined from its already very low level: 9.2 per cent (1964) to 4.5 per cent in 1976.

Table 19.10: Syria: Population and Labour Force, 1976

| Sex | Population | Labour Force | Proportional Share (per cent) | Crude Participation Rate (per cent) |
|---|---|---|---|---|
| Male | 3,971,800 | 1,657,300 | 90.7 | 41.7 |
| Female | 3,741,400 | 170,500 | 9.3 | 4.6 |
| Total | 7,713,200 | 1,827,800 | 100.0 | 23.7 |

Source: Office of the Prime Minister, Central Bureau of Statistics, *Statistical Abstract 1977* (Damascus, 1978), Table 3/1.

The unemployment rate appears low at 2 to 3 per cent, but is a minimal estimate. Reluctance to use official labour exchanges and problems of definition depress the rate falsely.

### (a) Economic Characteristics of the Labour Force

Agriculture is much the largest sector in terms of employment, accounting for about half of all employment on the basis of the figures in Table 19.11, but for rather more than that considering part-time agricultural employment and participation of women, who do not feature in these figures at all. The labour force data by main occupation illustrate again agriculture's overwhelming dominance of employment followed by production, transport and sales workers.

The absolute and proportionate numbers of those in the labour force with formal education is small but growing: 12 per cent altogether in 1964, 21 per cent in 1970 and 34 per cent in 1976 (Table 19.13). The crucial importance to further economic development of expanded educational programmes related to manpower requirements is forcefully

Table 19.11: Syria: Labour Force by Economic Sector, 1976

| Economic Sector | Number | Per cent |
|---|---|---|
| Agriculture, forestry, fishing, hunting | 916,440 | 49.8 |
| Mining, quarrying | 11,730 | 0.6 |
| Manufacturing | 210,620 | 11.5 |
| Electricity, gas, water | 9,600 | 0.5 |
| Construction, building | 129,660 | 7.1 |
| Commerce | 189,080 | 10.3 |
| Transport, communications | 78,220 | 4.3 |
| Finance, insurance, real estate, business | 10,010 | 0.5 |
| Community, social and personal services . | 238,640 | 13.0 |
| First-time job seekers | 44,950 | 2.5 |
| Total labour force | 1,838,950 | 100.0 |

Source: Office of the Prime Minister, Central Bureau of Statistics, *Statistical Abstract 1977* (Damascus, 1978), Table 3/4.

Table 19.12: Syria: Labour Force by Major Occupational Group, 1976

| Occupational Group | 1976 (Sample Survey) | |
|---|---|---|
| | Number | Per cent |
| Professional, technical and related occupations | 82,770 | 4.5 |
| Administrative and managerial | 2,010 | 0.1 |
| Clerical and related | 95,280 | 5.2 |
| Sales workers | 161,630 | 8.8 |
| Service workers | 32,000 | 1.7 |
| Agriculture, animal husbandry, foresters, fishers and hunters | 918,100 | 49.9 |
| Production and related, transport operators and labourers | 502,210 | 27.3 |
| First-time job seekers | 44,950 | 2.5 |
| Total labour force | 1,838,950 | 100.0 |

Source: Office of the Prime Minister, Central Bureau of Statistics, *Statistical Abstract 1977* (Damascus, 1978), Table 3/3.

demonstrated by these data and is reiterated in the Development Plan.

Table 19.14 classifies government employment by sex and shows that the government is much more favourable than the economy as a whole to the employment of women.

The government and public sectors employed about 280,000 people in 1976. Some 16 per cent were women, who comprised 9 per cent of

Table 19.13: Syria: Labour Force by Educational Status, 1976

| Educational Status | 1976 (Sample Survey) | |
|---|---|---|
| | Number | Per cent |
| Illiterate | 614,720 | 33.4 |
| Literate | 583,520 | 31.7 |
| Primary certificate | 316,880 | 17.2 |
| Intermediate certificate | 95,030 | 5.2 |
| Secondary certificate | 79,530 | 4.4 |
| Vocational certificate | 71,540 | 3.9 |
| Bachelor and master university degree | 63,350 | 3.4 |
| Doctorate | 3,230 | 0.2 |
| Not stated | 11,150 | 0.6 |
| Total | 1,838,950 | 100.0 |

Source: Office of Prime Minister, Central Bureau of Statistics, *Statistical Abstract 1977* (Damascus, 1978), Tables 3/5 and 3/12.

Table 19.14: Syria: Government and Public Sector Employment by Sex, 1976

| | Government and Public Sector Employment[a] | | Total Labour Force | |
|---|---|---|---|---|
| | Number | Per cent | Number | Per cent |
| Male | 235,390 | 84.2 | 1,657,280 | 90.7 |
| Female | 44,310 | 15.8 | 170,520 | 9.3 |
| Total | 279,700 | 100.0 | 1,827,800 | 100.0 |

Note: a. Data exclude employees of Departments of Defence and of the Presidency.
Source: Office of the Prime Minister, Central Statistical Bureau, *Statistical Abstract 1977* (Damascus, 1978), Tables 3/11 and 3/13.

the entire work-force (Table 19.14). The government and public sectors also tend to employ the more educated sections of the work-force (Table 19.15).

Unofficial sources provide estimates of the active armed forces (Table 19.16). Between 1960 and 1975 employment in the armed services increased at 15 per cent per annum, compared with 7 per cent for other government employees and 3.5 per cent for the labour force generally. In total, military and paramilitary personnel account for about 12 per cent of the total labour force in 1976. Between 12 and 15 per cent are accounted for by other government and public-sector employment.

Aggregated data on employment give an indication of the distribution of employment between the modern and traditional sectors. Table

Table 19.15: Syria: Government and Public-Sector Employment by Educational Status, 1976

| Educational Attainment | Government and Public-Sector Employment[a] | | Total Labour Force | |
|---|---|---|---|---|
| | Number | Per cent | Number | Per cent |
| Illiterate | 41,790 | 14.9 | 614,720 | 33.6 |
| Literate | 79,690 | 28.5 | 583,520 | 31.9 |
| Primary | 35,700 | 12.8 | 316,880 | 17.3 |
| Intermediate | 19,400 | 6.9 | 95,030 | 5.2 |
| Secondary | 28,790 | 10.3 | 79,530 | 4.3 |
| Post-secondary | 74,330 | 26.6 | 138,120 | 7.7 |
| Total | 279,700 | 100.0 | 1,827,800 | 100.0 |

Note: a. Data exclude military personnel.
Source: Office of the Prime Minister, Central Bureau of Statistics, *Statistical Abstract 1977*, Tables 3/12 and 3/15.

Table 19.16: Syria: Employment in the Armed Forces, 1967 and 1976

| | 1967 | 1976 | Annual per cent Increase 1967 to 1976 |
|---|---|---|---|
| Active military | 60,500 | 227,000 | 15.8 |
| Active paramilitary | 8,000 | 9,500 | 1.9 |
| Total active armed forces | 68,500 | 236,500 | 14.8 |

Source: International Institute for Strategic Studies, *The Military Balance 1967/1968*, and *1976/1977* (London).

Table 19.17: Syria: Employment by Type, 1976

| Type of Employment | Number | Per cent |
|---|---|---|
| Agricultural | 916,400 | 49.8 |
| Government and public sector | 279,700 | 15.2 |
| Armed forces and paramilitary | 236,500 | 12.8 |
| Unemployed | 45,000 | 2.5 |
| Private sector | 361,400 | 19.7 |
| Total labour force | 1,839,000 | 100.0 |

Sources: Tables 19.11, 19.14, 19.16 and 19.12.

19.17, based on a variety of sources, shows that public-sector employment — the government, public sector and military — together account for 28 per cent of the total. The civilian modern-sector work-force is some 361,000 persons, about a fifth of the total. This latter group represents the most productive sector of the economy, with a large proportion of skilled manpower. In this, the Syrian work-force resembles that of Egypt, where those working in agriculture, government and defence comprised 75 per cent of the work-force in 1976.

This distinction between different sectors of employment indicates the proportion of the work-force engaged in 'productive' employment which adds to the national income; it produces a surplus of product over inputs, or generates foreign exchange. Whether employment is productive in this sense or not depends on the nature of the sector: some parts of Syrian agriculture are economically productive, earning or saving foreign exchange, but much of it is near the subsistence level. Public-sector employment includes that in nationalised industry, some of which is productive. In contrast, government and defence workers, though possibly essential to the development and stability of the economy, do not contribute directly towards it. The proportion of the work-force employed as 'civilian modern sector' in Syria, as in Egypt, is limited to less than 20 per cent. This reflects the underdevelopment of Syria.

### (c) Syrian Workers Abroad

Syrians have, since the beginning of this century, travelled extensively abroad. The French left the legacy of their language, which facilitated Syrian emigration. Like the Lebanese, Syrians have emigrated to South America, Canada, Francophone West Africa, Europe, and of course within the Middle East. A second encouragement to emigrate for the more affluent of the country's citizens came in the 1960s with the increasingly strident socialism of the government. During that period, many small businessmen and merchants left Syria. Some moved to the Arabian peninsula, either taking up citizenship there or joining the growing semi-permanent community of non-national residents. Typically these migrants were well educated, and relatively few in number.

Distinct from this group are the Syrian migrants who, during the 1960s and 1970s, found employment in surrounding states, usually on a seasonal or temporary basis. These typically worked in Lebanon as house builders for part of the year, and undertook seasonal employment in Jordan and Turkey in agriculture. They comprise manual workers, usually semi-skilled or unskilled.

Throughout the 1970s and particularly after 1974, the labour demands of the oil-rich states began to have a growing impact on the Syrian labour market, drawing Syrians into a new experience of migration. The distance travelled to the place of work was further than before, the migrant better trained, the duration of work longer, and wages were higher. By 1975 some 50,000 Syrian migrants were working in the capital-rich states (excluding Iraq) (Table 19.18).

Kuwait, physically closest to Syria, employs more Syrians than Saudi Arabia, but since 1975 the position has changed. It is perhaps surprising that such a relatively small number of Syrians work in these countries. Whilst Syria's population was over 7 million in 1975, Jordan's was less than 3 million, yet three times as many Jordanians were working in the capital-rich states.

Table 19.18: Syria: Migrant Workers in Capital-Rich States, 1975

| Country of Employment | Migrant Workers | |
| | Number | Per cent |
| --- | --- | --- |
| Kuwait | 16,547 | 32.9 |
| Saudi Arabia | 15,000 | 29.8 |
| Libyan Arab Jamahiriya | 13,000 | 25.9 |
| United Arab Emirates | 4,500 | 9.0 |
| Qatar | 750 | 1.5 |
| Oman | 400 | 0.8 |
| Bahrain | 68 | 0.1 |
| Total | 50,265 | 100.0 |

Source: J.S. Birks and C.A. Sinclair, *International Migration and Development in the Arab Region* (ILO, Geneva, 1980), Table 10.

Despite the small overall number of migrants, the Syrian government has become alarmed by the departure of certain groups within the labour force, in particular skilled manual workers.[15] Consequently, strict negative controls have been instigated to reduce the numbers migrating, but these have been effective only in regard to those well educated or presently in government employment, typically professional, technical or skilled office workers. This group's migration is relatively formal and requires a passport and exit visa; although they find it possible to evade government controls, it is not easy. As a result, many such potential migrants are held in Syria.

Much less amenable to government control are skilled and semi-skilled manual workers. Two avenues of migration are open to this group. First, they can travel informally to Jordan and work there. Secondly, government regulations prohibiting the migration of more skilled migrants can be evaded by the migrant providing the authorities with an inaccurate and reduced account of his personal skills and employment experience, thereby obtaining a passport and exit visa on false pretences.

Thus the groups most able to migrate are skilled, semi-skilled and unskilled manual workers, particularly those from the private sector. Those least able to migrate are well educated government employees, working in clerical or administrative jobs.

At first inspection the government concern about migration for employment seems unwarranted: of the 1.8 million employed persons in 1975 in Syria only 50,000 were working abroad, with an unknown number in Jordan and Iraq. As a proportion of the total work-force this number of migrants is low: 3 per cent. However, when this figure is expressed as a proportion of 'civilian modern sector' employment from which most of these migrants originate, it rises to 14 per cent. Moreover, if a large proportion of the 50,000 Syrians in oil-rich states consists of skilled manual workers — electricians, carpenters, welders, toolmakers, turners, fitters, mechanics — then the analysis draws to a different conclusion. It is entirely understandable that the government should be most concerned about their migration. The withdrawal of a high proportion of any type of labour from the work-force would have an impact on output, and migration of these workers could have a particularly acute effect. The deleterious impact of the departure of these workers on production is likely to be far greater than their numbers alone would suggest.

### 5 Conclusion

Examination of the Syrian economy highlights a series of weaknesses, not at first evident, which should be taken account of when assessing Syrian economic performance. The labour force, ostensibly a major asset to Syria, encompasses several such shortcomings. Many workers are poorly educated and a substantial number work in non-productive sectors. The advent of a genuine peace in the region would give Syria the opportunity to develop further her resources. However, an overriding concern of the government is that efforts to develop will be hampered by a severe lack of skilled labour; this, it is felt, will continue to be exacerbated by increased exports of labour to the capital-rich states. Although Syrian labour exports will continue, the regional perspective presented in the following section suggests that future problems caused by Syrian migration for employment will not be as acute as the planners fear.

## Notes

1. World Bank, *World Development Report, 1978* (Washington, DC, 1978).

2. T.T. Petran, *Syria* (Benn, London, 1972), particularly pp. 69 and 220.

3. Syrian Arab Republic, Office of the Prime Minister, Central Bureau of Statistics, *Socio-Economic Development in Syria 1960-70* (Damascus, 1973), pp. 23-8.

4. Calculation based on Office of the Prime Minister, Central Bureau of Statistics, *Statistical Abstract 1977* (Damascus, 1978), Tables 2/7, 2/16 and 4/7.

5. P. Beaumont, G.H. Blake and J.M. Wagstaff, *The Middle East: A Geographical Study* (Wiley, London, 1976), Chapter 13 and pp. 542-3.

6. M. Field, 'Moves for Economic Rationalisation', *Financial Times*, 16 November 1977, pp. 20-1; Anon., 'Syria: Economic Survey', *Middle East and North Africa 1977-78* (Europa Publications, London), pp. 669-74.

7. For more, if dated, information on the Syrian economy, see E.Y. Asfour, *Syria: Development and Monetary Policy* (Harvard University Press, Cambridge, Mass., 1959); B. Hansen, 'Economic Development of Syria' in C.A. Cooper and Alexander Cooper (eds.), *Economic Development and Population Growth in the Middle East* (Elsivier, New York, 1972); World Bank, *The Economic Development of Syria* (Baltimore, 1955); E. Kanovsky, *Economic Development of Syria (The Economy of Syria)* (Tel Aviv, 1977).

8. Central Bank of Syria, Research Department, *Quarterly Bulletin, XIV*, 3 (1976), Table 17.

9. Calculations based on Office of the Prime Minister, Central Bureau of Statistics, *Statistical Abstract 1964*, Table 7.2, *Statistical Abstract 1967*, Table 10/6, *Statistical Abstract 1970*, Table 9/1, *Statistical Abstract 1977*, Tables 9/1, 9/2, 17/27, 17/39; 1963-76 is the longest period for which relevant comparable data are available. Extension of the period back to 1960 suggests an average annual inflation rate for the decade 1960-70 of about 2 per cent.

10. A. Cass, 'Syria: Socialism with a Levantine Face', *Financial Times*, 21 June 1978.

11. *Fourth Five-Year Economic and Social Development Plan, 1976-80*, Arab Office for Press and Documentation, Documents Series 1127 (Damascus, 1979); A. McDermott, 'Development Priorities Well Documented', *Financial Times* 16 November 1977, p. 22.

12. For more extensive treatment of Syrian agriculture, see *Financial Times*, Supplements on Syria: 10 March 1975, pp. 30-5, 18 November 1976, pp. 21-8 and 16 November 1977, pp. 19-26. Particularly M. Field, 'Agricultural Targets', *Financial Times*, 16 November 1977, p. 26, and J. Garner, 'Cotton under Pressure', *Financial Times*, 16 November 1977, p. 26.

13. A. McDermott, 'Modest Oil Producer', *Financial Times*, 16 November 1977, pp. 24-5; A. Cass, 'Oil and Mining', *Financial Times*, 10 March 1975, p. 34.

14. Calculations based on Directorate of Statistics, *Census of the Population 1960* (Damascus, 1962), Summary, Vol. 15, Tables 4, 5 and 7.

15. For example, see 'News from around the Region: Preparatory Meeting of Experts for the Survey of Arab Scholars, 11-13 June, 1977', *Population Bulletin*, 12 (January 1977) (Beirut, 1978), pp. 42-3; *MEED, 21*, 10, 11 March 1977: 'Syria's difficulties, however, are not merely financial. The shortage of skilled and semi-skilled labour will be an obstacle to implementation of the five year plan. "We've had a shortage – a bottleneck – since 1974, simply because our expansion was so rapid", said Abrash. 'But then we were hit by workers being attracted to the Gulf States, Saudi Arabia and West Germany, and our economy just cannot possibly compete at present with wages offered by Arab petroleum-producing

and European countries.' An unskilled building worker in Damascus might earn £Syr. 250 ($68) a month, while in Saudi Arabia he would probably earn at least five times as much. To deal with this, the authorities are thinking of increasing restrictions on the movement of skilled and semi-skilled workers.

PART V: CONCLUSION

# 20 ARAB LABOUR MARKETS: A BROAD ASSESSMENT

## 1 Introduction

The distinction made throughout this book between capital-rich, pseudo-capital-rich and capital-poor states has been used to characterise different groups of states each with comparable endowments of resources and, consequently, similar paths of economic development. The comparable demographic, labour market and social features of countries divided by this criterion have also been noted. Here key aspects of Arab labour markets are discussed thematically on a regional basis. They include the informal sector, the traditional sector, segmentation of the labour market and the concept of the Arab common market. This penultimate chapter on labour markets also makes a broad assessment of patterns and trends and indicates their significance.

## 2 The Informal Sector

### (a) The Characteristics of the Informal Sector

Informal-sector employment is common and increasing throughout developing countries. The poor countries of the Arab region offer no exception: informal-sector employment abounds in Cairo, Khartoum, Tunis, Damascus and Beirut, for example. The informal sector is roughly defined as being easy to enter, reliant on indigenous resources, organised on a small scale and often family basis, and is labour-intensive, using adapted technology and skills acquired informally. It exists in both urban and rural areas, and is typically proximate to centres of modern development.[1]

Until recently the informal sector was not seen as particularly relevant to the objectives of modern economic development; economists, planners and governments were primarily concerned to expand the modern sector. However, the inability of that sector to grow quickly enough to employ more than a small proportion of all job seekers together with the capacity of the informal sector to absorb quite large numbers has given it an enhanced respect.

In the Arab region, informal-sector employment is concentrated almost solely in capital-poor countries; in capital-rich states the number of petty traders, shoe shiners, small garages and so on is very small.[2]

Several reasons account for this. First, in these capital-rich states, official policy has been to employ all nationals in government service, if they so desire, irrespective of their skills or educational background. Secondly, severe barriers exist to the development of an informal sector by immigrants who might reasonably be expected to be in and out of formal employment quite regularly and so generate an informal sector. In particular, governments of capital-rich states do not permit residence of people who do not have a 'work permit'. This is obtainable only by the 'sponsorship' of a recognised employer in the modern sector. Sponsorship is both difficult to obtain and expensive, and as a result the development of the informal sector is curtailed.

Moreover, even if migrants who have evaded the work permit regulations do establish informal-sector ventures, these do not last. Either the informally employed fall foul of other licensing regulations, in which event they are commonly deported or, if the ventures are successful, they tend to be bought up by the private formal sector. Other barriers to informal-sector ventures in the capital-rich states include the high costs of overheads, especially land, rents and buildings, as well as the particular commercial laws of these countries which preclude non-nationals from personally owning enterprises. These barriers, and the active labour market policy of governments, backed up by their fiscal position and rapid spontaneous expansion of modern-sector private employment, mean that the generally ubiquitous informal sector is absent from capital-rich states. The only country which might be becoming an exception to this amongst the capital-rich states is Iraq, where rural urban migration is so rapid that a reservoir of informally employed is building up in the towns.

A quite different state of affairs exists in capital-poor states. Casual empiricism suggests that large numbers in the cities of these poorer countries derive a living from the informal sector. In rural areas, too, the informal sector is increasingly becoming a significant source of employment. This will be a significant factor in the rural employment structure of Egypt and Morocco, as well as the smaller capital-poor Arab states.

In the pseudo-capital-rich states, despite their feverish attempts to develop the modern economy, there are signs of growth in informal-sector employment. In Algeria, the dominance of capital-intensive projects of investment has led to only limited employment creation and hence underemployment and open unemployment. Inevitably the informal sector is growing. A different pattern exists in Bahrain and

Oman. Although labour importers, they have not applied residence permit regulations as strictly as some of their neighbours, nor are the levels of investible funds so high. In both these states, informal-sector employment of immigrant populations is beginning to appear. This is yet another respect in which the pseudo-capital-rich share characteristics of both capital-poor and capital-rich states.

Official figures pertaining directly to informal employment are virtually non-existent; by its nature the informal sector is not amenable to enumeration. It is only through a process of elimination that estimates of informal-sector employment are derived. In three capital-poor states where estimates have been made, the informal sector accounts for 11 per cent (Egypt, 1976), 14 per cent (Sudan, 1973) and 14 per cent (North Yemen, 1975) of all employment.[3] These estimates err on the conservative side, but in all cases the recent growth of informal-sector employment has made it equivalent to about half of all modern-sector employment.

Yet more significant than the present size of the informal sector in capital-poor states is its likely future growth. The proportion of labour market entrants able to find modern-sector jobs will diminish as time passes. Working in the informal sector will be their only alternative to outright unemployment.

The failure of the modern sector of these capital-poor economies over the past 30 years to provide sufficient employment is easily explained in general terms: the high cost of job creation, the fact that modern development typically creates limited but highly productive employment (being essentially capital-intensive); and the continuing high rates of population increase. Moreover, the widening disparity in terms of income and wealth between rural and urban areas has encouraged internal migration and hence more urban job seekers all contribute to the growing pool of those informally employed.

These are the fundamental causes of the past and future growth of the informal sector. But more recently one factor in particular has contributed to its growth and its rate of increase, namely the passive relationship that the capital-poor countries have with the capital-rich as suppliers of labour, on terms dictated by the latter. To see the significance of this, aspects of the process of international migration bear illumination. Typically, international migration comprises a series of steps, with migrants moving from villages to towns, then towns to cities, with the ultimate aim of international migration. A chain of migrating steps is established which ends abroad. However, a residue of unsuccessful migrants is left in the urban centres of the capital-poor states.

These aspiring migrants depend for their livelihood on the informal sector. Moreover, on their return, many successful migrants have acquired skills useful in towns rather than villages. Thus there is also a tendency for returnees to remain in cities, and not to return to villages. Moreover, many of the returned migrants acquire attitudes and aspirations that can only be fulfilled in cities.

At the same time, it is arguable that the economic development of the capital-poor states has been compromised in several ways by international migration, particularly because of the violence of the changes in the international demand for migrant labour. This is most easily seen in the effect of the sudden torrent of migrant workers' remittances after 1974 on the economies of the migrant-sending states. The exceptionally rapid increase in the flow of remittances and the generally informal mechanisms used to transfer the cash balances meant that there was little opportunity to channel these remittances into productive investment.[4] At the same time, the sudden increase in disposable income and the limited productive capacity of these economies created very high levels of inflation. The general absence of skilled labour has an effect on wages which rose, and this wage inflation was fuelled by the sudden boom in construction, financed by the migrant workers' remittances. Thus development was made more costly for capital-poor states by increased labour costs and inflation, and the impact of aid or grants was less beneficial than it would otherwise have been. Now the flow of remittances seems likely to fall almost as abruptly as it rose, thus engendering further disruption.

It is arguable that such disruptions, in particular inflation and domestic labour shortages, have compromised what little development these countries would otherwise have been capable of. Less development and hence less modern-sector employment has been possible than would otherwise be the case, and so the informal sector has been swollen further.

Finally, there is the crucial point that not only do the capital-rich states have the power to import the quantity and quality of labour which they require, but also they have almost complete flexibility in determining the duration of stay of migrants. Thus capital-rich states are able to re-export to the capital-poor labour which, through the vagaries of the business cycle or even a change of political or social policy, has become redundant to them. No such luxury is open to economic planners in capital-poor states who are obliged first to face compromised economic development through inflation and labour shortages, and quite possibly, secondly, the sudden return of migrant workers and a sharp decline in remittances. Under these circumstances the informal sector grows inexorably.

## (b) Future Development of the Informal Sector

The informal sector will grow in the capital-poor states, and remain non-existent in the capital-rich. The trend of development in the Arab world is towards a widening gap between capital-rich and capital-poor; as the latter become poorer, so the lack of resources will become more pressing, thus encouraging an enlarged informal sector. Rapid population growth, the net return of erstwhile migrants (larger numbers will return than are departing) and the increasing costliness of job creation will ensure that the demand for modern employment exceeds job opportunities in the capital-poor states, and by an ever greater margin. In future years, informal employment at subsistence levels is the likely livelihood of an ever-growing number of the peoples of the capital-poor. The rising costs of inputs in the capital-rich states, together with increasingly conscious efforts to formalise the labour market, backed up, of course, by large disposable public funds, will ensure a minimal level of informal-sector activity in the capital-rich states.

## 3 The Traditional Sector

### (a) The Nature of the Sector

Whereas informal-sector employment is found almost exclusively in capital-poor states, employment in the traditional sector is more evenly spread, having remained in the larger capital-rich states. Agriculture is the principal repository of traditional-sector employment, though modernisation of farming is beginning in many rural areas.

From Table 20.1 the extent of traditional-sector employment in the capital-poor states is evident. Traditional sector employment dwarfs both modern and informal sector employment. Yet much traditional sector employment yields barely a subsistence level of return. Not surprisingly, the traditional sector remains quite extensively in the pseudo-capital-rich states with the exception of Bahrain, where the length of time for which the island has been developing and the established education system have brought about the virtual eclipse of the traditional sector. With this has come, moreover, the decline of farming. In both Algeria and Oman, large traditional farming systems remain, largely unchanged by the modern order.

In the capital-rich states, with the particular exceptions of Saudi Arabia, Libya and Iraq, the traditional sector is small. Whereas in the

Table 20.1: Employment in the Traditional Sector of Selected Arab States, Various Years

| State | Employment in Traditional Sector (per cent of all employment) | Year |
|---|---|---|
| Yemen Arab Republic | 57.9 | 1975 |
| Sudan | 55.2 | 1973 |
| Egypt | 50.7 | 1976 |
| Syria | 50.0 | 1976 |
| Oman | 29.3 | 1975 |
| Jordan | 13.6 | 1975 |
| Saudi Arabia | 32.5 | 1975 |
| Libya | 25.4 | 1975 |
| Bahrain | 6.6 | 1971 |
| United Arab Emirates | 4.5 | 1975 |
| Qatar | 4.3 | 1970 |
| Kuwait | 1.5 | 1975 |

Sources: Derived from J.S. Birks and C.A. Sinclair, *International Migration and Development in the Arab Region* (ILO, Geneva, 1980); J.S. Birks and C.A. Sinclair, *Country Case Studies,* International Migration Project Working Papers (Durham, 1977/8).

capital-poor states the traditional sector principally comprises agri- culture, in the capital-rich fishing is also a traditional activity, and lesser though significant activities are boat building and weaving. In the small Gulf states traditional activities vanished almost overnight as oil wealth brought vastly more remunerative opportunities, which were seen by the indigenes as more prestigious and rewarding forms of em- ployment. The same processes precluding informal-sector development in capital-rich states are instrumental in the collapse of the traditional sector. The pace of transformation in some cases has been very rapid indeed. In 1968, in the United Arab Emirates, 18 per cent of all em- ployment was in traditional activities; by 1975 this had fallen to 4.5 per cent. A similar pattern can be traced, though not with the same accuracy, in all the small capital-rich states of the Gulf. In short, in all the small, rich Gulf states rewarding employment opportunities in the modern sector have led to the virtual disappearance of the traditional sector.

The larger capital-rich states of Saudi Arabia, Libya and Iraq do not conform to this pattern, however. In these states the traditional sector has shown remarkable durability. For example, in Saudi Arabia in 1966, agriculture, fishing, livestock and bedouins accounted for almost half of all employment. This employment was, at that time, best des- cribed as providing a subsistence income. Surprisingly, in 1975 more than half of the indigenous work-force was still engaged in that sector, the character of which had changed little, remaining predominantly traditional.

Since modern development began with the investing of oil revenues in the domestic economy, Saudi Arabian development has proceeded along dual-economy lines — the modern sector has forged ahead, associated with the development of urban centres and industrial areas. The rural agricultural sector has remained largely subsistence based, except for a few large-scale agricultural projects. Consequently, a large proportion of the Saudi Arabian national work-force has not participated full-time in the modern development of this most wealthy of Arab states. The reasons accounting for so many Saudi Arabian nationals remaining outside the modern sector have been enumerated (see Chapter 5). Similar explanations have also been advanced to explain the resilience of the traditional sector in Libya. On a smaller scale and at a lower level of wealth, the tendency of dual economic development with a persistent traditional sector has also been exhibited in the pseudo-capital-rich states, especially the Sultanate of Oman. In all these capital-rich and pseudo-capital-rich countries, the traditional- and modern-sector labour markets are not entirely independent, though. The two interact by virtue of members of the traditional sector participating in the modern, formally employed labour force, in an informal and part-time manner. Members of the rural economy have become short-term periodic migrant labourers, who move from their village homes to the urban areas in search of employment.

The rewards from these short-term periods of employment sustain the declining traditional sector. This part-time informal employment distributes income amongst a larger section of the national population. Saudi Arabian and Libyan nationals effectively gain a rent from being nationals and so gain a high return to labour, divorced from marginal productivity. This constrains their inputs to the modern sector, because even given their abnormally high returns to labour, the migrants soon see the opportunity cost of leisure and time spent at home as outweighing further cash earnings, and so withdraw again from the modern sector, returning to a more relaxed life in the rural areas.

*(b) The Future of the Traditional Sector*

In Saudi Arabia, Libya and Iraq the traditional sector is surviving temporarily. These economies have sufficient wealth, and their modern sectors will continue to grow so that eventually the traditional sector will be engulfed. The labour presently in the traditional sector will be absorbed into an expanded modern sector. The modern sector, the core of the economy, will expand, to engulf the peripheral, traditional economy.

In the pseudo-capital-rich states of Algeria and Oman, it is less easy to see the process of absorption of the traditional sector proceeding in this way. In both countries, the rate of expansion of the modern (presently urban) economy will slow. When it does, because of falling government income, relatively little finance will be available for the rural sector. Government spending in the rural sector will be further limited by high current account payments on social services and possibly also by subsidies to an ailing industrial sector.

The 'luxurious' traditional economy in the capital-rich states is in sharp contrast to that prevailing in the capital-poor states. In the former the income of the population is high, related to the wealth in the modern sector. In the latter, the capital-poor states, the income of those in the traditional sector is not augmented by earnings from periodic participation in the modern sector. In the capital-poor states, there are insufficient opportunities in the modern sector for those from the traditional sector to enter and leave it at will. Those in the traditional sector in the capital-poor states are reliant totally upon the resources of that sector and its technology.

Not only does international migration for employment represent almost the only escape from the traditional (and informal sectors) in the capital-poor states, it also underlies the survival of the traditional sector in the capital-rich states. It is only the imports of labour which the capital-rich countries of Saudi Arabia and Libya can afford which enable the survival of the traditional sector in Saudi Arabia. Indeed, it has been argued (Chapter 6) that imports of labour to Libya actually prevent a reduction in the numbers in the traditional sector there.

## 4 Segmentation of the Labour Markets in the Arab World

The traditional and modern, informal and formal sectors are part of wider segmentation of the labour market in the region. Arab labour markets are divided into several distinct and separate compartments. Entry into each compartment requires particular qualifications; market forces and political stances mean that the rules of admission tend to be enforced rigorously. Essentially, these divisions have been created by wealth, or the lack of it, by custom and religious precept. Here three divisions which exist on a regional basis are discussed, though study of any one country would reveal more subtle distinctions between segments of the market.

## (a) Sex

One of the most obvious and best known segmentations in the Arab world's labour markets is according to sex. In capital-poor, pseudo-capital-rich and capital-rich Arab states the labour market discriminates against women. Women have always worked and continue to work in the traditional sector: they are often seen working in the fields in Yemen, Oman, Saudi Arabia, Egypt and Sudan, to name only a few countries. Their labour is of considerable significance in traditional sectors which have experienced the outmigration of labour, for example Yemen, Oman and Egypt. In the absence of the male household head, women have been obliged to adopt roles and functions normally reserved for men.[5]

In the capital-poor countries, women have entered the modern sector to a limited degree. There are no official barriers to them, though social customs and practices restrict their freedom of career choice. As in the traditional sector, the expansion of women's role in formal employment in the modern sector is associated with outmigration of male labour. In the Sudan and Jordan, for example, women are increasingly widely employed in government, especially as replacement labour for those menfolk who have departed for employment in the capital-rich states.

It is in the capital-rich states where the number of active women is truly small. In general few women work outside their homes, and then only in particular occupations, for example nursing and teaching. Social and religious customs combine to exclude women from employment in 'mixed sex' environments, though in some states change is quite rapid, notably Kuwait and Bahrain. In Saudi Arabia and Libya, however, the contrary is the case, and social custom has recently been reinforced by government legislation. Women are now prohibited by law from working in the Kingdom and the Jamahiriya in all but a few occupations, despite the constantly increasing levels of educational attainments of women in these states.

The removal of women from the indigenous work-force effectively halves the size of the economically active group, so the crude participation rate of populations in these states is remarkably low, usually falling between 18 and 22 per cent. The very high dependency ratio implicit in these figures reflects the unusually high earning capacity of active male nationals in these capital-rich states. An element of this is the rent that nationals in employment in the public sector enjoy; remuneration is much higher than their marginal productivity would justify.

In the traditional sector, where productivity is low, and remuneration more closely related to economic product, women tend to participate more fully. This is especially the case in the capital-poor states, where traditional-sector incomes are not subsidised by periodic employment in the modern sector.

A considerable waste of resources is involved in the bias against women's employment, especially in the oil-rich states, where women are becoming extremely well educated. However, despite the dependence upon migrant labour in these oil-exporting states, national women will not be permitted to participate in the economy until social perspectives change – perhaps only in the face of a different financial situation. Despite their improving status in some states, such as Kuwait and Bahrain, no profound change in the economic participation of women will come about in the near future.

*(b) Nationals and Non-Nationals*

In capital-rich countries, apart from the traditional and modern, there are two other distinct labour markets. In one nationals work, in the other, migrant workers. This distinction has grown with modern development, and stems from the desire of governments to distribute oil wealth. The traditional relationship of sheikh to tribesmen has not, in essence, been altered by the advent of oil. The traditional duties of the sheikhly leader have been assumed by the government, whose modern responsibilities remain the provision of social services and employment. This attitude means that the conditions of employment for nationals are particularly favourable, wages being paid to nationals as a right almost irrespective of productivity. Many nationals therefore regard their job in the Ministry as a sinecure, which requires only infrequent personal attendance. The true duties of the individual are loyalty to government and an observance of the social mores – those values which were the essence of the traditional order. An unfortunate side-effect of the redistribution of wealth amongst nationals is that their desire or need to work productively is diminished. Their labour is effectively removed from the resources of the economy.

The essential tasks required to maintain and develop the economy are left to migrants. The consequent dependence on migrants in the capital-rich states is both quantitative and qualitative. Table 20.2 shows the extent of quantitative reliance to be high in several cases.

The labour market which non-nationals enter is, unlike that of nationals, a highly competitive one, where wages follow marginal pro-

Table 20.2: Capital-Rich States: Extent of Dependence upon Non-National Labour, 1975

| State | Nationals' Employment | Per cent of Total | Non-Nationals' Employment | Per cent of Total | Total Employment |
|---|---|---|---|---|---|
| Saudi Arabia | 1,026,500 | 57.0 | 773,400 | 43.0 | 1,799,900 |
| Libya | 449,200 | 57.5 | 332,400 | 42.5 | 781,600 |
| Kuwait | 91,800 | 30.6 | 208,000 | 69.4 | 299,800 |
| United Arab Emirates | 45,000 | 15.2 | 251,500 | 84.8 | 296,500 |
| Bahrain | 45,800 | 60.4 | 30,000 | 39.6 | 75,800 |
| Qatar | 12,500 | 18.9 | 53,800 | 81.1 | 66,300 |
| Total | 1,670,800 | 50.3 | 1,649,100 | 49.7 | 3,319,900 |

Source: J.S. Birks and C.A. Sinclair, *International Migration and Development in the Arab Region* (ILO, Geneva, 1980), Table 8.

duct very closely. Many nationalities from non-oil-endowed states are competing to work in the capital-rich states, and when choosing between potential migrants of a comparable skill level, relative productivity, transportation costs and other costs paid by employers in the capital-rich states are weighed. At times political considerations override such economic calculi, as certain nationalities are either regarded as *persona non grata* or are given preferential treatment in applications for work visas. At moments of intense demand for labour, such as occurred from 1973 to 1975, availability is the most relevant factor.

The tenure of employment within the non-national market is becoming increasingly limited. Governments are ever more concerned to limit the period of stay to exactly that required to fulfil the tasks of the appointment. The capacity of migrants to settle with their families has presented several countries of employment with a migrant community which outnumbers nationals, and the financial burden of providing social services, albeit at a meagre level, is considerable.

By separating the labour market into two segments, one where wages are paid in return for productivity, the other where they are also a rent paid to the possession of nationality, the government has ensured that whatever the terms on which migrants work in capital-rich states and whatever the blend of nationalities found there, the dependence upon their services will grow. Whenever additional labour is required, it will have to be imported. Moreover, devising and executing a coherent manpower strategy for the development of indigenous labour is at present a near impossible task. On a broader front, it can be argued that indigenous human capital in oil-rich states is actually deteriorating, despite the increasing educational attainment. As the nationals of capital-rich states become increasingly used to living off sinecure incomes, so their contribution to the economy is declining. At a time when the oil-rich states are worrying about their reliance upon imported labour, they are squandering indigenous human resources, and are not, moreover, mobilising them effectively for the future.

### 5 Occupational Mobility in the Arab Regions

*(c) Introduction*

The international migration of labour from the capital-poor to the capital-rich states of the Arab world has been a recurring facet of the analysis throughout this book. From the point of view of the individual migrant, departure from a capital-poor state to an oil exporter often, especially in the case of the more skilled migrant, compresses into a year a process which normally takes twenty, namely the promotion to a position of higher seniority. Thus, the expansion of international migration for employment after 1973 facilitates, in theory, study of occupational mobility in labour-sending countries. In practice, this is a difficult task, as data are so limited. However, the varied responses in terms of occupational mobility of the capital-poor states' labour markets are discernible. As examples from either end of a spectrum of varied occupational mobility, Egypt and Jordan are considered.

## (b) Egyptian Occupational Immobility

It is a curious paradox that, although Egypt has exported only a small proportion of her work-force (4 per cent in 1975), there are acute shortages of labour in Cairo, particularly of skilled craftsmen. It is most unlikely that domestic economic expansion or military conscription has brought about these shortages. Migration of Egyptians abroad for employment is generally seen as the cause of these labour shortages.

It seems likely that Egypt's labour market is highly compartmentalised, and movement between occupations much more limited than might be expected. As a result there is very little internal readjustment within the labour market to compensate for the exports of certain types of manpower. Thus vacancies which occur are not quickly filled, and labour shortages appear widespread, even although only a relatively small number migrate and although unemployment of other types of labour is pervasive.

A number of factors help explain this lack of occupational mobility. The first concerns lack of movement from the agricultural sector. It is asserted here that marginal products to labour in agriculture, though perhaps small, are positive. Consequently, today there are not large numbers willing to migrate to towns. There are severe discouragements to moving into Egyptian cities, including the high social cost of living in overcrowded and underserviced slums. This lack of rural to urban migration is also evidenced by the growth of low-income-generating informal-sector activities in rural areas. Frustrated would-be rural to urban migrants establish their informal non-agricultural activities in their home areas, rather than endure the costs and conditions of today in the large Egyptian urban centres.

Secondly, an important proportion of the labour market is accounted for by those in government service and public employment generally. From the point of view of this analysis – occupational mobility and the propensity to migrate internationally – these public-sector employees are essentially immobile occupationally. Although some migrant workers are indeed government secondees (such as teachers and technicians), their number is relatively small. The secure income, with annual increments, that government employment provides means that a public-sector employee maximises long-term economic returns by remaining in the post. He or she is therefore neither a potential migrant, nor has occupational mobility within the domestic labour market. The Egyptian public sector accounts for 75 per cent of non-agricultural employment. Therefore, only some 25 per cent of the labour force (about 3 million persons) are potential migrants for employment, or likely to fill the vacancies left by those who have migrated. Their number is particularly limited, because of the small private sector in urban Egypt, a consequence of government domination of the economy.

Not only is this group surprisingly small in number, but many are of low educational attainment, frequently illiterate, lacking in employment experience or often unemployed. However, only those of this population with work experience or skills are demanded as migrants. Furthermore, only these same can move easily to higher levels of occupational status within Egypt. The unemployed and inexperienced, the urban poor, find it difficult to migrate internationally. These poorly qualified Egyptians are only in demand internationally if their marginal cost and productivity compare favourably with alternative labour supplies. Similarly, those unqualified groups are slow to move to levels of higher occupational status.

Thus it is that the Egyptian labour market appears compartmentalised, and therefore has been slow to exploit the potential for exporting labour, and ineffective in replacing the domestic labour shortages in the Egyptian labour market which have come about as a consequence of those limited exports of manpower which have taken place. In sharp contrast to this is the Jordanian labour market, which might be thought to have shaped itself around international migration for employment.

### (c) Jordanian Occupational Mobility

The Jordanian labour market has exported a much higher proportion of its work-force abroad than has the Egyptian: about 28 per cent of the Jordanian domestic labour force was abroad in 1975, compared to the figure for Egypt of 4 per cent. The Jordanian tradition of migration is long, even before 1973 there were a large number of Jordanians abroad. Typically, Jordanians are well educated and so are in high demand in capital-rich states.

Within the Jordanian labour market, occupational mobility is high.

Unlike Egypt, the government in Jordan is small, and the Jordanian economy is run on a free enterprise basis. Since the rapid departure of so many migrants after 1973, both the private and public Jordanian markets readjusted very quickly. Upward mobility through promotion has been rapid. Confirmation of this is given by the inexperience and youth of many new appointees in government service. Changes of employment across occupational groups also appear common in Jordan. These are in response to high returns for labour in those areas of the labour market in which the shortfall and demand is greatest. There has also been a marked impact upon the pattern of training of school-leavers, who have availed themselves of technical and vocational courses in order to maximise their returns when seeking employment. This contrasts with the Egyptian case, where a more rigidly structured education system continues to produce labour market entrants who are ill qualified in terms of the demands of the economy and the outside world.

The Jordanian labour market also compensates for the outmigration of Jordanians by attracting numbers of Egyptians, Syrians and Pakistanis. These replacement migrants move into the vacuum left at the lower occupational levels of the Jordanian labour market by the upward mobility of Jordanian nationals. Thus the most common employment of replacement migrants is as unskilled labour, particularly on building sites and on the land. In the latter case the occupational shift of Jordanians – out of farming – has been accompanied by a geographical shift of population – rural to urban migration.

Although labour shortages have not been completely avoided in Jordan (with almost one-third of the labour force abroad, it would be impossible to avoid some shortfalls of specific types of labour) they are of a much smaller significance than might have been expected because of the rapid internal responses of the labour market. It is this responsiveness which has permitted the outmigration of such a larger proportion of Jordanian workers than has been possible in Egypt.

## (d) Conclusion

The Egyptian and Jordanian labour markets represent two extremes on a scale of occupational mobility which is identifiable within the Arab world. A greater degree of occupational mobility tends to minimise the harmful effects of labour outmigration upon the domestic economy. Thus far, occupational mobility has been examined in a time of labour shortage and increasing exports of manpower. This shortage of manpower within the region has brought about the export of very large proportions of the work-forces of the capital-poor and pseudo-rich states, as has been detailed in Parts III and IV.

These large exports of labour – which make the study of occupational mobility so significant – have been caused by the most labour-intensive phases of the capital-rich states' development plans, their construction phases. It is not clear, though, whether the capital-poor states will continue to experience a regional shortage of labour. A combination of a downturn in the construction phases of the development plans (likely to occur despite the 1979 oil price rises), combined with the substitution for Arab labour of more cost-effective (and politically desirable) Far Eastern workers, will mean labour shortages are not likely to prevail in the capital-poor states in the 1980s. The net return of their workers from the capital-rich states will generate unemployment once the current shortages are filled. This unemployment is likely to be especially problematical, as the unskilled will be the first to return.

Under these conditions of returning labour, it will be of more than academic interest to determine whether the same characteristics of labour market adjustments occur when manpower is reabsorbed by these labour supplying states as their workers are sent home by the capital-rich countries. Before considering the future of the overall demand for and supply of labour in the Arab world, it is pertinent to examine further some qualitative aspects of the region's labour market.

### 6 An Arab Common Labour Market – Myth or Reality?

The differential pace of development of individual countries in the region and uneven endowments of financial wealth and human resources are the essential background to labour migration in the region. Since oil has been exported migrants have travelled from the poor countries of the region to the newly rich to benefit from the larger rewards to labour in the latter.

The Arab world includes some 21 countries and over 131 million persons (1975). The region was well suited to engender spontaneous international migration within it. Throughout the region language and religion are common, though there are significant subregional variations. It is partly this (perhaps) superficial unity which means that many Arabs do not recognise national borders as delineating individuals as different from their relatives or fellow tribesmen across the border. Furthermore, familiar regional groupings in the Arab world such as 'the Levant', 'Greater Syria', 'the Arabian Gulf', the 'Hadramaut', 'the Empty Quarter', the Maghreb', 'the Mashreq' and 'Palestine' all rein-force the pan-national attitudes of Arabs. Travelling from Muscat to Dubai, from Baghdad to Beirut, Fez to Cairo, or from Sanaa to Mecca is a different proposition psychologically for an Arab and a European.

National boundaries are also made less relevant for Muslims by the religious injunction upon them to undertake the pilgrimage at some point in their lives. This involves a journey to Mecca. It is upon geo-graphical relationships with Mecca that the nomenclature of the Arab world is divided; hence Morocco, Algeria and Tunisia are the Maghreb (the west in Arabic), and Lebanon, Jordan and Syria are the Mashreq (the east in Arabic).

As a result of this view, what an outside observer would call a very casual attitude to 'international' travel is common amongst Arab pop-ulations. This informal attitude towards crossing borders is often a reality. Until recently, for example, Yemenis travelling to Saudi Arabia did not require documentation, nor do Syrians travelling to Jordan or Beirut. The view has been expressed on several occasions to the authors by members of leading Arab institutions that the term 'international migration' is a misnomer within the Arab world, the product of an un-knowing European mind. More accurate, these Arabs argue, is the term 'circulation of manpower'.

After 1973 the scale and intensity of labour migration heightened dramatically as oil-rich states began to invest their enhanced revenues in domestic development programmes. Little thought was given to the im-plications of importing such large numbers of migrants, generated by their development plans' demand for manpower: comparatively little control was exercised over the entry of migrant workers into the capital-rich states, and the degree to which they have become depen-dent upon migrant labour was shown on Table 20.2. By 1977/8, how-ever, a large slice of the key development projects was completed, and the rate of growth of the demand for labour was slowing. Moreover, a less sanguine view of the extent and life of oil revenues was emerging in the capital-rich states, together with a growing concern over the degree of dependence on migrant labour and their numbers. By 1978, development had changed not only the skyline of the capital-rich states, but also transformed their social composition. Almost inevitably, a less sympathetic view of labour immigration developed. Following this, the terms on which migrants came and when they should leave were defined ever more strictly. During 1978, Saudi Arabia, the largest labour importer, declared an amnesty during which time 'illegal' workers could register at the Ministry of Interior without official reprisal. Tens of thousands of migrants did so. Following this, further efforts have been made to formalise the immigrant sector of the labour market in the Kingdom.

As the controls placed by capital-rich governments on immigrant labour have increased, so has the sophistication of the means of selecting one migrant rather than another. Increasingly, Asians, and particularly Far Easterners, are preferred to Arabs. The Asian and Far Eastern workers are more cost-effective than Arab labour. Non-Arab migrant labour also presents host governments with a smaller number of unproductive dependents requiring the provision of social services.

For an Arab common labour market to exist there must be virtually unrestricted movement of labour from capital-poor Arab states to the capital-rich. This precondition was quite closely met in the past, when the movement of Arab workers was small scale, spontaneous and little interfered with by governments. Today, however, the key countries of employment are erecting increasing barriers to migration with the particular object of restraining the movement of Arab labour. The governments of the oil-exporting states are feeling increasingly that the political disadvantages associated with the employment of Arab labour from the capital-poor states of the region are becoming prohibitive. Whilst this political reality grows and remains significant, an Arab common labour market remains mythical.

## 7 Projections of Arab Labour Markets to 1985

### (a) Introduction

The concern with labour migration of national governments within the area has grown with perception of the advantageous and deleterious impacts of migration for employment upon their economic development and societies. As efforts to stimulate or limit migration grow in the capital-poor countries, and as the capital-rich countries attempt unilaterally to slow imports of Arab labour, so international transfers of labour feature increasingly in social and economic planning within the Arab world. Despite a contemporary concern with international migration for employment in virtually all countries of the Middle East, there has not yet been any regional or unified approach. However, these national policies have been slow to evolve beyond a short-term and piecemeal basis. As a result, government action in the Arab world directed towards labour movement has been pragmatic, changeable, inconsistent and often contradictory. The only characteristic that policies have shared is relatively ineffective application. It is because of this that the patterns of labour movement, resulting from some extraordinarily powerful labour market forces, have become deeply entrenched.

Throughout this book, several strong labour market trends have been identified. The one with which these projections is concerned is the increasing tendency of the capital-rich states to utilise non-Arab labour, and in particular Far Eastern labour, associated with enclave containment of these workers in work camps. Yet Far Eastern workers are not only employed within the Arab world as enclave labour forces. Companies from south-east Asia have tendered successfully and are meeting deadlines on non-enclave contracts; the provision of infrastructure in Riyadh, for example, is being effected by Far Eastern firms, as are major hotel and office building contracts in other capital-rich states. The market trend suggests that Far Eastern labour will increasingly be employed in the capital-rich countries by choice instead of Arab labour. Not only is Far Eastern labour more cost-effective; not only do Far Eastern companies offer very attractive 'enclave packages' to capital-rich countries, which minimise difficulties to indigenous planners, but the Far Eastern workers, by virtue of their preparedness to live in enclave developments, and return home after contracts are complete, offer overriding social advantages as a labour supply for which knowledge of Arabic is not essential.

It is with the probability of increased substitution of Far Eastern workers for Arab labour supplies that the analysis turns to projections of the labour markets in the major labour-importing states up to 1985. These projections quantify present market trends to demonstrate their future significance within the Arab world.

*(b) The Projected Demand for Labour in Major Labour Importing States, 1975 to 1985*

In this projection of the future demand for labour, the analysis focuses on six states which, up till now, have been principal importers of labour. These are Saudi Arabia, Libya, Kuwait, the United Arab Emirates, Qatar and Bahrain. The projection of labour demand for each of these states is based upon the growth of total employment between 1970 and 1975, amended in view of development plans, major projects, stated objectives and success in meeting past deadlines. Employment in 1975 and 1985 is shown on Table 20.3 for each state. Overall employment increases by 4.6 per cent per annum between 1975 and 1985. This amounts to some 1.9 million extra workers.

Table 20.3: Major Capital-Rich States: Total Employment Projected to 1985

| State | 1975 Number | Annual per cent Increase 1975 to 1980 | 1980 Number | Annual per cent Increase 1980 to 1985 | 1985 Number |
|---|---|---|---|---|---|
| Saudi Arabia | 1,799,900 | 5.0 | 2,297,200 | 3.5 | 2,728,400 |
| Libya | 781,600 | 5.8 | 1,036,000 | 4.5 | 1,291,000 |
| Kuwait | 299,800 | 4.7 | 377,100 | 3.2 | 441,400 |
| United Arab Emirates | 296,500 | 5.4 | 386,500 | 5.4 | 502,700 |
| Bahrain | 75,800 | 4.1 | 92,700 | 3.5 | 110,100 |
| Qatar | 66,300 | 9.9 | 106,300 | 5.5 | 138,900 |
| Total | 3,319,900 | 5.3 | 4,295,800 | 3.9 | 5,212,500 |

Source: Derived from material presented in this book.

### (c) The Projected Domestic Supply of Labour, 1975 to 1985

A proportion of total labour demand in these states was, in 1975, met by indigenous labour supplies. To estimate this for 1985, indigenous work-forces have been projected forwards at a rate consistent with growth between 1970 and 1975. However, this rate is adjusted to take into account likely changes in relevant economic or social variables (naturalisations, and the participation of women in the economy). The national work-forces of the six labour-importing states are projected to rise in total from 1,670,000 persons in 1975, to 2,200,000 in 1985, at an annual rate of 2.6 per cent (Table 20.4).

Therefore, the difference between demand and supply in Tables 20.3 and 20.4 give an estimate of the required number of migrant workers. The number of migrants, it is known, was 1,700,000 in 1975 (in these six states only) and so becomes 3,100,000 in 1985.[6]

### (d) The Projected International Supply of Labour, 1975 to 1985

In 1975, three-quarters of all migrant workers in these six states were Arabs (Table 20.6). The estimation of the future supply of Arab labour is based on a key assumption: by 1975 the majority of Arabs from the countries of origin who were able and willing to migrate, and whose skills were employable in the labour-importing states, were already abroad. Therefore, it is presumed that large extra reserves of Arab migrant labour did not exist after 1975. However, the high real wages in these states did attract an additional number of Arab migrants after 1975. These are shown in Table 20.5 under the heading 'once and for all increase'. This number is added to those already recorded as abroad

Table 20.4: Major Capital-Rich States: Employment of Nationals Projected to 1985

| State | 1975 Number | Annual per cent Increase 1975 to 1980 | 1980 Number | Annual per cent Increase 1980 to 1985 | 1985 Number |
|---|---|---|---|---|---|
| Saudi Arabia | 1,026,500 | 2.0 | 1,133,300 | 2.2 | 1,263,600 |
| Libya | 449,200 | 3.2 | 525,800 | | 609,500 |
| Kuwait | 91,800 | 5.0 | 117,200 | 3.2 | 137,200 |
| Bahrain | 45,800 | 4.5 | 57,100 | 3.2 | 66,800 |
| United Arab Emirates | 45,000 | 3.2 | 52,700 | 3.0 | 61,100 |
| Qatar | 12,500 | 4.5 | 15,600 | 3.2 | 18,300 |
| Total | 1,670,800 | 2.6 | 1,901,700 | 2.5 | 2,156,500 |

Source: Derived from material presented in this book.

in 1975. Apart from this increase, extra Arab migrants in the market are projected to increase by, in most cases, 3 per cent per annum from 1975 to 1985. Thus on Table 20.5, 1,300,000 Arab migrants abroad in 1975 are shown, and just over 1,900,000 'able and willing' Arab migrants are predicted by 1985.

*(e) The Resolution of Demand for and Supply of Labour in 1985*

At this point, where demand for labour is reconciled with the supply, the nature of the assumptions made becomes critical to the resulting picture.

Two scenarios are presented (see Tables 20.6 and 20.7). The first is one in which every able and willing Arab migrant finds employment in one of the capital-rich states. This demonstrates the maximum possible contribution of Arabs to the development of the labour-importing states.

*Scenario One: Maximum Penetration by Arab Migrant Workers of International Labour Markets.* Here, it is presumed that the entire number of 1.9 million 'able and willing' Arab migrants (derived from Table 20.5) are employed in the oil-exporting states. It is also assumed that the demand for the services of 'Europeans' rises to 70,000, where it is stable. It is predicted that the number of 'Iranians and others' falls from 86,100 in 1975 to 70,000 in 1985, as they are drawn back to Iran as development proceeds there. (Recent developments in Iran do not, it is felt, call this presumption into question over the period of the pro-

Table 20.5: Number of Arab Migrants Abroad in 1975 and Projected Numbers for 1985 by Country of Origin

| Country of Origin | 1975 Number of Migrants | Once and for All Increase | Annual Growth of Migrants Abroad (per cent) | 1985 Number Available |
|---|---|---|---|---|
| Egypt | 397,545 | 50,000 | 3.0 | 601,600 |
| Yemen (YAR) | 290,128 | 15,000 | 3.0 | 409,200 |
| Jordan and Palestine | 264,717 | 20,000 | 3.0 | 382,500 |
| Yemen (PDRY) | 70,630 | — | 3.0 | 95,000 |
| Syria | 70,415 | — | 3.0 | 95,000 |
| Lebanon | 49,661 | 5,000 | 3.0 | 73,000 |
| Sudan | 45,873 | 10,000 | 3.0 | 75,000 |
| Tunisia | 38,649 | 40,000 | 3.0 | 115,000 |
| Oman | 38,413 | — | 3.0 | 51,000 |
| Iraq | 20,625 | — | – 3.0 | 11,000 |
| Somalia | 6,547 | 5,000 | 3.0 | 15,000 |
| Morocco | 2,529 | — | 3.0 | 3,300 |
| Algeria | 18 | — | — | — |
| Total | 1,295,750 | — | 4.0 | 1,926,600 |

Source: Compiled by the authors from official and other sources.

jections.) The number of Asians (from the Indian subcontinent, including Nepal, Bangladesh and Sri Lanka) employed increases from 277,500
to 500,000 from 1975 to 1985 (Table 20.6).

Table 20.6: Resolution of Labour Demand and Supply: Maximum
Penetration of Capital-Rich States' Labour Markets (Scenario One)

|  | 1975 | | 1985 | |
|---|---|---|---|---|
|  | Number | Per cent | Number | Per cent |
| Total labour demand | 3,319,900 | 100.0 | 5,212,500 | 100.0 |
| of which nationals | 1,670,800 | 50.3 | 2,156,500 | 47.0 |
| residual demand for |  |  |  |  |
| migrants | 1,649,100 | 100.0 | 3,056,000 | 100.0 |
| of which Arabs | 1,236,600 | 75.0 | 1,926,600 | 63.0 |
| Asians | 277,500 | 16.8 | 500,000 | 16.4 |
| Orientals | 14,600 | 0.9 | 489,400 | 16.0 |
| European and American | 34,300 | 2.1 | 70,000 | 2.3 |
| Iranians | 86,100 | 5.2 | 70,000 | 2.3 |

Source: Derived from material presented in this book.

This leaves a deficit of some 489,400. This, it is postulated, is met
by workers from the Far East. Therefore, the relative market shares of
each group in 1980, if the capital-rich and pseudo-capital-rich states'
labour markets are presumed to be receptive of Arab migrant labour, to
the extent that Arab countries of origin are able to supply migrant
labour, is as follows: Arab migrants, 63 per cent (1975, 75 per cent);
Asian migrants, 16.4 per cent (1975, 16.8 per cent); Far Eastern
migrants, 16.0 per cent (1975, 0.9 per cent); European migrants, 2.3
per cent (1975, 2.1 per cent); Iranians and others, 2.3 per cent (1975,
5.2 per cent).

Two aspects of this pattern are important: first, the labour markets of
the labour-importing states will continue to rely on non-Arab labour to
an increasing extent; even if every available Arab migrant is accepted in
1985, there remains a shortfall of employment. Therefore, even if all
available Arabs are employed in these labour-importing states, their proportional contribution to the labour market falls. Secondly, this shortfall in the supply of labour will be met from the Asian subcontinent,
and increasingly from the Far East.

*Scenario Two: Limited Penetration by Arab Migrant Workers of Inter-
national Labour Markets.* The analysis of labour markets of labour
importers shows that they are becoming increasingly selective over the
nationalities employed because of wider issues associated with hosting

large numbers of migrants.

In scenario two it is assumed that, as a result of these market trends, the number of Arabs working in the labour-importing states remains constant and does not rise between 1975 and 1985. Arabs remain in employment, each one who retires or who returns home is replaced by another Arab migrant. However, every new job is given to an Asian or a Far Eastern migrant. In the light of the preceding pages this is quite possible; indeed, it is postulated by the authors to be the scenario closer to reality. In this more realistic scenario, the Arab migrants' share of the market in this group of labour importers falls from 75 per cent in 1975 to 40.5 per cent in 1985 (Table 20.7). Together, Asian and Oriental migrants increase in number from 1975 to 1985 from 292,000 (17.5 per cent) to 1,679,400 persons (55 per cent).

Table 20.7: Resolution of Labour Demand and Supply: A More Selective Labour Market in the Capital-Rich States, Less Open to Arab Labour (Scenario Two)

| | 1975 | | 1985 | |
|---|---|---|---|---|
| | Number | Per cent | Number | Per cent |
| Total labour demand | 3,319,900 | 100.0 | 5,212,500 | 100.0 |
| of which nationals | 1,670,800 | 50.3 | 2,156,500 | 41.4 |
| residual demand for migrants | 1,649,100 | 100.0 | 3,056,000 | 100.0 |
| of which Arabs: | 1,236,600 | 75.0 | 1,236,600 | 40.5 |
| Asians | 277,500 | 16.8 | 500,000 | 16.3 |
| Orientals | 14,600 | 0.9 | 1,179,400 | 38.6 |
| Europeans and Americans | 34,300 | 2.1 | 70,000 | 2.3 |
| Iranians | 86,100 | 5.2 | 70,000 | 2.3 |

Source: Derived from material presented in this book.

*(f) Conclusion*

Thus, by 1985 the labour market of the Arab world will have dramatically different characteristics to those which it had in 1975. Such is the pace of change in the Middle East that this should come as no surprise. The wider implications of this are dealt with in the conclusion to the book, Chapter 21.

### Notes

1. See S.V. Sethuraman, 'The Urban Informal Sector: Concept, Measurement and Policy', *International Labour Review, 114*, 1 (ILO, Geneva, 1976) for a defin-

ition of the informal sector.

2. Iraq is a notable exception to this description of capital-rich states.

3. J.S. Birks and C.A. Sinclair, 'Structures of Urban Employment in the Arab Middle East' in G.H. Blake and R.I. Lawless (eds.), *The Middle East City* (Croom Helm, London, 1980).

4. But see G. Nihan and R. Jourdain, 'The Modern Informal Sector in Nouakchott' *International Labour Review, 117*, 6 (ILO, Geneva, 1978) for a different perspective on the use of remittances. See also J.S. Birks and C.A. Sinclair, *Migration and Development in the Arab Region* (ILO, Geneva, 1980).

5. J.S. Birks and S.E. Letts, 'Women in Rural Arab Society: Old Roles and New in the Sultanate of Oman', *Journal of Gulf and Arabian Peninsula Studies, 3*, 10 (Kuwait, April 1977), pp. 49-65 (Arabic); C. Makhlouf-Obermeyer, *Changing Veils: A Study of Women in South Arabia* (Croom Helm, London, 1978).

6. Throughout this section, only migrants for employment are considered. Refugees, those migrating for educational purposes, tourists and those crossing borders for other reasons such as pilgrimage are excluded. Normally, figures quoted refer to migrant workers, excluding dependents. Where dependents are included, they are mentioned specifically.

# 21 CONCLUSION: THE NATURE OF THE CRISIS

## 1 Introduction

The uneven distribution of oil and population in the Arab region has resulted in wide variations of living standards and rates of economic growth. As the differences between rich and poor grow wider rather than narrower, oil wealth has begun to be a divisive force. This is surprising, because considerations such as aid transfers between Arab states, the scale of labour migration from poor countries to rich and the explicitly stated aim of Arab development for Arabs would suggest that oil wealth should coalesce Arab interests. Indeed, in the early 1970s, the region as a whole seemed well set to make general economic progress. The resources of the oil-endowed and the non-oil-endowed looked happily complementary, Sudan and Iraq possessing agricultural potential in abundance, the peninsula with sufficient energy and minerals to serve as a base for unprecedented industrial development, whilst Egypt and Morocco had the manpower to staff the region's industries.

However, far from growth and development occurring on a regional basis, disparities in living standards, wealth and income have increased in the 1970s. Consequently a new note of stridency has entered the regional debate on development questions. In short, the considerable wealth of the oil-endowed states in comparison with the growing poverty of the non-oil states has made oil wealth a divisive force in the Arab world.

Indeed, it is the authors' view that tensions within the Arab region are drawing the Arab world towards a new crisis, the symptoms of which can be seen most clearly in the field of manpower. So, in conclusion, the analysis turns to a consideration of the future shape of labour markets and the nature of the regional manpower problem which, as time passes, becomes more acute, and will become increasingly difficult for the Arab world to avert.

## 2 Capital-Rich Labour Markets

In the capital-rich states the pattern of economic development is well established. It is impossible to alter the general direction of economic development. Even quite profound political change is unlikely to alter the present pattern of industrialisation and infrastructure provision. This means that the demand for labour can be predicted with some confidence in broad outline. Thus the work-forces of the six major labour importers of Saudi Arabia, Libya, Kuwait, the United Arab Emirates, Qatar and Bahrain, which amounted in 1975 to about 3.3 million (of which 51 per cent were indigenous), will increase to 5.2 million in 1985. Crucially, of this number only 41 per cent will be nationals. The remainder of the work-forces will comprise imported labour.

Therefore, the capital-rich states will increase quite significantly their dependence on immigrant labour. Yet already worries about this reliance and its wider implications are growing. Of particular relevance is the fact that in these six capital-rich states, the number of migrant workers will double between 1975 and 1985, increasing by 1.4 million. Even if only a small proportion of these extra immigrant workers bring their dependents, then the immigrant communities as a whole will grow yet more rapidly. At present, moves to minimise the social and wider impact of migrants are constantly being sought. Single men, rather than families, are recruited and these are isolated in enclave developments. In some respects, this enclave and work camp containment of immigrant labour does, in a rather crude way, ease social pressures for nationals in the short term. However, even now large numbers of immigrants exist outside enclaves. These are, in some states, felt to be an undesirable political force which is strengthening.

Probably the deeper and less obvious impact of the imported labour upon indigenous human capital in these oil-exporting states will become significant in the longer term; the stunting of indigenous human capital which is concomitant upon the reliance on immigrants is of profound importance. As the extent of sinecure employment of nationals grows in the capital-rich states, so these states are suffering attrition of their ability and determination to meet the challenges posed by their own economic development. Awareness of this means that as ever-strengthening economic pressures reinforce present market trends, so political apprehension is more frequently expressed.

As this dependence on migrant labour is being questioned, so also is the very strategy of industrialisation. It has yet to be shown that the industrial ventures entered upon by the capital-rich states are all viable, particularly when an evaluation is made on a regional basis. The duplication of industrial effort might mean that some projects are not economic, in which case much investment will have been wasted. In this event, the past development which engendered the dependence on migrant labour will then be seen to have been altogether mistaken strategy.

## 3 Capital-Poor Labour Markets

The preceding section has raised the question of the economic viability of the nature of the path of development presently followed by capital-rich states and the wider implications of using migrant labour to achieve development. There are also cognate arguments for suggesting that the economic transformation of the capital-rich states has been, on balance, detrimental to the economic progress of the capital-poor Arab states.

The economies of the capital-poor states appear to have gained very little from the transformation of the capital-rich. Individual migrants for employment have benefited greatly and payments of aid and soft loans have also been considerable. But the capital-poor states have not enjoyed anything approaching economic transformation and in many instances, what little nominal growth there has been in the last decade has been more than annulled by inflation and population increase. One of the most tangible ways in which the capital-poor states have participated in the development of their more wealthy neighbours has been through international migration of workers. However, many of the supposed benefits of this participation have proved to have a sting in their tail. For instance, the conventional view that remittances represent a valuable source of foreign exchange might only be as apt as the assertion that remittances bring about an import-led boom and domestic inflation. Similarly, the benefits of exporting unemployment seem to turn, with almost astonishing rapidity, into shortages of manpower which appear significant enough to prejudice economic development.

The selectivity of labour migration means that its impact on the economies of the countries supplying labour is greater than numbers alone would suggest. One result of the diminished productive capacity is to reduce the beneficial impact of grants and aid. Thus it appears that through the process of international migration the economies of the capital-poor states have been weakened, that inflation has been raised, that domestic capital formation has been reduced and that labour has become disenchanted with rewards available domestically.

But this disruption of the labour markets of the capital-poor states is not the end of the story. The capital-rich states are now turning away from Arab labour. The analysis of the labour markets of the labour importers shows clearly that more labour from the Far East is being employed, and that Arab labour will be discarded as it is replaced by the most cost-effective and politically desirable Far Eastern work-forces.

The result of the net return of labour to the capital-poor states in the 1980s, compounded by their lack of growth in the 1970s, will be widespread unemployment on a scale which will make the labour surpluses of the 1960s, prior to the burgeoning demands of the capital-rich states, seem to have been altogether more manageable. This unemployment will be the most painful expression in the 1980s of the widening gap between rich and poor Arab states in the1970s.

Thus we see problems of crisis dimensions in both capital-rich and capital-poor states, in each case first being manifest through the labour markets in the 1980s. Just at the time when the economic objectives of the capital-rich states are coming to fruition, so dissatisfaction with the social and political consequences of their chosen path of development will be highest. Nationals will come to fear complete loss of political and economic control of their countries. Contemporaneously, poverty and unemployment will be experienced in the capital-poor states on unprecedented scales, to the extent that their political fabric and stability will be threatened. The geographical proximity of the capital-rich states will mean that their own domestic economic problems will be compounded by the threat from the social unrest following from the lack of economic success in the capital-poor. The manpower crisis of the 1980s will quickly become a political crisis throughout the Arab region.

# BIBLIOGRAPHY

Abadan-Unat, N. 'The Modernization of Turkish Women', *Middle East Journal, 32*, 3 (1978), pp. 291-306

Abdel Jaber, T. *The Brain Drain Problem in the ECWA Countries* (UNECWA, Beirut, 21 July 1978)

Abdel Rahman, E., Taha, Ali and Mehaisi, Mohammed el Hassan *Higher Education and Development in the Sudan, A Review of New Policy* (Economic and Social Research Council, Khartoum, December 1976)

Abdullah, M.M. *The Modern History of the United Arab Emirates* (Ad Orientem, Delhi, 1978)

Adler, S. *International Migration and Development* (Saxon House, London, 1977)

Algeria: Commissariat National aux Recensements et Enquête Statistique *La Population Active au Recensement de 1966* (Algiers, 1970)

——-, *Etude Statistique Nationale de la Population, 1969/70* (Algiers, April 1974)

Algeria: Ministère de l'Education *Informations Statistiques* (Algiers)

Algeria: Ministère de l'Enseignement Supérieur et de la Recherche Scientifique *Bulletin Statistique* (Algiers)

Algeria: Secrétariat d'Etat au Plan, *Données Globales sur l'Evolution de l'Economie Nationale, Année 1976 et Provisions de Réalisation de l'Année 1977* (Algiers, November 1977)

Allan, J.A., McLachlan, K. and Penrose, E.T. *Libya. Agriculture and Economic Development* (Frank Cass, London, 1973)

Allman, J. and Hill, A.G. 'Fertility, Mortality, Migration and Family Planning in the Yemen Arab Republic' (Sanaa, mimeograph, March 1977)

Amicale des Algériens en Europe *Nouvelles Perspectives pour l'Emigration Algérienne,* 8e Assemblée Générale des Cadnes, Nancy, 12-13 Fevrier 1977 (Paris, 1977)

Al Amin, M.K.M. 'A Plan for Increasing Employment in the Sudan' (unpublished thesis, Arab Planning Institute, Kuwait, 1974)

Anon. 'Syria: Economic Survey', *Middle East and North Africa 1977-78* (Europa Publications, London)

*Arab Economist* (Beirut)

Asfour, E.Y. *Syria: Development and Monetary Policy* Harvard University Press, Cambridge, Mass., 1959)

Askari, H. and Cummings, J.G. *Middle East Economies in the 1970s: A Comparative Approach* (Praeger Special Studies, New York, 1976)

Azzi, R. 'Bahrain Dinar, a Gulf Currency', *Orient, 12*, 4 (Hamburg, 1971), pp. 3-5

Al Baharna, H.M. *The Arabian Gulf States: Their Legal and Political Status and their International Problems* (Librairie de Liban, Beirut, 1975)

Bahrain: Ministry of Finance and National Economy, Statistical Bureau *Fourth Population Census of Bahrain* (Manama, 1966)

—— , *Statistics of the Population Census, 1971* (Manama, n.d.)

—— , *Statistical Abstracts* (Manama)

Bahrain Petroleum Company, Annual Report, 1973/74 (Bahrain, 1975)

Balamoan, A.G. *Migration Policies in the Anglo-Egyptian Sudan 1884-1956 – The first part of a history of human tragedies on the Nile* (Harvard University Press, Cambridge, Mass., 1974)

Beaumont, P., Blake, G.H. and Wagstaff, J.M. *The Middle East: A Geographical Study* (Wiley, London, 1976)

Belgrave, C. *Personal Column* (London, 1960)

Belgrave, J.H.D. *Welcome to Bahrain* (Auguston Press, Beirut, 1970)

Benhadi, A. 'La politique Marocaine de barrages', *Annuaire de l'Afrique du Nord, 14* (Paris, 1976)

Beshai, A.A. *Export Performance and Economic Development in Sudan, 1900-1967* (Ithaca Press, London, 1976)

Beshir, M.O. *Educational Policy and the Employment Problem in the Sudan, 1977* (Economic and Research Council, Khartoum, 1978)

Bidwell, R. *The Two Yemens* (Brill, Leiden, 1978)

Birks, J.S. 'Aspects of Demography Related to Development in the Middle East', *Bull. British Society for Middle Eastern Studies, 2* (1976), pp. 79-87

—— , 'Development or Decline of Nomads: the Example of the Bani Qitab', *Arabian Studies, V* (1978)

Birks, J.S. and Letts, S.E. 'Dying Oases in Arabia', *Tijdschrift voor Economische en Sociale Geografie, lxviii, 3* (1977), pp. 145-51

—— , 'Women in Rural Arab Society: Old Roles and New in the Sultanate of Oman', *Journal of the Gulf and Arabian Peninsula Studies* (Kuwait), *III*, 10, pp. 101-12 (Arabic)

Birks, J.S. and Sinclair, C.A. *Country Case Studies, Oman, Kuwait, Jordan, Qatar, Sudan, Egypt, Bahrain, United Arab Emirates, Libyan Arab Jamahiriya, Saudi Arabia*, International Migration Project

Working Papers (Durham, 1977 to 1978)

—— , *Movements of Migrant Labour from the North of the Sultanate of Oman*, International Migration Project Topic Paper (Durham, 1977)

—— , *Aspects of the Demography of the Sultanate of Oman*, International Migration Project Topic Paper (Durham, 1977)

—— , *A Summary of Provisional Findings: Empirical Patterns, Past Trends and Future Development*, International Migration Project Working Paper (Durham, 1978)

—— , *The Sultanate of Oman: Economic Development, Domestic Labour Market and International Migration*, World Employment Programme Working Paper (ILO, Geneva, 1978)

—— , *The Nature and Process of Labour Importing: The Arabian Gulf States of Kuwait, Bahrain, Qatar and the United Arab Emirates*, World Employment Programme Working Paper (ILO, Geneva, 1978)

—— , *Human Capital on the Nile: Development and Emigration in the Arab Republic of Egypt and the Republic of the Sudan*, World Employment Programme Working Paper (ILO, Geneva, 1978)

—— , *The Kingdom of Saudi Arabia and the Libyan Arab Jamahiriya: The Key Countries of Employment*, World Employment Programme Working Paper (ILO, Geneva, 1979)

—— , 'International Labour Migration in the Arab Middle East', *Third World Quarterly, 1*, 2 (April 1979), pp. 87-99

—— , 'Structures of Urban Employment in the Arab Middle East' in G.H. Blake and R.I. Lawless (eds.), *The Middle East City* (Croom Helm, London, 1980)

—— , *International Migration and Development in the Arab Region* (ILO, Geneva, 1980)

Birks, J.S., Sinclair, C.A. and Socknat, J.A. *Country Case Study: The Yemen Arab Republic*, International Migration Project Working Paper (Durham, 1978)

Blacker, J.G.C. 'A Critique of the International Definitions of Economic Activity and Employment Status and their Applicability in Population Consensus in Africa and the Middle East', *Population Bulletin for Western Asia, 14*, (June 1978) pp. 47-56

Blake, G.H. 'Libya and the Arab World', *Bulletin of the Faculty of Arts, University of Benghazi, IV* (Benghazi, 1972)

Böhning, W.R. *Elements of a Theory of International Migration and Compensation*, World Employment Programme Working Paper (ILO, Geneva, 1978)

Bowles. F. *et al., Higher Education in the Sudan* (UNESCO, Paris,

1974)

Braibanti, R. and al Farsy, F.A. 'Saudi Arabia: A Development Perspective', *Journal of South Asian and Middle Eastern Studies, I*, i (Fall 1977), pp. 3-43

British Council *Education Profile on Algeria* (Education Liaison Unit, London, May 1977)

British Petroleum *Statistical Review of the World Oil Industry* (BP, London, 1976)

Bulloch, J. *Death of a Country: the Civil War in Lebanon* (Brill, Leiden, 1977)

Burrell, R.M. *et al. The Developing Agriculture of the Middle East – Opportunities and Prospects* (Graham and Trotman, London, 1976)

Cass, A. 'Oil and Mining', *Financial Times*, 10 March 1978

——, 'Syria: Socialism with a Levantine Face', *Financial Times*, 21 June 1978

Cherkaoui, S. 'Human Resources as a Factor in the Development of Morocco' (unpublished MPhil thesis, Cairo, 1975)

Choucri, N. 'Labour Transfers in the Arab World: Growing Interdependence of the Construction Sector', paper presented to the *Seminar on Population, Employment and Migration in the Gulf Countries* (Arab Planning Institute, Kuwait, 1978)

Clark, D.O. and Mertz, R.A. *The Coastal Countries of the Arabian Peninsula: A Guide to the Academic Placement of Students from Kuwait, Bahrain, Qatar, United Arab Emirates, Sultanate of Oman, People's Democratic Republic of Yemen and Yemen Arab Republic in Educational Institutions in the USA* (American Association of Collegiate Registrars, Washington, DC, 1974)

Clemenceau, P. and Hadjadj, B. *Contribution a l'étude des problèmes de l'emploi et de la formation en Tunisie* (Ministère du Plan, Tunis, 1976)

Cole, D.P. *Nomads of the Nomads: The Al Murrah Bedouin of the Empty Quarter* (Aldine, Chicago, 1975)

Courbages, Y. and Fargues, P. *La Situation Démographique au Liban* (Centre for Palestinian Research, Beirut, 1974)

Cummings-Bruce, N. 'Rise in 1977 Payments Surplus May Ease Cash Flow Worries', *MEED*, 28 April 1978, p. 4.

Davies, H.R.J. 'The West African in the Economic Geography of the Sudan', *Geography, 49* (1964)

De Mas, P. 'The Place of Peripheral Regions in Moroccan Planning', *Tijdschrift vor Economisch en Sociale Geografie, 69* (Summer 1978), p. 80

Dialto, S. 'Les expulsions en Afrique', *Jeune Afrique, 79* (1975)

Al Din, S.A. *An Appraisal of the Five Year Plan* (Economic and Social Research Council, Khartoum, 1976)

Dorance, G.I. 'Population Growth in Egypt, 1800-2000: An Essay in the Quantification of Trends' (unpublished MA thesis, Durham, 1975)

Durham University Oman Research Project Reports (unpublished)

Economist Intelligence Unit, *Oil in the Middle East* (EIU, London, 1977)

——, *Quarterly Economic Review* (London)

Edens, D.G. *Oil and Development in the Middle East* (Praeger, New York, 1979)

Edens, D.G. and Snavely, W.P. 'Planning for Economic Development, Saudi Arabia', *Middle East Journal, 24* (1970), pp. 17-30

Egypt: Central Agency for the Public Mobilization of Statistics *Statistical Yearbooks* (Cairo)

——, *The Increases of Population in the United Arab Republic (Cairo, September 1969)*

——, *Preliminary Results of the General Population Census, 22-23 November* (Cairo, 1976)

Egypt: Ministry of Education, Statistical Division *(Development and Flow of General Education Since the Middle of the 20th Century, 1950/51 to 1976/77* (Cairo, 1977)

Egypt: Ministry of Planning, *Five Year Plan: 1978-1982*, Vols. I–XII (Cairo, 1977) (Arabic)

Fabunmi, L.A. 'Nigerians on the Nile', *West Africa* (4 August 1956)

Farhaly, O.I., Palmer, M. and Chackerian, R. *Political Development and Bureaucracy in Libya* (Lexington Books, Toronto, 1977)

Farley, R. *Planning for Development in Libya: The Exceptional Economy in the Developing World* (Praeger, New York, 1977)

Farrag, A.M. 'Migration between Arab Countries' in *Manpower and Employment in Arab Countries, Some Critical Issues* (ILO, Geneva, 1976), pp. 84-109

Al Farsy, F.A. *Saudi Arabia: A Case Study in Development* (Stacey, London, 1978)

Fenelon, K.G. *The United Arab Emirates: an Economic and Social Survey* (Longman, London, 1976)

Field, M. 'Moves for Economic Rationalisation', *Financial Times*, 16 November 1977

——, 'Agricultural Targets', *Financial Times,* 16 November 1977

Filahi, M. *The Sedenterization of Nomadic Populations* (Riyadh, 1963)

*Financial Times* (London)

Findlay, A. *Country Case Study: Tunisia,* International Migration Project Working Paper (Durham, 1978)

——, Findlay, A. and Lawless, R. *Country Case Study: The Kingdom of Morocco,* International Migration Project Working Paper (Durham, 1978)

First, R. *Libya: the Elusive Revolution* (Penguin Books, Baltimore, 1974)

Fischer, G. and Muzaffar, A.M. 'Some Basic Characteristics of the Labour Force in Bahrain, Qatar, United Arab Emirates and Oman' a paper presented to the *Conference on Human Resources Development* (Arab Planning Institute, Kuwait, 1975)

Fouad, M.H. 'Petrodollars and Economic Development in the Middle East', *Middle East Journal, 32,* 3 (1978), pp. 307-21

Fyfe, A. 'Development Bond Satisfies Main Needs', Supplement on Bahrain, *The Times,* 16 December 1977

Gadir Ali, A.A. *A Note on the Brain Drain in the Sudan* Economic and Social Research Council, Khartoum, December 1976)

Garner, J. 'Cotton under Pressure', *Financial Times,* 16 November 1977

Graham, H. *Arabian Time Machine, Self Portrait of an Oil State* (Heinemann, London, 1978)

Guine, A. (ed.) *Rapport 1975-76 sur l'Economie Syrienne,* (Office Arabe de Presse et de Documentation, Damascus, n.d.)

*Gulf Handbook* (London)

Gupta, M.G. *Non-Libyans' Employment and its Costs and Benefits in the Socio-Economic Development of the Country* (Department of Social and Economic Planning, Demography and Manpower Planning Section, Tripoli, 1976)

Al Hamer, A.M. *The Development of Education in Bahrain, 1940-1965* (Oriental Press, Bahrain, 1969)

Hamza, F. *The Heart of Arabia* (1933)

Hansen, B. 'Economic Development of Syria' in C.A. Cooper and Alexander Cooper (eds.), *Economic Development and Population Growth in the Middle East* (Elsevier, New York, 1972)

Hansen, B. and Marzouk, G.A. *Development and Economic Policy in the UAR (Egypt)* (McGraw Hill, Amsterdam, 1965)

Hassoun, I.A. 'Western Migration and Settlement in the Gezira', *Sudan Notes and Records xxxii* (1952), pp. 60-112

Hazelton, J.E. 'Gold Rush Economies: Development Planning in the Persian/Arabian Gulf', *Studies in Comparative International Develment, 13,* 2 (New York, 1978), pp. 3-22.

Heard-Bey, F. 'The Gulf States and Oman in Transition', *Asian Affairs*, *59*, 3, 1 (February 1972), pp. 14-22

—— , 'Social Changes in the Gulf States and Oman', *Asian Affairs, 59*, 3, 3 (October 1972), pp. 309-16

—— , 'Development Anomalies in the Bedouin Oases of al-Liwa', *Asian Affairs, 61*, 5, 3 (October 1974), pp. 272-86

—— , 'Arab Women in the United Arab Emirates', *Arab Women*, Report No. 27 of the Minority Rights Group (London, December 1975)

Helaissi, A.H. 'The Bedouins and Tribal Life in Saudi Arabia', *International Social Science Journal, 11* (1959), pp. 532-9

*Herald Tribune*, Banking and Finance in the Arab World, 15 May 1979

Hill, A. 'The Demography of the Kuwaiti Population of Kuwait', *Demography, 12*, 3 (1975)

—— , 'The Demography of the Population of Kuwait', *Population Bulletin of the United Nations Commission for West Asia, 13* (July 1977), pp. 42-55

Hoagland, J. 'Saudi Arabians Push $100 Billion Development Plan', *Washington Post*, 13 April 1975

Hobday, P. *Saudi Arabia Today: An Introduction to the Richest Oil Power* (Ad Orientem, Delhi, 1978)

Holt, P.M. *A Modern History of the Sudan* (Grove Press, New York, 1974)

Hyde, G.D.M. *Education in Modern Egypt; Ideals and Realities* (Brill, Leiden, 1978)

International Bank for Reconstruction and Development, *The Economic Development of Kuwait* (Johns Hopkins, Baltimore, 1965)

International Institute for Strategic Studies, *The Military Balance, 1977-1978* (London)

International Labour Office *Growth, Employment and Equity, a Comprehensive Strategy for the Sudan* (ILO, Geneva, 1976)

—— , *Labour Force Estimates and Projections* (ILO, Geneva, 1977)

International Monetary Fund *International Financial Statistics* (Washington, DC)

Iqbal, S.M. *The Emergence of Saudi Arabia* (Ad Orientem, Delhi, 1977)

Iraq: Ministry of Planning *Man: The Object of Revolution* (Baghdad, 1978)

—— , Central Statistical Office *Annual Abstract of Statistics* (Baghdad)

Jordan: Central Bank of Jordan *Monthly Statistical Bulletin* (Amman)

Jordan: Department of Statistics *Statistical Yearbooks* (Amman)

—— , *The Multipurpose Household Survey, January to April 1976*

(Amman, 1976)

Jordan: Ministry of Education *Education in Jordan in Figures, 1976-1977 (East Bank only)* (Amman, 1977)

Jordan: National Planning Council *Sample Survey of Households 1971* (Amman, May 1971)

———, *Preliminary Results of the 1975 Manpower Survey* (Amman, 1975)

———, *Five Year Plan 1976-1980* (Amman, 1976)

Kanovski, E. *Economic Development of Syria* (Tel Aviv, 1977)

Kassab, K.I. 'Manpower Development in Iraq 1976-1980', a paper presented to the conference on *Population, Migration and Employment*, Arab Planning Institute/International Labour Office (Kuwait, December 1979)

Keddeman, W. and Gader Ali, A.A. *Employment and Incomes in Rural Sudan* (Economic and Social Research Council, Khartoum, 1978)

Al Khayat, S.M.A. 'Aspects of Lebanese Labour Movement Post the Labour Law of 1946' (unpublished MBA thesis, Beirut, 1971)

Khouja, M.W. and Sadler, P.G. *The Economy of Kuwait* (Macmillan, London, 1979)

Kidd, C.V. and Thurston, J.L. *Higher Education and Development in the Sudan* (Institute of Higher Education, New York, 1977)

Knaverhase, R. 'Saudi Arabia's Economy at the Beginning of the 1970s', *Middle East Journal, 28* (1974), pp. 126-40

Kuwait: Central Bank *Annual Reports* (Kuwait)

Kuwait: Ministry of Education *Annual Reports* (Kuwait) (Arabic)

Kuwait: Ministry of Finance and Oil *The Oil of Kuwait, Facts and Figures* (Kuwait, 1970)

———, *General Budget Report to Parliament, 1971/72* (Kuwait, 1971) (Arabic)

Kuwait: Ministry of Planning, Central Department of Statistics, *Population Census, 1975* (Kuwait, May 1976) (Arabic)

Kuwait: Planning Board *Census, 1965, 1970* (Kuwait) (Arabic)

———, Statistical Department *Statistical Abstracts* (Kuwait)

Lawless, R.I. *New Agricultural Projects in the Libyan Arab Republic: A Survey* (Durham, 1975)

———, 'Industrialisation in the Maghreb, Progress, Problems and Prospects', *Maghreb Review* (London, 1976), *1*, 3, p. 11.

———, *Country Case Study: Algeria*, International Migration Project Working Paper (Durham, 1978)

Lebanon: Direction Centrale de la Statistique *L'Enquête par sondage sur la population active au Liban, Novembre 1970* (Beirut, 1972)

Lee, E. and Radwan, S. *The Anatomy of Rural Poverty: Egypt, 1977* (ILO, Geneva, 1980)

Lees, F.A. and Brooks, H.C. *The Economic and Political Development of the Sudan* (Macmillan, London, 1977)

Libya: Ministry of Education *Educational Statistics* (Tripoli) (Arabic)

Libya: Ministry of Information *Oil and Planning* (Tripoli, 1968)

Libya: Ministry of Labour *Labour Force Statistics, 1974* (Benghazi, n.d.)

Libya: Ministry of Planning and Scientific Research *National Income Accounts* (Tripoli, 1976) (Arabic)

——, *Economic and Social Transformation Plan (1976 to 1980)* (Tripoli, 1976)

——, *Statistical Abstracts* (Tripoli)

——, Census and Statistical Department *Some Preliminary Results of the 1973 Population Census* (Benghazi, 1975)

Libya: Tripoli Chamber of Commerce *Quarterly Bulletin* (Autumn 1977)

Llewelyn-Davies, Weekes, Forestier-Walker *National Housing Policy Study* (Bahrain, 1974)

Lorimer, J.G. *Gazetteer of the Persian Gulf, Geographical and Statistical* (Calcutta, 1908), Vol. 2

Mabro, R.E. *The Egyptian Economy, 1952-1972* (Oxford University Press, London, 1974)

——, 'Employment, Choice of Technology, Sectoral Priorities', *Manpower and Employment in Arab Countries, Some Critical Issues* (ILO, Geneva, 1976)

——, 'Increased Opportunities in Wake of Strife', Supplement on Egypt, *The Times*, 7 December 1977

*Maghreb Selection* (Paris)

Mahdary, H. 'The Patterns and Problems of Economic Development in Rentier States: The Case of Iran' in M.A. Cook, *Studies in the Economic History of the Middle East from the Rise of Islam to the Present Day* (Oxford University Press, Oxford, 1970) pp. 428-67

Makdisi, S.A. 'An Appraisal of Lebanon's Post-War Economic Development and a Look to the Future', *Middle East Journal*, 31 3 (1977), pp. 267-80

Makhlouf-Obermeyer, C. *Changing Veils: A Study of Women in South Arabia* (Croom Helm, London, 1978)

Al Mallakh, R. 'The Economics of Rapid Growth: Libya', *Middle East Journal* (Summer 1969)

——, *Qatar, the Development of an Oil Economy* (Brill, Leiden,

1979)

Mather, D.B. 'Aspects of Migration in the Anglo Egyptian Sudan' (unpublished PhD thesis, London, 1953)

McDermott, A. 'Development Priorities Well Documented', *Financial Times*, 16 November 1977

McLachlan, K.S. 'Iraq' in R.M. Burrell *et al., The Developing Agriculture of the Middle East* (Graham and Trotman, London, 1976) pp. 41-53

McLoughlin, P.F. 'Economic Development and the Heritage of Slavery in the Sudan', *Africa, 32*, 4 (1962) pp. 355-91

Mead, D.C. *Growth and Structural Change in the Egyptian Economy* (Illinois, 1967)

MEFIT *Regional Plan of Khartoum and Master Plan for the Three Towns* (Rome, 1974)

Mertz, R.A. *Education and Manpower in the Arabian Gulf* (American Friends of the Middle East, Washington, DC, 1972)

*The Middle East* (London)

*Middle East Economic Survey* (Nicosia) (*MEES*)

*Middle East Annual Review* (London)

*Middle East Economic Digest* (London) (*MEED*)

Minces, J. 'La femme dans le monde arabe', *Espirit 22* (1978), pp. 62-6

Moorhead, J. *In Defiance of the Elements: A Personal View of Qatar* (Quartet Books, London, 1977)

Morocco: Banque du Maroc, *Exercices* (Rabat)

Morocco: Secrétariat d'Etat au Plan, *Recensement Général de la Population et de l'Habitat, 1971* (Rabat, 1971)

—— , *Plan de Développement Economique et Social 1973-1977* (Rabat, 1973)

Motassime, A. 'La politique de l'enseignement au Maroc de 1957 a 1977', *Maghreb-Machrek, 79* (1978), p. 40

Mulat, T. *Educated Unemployment in the Sudan*, Education and Employment Project Working Paper (ILO, Geneva, 1975)

Mustafa, M. 'Manpower and Employment Problems in Developing Countries: A Case Study of the Sudan' (unpublished MA thesis, Boston, May 1973)

Nassef, A.F. 'Internal Migration and Urbanisation in Egypt', *Urbanization and Migration in some Arab and African Countries*, Cairo Demographic Centre, Research Monograph Series (Cairo, 1973)

Negadi, G., Tabutin, D. and Vallin, J. 'Situation démographique de l'Algérie', *La Démographie Algérienne* (Algiers, 1972), pp. 13-30

Newbold, Sir D. *The Making of the Modern Sudan* (Greenwood Press,

Connecticut, 1974)

Nihan, G. *Le Secteur Non Structure; Signification, Aire d'Extension du Concept et Application Experimentale*, World Employment Programme Working Paper (ILO, Geneva, 1979)

—— and Jourdain, R. 'The Modern Informal Sector in Nouakchott', *International Labour Review, 117*, 6 (ILO, Geneva, 1978)

Nimeri, S. *The Five Year Plan (1970-75): Some Aspects of the Plan and its Performance* (Development Studies and Research Centre, Khartoum, May 1977)

Nolte, R.H. 'From Nomad Society to New Nation: Saudi Arabia' in K.H. Silvert (ed.), *Expectant Peoples: Nationalism and Development* (New York, 1963), pp. 77-95

OCDE, *Migrations et transfests de technologie: étude de cas Algerie, Maroc, Tunisie et France* (Paris, 1975)

Oman: Michel Ecochard Planning Office *Study of the New Capital, Interim Reports* (Paris, 1973)

Oman: Ministry of Communications *Water Resources Survey of Northern Oman* (Muscat, 1975)

——, Italconsult *Oman Transport Survey, Interim Report* (Rome and Muscat, 1974)

Oman: Ministry of Planning, *Statistical Yearbooks* (Muscat)

——, *National Economic Development Plan for the Sultanate of Oman* (Muscat, n.d.)

Oman: Whitehead Consulting Group *Sultanate of Oman: Economic Survey* (London, 1972)

Organization of Arab Petroleum Exporting Countries *Fourth Statistical Report 1975-76* (Vienna, 1977)

Otaiba, al M.S. *Petroleum and the Economy of the United Arab Emirates* (Croom Helm, London, 1977)

Peddle, Thorp, Chapman and Taylor *Employment and Population Estimates for Jebel Ali Industrial Complex* (Dubai, 1977)

Peterson, J.E. *Oman in the Twentieth Century: Political Foundations of an Emerging State* (Croom Helm, London, 1978)

Petran, T.T. *Syria* (Benn, London, 1972)

*La Presse* (Paris)

Qatar: Ministry of Education, Statistical Department *Annual Reports* (Doha) (Arabic)

Qatar: Ministry of Information *1970 Census* (Qatar, 1970)

——, *Qatar in the Seventies* (Doha, May 1973)

Al-Qazza, A. 'Development of Higher Education in Iraq, 1900-1972', *Third International Conference of the Center for Arab Gulf Studies*

(Basrah, March 1979)

Rassam, A. *National Development and the Arab Woman: Contradictions and Accommodations*, paper prepared for the Symposium of Centre for Arab Gulf Studies (Basrah, March 1979)

The Royal Institute of International Affairs *The Middle East, A Political and Economic Survey* (London, 1950)

Rumaihi, M. *Bahrain: Social and Political Change since the 1st World War* (Bowkers, London, 1977)

Sadik, M.T. and Snavely, W.P. *Bahrain, Qatar and the United Arab Emirates: Colonial Past, Present Problems and Future Prospects* (Lexington Books, Massachusetts, 1972)

Al Saleh, N.P. 'Some Problems and Development Possibilities of the Livestock Sector in Saudi Arabia: A Case Study in Livestock Development in Arab Lands' (unpublished PhD thesis, Durham, 1976)

Sales, M.E. *Country Case Study: Syria,* International Migration Project Working Paper (Durham, 1978)

Sanyal, B.C. and Versluis, J. *Higher Education, Human Capital and Labour Market Segmentation in the Sudan,* World Employment Programme Working Paper (ILO, Geneva, 1976)

Saudi Arabia: Central Planning Organisation *Population and Housing Census 1962/63* (Riyadh, 1963)

———, *Economic Report* (Riyadh, 1965)

———, *Development Plan, Kingdom of Saudi Arabia* (Riyadh, 1974)

Saudi Arabia: Ministry of Education *Towards an Appropriate Strategy for Training Skilled and Semi Skilled Workers* (Riyadh, April 1974)

Saudi Arabia: Ministry of Finance and National Economy *Census of Population in the Kingdom of Saudi Arabia, 1974* (Dammam, 1978)

Saudi Arabian Monetary Agency *Annual Reports* (Riyadh)

*Saudi Economic Survey* (Dammam)

Sayigh, Y.A. 'Problems and Prospects of Development in the Arabian Peninsula', *International Journal of Middle East Studies, 2* (January 1971), pp. 40-58

———, *The Economies of the Arab World* (Croom Helm, London, 1978)

Sethuraman, S.V. 'The Urban Informal Sector: Concept, Measurement and Policy', *International Labour Review, 114*, 1 (ILO, Geneva, 1976)

Shaw, P. 'Migration and Employment in the Arab World: Construction as a Key Policy Variable', paper presented to the *Seminar on Population, Employment and Migration in the Gulf Countries* (Arab Planning Institute, Kuwait, 1978)

Shell Briefing Service *Oil and Gas in 1977* (London, 1978)

Sinclair, C.A. 'The Future Development of Highly Qualified Manpower in the Gulf States', paper presented to the *Conference on Human Resource Development* (Bahrain, 1975)

———, 'Education in Kuwait, Bahrain and Qatar: An Economic Assessment' (unpublished PhD thesis, Durham, 1977)

———and Socknat, J.A. *An Estimate of the Population of the Yemen Arab Republic and the Number of Workers Abroad* (Sanaa, 1975)

———, *Assessment of Manpower Development and Policy and Programme Suggestions for the Yemen Republic* (Sanaa, 1976)

———, *Migration for Employment Abroad and its Impact on Development in the Yemen Arab Republic*, International Migration Project Topic Paper (Durham, 1978)

Skeet, I. *Muscat and Oman: The End of an Era* (London, 1974)

Socknat, J. *An Inventory and Assessment of Employment Orientated Human Resources Development Programs in the Gulf Area* (Ford Foundation, Bahrain, 1975)

———, *Labour Market Conditions and Prospects in the Gulf States and Saudi Arabia* (Central Planning Organisation, Amman, 1975)

Souriau, C. 'Femme et politique en Libye', *Revue Française d'Etudes Politiques Méditerranéanes* (Paris, 1977), pp. 81-104

Steffan, H. *Preliminary Report No. 5, Data Bank of Yemen's Population and Housing Census* (Zurich, May 1977)

———, *et al. Final Report on the Airphoto Interpretation Project of the Swiss Technical Co-operation Service, Berne* (Zurich, April 1978)

Stevens, J.H. 'The Role of Major Agricultural Projects in the Economic Development of Arabian Peninsula Countries', *Proceedings of the Seventh Seminar for Arabian Studies* (1973), pp. 140-4

Sudan: Bank of Sudan, *Annual Reports* (Khartoum)

Sudan: Department of Statistics, *First Population Census of the Sudan, Nine Interim Reports and Two Supplements* (Khartoum, 1956)

———, *Population Projections* (Khartoum, 1969)

———, *Household Sample Survey in the Sudan, 1967-68* (Khartoum, 1970)

———, *Preliminary Results of the 1973 Population Census* (Khartoum, 1977)

———, *Educational Yearbooks* (Khartoum) (Arabic)

Sudan: Higher Grants Commission *Manpower in Sudan's Six Year Plan for Economic and Social Development, 1977/78 to 1982/83* (Khartoum, n.d.)

Sudan: Ministry of Agriculture, Department of Agricultural Economics

*Agricultural Statistics, 1974* (Khartoum, 1975)

Sudan: Ministryof Education 'The Six Year Plan 1977/78 to 1982/83' (Khartoum, mimeograph, n.d.)

Sudan: Ministry of Planning *National Income Accounts and Supporting Tables* (Khartoum)

——, *The Five Year Plan of Economic and Social Development (1970 to 1975)* (Khartoum, 1970)

——, *Industrial Survey of Establishments Employing less than 25 Workers, 1970-71* (Khartoum, 1976) (Arabic)

——, *Six Year Social and Economic Development Plan for the Republic of the Sudan 1977/78 to 1982/83* (Khartoum, 1978) (Arabic)

Sudan: Ministry of Public Service *Establishments Survey, 1973* (Khartoum, 1974)

Sudan: *Report of the Committee for the Study of Staff Affairs, 1975* (University of Khartoum, Khartoum, 1976)

*Sudanow* (Khartoum)

Sultan, A. 'Development Plan', *MEED*, Special Supplement on Libya, 18 February 1977

Syria: Central Bank, *Quarterly Bulletin* (Damascus)

Syria: *Fourth Five-Year Economic and Social Development Plan, 1976-80,* Arab Office for Press and Documentation, Documents Series 1127 (Damascus, 1977)

Syria: Office of the Prime Minister, Central Bureau of Statistics *Census of the Population 1960* (Damascus, 1962)

——, *Socio-Economic Development in Syria 1960-70* (Damascus, 1976)

——, *Statistical Abstracts* (Damascus)

Szyliowicz, J.S. *Education and Modernisation in the Middle East* (Cornell, New York, 1973)

Tabbarah, R. 'Rural Development and Urbanization in Lebanon', *Population Bulletin*, United Nations Economic Commission for West Asia, *14* (Beirut, June 1978), pp. 3-25

Townsend, J. *Oman: The Making of a Modern State* (Croom Helm, London, 1977)

Tunisia: Banque Centrale de Tunisie *Statistiques Financiers* (Tunis)

Tunisia: Ministère du Plan *Recensement général de la population et des logements* (Tunis, May 1975)

——, *Cinquième plan de développement, 1977-81* (Tunis, 1977)

Turing, P. 'Two Universities Crown Educational System', *The Times*, Supplement on Jordan, 11 August 1978

United Arab Emirates: Ministry of Education *Annual Reports* (Abu

Dhabi) (Arabic)

United Arab Emirates: Ministry of Information *Census 1968* (Abu Dhabi, 1968)

United Arab Emirates: Ministry of Planning *Census, 1975* (Abu Dhabi, 1976)

——, *Establishment Survey, 1975 and 1977* (Abu Dhabi, 1978)

United Nations *Population and Vital Statistics Report*, Statistical Papers, Series A (New York, April 1967)

——, *Trends and Prospects in Urban and Rural Population, 1950-2000* (New York, November 1975)

United Nations Economic Commission for Western Asia *Demographic and Related Socio-Economic Data Sheets for Countries of the Economic Commission for Western Asia* (Beirut, January 1978), No. 2.

United Nations Industrial Development Organization *Comparative Study of Plan of Arab States* (Vienna, 1976)

United Nations Inter-Disciplinary Reconnaissance Mission *Bahrain* (Beirut, 1973)

United Nations Organization, Statistical Office, *Statistical Yearbook 1976* (New York, 1977)

United Nations Statistical Council *Demographic Yearbook, 1976* (New York, 1977)

United States, Bureau of Census, Department of Commerce *Summary of Census Data* (Washington, DC, n.d.)

Warnock, E. *et al., Middle Eastern Muslim Women Speak* (Austin, University of Texas, 1978)

Al Wassim, A.A. 'Spatial Patterns of Population Dynamics in Egypt: 1947-1970' (unpublished PhD thesis, Durham, 1977)

Waterbury, J. *Egypt: Burdens of the Past, Options for the Future,* American Universities Field Staff Report (Cairo, 1978)

Whelan, J. 'International Monetary Fund Urges Broader Base for the Omani Economy', *MEED*, 15 June 1979

Whitehead Consulting Group *Sultanate of Oman: Economic Survey* (London, 1972)

Williams, M.J. 'The Aid Programs of OPEC Countries', *Foreign Affairs*, 54, (1976) pp. 308-24

Winder, R.B. *Education in Al Bahrayn – The World of Islam* (London, 1959)

World Bank *World Development Report 1978* (Washington, DC, August 1978)

——, *Yemen Arab Republic: Development of a Traditional Economy*

(Washington, DC, 1979)

Wright, J. *Libya* (London, 1969)

Yacoub, I. 'Family Planning in Bahrain', *ECWA First Population Conference* (Beirut, 1974)

Yasin, M. *A Review of the Manpower Situation of Lebanon* (ILO, Geneva, 1976)

Yemen (PDRY): Central Bank of Yemen *Annual Report, 1977* (Aden, 1978)

Yemen (PDRY): Central Statistical Organisation 'Preliminary Results of the 1973 Census' (Aden, mimeograph, n.d.)

Yemen (YAR): Central Planning Office *Population Statistics of the Yemen Arab Republic* (Sanaa, 1976)

―― , *Statistical Yearbooks* (Sanaa)

―― , *Five Year Development Plan, 1976/77 to 1980/81* (Sanaa, 1976)

Youssef, N.H. *Women and Work in Developing Countries* (Connecticut, 1977)

Zarrugh, A.M. 'The Development of Public Education in Libya, 1951-1970, with Special Reference to University Education' (unpublished PhD thesis, Durham, 1978)

# INDEX

For Product Safety Concerns and Information please contact our EU
representative GPSR@taylorandfrancis.com Taylor & Francis Verlag GmbH,
Kaufingerstraße 24, 80331 München, Germany

Printed and bound by CPI Group (UK) Ltd, Croydon, CR0 4YY
01/05/2025
01858342-0017